Hume, Smith, Burke,
Geijer, Menger,
d'Argenson,
et EJW cetera

Hume, Smith, Burke, Geijer, Menger, d'Argenson, et EJW cetera

Edited by
Daniel B. Klein &
Jason Briggeman

CL Press
A Fraser Institute Project
Vancouver

CL Press

Published by CL PRESS
A project of the Fraser Institute
1770 Burrard Street, 4th Floor
Vancouver, BC V6J 3G7 Canada
www.clpress.net

Hume, Smith, Burke, Geijer, Menger, d'Argenson, et EJW cetera
Edited by Daniel B. Klein and Jason Briggeman

© 2022 by CL Press

ISBN: 978-1-957698-01-4

Cover design by John Stephens

Contents

Preface

This volume contains a selection of 15 items published in *Econ Journal Watch* between 2011 and 2022. David Hume and Adam Smith loom large. Aside from forewords, only four of the items are scholarship original to *Econ Journal Watch*. But those four deal with Hume or Smith. Of the other items, two are by Edmund Burke. We hope the potpourri appeals to readers interested in such figures. The items are arranged by chronological aspect (either authorship or topic).

All of the items can be found online at econjwatch.org. The items have been newly typeset, but otherwise changed very little (for example, a few references have been updated). Acknowledgments are given with each item. Beyond that, we would like to express our thanks to the contributors to this volume, Benoît Malbranque, Jacob Hall, Enrique Guerra-Pujol, Scott Drylie, Frederic Sautet, Erwin Dekker, and Stefan Kolev. As ever, we are grateful to the Fraser Institute for their support of both EJW and CL Press and to individuals and foundations who support both projects.

Rather than remarking on the various items, we simply compile their abstracts, immediately following this Preface.

We hope the reader finds the collection both immediately agreeable and durably useful.

Chapter Abstracts

Chapter 1: René Louis de Voyer de Paulmy, Marquis d'Argenson and Anonymous (a Bellonian), "The General Directing of Trade Cannot Be a Science: D'Argenson's 1751 Commentary Essay and the Response to It" (September 2021)

René Louis de Voyer de Paulmy, Marquis d'Argenson (1694–1757) published a wonderful essay in French in 1751, expounding that knowledge problems foil any pretense of making the general directing of trade into a science. The essay was published in English, translated by Tobias Smollett, in 1754 and reprinted in 1762 in Edmund Burke's *The Annual Register*. Here Smollett's translation is reproduced with minor changes made by Benoît Malbranque based on the 1751 French publication and an original manuscript text of the essay. Malbranque also provides here a first-ever translation of a response by an unknown author who argued that, yes, the directing of trade can be a science. The exchange between d'Argenson and the anonymous author raises issues about the meaning of 'science' and who it is that can justly claim to speak in the name of science.

Chapter 2: Hew Dalrymple (pseud.?), "Information for the Hair Dressers in Edinburgh; Against the Incorporation of Barbers—The Second Edition" (September 2018)

Here reproduced is a rollicking, yet virtually unknown, Edinburgh pamphlet of 1758, a liberal criticism of what we nowadays term occupational licensing. The pamphlet presents itself as an official court document (an 'Information'), but John Cairns and the editor of this republication conjecture that it is a rambunctious variant of such a document. Irrespective of its original function, the pamphlet uses irony to make serious points. The "hair dressers" and "wigmakers" seek liberty to cut hair. The "barbers," traditionally auxiliary to surgeons, assert an exclusive privilege not only to shaving but also to hair-cutting.

The pamphlet teaches key insights: Exclusive privileges reduce quality, supply, convenience and availability, and innovation; their rationales go obsolete; they are inevitably rather arbitrary, generate turf battles, and are a source of social "Rancour" and hypocrisy; they are used opportunistically to seek rents. The pamphlet provides rich context and argues specifics, yet expresses broad liberal principles, calling such exclusive privileges "a Restriction of natural Freedom" and "almost a Reproach to the Constitution."

Chapter 3: David Hume, "Hume's Manuscript Account of the Extraordinary Affair Between Him and Rousseau" (September 2021)

Published here is David Hume's original manuscript account of his tangle with Jean-Jacques Rousseau. Hume was quite dissatisfied with the rushed version of the account, published in London in 1766, which, apart from the letters therein, was in the main a retranslation of a French translation of Hume's manuscript. Hume "expresses himself bluntly and forcibly," as one scholar said about this never-before-published manuscript.

Chapter 4: Daniel B. Klein, "To Tolerant England and a Pension from the King: Did Hume Subconsciously Aim to Subvert Rousseau's Legacy?" (September 2021)

David Hume conducted Jean-Jacques Rousseau to England, landing in Dover 11 January 1766. Hume worked doggedly to settle Rousseau in England and procure a pension from the King of England, George III. But, from especially April 1766, the relationship quickly went from awkward eccentricity to bitter enmity, culminating in Rousseau's remarkable letter of 10 July, and then publication of Hume's account of the affair, and enormous notoriety. Here Daniel Klein suggests that, had Rousseau fallen in with—or become a pet of—the establishment in England, his legacy would have been diminished, and that Hume could sense that. Settling down in England, in arrangements crafted by Hume, and enjoying a royal pension would have undermined Rousseau's persona as an audacious radical critic of refinement, of modern commercial society, of established aristocracies, and of England in particular. He would be seen—or portrayed—as accepting and assimilating to that which he scorned and pretended to expose. Klein develops the hypothesis that an impetus behind Hume's efforts was to subvert Rousseau's legacy. If such impetus existed, it was probably largely subconscious. One line of evidence is that Hume continued to work to salvage the plan, or parts of it, as much as a year after mutual enmity had become common knowledge. Also, unlike previous treatments of the affair, Klein makes use of an insertion Hume had prepared for a never-realized second edition of the published account, an insertion alluding to Themistocles in Persia.

Chapter 5: "Glimpses of David Hume" (September 2017)
Here collected are anecdotes and miscellanea about David Hume. Most of the 25 items presented here may also be found in James Fieser's marvelous 10-volume compilation *Early Responses to Hume* (Thoemmes Press, 2nd revised edition 2005), volumes 9 and 10 containing material about Hume's life and reputation. Included here also are Hume's 1775 "Advertisement" disavowing *A Treatise of Human Nature*, and an excerpt from the Conclusion of Book I of that work.

Chapter 6: Jacob R. Hall, "From Hume to Smith on the Common Law and English Liberty: A Comment on Paul Sagar" (March 2022)
Paul Sagar, in his 2021 *Political Theory* article "On the Liberty of the English: Adam Smith's Reply to Montesquieu and Hume," discusses the role that the common law plays in Smith's account of English liberty. In doing so he fashions something of a divide between Smith and David Hume with respect to their views on the development of liberty in England. As Jacob Hall sees it, here, the divide between Smith and Hume is less than Sagar suggests, if it exists at all. Hall highlights Hume's discussions of English common law in his *History of England*. In doing so, Hall makes more apparent the shared sentiments between Hume and Smith on the importance of the legal system for the development of English liberty. Rather than replying to Hume, Smith should be seen as developing on Hume's ideas and disseminating the results, by way of both his Glasgow classroom and *The Wealth of Nations*. Not once does Sagar cite volumes 1 and 2 of Hume's *History of England*, though they contain much that dovetails with and no doubt fed Smith's interpretations.

Chapter 7: F. E. Guerra-Pujol, "Adam Smith in Love" (March 2021)
Who were Adam Smith's lost loves? F. E. Guerra-Pujol puts Smith's love life into historical context by briefly describing the strict ecclesiastical regulation of sex as well as the expansive jurisdiction of parish churches over people's sex

lives in the Scotland of his youth. Next, Guerra-Pujol reassembles all the available evidence, draws inferences, and presents some conjectures. It is reasonable to conclude that Smith had at least two romantic relationships, possibly more, though we know very little about the women or the precise nature of these relationships.

Chapter 8: Scott Drylie, "Professional Scholarship from 1893 to 2020 on Adam Smith's Views on School Funding: A Heterodox Examination" (September 2020)

Scott Drylie critically examines a set of 191 interpretations dating from 1893 to 2020 that characterize Adam Smith's views regarding taxpayer financing of schooling for youngsters. Drylie finds that the interpretation of Smith as an advocate of taxpayer funding predominates, and that it has done so consistently over this time frame of professional Smithian scholarship—making a sort of orthodoxy. But one passage prompts the question as to why. The passage is Smith's final words on the subject. Drylie focuses on the treatment of this passage which places the options of taxation and voluntary funding (user fees and charity) in a complex equipoise. Those who dissent from orthodoxy more often cite and examine this passage. Those who perpetuate the orthodoxy fail to give the passage an attentive reading, widely omit it, sometimes suppress the heterodox portion of it, and abstain from engaging with those who find it evidentiary of an alternative view. Drylie complements the study with a literature review for the reader's further exploration, and he poses some challenges to the orthodox view.

Chapter 9: Pierre-Samuel Dupont de Nemours, "Remarks from 1809 by Dupont de Nemours on Adam Smith" (May 2011)

This document offers an English translation of remarks that Pierre-Samuel Dupont de Nemours made in 1809, remarks principally about Adam Smith. Dupont suggests repeatedly that Adam Smith fudged some points in *The Wealth of Nations*, because, says Dupont, Smith "thought that in order to maintain public peace, one should not assault infirm eyes with a bright light turned too directly towards them." This document from 1809 makes a nice companion to the 1788 letter from Dupont to Smith, translated and discussed by Prasch and Warin (2009), in which Dupont wrote: "By assaulting their eyes with a bright light, we would reconstitute their blindness."

Chapter 10: Ian Simpson Ross, "Glimpses of Adam Smith: Excerpts from the Biography by Ian Simpson Ross" (January 2016)

This article presents excerpts from the grand biography *The Life of Adam Smith* by Ian Simpson Ross, with the kind permission of its publisher Oxford University Press.

Chapter 11: Edmund Burke, "Thoughts and Details on Scarcity" (March 2019)

In 1800, three years after Edmund Burke's death, his executors assembled this tract from a memorial Burke wrote to Prime Minister William Pitt in 1795 and other draft material intended for the public. The material began as a timely warning against interventionist measures in the face of dearth, including a locally administered minimum-wage scheme (referred to as a "tax" by Burke, because employers pay more for labor). The markets treated are chiefly those for labor, food, and spirits. The result is Burke's most general expression of his views in political economy, showing a sensitive appreciation of the particularism of social affairs and local, disjointed knowledge. He warns: "The moment that Government appears at market, all the principles of market will be subverted," and he articulates the intervention dynamic. Perhaps the most important aspect of the piece is Burke's attitude about standing firm on principles against the governmentalization of social affairs, in the face of foolish popular and political impulses and prejudices. The piece ends with the words: "My opinion is against an over-doing of any sort of administration, and more especially against this most momentous of all meddling on the part of authority; the meddling with the subsistence of the people." According to the Preface of the executors (not included here), Burke's words had a persuasive effect on opinion and policy decisions.

Chapter 12: Edmund Burke, "Scattered Hints Concerning Philosophy and Learning" (September 2022)

In this little-known writing, a young Edmund Burke shares some reflections on virtues for those species of action we call thinking, understanding, believing, learning, and discoursing. The piece dates from the 1750s, and is reproduced, with some omissions, from the slim book published by Cambridge University Press in 1957 titled *A Note-Book of Edmund Burke*: Poems, Characters, Essays and Other Sketches in the Hands of Edmund and William Burke Now Printed for the First Time in Their Entirety and Edited by H. V. F. Somerset. Burke says that a wide learning spares us of "false admirations that a more general knowledge would go a great way to Cure," and that acquaintance with numerous sciences prompts us "rather to master those principles that govern almost all of them than to sift into those particulars that direct and distinguish each of them separately."

Chapter 13: Erik Gustaf Geijer, "An Economic Dream" (September 2017)

Reproduced here is an 1847 article, in translation, the last that Erik Gustaf Geijer published during his lifetime. A Swede, Geijer—pronounced "yay-yer"—writes: "What is the *new order of things?* With each day, its *law* evolves more clearly; its *substance* is already so apparent that one can thereof judge its nature and the spirit of progress. This substance is the *day-by-day, constantly evolving, all-encompassing fellowship and interaction of human powers and needs.* This new, but actually ancient law of labour is that of *intelligence*, which works in expanding circles."

Chapter 14: Carl Menger, "The Social Theories of Classical Political Economy and Modern Economic Policy" (September 2016)

This is the first-ever English translation of an 1891 essay by Carl Menger published in the most important newspaper of the Habsburg Empire, the *Neue Freie Presse*. Menger writes the piece as a defense of classical political economy in general and of Adam Smith in particular, focusing on misinterpretations of Smith's work by the Younger Historical School in Germany. The essay reveals that Menger saw himself as working in a liberal tradition going back to Smith and classical political economy, rather than as a marginalist revolutionary who broke with classical political economy. It is a rare instance where Menger, holding the chair of economic theory at the University of Vienna, publicly expresses recommendations on economic policy. The essay represents Smith and the other classical political economists as socially motivated scholars concerned with just reforms to benefit ordinary people. Menger argues that the classical political economists were inclined toward liberal reforms but were by no means rigid exponents of laissez-faire. The essay is preceded here by an introduction authored by the translators Erwin Dekker and Stefan Kolev.

Hume, Smith, Burke,
Geijer, Menger,
d'Argenson,
et EJW cetera

The General Directing of Trade Cannot Be a Science: D'Argenson's 1751 Commentary Essay and the Response to It

Foreword

Benoît Malbranque

René Louis de Voyer de Paulmy, Marquis d'Argenson (1694–1757), played an important though rather overlooked place in the history of classical liberalism in France. Original and incisive at a time when systematizing was the vogue—though not yet in economics (the physiocrats were just about to appear)—he hampered his long-term recognition by scarcely ever publishing his writings, which were voluminous. To this day his private journal and memoirs are the best resource available to study his thought. Text from his journal and memoirs was published three times in France, and a selection in English in 1789, before, alas, the originals along with most of his remaining manuscripts burned in a fire during the 1871 Commune de Paris. In 1901 a two-volume edition of his journal and memoirs appeared, based on the published French materials.[1]

D'Argenson was from a family well-connected in the spheres of power. His father, Marc-René de Voyer de Paulmy (1652–1721), had been a ministre

---

1. D'Argenson's *Journal* first appeared in 1825, along with a selection of other writings (*mémoires*); two new editions were later published, in 1857–1858 (6 volumes) and 1859–1867 (edited by E. J. B. Rathéry, 9 volumes; hereafter cited as "éd. Rathéry"). The 2-volume abridged English edition bears the title *Journal and Memoirs of the Marquis d'Argenson* (d'Argenson 1901), although the additional *mémoires* added to the French editions were not included. Also, the son of our d'Argenson edited a volume titled *Essais dans le goût de Montagne*, which includes some notes found in the papers of his father, and which was translated and published as *Essays, Civil, Moral, Literary and Political* (d'Argenson 1789).

d'État and was lieutenant-general of police from 1697 to 1718. His brother, Marc-Pierre de Voyer de Paulmy, served as minister in charge of defense. And D'Argenson himself became minister of foreign affairs, 1744 to 1747.

Yet d'Argenson's appetite for power was very moderate. He had a preference for ideas. As a personal friend of the pacifist and free-trade advocate Abbé de Saint-Pierre (1658–1743), d'Argenson was a member of the Entresol club, created in 1724, where ideas were debated and manuscripts discussed, including drafts of Montesquieu's *Spirit of Laws*, thirteen years before its publication. In this cozy and free atmosphere ideas were bold and radical, on topics ranging from belles-lettres to economics and politics. "One day the government will ask us to mind our own business,"[2] said d'Argenson, who was advocating for prudence and moderation; the club was closed in 1731. After serving as foreign affairs minister, d'Argenson lived a solitary life and continued writing a journal and memoirs. He was a keen observer of the poor economic conditions of most of the rural populations. He died in 1757.

In government d'Argenson saw good men turned down and sound economic policy refused. He was a liberal who understood the need for stability and functionality in government. In a journal entry from 1731, he commented on the tax reform set up by the intendant of Caen: "He wanted to change the whole of the assessment of the arbitrary taxes, especially that of the poll-tax. Those he thus relieved did not thank him; they thought, as usual, it was only justice; and those whose tax he increased uttered such loud cries, wanting to eat him up, that the echo of them besieged both throne and Court."[3]

Year after year d'Argenson echoed the growing dissatisfaction of the country and expressed his concerns for the future. Yet he was of the opinion that "it would require tremendous faults and incidents for a king to lose his throne" (1764, 41), and he carried on naively, fitting Tocqueville's description of the lead-up to the French Revolution, "there never were events greater, better prepared, longer matured, and yet so little foreseen" (1856, 12). Tocqueville quotes d'Argenson twice in his great work and likely was influenced by him.

In 1901, the English translator of d'Argenson's journal marveled at his foresight and observations. "These notes and reflections," she wrote, "give an

---

2. Journal du marquis d'Argenson, 10 décembre 1731 (éd. Rathéry, I:103).
3. Journal, 1731 (éd. Rathéry, I:80–81; d'Argenson 1901, I:66).

invaluable picture, not elsewhere to be found, of the dull corruption, political and social, of the first forty years [i.e., 1715–1755] of [Louis XV's] sixty years' reign—the wonder is that Louis XV was allowed to reign so long and that Louis XVI ever came to the throne" (Wormeley 1901, 40).

D'Argenson did not keep his ideas entirely to himself. He was largely read by those who had received copies of his manuscripts, such as Pierre-Samuel Dupont de Nemours (1984, 168). D'Argenson's *Considérations sur le gouvernement* were published posthumously in 1764.[4]

One piece that was published by d'Argenson during his life expressed his thoughts on the merits of free trade. Written in French, it was initially published in 1751 and did receive some attention. What prompted d'Argenson to write and publish this piece?

Around 1750, in Italy, a chaotic monetary situation motivated several writings on economic matters,[5] among them a widely read tract by Girolamo Belloni (1688–1760), published in Rome in 1750 under the title *Del commercio*.[6] After considering the nature of money, Belloni turns his attention to public policy, advocating tariffs and a monitored balance of trade. The tract was soon translated into many languages, appearing in English (1752),[7] German (1752), and French (1751; 1755; 1756; 1765). *Del commercio* was "the first Italian book on economics to have been successful in France," according to a recent survey on Italian economic thought (Bianchini 2002, 3).

In France the *Journal Œconomique* published in its March 1751 issue an article, summarizing Belloni's argument, written by an unknown author—a Bellonian, if you will—who likely hailed from Italy. D'Argenson seized the opportunity to comment critically upon Belloni, writing an essay that put forward a laissez-faire outlook, one which he had been developing in his private writings. D'Argenson's essay was published anonymously in the *Journal*

---

4. Adam Smith had a copy in his personal library (Mizuta 2019, 388).

5. Giovanantonio Fabbrini, *Dell'indole e qualità naturali e civili della moneta e de' principi istorici e naturali de' contratti. Dissertazioni*, 1750; Girolamo Belloni, *Del commercio*, 1750; Carli Gian Rinaldo, *Dell'origine del commercio della moneta e dell'istituzione delle zecche d'Italia sino al secolo decimosettimo*, 1751; Ferdinando Galiani, *Della Moneta*, 1751.

6. It contains a Latin translation by Nicolas Rubbi.

7. The translation in English was published in 1752 under the title: *A dissertation on commerce. Clearly demonstrating the true sources of national wealth and power, together with the most rational measures for acquiring and preserving both. The whole deduced from the nature of trade, industry, money and exchanges. Tr. from the Italian of the celebrated Marquis Jerome Belloni.*

Œconomique issue of April 1751. An English translation by Tobias Smollett was published in 1754, and an Italian translation appeared two years after that.[8] Smollett's English translation was also reprinted in 1762 in *The Annual Register*,[9] the chief editor of which was Edmund Burke.

In my opinion, d'Argenson's essay is one of the best compact statements of laissez-faire French classical liberalism. It highlights wholesome autocorrective tendencies in free markets and remarks on how the alternative lacks such virtues; it fairly compares freedom and unfreedom, rather than assessing freedom against an irrelevant perfection. The date of the French original, 1751, reminds us that the central spine of liberal political economy—a presumption of liberty, corresponding ideas of beneficial spontaneous mechanisms, and a sober view of government—though ripened by the Physiocrats and Adam Smith (beginning in his jurisprudence lectures), had been bubbling up pervasively, for example in the writings of the Dutchman Pieter de la Court (1618–1685), earlier in the Salamancans, and so on.

D'Argenson questions whether the "general direction of trade" can be a science. He suggests that the general direction of trade is "beyond our reach," epistemically. When we reach beyond our inherent limitations in metaphysics, we merely waste our time. But in policy, he says, we take steps down the road to serfdom:

> [T]he general direction of trade cannot be a science; for it is impossible. Oftentimes, when we dive into sciences beyond our reach, ...we are quit for so much loss of time; but in policy, such false presumptions carry us a great way down the fatal paths of ruin and destruction. We ought to be persuaded that, in order to attain to that knowledge which is requisite for the direction of commerce, it is not enough to know the different interests of different nations, provinces and societies; but we must also understand the interests and connections of individuals, together with the quality and value of each commodity.

D'Argenson goes on to say that we "arrogate" to ourselves a pretense of knowledge. His essay helps us see that liberal arguments based on the disjointedness of knowledge and human conceits are older than we might realize.

---

8. "Critica di un oltramontano alla dissertazione del sig. Marchese Belloni sul commercio," *Magazzino toscano d'instruzione e di piacere*, December 1756.

9. *The Annual Register, or a View of the History, Politics, and Literature for the Year 1762* itself went through numerous editions, the fifth appearing in 1787.

"[T]he instinct of the bee," d'Argenson writes sarcastically, "does more in this particular, than the genius of the greatest politician."

After d'Argenson's essay commenting on the Bellonian's article was published anonymously in the April issue of *Journal Œconomique*, in the June issue was published a response by the Bellonian to d'Argenson.

The Bellonian's response is respectful and takes up d'Argenson's claim that the direction of trade cannot be a science. The exchange naturally raises issues about meanings of the word *science*. It also raises issues about how self-image or selfhood might motivate beliefs on either side of the exchange. Would d'Argenson say that his claim is a matter of science? Would he purport to being scientific in making his claim that the general direction of trade cannot be a science? The exchange raises questions about what work "general" is doing in the expression "general direction of trade."

But the Bellonian's response is also interesting on other counts. It highlights how the matter of freedom (*liberté*) is distinct from the issue of monarchy versus republic, writing: "the significant difference between these two forms of government is not freedom itself; freedom is equally necessary in both, since she alone can provide the tranquility which man needs to do his work and to enjoy the fruits of his labor." Also, the response notes how, historically, the sovereign's attention to commerce followed the transition from paying tributes in kind to paying tributes in money: "When the sovereigns drew, in fruits from the earth or in works of art, the tributes which their subjects must absolutely pay to them, it was very indifferent to them whether or not the people carried on any trade: but since they are now asking them for money, which commerce alone can procure them, it is very important for princes to see that commerce flourishes in their States". The fisc impels governmental involvement in trade. In a spirit of friendly and reasonable engagement, the response makes several points that we associate with economic nationalism. The response ends by affirming the importance of the "balance of power" concept in European international relations.

D'Argenson later prepared a rejoinder to the Bellonian, but he did not publish it, and it was presumably lost in the fire of 1871.[10]

---

10. Rathéry, the editor of d'Argenson's *Journal et Mémoires*, mentions the existence of an unpublished answer to the rebuttal of his first Observations (éd. Rathéry, I:xxxii). It has not been found in the remaining d'Argenson papers kept in the Archives Nationales or in the bibliothèque de Poitiers (Fonds d'Argenson).

Notes on the texts

The following English text of d'Argenson's essay keeps close to Smollett's version of 1754. I have compared the 1754 English version both to the 1751 published French version and an original manuscript version. Smollett's version had but a single (English) word in italics (namely, "*Police*"), but the published 1751 French original made frequent use of italics, and I have for the most part reinstated the 1751 italics. Also, based on the 1751 version, I have for the most part restored the original paragraph breaks and, on occasion, the punctuation, as when the removal of commas or the splitting of a particular sentence appeared to me as unreasonable decisions on Smollett's part. Also, for modern readers, I made a few very minor changes, such as the removal of a few commas. I changed Smollett's wording in just a few very minor instances.

Below d'Argenson's essay, I have rendered the Bellonian's response to d'Argenson into English for the first time, and into American English ("labor"), whereas the present version of d'Argenson retains the British of Smollett's 1754 version ("labour"). In the texts presented here, the words "trade" and "commerce" are both always translations of *commerce* in the original French texts. Smollett frequently translated *commerce* as "trade" (rather than as "commerce"). In translating the response, I too often use "trade," to echo the d'Argenson text, notably in the expression "the direction of trade."

In both texts that follow, I occasionally insert clarifying remarks in brackets [like these], and none of the footnotes are original; rather all of the footnotes have been introduced by me and represent my voice.

The General Directing of Trade Cannot Be a Science[11]

René Louis de Voyer de Paulmy, Marquis d'Argenson
edited by Benoît Malbranque
translated by Tobias Smollett

Sir [that is, the editor of *Journal Œconomique*],

In your journal for March, 1751, you have inserted a Dissertation upon trade, by the Marquis Belloni, which I have read several times, as an excellent piece; the substance of all the best remarks which have been made by our modern politicians on that subject, containing advice to sovereigns touching the direction of commerce, manufactures and the circulation of money.

But ought not he first to have considered whether it is more necessary to direct all those things with so much care and concern as he proposes, or to let them take their own way, under proper protection[12] only? How many general and particular manufactures have been established and brought to perfection by liberty alone, each having been carried *on in its own right*; every individual is led by honour and advantage, and thence results a *great whole*, which never is the consequence of a general direction. If, on the contrary, the government should be too watchful and solicitous, and laws too much extended or too minute should happen to disturb particular manufactures, in terrifying by penalties (often injudiciously inflicted) or recompensing by prices (ill adjudged), you substitute intrigue instead of emulation. How many things are now carried on with tolerable success, merely from having hitherto escaped a pretended legislative *police*, which instead of advancing, retards the progress of industry and improvement![13]

---

11. Smollett's translation was originally published as "A Letter to the Author of the Journal, Concerning the Dissertation upon Commerce, by the Marquis Belloni," in *Selected Essays on Commerce, Agriculture, Mines, Fisheries, and Other Useful Subjects*, London: D. Wilson and T. Durham (1754): 328–335.

12. *Protection* is not to be mistaken with *protectionism*, for it mostly referred to the protection of commercial ships by the navy, therefore enabling free-trade, not limiting it. At the same time Vincent de Gournay was also arguing for the combined policy of "liberty and protection," claiming that "everything grows and flourishes through a free and protected trade" (2017/1753, 55.).

13. "The very few things which can be said to be remotely satisfactory in France," d'Argenson writes elsewhere, "are those in which regulatory police has not penetrated and which

Observe how trade flourished in the republics, until its prosperity was interrupted by other political causes foreign to commerce (such as wars, national debt and oppression); the reason was, those republics have a spirit ever healthy, ever active, which is *liberty*; and this, far from diminishing, actually constitutes the public strength; it represses evil and maintains distributive justice, and the evil being repressed, the good appears and predominates: yes, the *removal of obstacles* is all that is necessary to the success of trade.

It asks nothing of the public, but good judges, the discouragement of monopoly, an equal protection to all the subjects, an invariable value of coin, roads and canals: besides these articles all other cares are vicious; and this vice is the more pernicious to a state, as it flows from an ill conducted zeal: this zeal has partisans, officers in employment and authority, and it requires whole ages to undeceive them of their errors.

Trade is the science of individuals; but the general direction of trade cannot be a science; for it is impossible.[14] Oftentimes, when we dive into sciences beyond our reach, such as the general system of the universe, infinitude, the union of spirit and matter, etc., we are quit for so much loss of time; but in policy, such false presumptions carry us a great way down the fatal paths of ruin and destruction. We ought to be persuaded that, in order to attain to that knowledge which is requisite for the direction of commerce, it is not enough to know the different interests of different nations, provinces and societies; but we must also understand the interests and connections of individuals, together with the quality and value of each commodity. He therefore, who is mistaken in the least article, will direct amiss, and enact preposterous laws.[15] Who then shall pretend to this integral and universal capacity? *Non*

---

remained free from taxation and monopoly" (1765, 261–262).

14. Along these lines the physiocrats and Turgot later expounded on the impossibility of government planning. See for example "Letter on the 'marque des fers'" (Turgot 1977/1773, 187).

15. "Ministers wish to conduct trade through their orders and regulations," noted d'Argenson in 1742, "but to this end one would need to fully know the interests of trade, not just from nation to nation, but county to county, town to town, and individual to individual; for without such a knowledge, half-science is far worse than ignorance in terms of the effects it produces" ("Mémoire à composer pour délibérer le pour et le contre, etc.," July 1742, in éd. Rathéry, IV:456).

At the beginning of the 18th century, Pierre de Boisguilbert (1646–1714), who influenced d'Argenson through Saint-Pierre, argued in favor of *laissez-faire*, understood as "letting the natural flow of things" in all economic matters, where the best outcomes, he claimed, were *datur scientia.*[16] Nevertheless the directors of trade arrogate this to themselves; and if this arrogance be faulty, and they consult their caprices more than their understanding, the result will be laws that cramp the commerce and favours unjustly conferred. Sometimes the council of commerce of a nation or province sees the common interest only through the eyes of their deputies; these sometimes propose private or particular advantages to their own towns or persons, to the prejudice of other towns and the rest of the subjects; and sometimes it is to be feared, they lay it down as a maxim to aggrandize what is great, annihilate what is little, and utterly banish equality.

It is reported of M. Colbert, that when he convened several deputies of commerce at his house and asked what he could do for the benefit of trade, the most sensible and plainest spoken man among them[17] replied in these three words: "Let us alone."[18] Have we ever sufficiently reflected upon the good sense of that short answer? This is no other than a kind of commentary upon it.

Apply it to everything that is done for trade, and to what chiefly destroys it in monarchies, and examine its effects: you will soon find how little fruit and success is reaped from all those cares of restraint, inspection and regulation; the republics have made greater advances in trade, almost without laws and constraint, than other countries when countenanced by the ablest ministers; the instinct of the bee does more in this particular, than the genius of the greatest politician;[19] the capital of a republican state, increases every day, by

---

always produced by themselves, "without the intervention of any superior authority, which must be banned when dealing of any sort of production, since nature, far from obeying human orders, always rebels again them, and never miss an opportunity to avenge itself by means of food shortage and misery" (*Traité de la nature, culture, commerce et intérêt des grains, etc.*, 1707, in Boisguilbert 1966, II:871).

16. Nonexistent is such science.

17. Thomas Le Gendre, a rich merchant from Rouen.

18. *Laissez-nous faire* later served as the rallying point for the physiocrats. "Let things be, let things go [*laissez faire et laissez passer*]," writes Le Trosne, "all the economic policy regarding industry and trade is contained in these words" (1768, 158). In his naturally excessive style, another writer, Nicolas Baudeau, spoke of "this divine phrase, let them be (*laissez-les faire*), that deserves to be engraved in gold letters on a marble column which would be placed on the grave of its author, and in front of which we would burn, instead of the regular incense, the massive volumes of laws under the yoke of which all the manufactures and industries of Europe are suffering" (1771, 208–209).

19. In another piece, published after his death, d'Argenson drew a parallel with a bee hive, to

economy, agriculture, industry, brokerage, manufacture, and everything that is understood by the idea of trade.

There are degrees by which we ascend successively from what is simple to what is improved, and from this last to the perfection of art; these the multitude will climb of themselves, by communication, example and emulation: they never fail to follow the different steps, and never mistake when left to their own conduct; but when people pretend to show them the road and direct them, woe be to him who mistakes![20] The needful is neglected, in order to proceed to what is superfluous before the time. Without mentioning particular nations, how many errors of this kind have been committed to the destruction of mankind![21] How many colonies have been peopled at the expense of the continent![22] While some places enjoyed abundance, how many others have been quite deserted! How many arts have been admired at the expense of neglecting the gifts of nature elsewhere; fine palaces built, and statues erected, but lands without culture, and villages without inhabitants.[23]

---

explain what was later famously associated with Smith's invisible hand. There, he says, "each insect acts according to its instinct, and what results from their actions is a great produce for the needs of their small society; but this was not brought about by orders, or by generals who forced each individual to follow the views of their leader" (1765, 41).

20. Elsewhere, d'Argenson expounded: "To let things be, should be the moto of every political authority since the world is civilized. Men emerged from barbarism, they cultivate arts very well; they have laws, models, they test different methods and practices to discover which one suits best. Let them be, and you will see that where this maxim is better followed, its effects are clearly visible. In a republic, individuals flourish and grow richer, private property is protected, and useful arts thrive. The same applies to our autonomous counties (*pays d'État*), for every time authority is kept at bay and human freedom is operating, things take off and grow rapidly" (1857–1858, V:364.).

21. Of course d'Argenson had the flawed policies of France in mind, but even in an anonymous article precautions had to be taken. In the same year of 1751, Montesquieu's *De l'esprit des lois* was banned by the Roman Catholic Church.

22. D'Argenson's inclination against colonization is expressed elsewhere: "If I were king, those colonies we possess, I would rather exchange them against a single pin! I would transform them into small republics under my protection, so that our merchants could trade with them, and increase the value and fame of our national products. I would do the same for the colonies that our India Company has created in Africa and Asia" (1857–1858, V:371).

23. The palace chiefly in mind would be Versailles, where d'Argenson disliked being. In his journal he constantly vilified its excessive luxury, and in the *Considérations* he wrote that "at court, it is a disgrace even to be suspected of being frugal" (1765, 172). Meanwhile descriptions of the misery of the people, especially in rural areas, are everywhere in d'Argenson's journal.

These are the effects of the grand science of trade.

The Marquis Belloni thinks it might be of service to trade, to set up custom-houses, and load one kind of commodity with higher duty than another; to exclude foreign merchandize, and favour our own by encouraging the exportation of them. This practice is but too well known in Europe; but the nation who introduced it first, has necessarily prescribed the example to others; each is willing to do the same injury to the right of nations which itself suffers: foreign manufactures were prohibited that one country might not become tributary to its neighbours; so that the Europeans, as they increased in the knowledge of trade, took measures for breaking all communication among themselves, and in time of profound peace suffer all the effects of an universal war. No, it is not the good of trade that advises these measures, but some *private interest* which too often gets the better of *public advantage*. If once the multitude is allowed to take their own way,[24] it will soon undeceive the world in this particular, to the great advantage of society, and show that the passage of merchandize from one state to another ought to be as free as that of air and water.[25] All Europe ought to be no other than a general and common fair; the person or nation which should make the best commodity could find the greatest advantage.[26] The distance and expense of carriage are sufficient reasons for any nation to prefer its own goods to those of others; and where these obstacles cease, the stranger is preferable to our own countryman, otherwise you ruin instead of favouring subjects in their trade. The custom-house duties will always have a bad effect, for the finances of the

---

24. D'Argenson was in favor of some sort of political representation: "My suggestion is to try giving the public a bigger role in government, and to see what happens" (1765, 172).

25. In a draft from 1742, d'Argenson noted how he should undertake a treatise on trade by considering "that one never bothers about air: it goes out and comes in, and yet is never found missing in the country. It is nonetheless a very necessary commodity" ("Mémoire à composer pour délibérer le pour et le contre, etc.," July 1742, in éd. Rathéry, IV:453; see also d'Argenson 1857–1858, V:383).

26. "Foreign trade can only be based on mutual need. When all doors will be opened it will flourish to the highest degree" (d'Argenson 1765, 185). D'Argenson's papers contained another judgment on this: "It is time for us to make a decision. Every nation hates and envies us. As for us, may we not envy them if they prosper, for it is good for them and good for us too: they will buy more of our products and will bring us more of their own, along with their money. It is indeed a despicable idea to wish for the prosperity of our nation by means of crushing down others; it can only please the malice and evil lying in our heart, and our own interest is in the very opposite" (1857–1858, V:372).

nation ought to be raised from the consumption only; as all duties levied upon the transportation (be what they will) never fail to distress the trade.

But presumption and self-love are so predominant among men, that they prefer a small advantage acquired by sophistry, subtlety or malice, to all that nature and humanity would afford with much more abundance and integrity; though their understanding was undoubtedly given them not to domineer but to regulate liberty. Yes, a regulated and enlightened *liberty* will always do more for the trade of any people, than the most intelligent domination: a single man sees more clearly into the interests of his own trade, and conducts it better than ten associates, whose interests are always divided and often opposed to each other. If he goes too far, if he usurps over or injures his neighbours, they can stop and restrain him with the assistance of justice; and this constitutes the equality, policy and balance that are necessary to trade: whereas our legislators can only perceive so many different interests in a confused manner. *Liberty* will enrich the merchants, and these becoming more or less wealthy, according to their talents, will endeavour to bring their manufactories to perfection. The regulations made for manufactories ought to be as so many instructions to those who are in search of this perfection, in the same manner as the books that treat of arts and sciences. There must be all sorts of degrees of goodness in the manufactories, according to the taste and circumstances of the purchasers:[27] imperfection and fraud discredit the manufacturer, while diligence and honesty enrich and bring them into vogue.[28] For these reasons commerce claims liberty instead of those penal laws, duties and interdictions by which it is discouraged.[29]

Trade itself is no other than an abstract idea lately known, as well as *circulation* and *credit*. We seem to make new divinities, like the Greeks, in order to adore them: our fathers, who had less idolatry and philosophy, but more wisdom, were richer by their economy and labour, than we by our sciences

27. "In clothing as in everything else," Vincent de Gournay similarly claimed in 1754, "room must be made for good, average and mediocre quality... If a seemingly bad fabric is sold, it is proof that it is not bad; if it is not sold, the maker is punished instantly and will make amends" (2008/1754, 195).

28. "The best indicator of utility is the public at large, it is the support consistently obtained from those who have an interest. Everyone feels what his own interest is, everyone takes action for his own benefit, and it is in this general agreement that we discover the truth" (d'Argenson 1857–1858, V:382–383).

29. "To lead industry against its will is to wish its downfall" (éd. Rathéry, VI:424).

of exchange, brokerage, and stock-jobbing. Perhaps our posterity, undeceived by experience, will laugh at the disease that now prevails in several nations, of endeavouring to reduce the principles of trade into a system:[30] and will place it in that rank which we now assign to the Crusades, and which we shall soon give to the folly of the *political balance* of power in Europe.[31,32]

Yes, the Directing of Trade Can Be a Science[33]

Anonymous (a Bellonian)
translated by Benoît Malbranque

Sir,

You do not surprise me when you claim that you have read several times the dissertation on commerce of the marquis Belloni, and that you regard it as an excellent piece, for it is indeed a masterpiece which has all the qualities to deserve this name. The marquis Belloni, a descendant of Roman merchants, surrounded by universal esteem for their probity and intelligence, is a merchant himself, and with a new brilliance he unites in his person the talents and virtues of his ancestors. It is his rare merit that owes him the affection with which His Holiness[34] honors him, and of which He wanted to give him incontestable proof, by conferring on him recently the title of Marquis. Therefore, his dissertation on commerce is not the fruit of idle speculation, but of deep study and thoughtful practice; his enlightened mind has penetrated the causes of what experience has shown him, and he

---

30. "A nation can slip into bad habits under bad governments, just like ill-bred children. These habits can disappear eventually, but they will impact the character for a long time" (1765, 81).
31. The response later criticized d'Argenson for this comment. It is worth noting nonetheless that d'Argenson had been Foreign Affairs Minister from November 1744 to January 1747.
32. This last sentence, like others, was omitted in the Italian translation (1756), which is more of an adaptation: it does not always follow the text perfectly, although all in all it gives a fair picture.
33. Originally published as "Réponse de l'auteur du Journal économique à la Lettre qui lui a été adressée au mois d'avril dernier, au sujet de la dissertation sur le commerce de M. le marquis Belloni" (which would translate as: "Response by the author in the *Journal oeconomique* to the letter addressed to him in April, concerning the dissertation *On commerce* by the marquis Belloni"), *Journal Œconomique*, June 1751: 130–149.
34. The Pope Benedict XIV, head of the Catholic Church from 1740 to 1758.

only took the pen after having discovered the connection between principles and their effects, and how they derive naturally from each other. It is the reason why, when aiming at establishing the true means of supporting and stimulating trade, he began by demonstrating the true nature of trade, so that there would be no misunderstanding regarding these means, and that trade could be governed according to its nature. Consequently, I am surprised, Sir, that without contradicting his fundamental principles, you would raise doubts about the fair consequences he draws from them. You are not inclined to approve of sovereign authority interfering in the conduct of commerce; chambers of commerce and custom-houses seem disastrous to you.

Before taking the defense of the marquis Belloni, I must clear up an ambiguity that I have caused. His views being comprehensive, he deals of both republics and monarchies, and says so positively. But monarchies being more common in the world, I considered them solely, and I had all the more reason to do so, since, if you examine the matter well and with some attention, there is nothing that the author says about monarchies that is not applicable to republics. Indeed, the significant difference between these two forms of government is not freedom itself; freedom is equally necessary in both, since she alone can provide the tranquility which man needs to do his work and to enjoy the fruits of his labor. It would be easy to prove that one is freer under the rule of a single sovereign, than under the rule of several leaders, and that the *regulated and enlightened* monarchical authority is infinitely above the republican authority, however wise we may suppose it to be. But what, according to some, gives the preference to the republic over the monarchy, is that in the latter the sovereign authority is always vigilant and alert, and acts by itself; while in the former the authority stays sometimes asleep, and discharges on ministers the care which should be exerted directly. These ministers sometimes set themselves as rulers who, when they consider only their own interests, have their wars and their leagues, their truces, their peace and their alliances; the body of the state is tormented by these irregular movements, and it suffers, until the head wakes up: but as soon as it resumes its functions, all things go back in running order, public health is quickly restored, and this is a real and often felt advantage which the republics have hardly ever enjoyed, for their internal troubles usually bring about the ruin of the State.

So do not set yourself, Sir, the prerequisite of a republic to make commerce flourish: the regulated and enlightened liberty which it requires can be found elsewhere. The first commercial state was monarchical; and when you say that *the republics have made greater advances in trade, almost without laws and constraint, than other countries when countenanced by the ablest ministers,* you agree in spite of yourself that at least some laws, and some constraint, are necessary in order for free trade to be regulated and enlightened. But who will dictate these laws if not the sovereign authority? And what change would it make for these laws in themselves, whether the authority rests in one or more hands? In vain on this subject do you suppose in monarchies all kinds of abuses which you believe are not to be found in republics. I do not allow myself to be surprised by this picture; I know that everywhere men are inclined to license when they obey, and prone to error when they command; and that for this reason we cannot over-enlighten some and contain others too much: these two points form the source of the public good. Just as the subject must respect the limits which are prescribed for him, the sovereign authority must see everything, examine everything, know everything in order to weigh the interests of all parts of the State, and to direct, by a general impression, the movements of individuals, so that the profit which a province will receive, for example, from trade, will not be so limited that it remains absolutely unknown to others, let alone becomes harmful to them. This care is as indispensable in a republic as in a monarchy, and this is the only management of trade that the marquis Belloni promotes.

But you, Sir, do not want any management whatsoever, and you assure that your republics, *almost without laws,* have made trade flourish without any knowledge; because you argue that this knowledge is impossible. *Trade,* you say, *is the science of individuals; but the general direction of trade cannot be a science; for it is impossible.* To this reasoning I will only oppose the following: *War is the science of soldiers, but the conduct of war cannot be a science, for it is impossible.* One would explain this impossibility like you prove that of the direction of trade. You say: *We ought to be persuaded that, in order to attain to that knowledge which is requisite for the commerce of direction* (would it not have been better to say this direction of trade?[35]) *it is not enough to know the different interests of different nations, provinces and societies; but we must also understand the interests and connections of individuals, together*

---

35. The original 1751 French edition of d'Argenson's article had the curious words "*pour connaître ce commerce de direction*" (to know this commerce of direction), which is very likely to have been a mistake, by him or the editor or the *Journal oeconomique.* Indeed the 1754 English translation says "the direction of commerce."

with the quality and value of each commodity. One would therefore add: *We ought to be persuaded that, in order to be able to conduct a war, it would not suffice to compare the forces from nation to nation, from armies to armies, from frontiers to frontiers, it would also be necessary to know the degree of force and the disposition of opposing soldiers, as well as the quality and value of their weapons.* While waiting for someone to point out the fault lying in this comparison, I have the right to speculate that the science of the direction of trade is indeed possible, and to try to prove its necessity in a few words.

When the sovereigns drew, in fruits from the earth or in works of art, the tributes which their subjects must absolutely pay to them, it was very indifferent to them whether or not the people carried on any trade: but since they are now asking them for money, which commerce alone can procure them, it is very important for princes to see that commerce flourishes in their States, and to ensure that *active* commerce prevails over *passive* commerce; for otherwise the people, being without money, however goodwill they might have, will not be able to pay their respects to their prince, and the prince without finances will not be able to defend them against the actions of their neighbors. It is therefore obvious that, in its own interest, the sovereign power must support foreign trade, extend interior commerce wherever it is not yet activated, animate both, and direct it to the general good of the State; and this can only be performed when the authority has acquired a general knowledge of trade, and by means of the various chambers of commerce that it establishes, from which information can be received, and which shall pass its orders wherever they need to be known.

This is the spirit of the institution of chambers of commerce: their purpose is the public good: they can achieve it, having the necessary credit and authority. If you find some chambers of commerce who take an opposite route, the marquis Belloni abandons them at your discretion; the fact that they can be useful is enough for him to be entitled to ask for their establishment.

As for customs, they have always been regarded among the most legitimate rights that princes levy in their states, and I am sure that if you had looked at antiquity, you would have spoken of it differently. You would have seen that in those early days when, as I have just said, kings received in kind the tributes of their subjects, merchants went to them, as much for permission to sell their goods as to buy from their stores, and never approached them without giving them presents. These gifts were too essential to be voluntary:

they were rather honest customs that the prince himself raised. He later had them levied by his officers, when the kingdoms began to expand, and the merchants no longer went directly to their capitals, but stopped on the border or in other towns. They were still asked everywhere for the prince's presents, which imperceptibly took the name of rights. Finally, money having become a common commodity, and kings having began to ask money from their subjects, they demanded all the more from merchants, to allow the entry of foreign goods. The marquis Belloni, when approving of them, did not do anything but in accordance with the custom of all times and all places; and the correct discernment which he makes between foreign goods and those of the country, clearly removes any occasion for misunderstanding.

Indeed, it is between the citizens of a single State that he could agree to have all goods shared commonly *like air and water*, because they would carry the same burden, and their interests would be common. But the danger of such freedom with foreign nations is so obvious that I do not believe it is possible not to perceive it. Allowing the entry of all foreign fabrics of silk and wool, manufacturers from outside, will cause the ruin of those at home: and do not say that the esteem that men in general have for anything that comes from distant countries will engage the foreigners to value your products.[36] The country where the materials are more beautiful will always win in the end; this country will fill itself with money at the expense of others. This is the advantage that the Indies have over the rest of the world. The state being stripped of money, where will the prince find enough to feed his armies, or to maintain his artillery? With what will he reward his officers, support the splendor of his crown, make the necessary advances, either for the advancement of science or for the good of commerce itself? The effect of customs is to prevent money from going out in excess for things that can be called unnecessary. The absolute defense against some foreign goods does not produce, as you seem to think, *all the evils of war*: this is but curious overstatement. It is one of the evils of war that raw and necessary materials are prevented from being exchanged from one country to another:

---

36. Before the Revolution of 1789, the French had been very keen at admiring other nations and welcomed with open arms anything coming from far away. "Our nation," wrote Charles Perrault in 1688, "has always been accused of excessively loving foreign peoples" (Perrault 1693, I:5). Back in 1614, an Englishman portrayed this French hospitality in a curious piece (see Barclay 1633, 55–56).

but it is the wisdom of legislators who are more clairvoyant than one might think, to ensure that a people, deprived of a superfluity which only serves to nourish luxury, learns to be satisfied with what its native land provides. On this subject, we must make a very essential distinction between the different powers: some occupy large areas, like the monarchies of France and Spain, etc.; others occupy only small areas, like the republics of Holland, Genoa, Venice, etc. Although absolutely speaking large states can survive on their own, those whose boundaries are narrow and who live on ungrateful lands, are obliged to have recourse to trade to feed their peoples. They can only support themselves through a perpetual exchange of all the productions of other countries. So to speak they are nothing but the shopkeepers and the merchants of the rest of the world. It is therefore necessary for them to have a share in everything, and that in their country everything enters and leaves easily. However, even in these States, the customs duties mentioned earlier are no less authorized, and the difference between these rights is yet another proof of the special care which the sovereign power takes and must take for the direction of trade with the view of the general interest of the State.

If there was a nation wise enough to limit itself to the productions of its country, one would soon see with astonishment, by the works that its industry would produce with its own materials, how rich nature is everywhere. Thus, bring us back the golden age, Sir, or give up the idea of forming one society of all the peoples of Europe. Nations are divided and will never rejoin together; various events can cause them to merge into each other, but as long as they remain distinct, their interests will always be separate, and the nation that most easily does without others will always be the wisest and the most powerful.

I notice that you have recognized that the abolition of customs would create a deficit in the prince's finances; yet the cure that you suggest seems worse than the disease. After letting foreign goods enter free of charge, you want to levy taxes on consumption. But if by consumption we are to understand the flow of goods and products within the country, whether food, clothing, or lodging, and the necessary export of their superabundance, can you ignore that by levying taxes on it, you actually make it impossible for the craftsman to work economically, and that you make life harder for an entire nation? Buyers will pay products at a higher price, while sellers will sell and manufacture less, since high prices discourage buyers, and little selling discourages labor. This is the inevitable effect of consumption taxes. Due to these taxes, the products necessary for life, which the country produces, or which are manufactured there, will lose the advantage that they should naturally have over foreigners; those products would then only be used insofar as absolutely necessary; there is no need to cite examples; hence the decrease in trade which always carries with it the abandonment of agriculture and the ruin of the arts. Such is the state to which you will reduce your own country, because of the favor given to foreign goods, which on the other hand will take away all the money from the state; this is as was noted by M. [Jean-Baptiste] Colbert, who the marquis Belloni quoted on this issue: *Even if*, said this great minister, *one would surround a kingdom with a high wall to contain the money from going out, if in this wall there is a small crack, all the money of the kingdom will flow through this opening.* But if you discourage your laborers and artisans, if you let foreign goods enter freely, how will you keep the money from coming out? How will you get money from outside? How will the prince obtain from his subjects the money that they will no longer have?

After this long introduction on the general management of trade, on the chambers of commerce, and on customs, one cannot help but feel surprised, Sir, to hear you treat trade as a new divinity that we made in order to adore it. What will become of this *science of individuals*? Did you cry out so loudly in favor of *freedom* to establish but a pipe dream? As for credit and agio, which the marquis Belloni does not cover, I will not make any comment on it, so as not to leave my subject, which is only to defend the principles of this illustrious merchant: yet I cannot possibly refrain from talking about the circulation of specie, which you treat no differently than trade itself.

We call circulation of specie its passage from one hand to the other: it takes place when the prince and the rich, receiving their income in one hand, spend them with the other, whether for the maintenance of the State, or for the needs and conveniences of life: then the entrepreneurs, employees and merchants carry over to the provinces and return to the common people the sums which have been drawn from them, and which will return again to the first hands, by the same channels, continually emerging through the same channels to replenish in their course and to benefit all parts of the State: just like water, which is necessarily discharged from the earth by evaporation, and subsequently moistens it back by means of dews and rains. This, Sir, is what circulation is: this is what you regard as an insubstantial idea. It is evident that trade alone, especially foreign trade, can animate it by means of consumption;

it is no less obvious that the prince has a very urgent interest in facilitating it, and consequently in keeping an eye on trade—all operations that he cannot do without having first acquired a general knowledge of it: not as to direct it in all its detail, as you suppose, but as a whole, as prescribed by the marquis Belloni.

I will end my answer by asking, Sir, for the permission to say, regarding the rather critical tone you took at the end of your letter, that one must have poorly reflected on history to treat as a folly the idea of the balance of powers. The Greeks were always very eager to maintain this balance, when the republics of Athens and Lacedaemon fought for the empire of Greece. Alexander's successors waged many wars, signed treaties and alliances among themselves only to maintain a fair balance. It was short-lived between Rome and Carthage: but it existed between these two republics, from the first to the second Punic war. This balance was perfectly observed in Italy until Charles VIII, aiming at the kingdom of Naples, eventually broke it: he had the support of Charles V and Francis I until the battle of Pavia; and it was to reestablish it that the emperor's allies then crossed over to France. Again, in the last century it has been the object of much attention, because the forces of France were growing rapidly and the neighboring states thought it necessary to take measures to ensure their safety: but there is no one who is not convinced by reading history, that the moderation of Louis XIV did more for them than their constantly renewed leagues. If it can be broken by the prosperity of a political power, is it a reason to treat the balance of power as a pipe dream and extravagance? It is not necessary that it subsists without interruption to give it reality; it is enough that it has existed from time to time, and that the effects have been satisfactory. A wise politician observes states in their birth; he sees them grow, sometimes stagnate for a long time, and finally thrive, and he recognizes that all things are set in motion by a higher cause which forms them, preserves them and leads them to their end by means which are as impenetrable as his views.

References

Anonymous (a Bellonian). 1751a. Dissertation sur le commerce, tirée de celle du Marquis Belloni, publiée à Rome en 1750. *Journal Œconomique*, March: 93–121.

Anonymous (a Bellonian). 1751b. Réponse de l'auteur du Journal économique à la Lettre qui lui a été adressée au mois d'avril dernier, au sujet de la dissertation sur le commerce de M. le marquis Belloni. *Journal Œconomique*, June: 130–149.

Barclay, John. 1633. *The Mirrour of Mindes, or, Barclay's Icon Animorum.* London: Thomas Walkley.

Baudeau, Nicolas. 1771. *Première introduction à la philosophie économique.* Paris: Didot, Delalain, Lacombe.

Belloni, Girolamo. 1750. *Del commercio.* Rome.

Belloni, Girolamo. 1752 [1750]. *A Dissertation on Commerce* [*Del commercio*]. London: R. Manby.

Bianchini, Marco. 2002. *Bonheur public et méthode géométrique: Enquête sur les économistes italiens, 1711–1803*, trans. Pierre Crépel. Paris: INED.

Boisguilbert, Pierre de. 1966. *Pierre de Boisguilbert ou la naissance de l'économie politique*, 2 vols. Paris: INED.

[D'Argenson, René Louis de Voyer de Paulmy, Marquis]. 1751. Lettre à l'auteur du Journal œconomique au sujet de la Dissertation sur le commerce de M. le Marquis Belloni. *Journal Œconomique*, April: 107–117.

[D'Argenson, René Louis de Voyer de Paulmy, Marquis]. 1754 [1751]. A Letter to the Author of the Journal, Concerning the Dissertation upon Commerce, by the Marquis Belloni. Translated by Tobias Smollett. In *Selected Essays on Commerce, Agriculture, Mines, Fisheries, and Other Useful Subjects*, 328–335. London: D. Wilson and T. Durham.

D'Argenson, René Louis de Voyer de Paulmy, Marquis. 1764. *Considérations sur le gouvernement ancien et présent de la France.* Amsterdam: Rey.

D'Argenson, René Louis de Voyer de Paulmy, Marquis. 1765. *Considérations sur le gouvernement ancien et présent de la France*, 2nd ed. Amsterdam: Rey.

D'Argenson, René Louis de Voyer de Paulmy, Marquis. 1789. *Essays, Civil, Moral, Literary and Political.* London: Logographic Press.

D'Argenson, René Louis de Voyer de Paulmy, Marquis. 1857–1858 [1825]. *Mémoires et journal inédit du marquis d'Argenson, ministre des affaires étrangères sous Louis XV*, ed. M. le Marquis d'Argenson, 6 vols. Paris: P. Jannet.

D'Argenson, René Louis de Voyer de Paulmy, Marquis. 1859–1867 (éd. Rathéry). *Journal et mémoires du marquis d'Argenson*, ed. E. J. B. Rathéry, 9 vols. Paris: Renouard.

D'Argenson, René Louis de Voyer de Paulmy, Marquis. 1901. *Journal and Memoirs of the Marquis d'Argenson*, ed. E. J. B. Rathéry, trans. Katharine Prescott Wormeley, 2 vols. Boston: Hardy, Pratt & Company.

Dupont de Nemours, Pierre-Samuel. 1984. *The Autobiography of Du Pont de Nemours*, trans. Elizabeth Fox-Genovese. Wilmington, Del.: Scholarly Resources.

Gournay, Vincent de. 2008 [1754]. Remarques. In *Traités sur le commerce*, by Josiah Child. Paris: L'Harmattan.

Gournay, Vincent de. 2017 [1753]. Réflexions sur la contrebande. In *Mémoires et lettres de Vincent de Gournay.* Marcq-en-Barœul, France: Institut Coppet.

Le Trosne, Guillaume-François. 1768. *Lettres à un ami.* Paris: Desaint.

Mizuta, Hiroshi. 2019. Adam Smith's Library: General Check-List and Index. *Econ Journal Watch* 16(2): 384–474.

Perrault, Charles. 1693. *Parallèle des Anciens et des Modernes*, 2nd ed. Paris: Coignard.

Tocqueville, Alexis de. 1856. *The Old Regime and the Revolution*, trans. John Bonner. New

York: Harper & Brothers.

Turgot, Anne Robert Jacques. 1977 [1773]. Letter on the "Marque des Fers." In *The Economics of A. R. J. Turgot*, ed. and trans. P. D. Groenewegen. The Hague: Nijhoff.

Wormeley, Katharine Prescott. 1901. Translator's Note. In *Journal and Memoirs of the Marquis d'Argenson*, by René Louis de Voyer de Paulmy, Marquis d'Argenson, I:39–40. Boston: Hardy, Pratt & Company.

Information for the Hair Dressers in Edinburgh; Against the Incorporation of Barbers— The Second Edition

Foreword

Daniel B. Klein[1]

Searching for something in Eighteenth Century Collections Online, I stumbled upon a 1758 pamphlet whose last page purports authorship of "Hew Dalrymple." The British Library deems that a pseudonym and the pamphlet itself a "squib" or spoof.

The pamphlet seems to have passed directly into oblivion; as of September 2018 it had just two Google Scholar citations, both ancillary (Festa 2005, 65; Markiewicz 2014, 151, 208).[2] Yet the pamphlet is a wonderful liberal criticism of what we term occupational licensing.

The pamphlet favors freedom in an Edinburgh turf battle. The "hair dressers" and "wig-makers" seek liberty to cut hair. The "barbers," in rent-seeking fashion, assert an exclusive privilege to cut hair. Historically, barbers were principally concerned with shaving auxiliary to surgery, surgery often calling for shaving of hair. Barbers also pulled teeth, let blood, stitched up minor wounds, etc., as well as cut hair, and of course gave shaves.

"Industry needs no other Spur than the Profit and Honour attending her," says the pamphlet author. The barbers' claimed exclusive privileges are "a Restriction of natural Freedom" and "a Reproach to the Constitution." The author asks the judges of Edinburgh, in interpreting the law, to "give a free

---

1. I am very grateful to Professor John W. Cairns for his generous help, to the librarians alluded to in a footnote below, and to Stephen Delli Priscoli for typing up the pamphlet.
2. Another ancillary citation, not captured by Google Scholar, is Williams (2016, 56 n.9).

and uninterrupted Course to the Bent and Genius of the People." The author highlights that the hairdressers seek merely the freedom to practice, not a privilege of their own against other cutters of hair.

The author teaches key insights against occupational licensing: The privileges reduce quality, supply, convenience and availability, and innovation. Consumer-protection rationales are fraudulent, and, at any rate, rationales go obsolete. The privileges are inevitably rather arbitrary, a source of social "Rancour" and hypocrisy. They are used opportunistically to seek rents.

The pamphlet highlights the expertise required by the original 1505 charter ("Seal of Cause") of surgeons and barbers, including that the candidate "know perfectly" how to "make *Phlebotomia* in due time; and also, that he know in [which] Member the Sign has Domination for the Time." Thus, entrance required "being acquainted with astrology in order to be able to bleed and operate satisfactorily" (Scott-Moncrieff 1912, 253).

Here are some pointers on the pamphlet's language:

- *Defenders* – the hairdressers and wig-makers.
- *Pursuers* – the barbers.
- *Preses* – the president or presiding officer of a meeting or group.
- *Box-master* – treasurer.
- *your Lordships* – the judges, known as Lords of Session, hearing the case.
- *Seal of Cause* – charter.
- *Emulation* – competition.
- *Cujus est finis, ejus sunt media* – he who intends some end should choose the means of achieving it.
- *Laputa* – in *Gulliver's Travels* (Swift 1726), a floating island, whose male inhabitants relish intellectual and mathematical abstractions, but impractically.
- *quondam* – former.
- *quhilk* – which.
- *Beker* – bowl.
- *Prescription* – a right, privilege, or presumption derived from custom.
- *in foro contradictorio* – where a court decision has been given after litigation by both parties.
- *Curdowers* – those working at a trade within a burgh in which they are

not burghers.

- *Mantua-makers* – makers of women's clothing.
- *taylors entering the mantua-makers* – tailors admitting the makers of women's clothing to the corporation (and taking specified dues from them).
- *took Pepper in the Nose* – took umbrage.

The status of the document as an official court document (an 'Information') remains highly uncertain; there is no complete inventory of official documents of the kind it pretends to be. Again, librarians have recorded it as a pseudonymous "squib."[3] To explore the matter further, I reached out to Professor John W. Cairns of the University of Edinburgh, an expert in Scots law of the time, who has, on short notice, responded avidly, as he could. The pamphlet assumes the form of a proper 'Information,' and it uses names that do appear in decreets on litigation about exclusive barbering privilege in Edinburgh and its suburbs.[4] From certain sources (e.g., Scott-Moncrieff 1912 and similar antiquarian pieces by G. A. Fothergill and C. H. Creswell), it seems that the pamphlet's historical information about the law and development of the trades is sound enough.

Cairns and I have a theory, built on curious features of the pamphlet. One of the curious things is that the title page of the pamphlet says "The SECOND EDITION;" no other edition is known to the British Library or elsewhere, which is not surprising; but more important is that Cairns has never before seen a second edition of an 'Information.' Other curious features

---

3. The prominent Hew Dalrymple of the time was Sir Hew Dalrymple (1712–1790), Second Baronet, of North Berwick; perhaps the pamphlet's author used the name "Hew Dalrymple" as a jest of some sort. A kind librarian of the British Library (Rare Books and Music Reference Team) explained that both "Explore the British Library" and the "English Short Title Catalogue" indicate "Hew Dalrymple" to be a pseudonym, though no reason is given; but he advised that he and colleague felt that it made sense to conclude that the pamphlet was not written by the Sir Hew Dalrymple, and a similar assessment was offered by a librarian at the National Library of Scotland (Rare Books, Maps, and Music Collections). I thank these librarians for the fine help on the matter.

4. *See* Society of Barbers of Edinburgh Archive, Litigation 1722–1829 series, held by the Royal College of Surgeons of Edinburgh Library, notably the January 16, 1750, "Decreet: the Incorporation of Barbers of Edinburgh against Low, Boyd and all wigmakers in Edinburgh" Reference no. SB 7/4 and the January 7, 1761, "Decreet and precept: the Incorporation of Barbers of Edinburgh against certain wigmakers of the city," reference no. SB 7/5.

are the ideological pointedness and, especially, the rollicking, over-the-top spirit. Finally, there is the extensive italicization throughout the pamphlet. Our theory is that the pamphlet is a take-off—hence "second edition"—of an official document from goings-on circa 1757, and that italics are used for additions or changes from the original official 'Information' (though not only for that). Where that theory would leave the pamphlet's purported authorship, "Hew Dalrymple," is unclear. Further investigation may resolve some of the mystery.

The pamphlet appeared when liberal principles were ascendant, and, indeed, when the guild privileges were falling apart. The matter before the judges is particular and circumscribed, but just principles would "throw open the Door to every *Footman*," the author says, and: "no *Detriment*, but much *Benefit*, would arise to the Nation in general" if "*every* Man of *every* Profession, had it in his Power to *exercise* the same, when, and where he pleased."

Adam Smith called for reform "where every man was perfectly free both to chuse what occupation he thought proper, and to change it as often as he thought proper" (WN, 116).[5] The words of the pamphlet also resemble Smith's more general avowals—leaving every man "perfectly free to pursue his own interest his own way," "allowing every man to pursue his own interest his own way"—in propounding, respectively, "the obvious and simple system of natural liberty" (ibid., 687) and "the liberal plan of equality, liberty, and justice" (664).

---

5. *See* Smith on long apprenticeships and labor-market privileges (WN, 116–152)—"a plain violation of this most sacred property" (WN, 138)—and on the "privileges of graduation" (WN, 762, 780; LJ, 84, 363–364, 472, 497–498, 529; *Corr.*, 173–179). Today the leading scholar of occupational licensing is Morris Kleiner (2006; 2013; 2014; Kleiner and Krueger 2013; Kleiner and Vorotnikov 2017) and the leading organization battling it in court is the Institute for Justice. *Econ Journal Watch* has published several articles on the topic including Svorny 2004; Stephenson and Wendt 2009; Reinhardt 2014.

Information for the Hair Dressers in Edinburgh; Against the Incorporation of Barbers— The Second Edition

Hew Dalrymple (pseud.?)

7th March 1758.

INFORMATION

FOR

ALEXANDER LOW, WALTER BOYD, JOHN CHINEBOW, and JAMES MACFARQUHAR, all Wig-makers in *Edinburgh*, Defenders;

AGAINST

The Preses, Box-master, and remanent Members of the Incorporation of BARBERS of *Edinburgh*, Pursuers.

The Barbers of *Edinburgh*, upon Pretences equally groundless and extravagant, having taken it into their Heads, that the exclusive Privilege, which they have always enjoyed, of clearing the Face from that uncleanly and unbecoming *Excrement*, the *Beard*, gave them also a Right to lop and prune the ornamental Hair of the *Head*, in so far as was necessary for the proper dressing and adorning thereof, did exhibit a Complaint, against the Defenders, before the Magistrates of *Edinburgh*, for alledged Incroachments, made upon this, *their particular Province of the human Body*.

The Magistrates, *always ready*, and *always willing*, to support and extend the *Privileges* and *Pretences* of their Incorporations, did pronounce an Interlocutor, declaratory of the Privileges of the Barbers, and finding that they are in the Possession, and have the sole and exclusive Privilege of trimming and barberising, or, of cutting Hair and taking off Beards, within this City. And, in consequence of that, they thought proper, by a subsequent Interlocutor, to inflict a Fine on the Defenders, for having transgressed against the Incorporation, and incroached upon their Privileges, and to prohibit them from cutting Hair, within the City, in all Time coming, under a Penalty of 6 *l. Scots* for each Fault.

The Defenders advised, that the *Beard* and the *Hair* of the Head, as being ruled by *different Planets*, ought also to be under the Direction of *different sublunary Agents*, brought the Cause, by Advocation, before your Lordships:

29

And the Barbers having consented to the Advocation, the Cause was debated before the Lord *Bankton*, Ordinary: And his Lordship, having taken it to report, and ordered Informations upon the *important Question*, the following State of the Case is humbly offered upon the Part of the Defenders.

The Defenders are, all of them, Freemen and Burgesses in the Town of *Edinburgh;* and, as such, are intitled to exercise every lawful Art and Calling, of which no exclusive Privilege has been granted to an Incorporation. The Making Wigs and the Dressing Hair is yielded to them by the Barbers; so that the single Question is, Whether the cutting of the Hair, to render it proper for dressing, is more *germain* to the Profession of a *Hair-dresser*, or to that of a *Beard-shaver?* and whether there is any exclusive Privilege granted to the Barbers, and possessed by them, as to this Particular?

And, in arguing this Question, your Lordships will not fail to consider the Effect of an exclusive Privilege. It is, at any Rate, a Restriction of natural Freedom: It is a great Bar to Industry; and, in a free and trading Nation, almost a Reproach to the Constitution. In the Days of our Ancestors, such was the idle and barbarous Disposition of the People, that every useful Art and Calling would have been totally neglected, unless the Legislature had fallen upon the Expedient of establishing Incorporations, and granting to them Immunities and exclusive Privileges. But although this Remedy prevented the total Destruction of Arts, it had this bad Effect also, to prevent their Increase and Growth to Perfection. It left little or no Room for Emulation: Nay, it checked the very Seeds of that Virtue, and an aspiring Spirit was looked upon as a dangerous Thing. Mediocrity was safe, and none attempted to get above it. For Corporations considered themselves as Republics, in which it is the Interest of the whole, to crush the growing Power or Merit of Individuals.

But the Tables are so far turned, and the World so far sensible of the Error, that, in some of the Arts at least, indeed all the mechanical ones, Industry needs no other Spur than the Profit and Honour attending her. Therefore, the continuing these exclusive Privileges is as absurd, as it would be to continue a Person, in the Vigour of Health, under the Regimen and Medicaments that were necessary when he languished beneath a mortal Disease. And therefore it has been Matter of Speculation, and very well deserves the Attention of the Legislature, whether it would not be proper to beat down all these *Gothick* Inclosures, and give a free and uninterrupted Course to the Bent and Genius of the People.

But, as your Lordships are not possessed of legislative Power, you cannot do this, though you are possessed of an interpretative Power, which enables you to do a great deal. One general Rule you follow, which is, never to extend exclusive Privileges, farther than they are clearly and explicitly founded in the Grant; and where there is any Doubt or Ambiguity, it is a Maxim of universal Law, to give Judgment on the Side of natural Liberty; and surely, if these Maxims can ever be applied in the utmost Latitude of Interpretation to any Case, they must in the present, where the Demands of Exclusion are so *unreasonable*, and the Request of Freedom so *natural*, and withal so *trifling*.

For all that the Defenders demand is, That, as they have confessedly a Right to dress Hair within the City, they should also have the Liberty of using the *Scissars*, to make it fit for the Operation of dressing, and they claim this upon the Import of that Maxim of natural Equity, *Cujus est finis, ejus sunt media*. On the other hand, the Barbers, who have the same Privilege of dressing with the Defenders, *together with that exclusive one of using the Bason and Suds, and of taking every one of his Majesty's Subjects, even the highest, by the Nose, with Impunity*, are unconscionable enough to demand, that they, and they only, should have the Power of cutting the Hair, which, in Consequence and Effect, would destroy the Defenders Business of dressing altogether: For no body would choose the Trouble and Expence of two different Operators; or, if any one was whimsical enough to have a Barber to cut his Hair, and one of the Defenders to dress it, the Consequence would be, that, *what with cutting to spoil the dressing, and dressing to shame the cutting, the poor Patient would soon be reduced to the Condition of the Man in the Fable, who, to his Misfortune, had both an old Wife and a young;* or, at best, *would look like one of the mathematical Inhabitants of* Laputa, *with the Hair on the one Side of his Head three Inches shorter than that on the other.*

Such fatal Consequences from the *Rancour* of contending Powers are to be avoided. And a just Interpretation of the Rights and Privileges established to the Barbers by their Seal of Cause, and the subsequent Act of Council founded on by them, will enable your Lordships to interpose your Authority for that Purpose. The Seal of Cause is granted in the 1505 to the Surgeons and Barbers, as a joint Society; and, it is to be remarked, that although the Barbers would now endeavor to *degrade* themselves to a Level with common *Friseurs*, yet, in their Original, they are of high Rank, *no less than Cadets of the Surgeons;* for Shaving was invented by the Sons of *Machaon*, and was by them used to clear away the Hair from these Parts of the human Body, that had been casually wounded. But, in Process of Time, *when the Degeneracy of Manners brought feminine Beauty into Repute, and transformed the rough Warriour into a whining Lover, then, and not till then, the Chins of Men were brought under the Barbers Yoke; and some Philosophers affirm, that the ignominious Treatment, which all Men must submit to from the Gentlemen of that Profession, was decreed as a Punishment for this Degeneracy, and a proper Badge of the Subjection of our Spirits, which evaporated with our Beards, and was conformable to the* Gothic *Custom of asserting Dominion over a Vassal, by leading him out of Court by the* Nose, which is now become a proverbial Expression. But, be that as it will, *the Beards, which had been often tugged in their Country's Cause, were thrown neglected aside, to make Way for the smooth and delicate Touch of a nimble-fingered Lady, upon the Lip and Cheek of her Paramour.*

In this Business were Surgeons first employed. But, as it was entirely mechanical, requiring neither Judgment nor Genius, the principal Persons of the Profession neglected it altogether, and it came to be left to the *Underlings*, who acquired the Name of Barbers, from that Operation in which they were only or chiefly employed; but still they retained a Connexion with their *quondam* Profession, and were understood to be in some Degree skilled in the lower Branches of Surgery, and practiced no other than that, and shaving. And therefore it is, that, in the Application to the Magistrates, in consequence of which the Seal of Cause was granted to the Incorporation, after a Demand of a general Prohibition against all Persons, for occupying or using any Part of the Surgery and Barber-crafts, until examined and admitted; the Particulars of the Examination and Profession to be incorporated are as follows:

> That the Candidate should know *Anatomia*, Nature and Complexion of every Member of the human Body. And, in like Manner, that he know all the Veins of the samen, that he may make *Phlebotomia* in due time; and also, that he know in quhilk Member the Sign has Domination for the Time: For every Man ought to know the Nature and Substance of every Thing that he works, or else he is negligent.

And it is there expressly declared, "That nae Barber, Master or Servant, haunt, use, nor exerce the Craft of Surgery, without he be expert, and know perfectly the Things above written." And the Deliverance of the Magistrates upon this Supplication, proceeds on a Narrative,

> That they think the same consonant to Reason, and nae Hurt to his Highness

the King, nor to any of his Lieges; and therefore they consent, and grant these
Privileges to the Crafts of Surgery and Barbers, and in so far as they may, or
have Power, confirm, ratify, and approve the said Statutes, Rules and Privileges,
in all Points and Articles.

This Seal of Cause is the Charter of the Privileges, both of the Incorporation of Surgeons and Barbers, and, in so far as it goes, they have an
exclusive Privilege, but no farther. And from the above Enumeration of
Particulars, it is clear that the Privilege now demanded was neither given, nor
meant to be given; all the Articles of Skill and Knowledge required, respect the
particular Branches of Surgery, which it was necessary Barbers should know;
it was superfluous to mention Shaving, because the Name of Barber imported
and included that; but further than Shaving, and particular Parts of Surgery,
no exclusive Privilege was given.

And it is impossible to suppose, that the Use of the *Scissars* in lopping the
Hair of the Head, was meant to be given by the Seal of Cause. For altho'
in its original Institution, the Barber-craft, as being invented by Surgeons,
and for a long Time practiced by them; and a Sort of dangerous Nicety in
using the sharp Instrument, *a Razor*, made it proper to confine the Business
to those who had some Pretences to Skill in Surgery, yet that can never apply
to lopping and trimming the Hair of the Head; for that Operation has no
Connexion with the Profession of Surgery; either in Point of *Nicety* or *Danger;*
the Instrument, with which it is performed, is a very simple one, the least
dangerous of all edged Tools, and so far from being only fit for the Hand of
a Surgeon and Barber, that even *our rude Ancestors* have ventured to trust that
terrible Weapon, a Pair of Scissars, in the Hands of every Housewife, and of every
Girl who goes to School to learn to *stitch*.

But the Profession of Hair-cutting could not possibly have entered into the
Privileges of the Barbers and Surgeons. For, besides that it has no Concern
with their Profession, it was no regular Employment, any more than Hair-
dressing, at the Time these Privileges were granted. We had no *Essay-writers*
in those Days; and therefore it is impossible to know, with Certainty, the
precise Time when this useful Art arose into a Profession. And therefore all
our Authority is Tradition, supported by what appears to be very weighty
Evidence, the *Portraits* of the Times. The tradition goes, *that the Mistress of the
Family was Hair-cutter to the whole, to which she had an exclusive Privilege, as being*

Proprietor of the Scissars; and the Method she took, when the Tresses of any of the Family grew redundant and luxurious, was to clap a Beker upon their Heads, and cut all away under Edges of it. Accordingly we see, that in all *Portraits*, down to the Time that *Wigs* came in Fashion, the only *Culture* and *Manœuvre* which the Hair received, was *shedding* it in the Middle of the Head with a Comb, and *squaring* it round the *Bottom, like the modern Method of Jockeys with their Horse Tails.*

But the Introduction of *Wigs* introduced quite a different *System of Hair-cutting*, above the Reach of the *Landlady's Skill; Wigs* were first used by those, who, by Disease, or Accident, were deprived of their Hair; and although, at first, it would, no doubt, be attempted to make them resemble the natural Growth of the Hair, yet, when *Wigs* came to be a fashionable Dress, *the poor Hair was tortured and twisted ten thousand Ways, in order to make it resemble a Wig;* thus it was, that the modern Professions of Hair-dressing and Hair-cutting were introduced. The Barbers did not pretend to an exclusive Privilege of making *Wigs*, when *Wigs* came into Fashion, nor yet to dressing Hair in the Form of *Wigs;* but, because *Scissars are sharp*, therefore, they must have a Right to *prune* and *lop* the Hair, to prepare it for that sort of Dressing, than which there can hardly be a more absurd or senseless Pretence.

The Barbers argue, That the Privilege of cutting the Hair comes in Place of shaving the Head, which they had a Right to in the more barbarous Times, before the modern Method of Dressing was invented; but this is a Sort of *Anachronism;* shaving the *Head*, and dressing the *Hair*, being introduced at, or very near, the same Time, and none of them very remote; and of this *Portraits* are a Proof: For no sooner do we observe *Wigs* in *Portraits*, but so soon, there appears a remarkable Difference in the *Oeconomy* of the *Hair*, and neither of them at a very distant Period; for King *Charles* II. is the first of our Monarchs, *who makes his Appearance in a Bush of borrowed Hair.*

Therefore the Defenders apprehend, that there arises no Argument from the Seal of Cause in Favours of the Exclusion here claimed, for, that there is not the smallest Appearance that such exclusive Privilege was given to the Incorporation, or could be meant to be given, as it had no Sort of Connection with the Profession of *Surgeons* and *Barbers*, as it did not exist at the Time, and when it afterwards came to exist, it was as unconnected with the Occupation of a *Barber*, as that of a *Taylor* with a *Weaver*, or any other Vocation the most opposite.

The Pursuers, the Barbers, laid a great Part of their Argument upon an

Act of the Town-council in 1682, recommending it to the Surgeons, to admit a sufficient Number of Persons qualified to *trim* and *barberize*, which Terms are afterwards explained by cutting *Hair*, and *shaving Beards;* and from this they contend, that the cutting of Hair was, and had been always esteemed as the proper Business of the Surgeons and Barbers, and that none could be permitted to exercise the Employment, who was not admitted a Freeman of the Incorporation.

As to which, it is not imagined your Lordships would suppose a Privilege of this Kind granted by Implication, or that a recommendatory Act of Council is any Proof, or would give any Right, which an Incorporation had not before: That they had it not before, is evident from the Seal of Cause, at the Date of which it was not a Profession, and, when it came to be one, it was taken up, and exercised by any Person who had a-mind, that was free of the Town. Just so it was with *Wig-making;* the Barbers never pretended any exclusive Privilege to that, though one should think they have full as good a Right to the one, as to the other.

The Argument taken from this Act of Council, so far as the Defenders see, resolves into Prescription; but the Prescription of an exclusive Privilege of this kind, they apprehend, is not at all a favourable one, and, at best, would require a much stronger Possession than is here founded on. The rather, that the Business pretended to be acquired by Prescription, is quite separate and distinct from that, for which the Incorporation was erected. If any Incorporation should acquire Right, by Possession, to any particular Business intimately connected with its own, the Proof of the Possession would not require to be so clear and strong, as your Lordships would think necessary, if the Right pretended to be acquired was utterly inconnected, and independent of the original Profession of the Incorporation; for the easy Progression in the one Case, in some Measure supplies a trifling Defect in Proof, as in the other, the Reverse makes a convincing Evidence necessary.

And what is the Proof founded on here? In the 1st Place, the Act of Council 1682; but, that being only a Recommendation, can have no Effect, either the one Way or the other; it gives no exclusive Privilege, and proves none; and so far as the Defenders know, the only Proof that could establish such a Right by Prescription, is the actual prohibiting and preventing all Mortals from using the Privilege claimed, for the Term of Prescription, and that too by judicial Acts, and *in foro contradictorio.*

The Barbers have attempted to prove, that they have been in the Use of excluding others from this Profession by judicial Acts. They first found upon a Decreet of your Lordships in the 1722, separating the Surgeons from the Barbers; but that Decision has plainly no Relation to the present Question, only adjusting the different Rights of the Surgeons and Barbers, as a Commonwealth; and the Act of Council proceeding thereon is no broader than the Seal of Cause. It does indeed enact that no Man shall be received to a Participation of the Rights and Privileges of the Society of Barbers, without first being admitted by the Society, and gives the Barbers a Power to curb all Incroachers upon the Privileges established by their Seal of Cause, and your Lordships Decree; but what these Privileges were, is in no Shape mentioned, further than by Reference to the Seal of Cause, which has been above explained to your Lordships.

But, from this Act of Council the Defenders apprehend, that the Argument arises in their Favours; for, the referring the Privileges entirely to the Seal of Cause, plainly shows, that they had acquired Right to no other, than such as were therein granted; and as the cutting of *Hair* neither was, nor could be granted by the Seal of Cause, therefore, it was not acquired by the Barbers: And this is further clear, from the Barbers having neglected to get this new Right ascertained by your Lordships Decree, and the Act of Town-council upon it, which it is impossible to imagine they would have misled, had they not been conscious of the Absurdity of the Pretension.

And, with respect to the Complaints and Decrees obtained before the Magistrates in the 1742, and 1743, these can as little affect the Question; for the Question there, was not between the *Barbers* and *Wig-makers* of *Edinburgh*, but between the Barbers of *Edinburgh* and Barbers of *Canongate*, Unfreemen of *Edinburgh* and Barbers of *Canongate*, Unfreemen of *Edinburgh*, or *Curdowers;* and the Complaints are exhibited against them, not only for shaving and cutting, but also for dressing of *Hair*, and making of *Wigs* within the Town; so that this was properly an Incroachment on the Privileges of the Town, and not solely the Privileges of the Barbers; but that cannot affect the Defenders, who are Burghers, and pay the same publick Taxations that the Barbers do.

But admitting in the Argument, that this exclusive Right to cut Hair had been established by the Seal of Cause, and that the *Barbers* had been in Possession of it, while it remained a *rude* and *barbarous Art*, performed by the Assistance of the *Beker*, in Manner above mentioned; yet upon such a

Change of Circumstances, as has now taken Place, in the *Government* and *Oeconomy* of the Hair, your Lordships will consider it as a new Employment, and consequently will not exclude the Defenders from the Profession of it.

There was a Case lately determined before your Lordships, upon the same Principles, between the *Taylors* and the *Mantua-makers* of *Perth*. The Taylors, for some *signal Services* performed to King *William* the *Lion*, had got from him a Grant in the most ample Form, to make all Sorts of *Men* and *Womens Apparel*, and to exclude all others from doing it within the Town of *Perth;* and this they peaceably and uninterruptedly *enjoyed*, for many Centuries. At last, *a Set of female Adventurers arose*, who called themselves *Mantua-makers*, and *bereaved* the *Taylors* of the better Half of their *Perquisite*, the *Womens Work*. The *indignant Taylors* complained to your Lordships, and the Plea put in for the *Damsels* was, that the Taylors refused to *enter them*, except upon Payment of a *larger* Sum, than they imagined all the *Benefit* the *Taylors* could give them *was worth;* and further, that by the present *Mode* of *Dress*, used by the *Ladies*, the making of *Mantuas* was too intricate, either for the *Head* or *Hand* of a *bungling Taylor*, although he might have been very proper for *equipping a Woman* in the *Days of Yore*, when a *Blanket* and a *Brotch* was all her *Dress* and *Ornament*.

On the other hand, the *Taylors* defended their Privileges *valiantly, as became them*, under the *Intrenchment* of their Seal of Cause, and the *uninterrupted Possession* they had had of *taking Measure of the Ladies;* they complained of the *Mantua-makers*, as being of that Sort of People, who, if give them an *Inch*, will take a *Yard*, for that they had offered to *enter them to the full Enjoyment of all their Rights and Privileges, for a smaller Consideration than they had a good Right to demand* by the NATURE OF THEIR FREEHOLD, *and the Value of the* BENEFIT proposed to be *communicated;* and they took *Pepper in the Nose*, at the Charge of *Incapacity* and *Insufficiency* brought against their *Craft*, exclaiming against the *Luxury of the Age*, and *presaging Ruin to that Nation*, where the *Women* could not be satisfied with the *Work of the Men*. But, to remove the *Objection*, these *Knights of the Thimble*, hardily *challenged their Petticoat Party to run a Tilt with* YARD *and* NEEDLE, or, in other Words, to a *comparative Trial*, in which, if the *Damsels* were *defeated*, they, by the Articles of *Combat*, were to *yield* up the *Ladies* to the *Will* of the *Taylors*, or to be INCORPORATED with them.

Your Lordships see, that this Plea of the Mantua-makers resolved into the same with what the Defenders now make. For, as the *modern* Method of *Dress*, used by the *Ladies*, occasions a separate and distinct Art in the making of it up, from that which the *Taylors* had received by their Charter, so the dressing of Hair, as it is now practised, is altogether another Profession from that which the Barbers pretend they had by their Seal of Cause: And as your Lordships *sustained* the *Mantua-makers Plea*, upon the *Incapacity* of the *Taylors* to *work Womens Work;* or rather, because you thought the Mantua-makers might, and could do it better, all that is incumbent on the Defenders, upon the Principle of that Decision, is, to show, not, that the Barbers are utterly incapable to cut Hair, but that they are improper Persons to be employed in that Business; or at least, that the Defenders are more proper than they.

And, at first Sight it must occur to your Lordships, that *a greasy Barber*, covered all over with *Suds*, and the *excrementitious Parts of the Beards of nasty Mechanicks*, is no very proper *Utensil* for the *Dressing-room* of a *Gentleman*, and much less of a *Lady*. The *Sight* is enough to some, the *Smell* loathsome to many, and the *Touch* intolerable to all. On the other Hand, the Defenders, who make the cutting and dressing of *Hair*, and making of *Wigs*, their sole Employment, have none of these *nausea* about them: It is their Study and Endeavour to keep themselves *sweet* and *clean*, that they may not prove *offensive* to their *Employers;* and therefore, in Point of Conveniency, they seem to be the properest Persons for that ornamental Business. They do not insist, that the Barbers should be excluded from it altogether, and if any Body chuses a Barber to cut and dress his *Hair, much good may it do him;* but they apprehend, that, as they have a Right to dress Hair, and are the properest Persons for that Business, they should also be allowed the Privilege of Cutting, without which the other can be of little Use to them.

The Defenders confess, that the Argument of Conveniency arises from the *Manners* of the present Age, or if the Barbers will have it so, *from the Luxury;* but it is never the worse for that, for the whole Arts and Sciences have no better Foundation, and the *Barbers* themselves are obliged to it for the best Part of their Employment; and if we must be *luxurious* and *effeminate*, it is better so with *Taste* and *effeminate*, it is better so with *Taste* and *Elegance*, than without it. The *Barbers* don't object to the *cutting* or *dressing* of *Hair* altogether; as much of that, and let it be as *nicely*, and as *expensively* done as possible, provided they, with their *greasy Aprons*, have the doing of it; as if a Person could atone for the greatest Height of *Intemperance*, by taking a *dirty* and *disagreeable* Road to arrive at it. The *Barbers* are precisely like the *patriot Statesmen* of the present Age, who *rail* at the *Manners* of the People, and the *Measures* of the *Government*, when they are out, and *promote* and *encourage* the same *Measures*, whenever they get in.

And whereas it was alledged before the Lord Ordinary, that the Defenders Plea tended to throw open the Door to every *Footman*, who had got the Art of *cutting* and *dressing Hair*, and should be disposed to set up Shop in these Professions; the Defenders do humbly contend, that supporting this were a certain *Consequence*, and that *every* Man of *every* Profession, had it in his Power to *exercise* the same, when, and where he pleased, no *Detriment*, but much *Benefit*, would arise to the Nation in general, from it. But as this is no proper Consideration for your Lordships, so it can have no Place in Fact of the present Question, because the Privileges of the Town exclude all *Unfreemen* from exercising any Employment within it.

Upon the whole, the Defenders are Freemen of *Edinburgh*, their Right to dress Hair is not contraverted, and they humbly submit it to the Court, if they are not the properest Persons to be employed in that, and its Accessary the Cutting: The Barbers have no Right, by their Seal of Cause, to this; it is a distinct Employment from theirs, neither have they proved such Possession, as will support their Claim of an exclusive Privilege.

IN RESPECT WHEREOF, &C.

HEW DALRYMPLE.

References

Festa, Lynn. 2005. Personal Effects: Wigs and Possessive Individualism in the Long Eighteenth Century. *Eighteenth-Century Life* 29(2): 47–90.

Kleiner, Morris M. 2006. *Licensing Occupations: Ensuring Quality or Restricting Competition?* Kalamazoo, Mich.: W. E. Upjohn Institute for Employment Research.

Kleiner, Morris M. 2013. *Stages of Occupational Regulation: Analysis of Case Studies.* Kalamazoo, Mich.: W. E. Upjohn Institute for Employment Research.

Kleiner, Morris M. 2014. Morris Kleiner on Occupational Licensing [interview by Lawrence H. White]. *EJW Audio, Econ Journal Watch*, July 19.

Kleiner, Morris M., and Alan B. Krueger. 2013. Analyzing the Extent and Influence of Occupational Licensing on the Labor Market. *Journal of Labor Economics* 31: S173–S202.

Kleiner, Morris M., and Evgeny S. Vorotnikov. 2017. Analyzing Occupational Licensing Among the States. *Journal of Regulatory Economics* 52(2): 132–158.

Markiewicz, Emma. 2014. *Hair, Wigs, and Wig Wearing in Eighteenth-Century England.* Ph.D. thesis, University of Warwick (Coventry, UK).

Reinhardt, Uwe E. 2014. Does Occupational Licensing Deserve Our Approval? A Review of Work by Morris Kleiner. *Econ Journal Watch* 11(3): 318–325.

Scott-Moncrieff, R. 1912. Notes on the Corporation of Surgeons and Barbers of the City of Edinburgh. *Proceedings of the Society of Antiquaries of Scotland* 46: 247–257.

Smith, Adam. 1976 [1776] (WN). *An Inquiry Into the Nature and Causes of the Wealth of Nations*, eds. D. D. Raphael and A. L. Macfie. Oxford: Oxford University Press.

Smith, Adam. 1978 (LJ). *Lectures on Jurisprudence*, eds. R. L. Meek, D. D. Raphael, and P. G. Stein. Oxford: Oxford University Press.

Smith, Adam. 1987 (*Corr.*). *Correspondence of Adam Smith*, eds. Ernest C. Mossner and Ian Simpson Ross. Oxford: Oxford University Press.

Stephenson, E. Frank, and Erin E. Wendt. 2009. Occupational Licensing: Scant Treatment in Labor Texts. *Econ Journal Watch* 6(2): 181–194.

Svorny, Shirley. 2004. Licensing Doctors: Do Economists Agree? *Econ Journal Watch* 1(2): 279–305.

Swift, Jonathan. 1726. *Gulliver's Travels*. London: Benjamin Motte.

Williams, Seán M. 2016. E. T. A. Hoffmann and the Hairdresser Around 1800. *Publications of the English Goethe Society* 85(1): 54–66.

Hume's Manuscript Account of the Extraordinary Affair Between Him and Rousseau

Foreword

Daniel B. Klein, Jason Briggeman, and Jacob R. Hall

In 1762, David Hume learned that Jean-Jacques Rousseau was interested in relocating to Britain and proceeded to help make that happen. The two men began to correspond in 1762 and first met in Paris in 1765. They traveled together from Paris to England in January 1766. Hume arranged lodging for Rousseau, otherwise tended to him, and successfully procured a pension for him from King George III.

Within a few months, however, things turned very sour. In June and July Rousseau wrote hateful letters to Hume accusing him of having plotted for his disgrace and humiliation by way of petty torments. Rousseau's long letter of July 10, 1766 was a complete and irrevocable declaration of enmity toward Hume, and was written in a manner of a memorial, as though for publication.[1]

Even after the blowup, Hume continued to work to maintain the plan of a royal pension, and to keep Rousseau settled in England. Rousseau remained in England until May 21, 1767, but never accepted a single payment of the pension. A timeline is shown in Table 1. Immediately after the blowup of July 1766, Hume was unsure whether to give the public an account of the affair, so as to contest Rousseau's version and defend himself against accusation and besmirchment. Adam Smith was among those who advised him not to. But Hume decided otherwise. The result was a pamphlet, most being correspondence between Hume and Rousseau. The account was published in

---

1. The 1766 French version of the account is the Hume 1766a item in the reference list here. The 1766 English version is the Hume 1766b item. The new presentation is listed as Hume 2021/1766.

French in Paris in October 1766 (Hume 1766a), and in English in London in November 1766 (Hume 1766b). The English version was about 23,700 words.[2]

TABLE 1. Timeline of Hume-Rousseau affair

2 July 1762	Hume's first letter to Rousseau
4–5 January 1766	"Je tiens J. J. Rousseau" would have occurred in Senlis, France[3]
10–11 January 1766	Crossing the Channel together from Calais to Dover
22 March 1766	Rousseau arrives and moves into Wootton in Staffordshire, a little-used residence owned by Richard Davenport
12 May 1766	Rousseau's equivocal letter to Conway, not accepting (nor conclusively refusing) the pension
23 June 1766	Rousseau's first open declaration to Hume of enmity
10 July 1766	Rousseau's mammoth memorial/letter, the last to Hume
15 July 1766	Hume encourages Davenport to continue his accommodating of Rousseau
22 July 1766	Hume's last letter to Rousseau
2 September 1766	Hume reiterates to Davenport to continue his accommodating of Rousseau
21 October 1766	*Exposé succinct* published in Paris
November 1766	*Concise and Genuine Account* published in London
1 May 1767	Rousseau vacates Wootton
21–22 May 1767	Rousseau crosses from England to Calais
February–July 1767	Hume advises officials (successfully) to sustain/rehabilitate the offer of the pension

2. The version from manuscript presented here (Hume 2021), exclusive of our own endnotes, is about 20,000 words, the approximately 3,500-word difference from *CGA* (Hume 1766b) coming chiefly because not included are the French editors' 1766 Advertisement, the Latin motto from Seneca, the declaration of D'Alembert, the erratum, the 1766 footnotes deriving from editors and translators, and some footnotes presented as being of Hume's composing but, as far as the manuscript testifies, are not in fact. Some of these differences are noted in our endnotes but not reproduced there.

3. In the 10 July letter, Rousseau writes of "*Je tiens*" having happened "the first night after our departure from Paris" (see Hume 2021/1766, 318), which would be Senlis, but elsewhere he says, twice, Roye, France. Evidently, as Mossner (2001, 516 n.2) explains, it could not have happened there because they did not sleep in the same chamber.

The blowup between two of Europe's most illustrious intellectuals was bound to be an *affaire célèbre*. Today, it remains of interest to readers of Rousseau and Hume. The spectator feels divided sympathies with each of the two men, whose interpretations disagree wildly. Was Hume innocent in the matter? Was Rousseau? English-language treatments include Dena Goodman (1991), Ernest Mossner (2001, 512–532), Leo Damrosch (2005, 403–433), David Edmonds and John Eidinow (2006), Robert Zaretsky and John Scott (2009), James Harris (2015, 416–421), and Dennis Rasmussen (2017, 133–145); also, Klein (2021) speculates that among Hume's motives was an aim to diminish Rousseau's legacy.

The remainder of this Foreword is devoted to the lineage of the present text, its relation to other versions, and its editorial apparatus.

A valuable piece on Hume's account is Paul Meyer (1952), "The Manuscript of Hume's Account of His Dispute with Rousseau," published in *Comparative Literature*, which is cited by Mossner (2001, 530 n.1) but few others.[4] In August 1766, Hume assembled the account and made three copies, sending one to his friend Jean de Rond D'Alembert in Paris. Meyer writes: "All of these copies seemed to be lost, until I recently discovered the one belonging to D'Alembert in Paris... These papers are now in the National Library of Scotland" (1952, 342).

In April 2021, Klein wrote to the National Library of Scotland (NLS) and acquired a PDF containing photos of the original manuscript pages, grateful to NLS. We have made that PDF available online, with NLS's assent.[5] Its 85 pages contain images of the manuscript told of by Meyer. "This manuscript...is in the hand of a copyist, but the marginal notes...are in Hume's hand" (Meyer 1952, 343).

Before explaining the present use of that manuscript, we now turn to its relation to what was published in 1766. Readers of the *Concise and Genuine Account* (*CGA*) may not know it, but the connective narrative between the letters is a retranslation of a translation. Hume's connective narrative (and some of the footnotes) from Hume's original manuscript were translated into

---

4. As of 28 September 2021, Meyer 1952 showed just three Google Scholar citations.

5. Klein asked NLS whether posting the PDF of the Hume manuscript was allowed. They said that in this situation the determination was up to him and pointed him to posted guidelines, and we found no barrier to posting the PDF. We hope that open and free access to the material will prove useful to scholars working on Rousseau and Hume.

French (by Jean-Baptiste-Antoine Suard), and then the French pamphlet was retranslated into English (by an unidentified translator in London, coordinating with William Strahan).

About the time he sent a copy of the manuscript to D'Alembert, Hume wrote to Adam Smith, then in Paris: "Tell D'alembert I make him absolute Master to retrench or alter what he thinks proper, in order to suit it to the Latitude of Paris" (II:83).[6] Meyer writes: "The eventual outcome of these instructions was a translation entitled *Exposé succinct de la contestation qui s'est élevée entre M. Hume et M. Rousseau, avec les pièces justificatives,* completed by Suard under the direction of D'Alembert and Baron d'Holbach prior to October 6, and published in Paris later that month" (1952, 342). The *Exposé succinct* appeared in Paris on October 21, 1766.

Meyer then writes something key to understanding what happens: "Only at that point did Hume, who had previously considered publication in England unnecessary, take steps to have an English account of the dispute published" (1952, 342). Had Hume been resolved in August to publish also in English, he would have provided a copy of the manuscript also to Strahan, his publishing agent in London, for that purpose, and conferred directly with him and perhaps the translator, as he was then in London himself. But by October, when he finally resolves to proceed in English—without yet having seen the French version—he was in Edinburgh. Whether from a breakdown in communication with Strahan or from failures on the part of Strahan or the translator, Hume ends up writing an indignant letter to Strahan after all is said and done: "I have scarce met with anything that has given me more Displeasure" (II:112).

Extant letters from Hume to Strahan from October–November 1766 number five. In the first, of an unspecified day in October (II:95), Hume issues his first instruction. He did not include the manuscript itself with the letter—perhaps Hume did not have it immediately at hand as he dashed off his letter to Strahan. Rather, he tells Strahan he "shall immediately send you up a Copy of the original Manuscript" (II:96). Perhaps there was a delay in Strahan's receiving the manuscript. In the same letter, Hume tells Strahan to make use of both the manuscript and the French version, still unseen by Hume, a copy of which would be sent from Paris to Strahan:

---

6. We refer to the two volumes of Hume's letters (Hume 1932) with this style of citation.

> Get a discreet and careful Translator:[7] Let him compare exactly the French
> Narration with my English: Where they agree, let him insert my English: Where
> they differ, let him follow the French and translate it: The Reason of this is,
> that I allowd my Friends at Paris to make what alterations they thought proper;
> and I am desirous of following exactly the Paris Edition. All my letters must be
> printed verbatim, conformable to the Manuscript I [will] send you. (II:96)

On November 4, Hume, still in Edinburgh and not having heard anything
from Strahan, gets hold of the French version and, unhappy with it, reverses
his instructions to Strahan: "Contrary to my former Directions, I now desire
you *not* to follow the Paris Edition in my Narrative; but exactly the English
Copy which I sent you in Manuscript" (II:99–100, italics added). (Hume also
requested two changes, evidently entirely new, one a minor change to the
narrative, which was not made, and one, a footnote about Hume's combing
of Rousseau's incoming mail, which was made.) The third letter (II:106–107)
speaks of Andrew Millar's complaint about not being included in the project
and a minor insertion that was included as an erratum on the last page of
CGA. In the fourth letter of November 13 (II:361–362), Hume notes that
he had not heard from Strahan, repeats the revised instructions, and clarifies
that he should include three items that were not in his manuscript, namely,
the Paris editor's Preface, the declaration of D'Alembert, and the Latin motto
from Seneca; all were included in *CGA*.

CGA was published shortly thereafter, in November 1766. After seeing it,
Hume, still in Edinburgh, wrote on November 25 to Strahan:

> Nothing could more surprise me, Dear Strahan, than your Negligence with
> regard to this silly Pamphlet I sent you. You have never been at the Pains once
> to answer one of my Letters with regard to it; tho' certainly I intended you a
> Friendship by sending it to you: You never informed me, that [Thomas] Becket
> [a bookseller] had got over a Copy from Paris; You have never conveyd any of
> my Directions to the English Translator… (II:112)

The letter then becomes more indignant over "printing the Name of two
Ladies, who had expressly forbid it" and did not appear in the French version
(namely, the Comtesse de Boufflers-Rouverel and the Marquise de Verdelin).
We have not examined the materials so as to determine whether Hume

---

7. As J. Y. T. Grieg, the editor of Hume's letters, aptly notes: "[t]he translator was neither
discreet nor careful" (II:96 n.4).

is right that all of his instructions, even the initial instructions, were basically disregarded. But Meyer (1952, 343) seems to think that, particularly in the earlier portion, the English translator in the main simply translated the connective narrative and notes. Hume's concluding paragraphs in *CGA*, however, appear to match the manuscript quite exactly. On the whole, the presentation that follows here differs from *CGA* in ways thought important by Hume.

Before moving on, there is one more letter, from December 1766, about *CGA* to be noted, but it is to Becket,[8] not Strahan. Hume writes: "I cannot imagine that a Piece wrote on so silly a Subject as mine will ever come to a second Edition; but if it shoud, please order the following Corrections to be made" (II:116). Hume lists twelve changes. One, alluding to Themistocles in Persia, pertains to how one might understand "*Je tiens J. J. Rousseau*" and is treated in Klein (2021). *CGA* never appeared in a second edition, however.

As for the differences between Hume's manuscript account and *CGA*, there is "a decided discrepancy in tone" (Meyer 1952, 350). Hume's original version has the tone of "a man sitting down in a rage immediately after a violent quarrel and giving his version of it" (ibid.). Hume "is plainly beside himself at Rousseau's behavior, and expresses himself bluntly and forcibly" (ibid., 345). *CGA*, by contrast—and by way of the French editors, remember—gives a voice to Hume that is more detached, sometimes even circumlocutive. "Certain of Hume's indignant and spontaneous exclamations on reproducing Rousseau's charges against him are not given in the published texts at all" (347). Hume's original has him enumerating a dozen lies ("lyes") as footnotes to Rousseau's mammoth letter of July 10, 1766; such enumerating of points is absent from *CGA*. Also, "[t]he glowing terms in which Hume speaks of his own conduct towards Rousseau have been toned down" (345). The original is stouter and more authentic.

Our approach in "Hume's Manuscript Account..."

Our approach here is to provide the manuscript itself. It is *not* to use it, along with all other records, notably Hume's letters, to construct a version of the account that approximates what he would have wished for in *CGA*.

That said, we do insert a small number of editorial notes, appearing as

---

8. *CGA*'s imprint is "Printed for T. Becket and P. A. De Hondt."

endnotes, and a few of them speak to Hume's preferences as expressed in his letters.

How we produced "Hume's Manuscript Account..."

The 85-page PDF scan of Hume's manuscript from NLS was handed off to Briggeman, who produced the version presented here (Hume 2021), with the aid of Klein and Hall.

The words composed by Hume, original to the manuscript itself, including his narration and notes, were typed up by Briggeman. As for the words in the manuscript reproduced by Hume directly from Rousseau's letters—written in French and left in French in the manuscript—Briggeman lifted the English text found at Project Gutenberg. That Project Gutenberg page reproduces the text of the 1826 edition of volume 1 (of 4) of *The Philosophical Works of David Hume* (published in Edinburgh and London). It contains what appears to be a direct reproduction of *Concise and Accurate Account* (Hume 1766b). Though we have noticed the slightest of differences, we believe that the 1826 version, and hence the online Gutenberg version, basically matches *CGA*.[9] Thus, Briggeman lifted the English translation of Rousseau's letters from Project Gutenberg, and drew everything else from the manuscript.

Editorial apparatus of "Hume's Manuscript Account..."

- The numbers in braces, such as {1}, indicate the start of the manuscript page (a file of the manuscript images is available online).
- Words in brackets [like this] are our insertions into the text.
- All footnotes are Hume's and Rousseau's, and only from the manuscript. In his mammoth letter of July 10, Rousseau made four footnotes. In the entire manuscript, Hume made 33 footnotes (including the one presented as by D'Alembert). Hume did not use numbering for his notes but rather symbols, chiefly the symbol +, with the corresponding note provided in the margin of the page.

---

9. Thanks to José L. Tasset, we do correct one meaningful error in the 1826/Project Gutenberg text, which has Rousseau saying "I mean myself" where it should be "I mean yourself."

- The lettered, bracketed superscripts indicate our own notes, which appear at the end. In the endnotes, we call attention to a few of the more significant features of *CGA* not in the manuscript. Also, we speak of Hume's preferences as expressed in the six October–December letters to Strahan or Becket, when thought highly noteworthy.
- The text in Rachana font is that of Rousseau's letters.

Hume's Manuscript Account of the Extraordinary Affair Between Him and Rousseau

David Hume

edited by Daniel B. Klein, Jason Briggeman, and Jacob R. Hall[10]

Quick guide:

- *The numbers in braces, such as {1}, indicate the start of the manuscript page (a large PDF containing images of the manuscript pages is online).*
- *Words in brackets [like this] are our insertions into the text.*
- *The numeric footnotes are Hume's or Jean-Jacques Rousseau's, from the manuscript.*
- *The lettered, bracketed superscripts indicate our own notes, which appear at the end.*
- *The text in Rachana font is that of Rousseau's letters.*

For further detail, see the Foreword.

{1}[a] The beginning of my connexions with M. Rousseau was in 1762, when he was outlaw'd (decreté) in France by a Sentence of the Parliament. I then received a letter from a Person of merit at Paris [Comtesse de Boufflers-Rouverel],[b] informing me that M. Rousseau intended to go over to England

---

10. We are grateful to librarians at the National Library of Scotland for their assistance in our procuring a PDF scan of the original Hume manuscript and for clarifying the conditions for its posting online. We thank Luc Marest for translating a footnote, inserted by Hume, of French text from D'Alembert.

for Protection, and recommending him to my good Offices. I lived at that time in Edinburgh; But supposing that he had arrived in London according to his intentions, I wrote in the warmest terms to several of my friends in that City, bespeaking their favours for that Exile, and I wrote also to M. Rousseau himself, assuring him of my utmost Zeal in his service; inviting him to Edinburgh, if that Place could suit him; and offering him a Retreat in my House, {2} as long as he would deign to share it with me. There needed no other motive for this Act of Beneficence than the personal character given of him by the Person who recommended him, and his well known Genius and Talents, joined to his misfortunes, misfortunes which seemed entirely to proceed from the freedom of his phylosophic spirit, and the Jealousy of Persons in authority; I received the following answer.

M. Rousseau to M. Hume
Motiers-Travers, 19 February 1763

Sir, I did not receive till lately, and at this place, the letter you did me the honour to direct to me at London, the 2d of July last, on the supposition that I was then arrived at that capital. I should doubtless have made choice of a retreat in your country, and as near as possible to yourself, if I had foreseen what a reception I was to meet with in my own. No other nation could claim a preference to England. And this prepossession, for which I have dearly suffered, was at that time too natural not to be very excusable; but, to my great astonishment, as well as that of the public, I have met with nothing but affronts and insults, where I hoped to have found consolation at least, if not gratitude. {3} How many reasons have I not to regret the want of that asylum and philosophical hospitality I should have found with you! My misfortunes, indeed, have constantly seemed to lead me in a manner that way. The protection and kindness of my Lord Mareschal [George Keith], your worthy and illustrious countryman, hath brought Scotland home to me, if I may so express myself, in the midst of Switzerland; he hath made you so often bear a part in our conversation, hath brought me so well acquainted with your virtues, which I before was only with your talents, that he inspired me with the most tender friendship for you, and the most ardent desire of obtaining yours, before I even knew you were disposed to grant it. Judge then of the pleasure I feel, at finding this inclination reciprocal. No, Sir, I should pay your merit but half its due, if it were the subject only of my admiration. Your great impartiality, together with your amazing penetration and genius, would lift you far above the rest of mankind, if you were less attached to them by the goodness of your heart. My Lord Mareschal, in acquainting me that the amiableness of your disposition was still greater than the sublimity of your genius, rendered a correspondence with you every day more desirable, and cherished in me those wishes which he inspired, of ending my days near you. {4} Oh, Sir, that a better state of health, and more convenient circumstances, would but enable me to take such a journey in the manner I could like! Could I but hope to see you and my Lord Mareschal one day settled in your own country, which should for ever after be mine, I should be thankful, in such a society, for the very misfortunes that led me into it, and should account the day of its commencement as the first of my life. Would to Heaven I might live to see that happy day, though now more to be desired than expected! With what transports should I not exclaim, on setting foot in that happy country which gave birth to David Hume and the Lord Mareschal of Scotland!

Salve, facis mihi debita tellus!

Hæc domus, hæc patria est.[c]

J. J. R.

I insert this letter, not from vanity; for I shall soon insert a Retraction of all this esteem; but to make the train of correspondence complete and to show that of a long time I had been disposed to render service to M. Rousseau.

I had no further correspondence with him, till about the middle of last Summer, when the following accident renewed it. {5} M.[de] la Marquise de Verdelin, an antient acquaintance of M. Rousseau's, having occasion to be in some of the Provinces of France bordering on Switzerland, seized the opportunity of paying a visit to the solitary Philosopher in his Retreat. He then told her that he found great difficulty to live in Neufchatel, by reason of the bigotry of the People, and the rage of the Priests against him; that he apprehended he would soon lie under the necessity of quitting it and of seeking shelter elsewhere, that England appeared, from its laws and Government, the only place which promised him a secure retreat; that Lord Mareschal, his antient Patron, advised him to throw himself entirely under my Protection, as he was pleased to term it; and that accordingly he had an intention of applying to me, if she thought that I would submit to the Burthen.

I was at that time charged with the Affairs of England at the Court of France: But having a prospect of soon returning home, I did not reject an application made in those circumstances {6} from a Man so celebrated for his genius and his misfortunes. As soon as M.^{de} de Verdelin informed me of M. Rousseau's situation and intentions, I made him a proffer of my services and good Offices, I received the following Answer,

M. Rousseau to M. Hume
In Strasbourg 4 Dec. 1765.

Sir, your goodness affects me as much as it does me honour. The best reply I can make to your offers is to accept them, which I do. I shall set out in five or six days to throw myself into your arms. Such is the advice of my Lord Mareschal, my protector, friend and father; it is the advice also of M.^{de} de Verdelin whose good sense and benevolence serve equally for my direction and consolation; in fine, I may say it is the advice of my own heart, which takes a pleasure in being indebted to the most illustrious of my contemporaries, to a man whose goodness surpasses his glory. I sigh after a solitary and free retirement, wherein I might finish my days in peace. If this be procured me by means of your benevolent solicitude, I {7} shall then enjoy at once the pleasure of the only blessing my heart desires, and also that of being indebted for it to you. I am, Sir, with all my heart, &c.

J. J. R.

But, besides the intention of employing my time and care in M. Rousseau's establishment, I had beforehand been contriving methods of serving him in the most effectual manner. M. Clairaut, a few weeks before his death, had shown me the following letter of M. Rousseau.

M. Rousseau to M. Clairaut
In Mortiers-Travers 3 March, 1765.

Sir, the remembrance of your former kindness, induces me to be again importunate. It is to desire you will be so good, for the second time, to be the censor of one of my performances. It is a very paltry rhapsody, which I compiled many years ago, under the title of *A Musical Dictionary*, and am now obliged to republish it for subsistence. Amidst the torrent of misfortunes that overwhelm me, {8} I am not in a situation to review the work; which, I know, is full of oversights and mistakes. If any interest you may take in the lot of the most unfortunate of mankind, should induce you to bestow a little more attention on his work than on that of another, I should be extremely obliged to you, if you would take the trouble to correct such errors as you may meet with in the perusal. To point them out, without correcting them, would be doing nothing, for I am absolutely incapable of paying the least attention to such a work; so that if you would but condescend to alter, add, retrench, and, in short, use it as you would do your own, you would do a great charity, for which I should be extremely thankful. Accept, Sir, my most humble excuses and salutations.

J. J. R.

I know at present with certainty, that this pretence of extreme poverty and distress was entirely groundless in M. Rousseau, and was nothing but an instance of Quackery, of a piece with many others of the same kind practiced by him, in order to render himself remarkable and interesting, and to excite the commiseration of the public. But being at that time wholly ignorant {9} of this artifice, I was struck with compassion, and a liberal indignation, that a Man of letters, and one so eminent, should be reduced, notwithstanding his frugal method of living, to the utmost extremity of want, and that this calamity was aggravated by sickness, by the approaches of old age, and by the unrelenting rage of Persecutors. I was sensible, that many People ascribed this Distress to the pride of M. Rousseau, which made him refuse all supply from his friends; but I considered, that this fault, if it was one, was a fault of the better side; that too many learned Men had prostituted their character by unworthy Applications to the Great; and that such pride, even tho' excessive, merited indulgence in a man of Genius, who, being conscious of an internal superiority, and enamoured of Independence, scorned to submit to the Assaults of Fortune, or expose himself to the insolence of Men. I endeavour'd therefore to serve him in his own way. I begged M. Clairaut to give me the letter: I carry'd it to several of M. Rousseau's Friends and Patrons at Paris: I proposed a scheme, to which I myself intended {10} to contribute, and by which M. Rousseau should be assisted without knowing it: It was to persuade him, that the Booksellers would give a larger Sum for his work than they really could be engaged to do; and to make up the difference. But this scheme, to which M. Clairaut's assistance was requisite, was frustrated by the sudden death of that profound Geometer and amiable Man.

Not discouraged, and still entertaining the same idea of M. Rousseau's extreme poverty, I was no sooner assured of his intention of retiring into England under my care, than I formed a Plan of executing a like artifice in his favour. I immediately wrote to my friend M. John Stewart of Buckingham street, that I had an affair to mention to him of so delicate and secret a nature, that I did not even care to commit it to paper, but that it should be told him by M. Elliot (now Sir Gilbert Elliot) as soon as that Gentleman returned from Paris. The Plan, which M. Elliot communicated under the strictest secrecy was, that M. Stewart should find out some discreet Farmer in the neighbourhood of his Country Seat, and make a bargain with him for the {11} board of M. Rousseau and his Gouvernante. Should take care that they had every convenience of life plentifully supply'd them, should limit himself to no Sum, tho' it might amount to 50 or 60 pounds a year, and should engage the farmer to keep the secret and pretend to M. Rousseau that he was contented with 20 or 25 pounds: I engaged to pay the difference. Soon after, upon M. Stewart's writing that he had found a Place which, he believed, would answer, I desired him to furnish the Rooms genteely and neatly at my Expence. But these Plans, which can not be suspected of any vanity, as secrecy was an essential part of them, were set aside, by the Offer of others more convenient and more agreable. They were however known to M. Stewart and to the Right Honble Sir Gilbert Elliot.

It may not perhaps be amiss on this occasion to mention another Plan of a like kind. I attended M. Rousseau to an agreable Country Place in Surrey, where we lived two days with Collonel Web. M. Rousseau was much taken with the privacy and natural beauties of the place: Upon which I, by means of M. Stewart, entered into Terms with the Collonel, for purchasing the House with a small Estate belonging to {12} it, in order to accommodate M. Rousseau. If it were safe, after what is past, to appeal to himself for any Fact, I would here venture to cite him: But however, the Story is also known to M. Stewart and to General Clark, and in part to Collonel Web.

But to take up the narration where it broke off, M. Rousseau's friends procured for him the king of France's Passport. He came to Paris: I conducted him to England, and employed my-self and many of my friends, for above two months, in discovering and adjusting Plans for his settlement. Every Humour of his was complyed with: Every Caprice studyed; No complaisance was wanting; no time was spared; and tho' many plans were frustrated and rejected, I deemed my-self sufficiently rewarded for all my pains by the amicable, grateful and even fond manner, in which he seemed to receive all my good Offices. At last, the present Scheme was settled: M. Davenport, a Gentleman of Fortune and distinction, as well as of merit, supply'd him with a House called Wotton, in which he himself {13} seldom resides, and he takes from his Guest a small board for himself and his Gouvernante. Immediately on M. Rousseau's arrival at the place, he wrote me the following letter;

Mr. Rousseau to Mr. Hume;
In Wootton 22, March, 1766.

You see already, my dear patron, by the date of my letter, that I am arrived at the place of my destination; but you cannot see all the charms which I find in it. To do this, you should be acquainted with the situation, and be able to read my heart. You ought, however, to read at least those of my sentiments with respect to you, and which you have so well deserved. If I live in this agreeable asylum as happy as I hope to do, one of the greatest pleasures of my life will be, to reflect that I owe it to you. To make another happy, is to deserve to be happy one's self. May you therefore find in yourself the reward of all you have done for me! Had I been alone, I might perhaps have met with hospitality; but I should have never relished it so highly as I now do in owing it to your friendship. Retain still that friendship for me, my dear patron; love me for my sake, who am so much indebted to you; love me for your own, for the good you have done me. {14} I am sensible of the full value of your sincere friendship: it is the object of my ardent wishes: I am ready to repay it with all mine, and feel something in my heart which may one day convince you that it is not without its value. As, for the reasons agreed on between us, I shall receive nothing by the post, you will be pleased, when you have the goodness to write to me, to send your letters to Mr Davenport. The affair of the carriage is not yet adjusted, because I know I was imposed on. It is a trifling fault, however, which may be only the effect of an obliging vanity, unless it should happen to be repeated. If you were concerned in it, I would advise you to give up, once for all, these little impositions, which cannot proceed from any good motive, when converted into snares for simplicity. I embrace you, my dear patron, with the same cordiality which I hope to find in you.

J. J. R.

A few days after I received the following letter from him.

M. Rousseau to M. Hume

In Wootton, 29th March, 1766.

You will see, my dear patron, by the {15} letter Mr Davenport will have transmitted you, how agreeably I find myself situated in this place. I might perhaps be more at my ease if I were less noticed; but the solicitude of so polite an host as mine is too obliging to give offence; and as there is nothing in life without its inconvenience, that of being too good is one of those which is the most tolerable. I find a much greater inconvenience in not being able to make the servants understand me, and particularly in my not understanding them. Luckily Mrs le Vasseur serves me as interpreter, and her fingers speak better than my tongue. There is one advantage, however, attending my ignorance, which is a kind of compensation; it serves to tire and keep at a distance impertinent visitors. The minister of the parish came to see me yesterday, who, finding that I spoke to him only in French, would not speak to me in English, so that our interview was almost a silent one. I have taken a great fancy to this expedient, and shall make use of it with all my neighbours, if I have any. Nay, should I even learn to speak English, I would converse with them only in French, especially if I were so happy as to find they did not understand a word of that language; an artifice this, much of the same kind with that which the Negroes pretend is practised by the monkeys, {16} who, they say, are capable of speech, but cannot be prevailed upon to talk, lest they should be set to work.

It is not true in any sense that I agreed to accept of a model from Mr Gosset as a present. On the contrary, I asked him the price, which he told me was a guinea and half, adding that he intended to present me with it; an offer I did not accept. I desire you therefore to pay him for it, and Mr Davenport will be so good as repay you the money. And if Mr Gosset does not consent to be paid for it, it must be returned to him, and purchased by some other hand. It is designed for Mr du Peyrou, who desired long since to have my portrait, and caused one to be painted in miniature, which is not at all like me. You were more fortunate in this respect than me; but I am sorry that, by your assiduity to serve me, you deprived me of the pleasure of discharging the same friendly obligation with regard to yourself. Be so good, my dear patron, as to order the model to be sent to Messrs Guinand and Hankey, Little St Helen's, Bishopsgate Street, in order to be transmitted to Mr du Peyrou by the first {17} safe conveyance. It hath been a frost ever since I have been here; the snow falls daily; and the wind is cutting and severe; notwithstanding all which, I had rather lodge in the hollow trunk of an old tree, in this country, than in the most superb apartment in London. Good day, my dear patron. I embrace you with all my heart.

J. J. R.

As M. Rousseau and I, had agreed not to be troublesome to each other by a regular commerce of letters, there remained no other subject of correspondence between us, but that of his Pension. The following is a succinct account of that Affair. One evening at Calais where we were detained by contrary winds, I asked M. Rousseau, whether, in case the king of England shou'd honour him with a Pension, he wou'd accept of it. He replyed, that there were some difficulties; but that he shou'd be entirely governed, in that affair, by the advice of Lord Mareschal. Upon this encouragement, I applyed, on my arrival in London, to the English Ministers, particularly to General Conway, Secretary of State, and to General Greene, Secretary {18} and Chamberlain to the Queen. They apply'd to their Majesties, who graciously yielded to the Proposal, desiring only that the Pension shou'd be a sort of secret, for fear of giving offence. M. Rousseau and I, both wrote to Lord Mareschal, and he said, that the secrecy was the Circumstance the most agreeable to him. Lord Mareschal's consent arrived, as might easily be imagined; M. Rousseau a few days after, went to the Country; and General Conway's bad state of Health prevented for some time, the Affair, from being terminated.

Meanwhile I was very uneasy to find, that the inquietude of my friend's temper kept him from enjoying that repose, which the security and Hospitality of England so much invited him to indulge: I saw with infinite regreat that he was born to live in tempests and tumults; and that the disgust, ensuing on absolute ease, safety and retreat, wou'd soon make him a torment to himself, and to all about him: But I little expected, at the distance of 150, Miles, and employing my-self constantly in his service, to be the victim of his rage and malevolence. There had been a feigned {19} letter of the King of Prussia's wrote last winter at Paris: It was as follows

The King of Prussia to M. Rousseau,

My Dear John James,

You have renounced Geneva, your native soil. You have been driven from Switzerland, a country of which you have made such boast in your writings. In France you are outlawed: come then to me. I admire your talents, and amuse myself with your reveries; on which, however, by the way, you bestow too much time and attention. It is high time to grow prudent and happy; you have made yourself sufficiently talked of for singularities little becoming a truly great man: show your enemies that you have sometimes common sense: this will vex them without hurting you. My dominions afford you a peaceable retreat: I am desirous to do you good, and will do it, if you can but think it such. But if you are determined to refuse my assistance, you may expect that I shall say not a word about it to any one. If you persist in perplexing your brains to find out new misfortunes, choose such as you like best; I am a king, and can make you as miserable as you can wish; at the same time, I will engage to do that which {20} your enemies never will, I will cease to persecute you, when you are no longer vain of persecution.

Your sincere friend, Frederick.

This letter was wrote by the Honble Horace Walpole, above three weecks before my departure from Paris, but M. Walpole tho' he lived in the same inn with me, and tho' we saw one another often, yet from a delicacy to me, very suitable to his usual humanity and politeness, had entirely suppressed the Piece. After my departure, he showed it to some of his friends; A copy was stolen: The poignancy of the satyre, and the justness of the application pleased every body: It had great success at Paris: Copies were multiplyed; and dispersed all over Europe. I saw it for the first time at London, where it was in every body's hands.

I believe every one will allow, who knows the liberty of England that such a piece of pleasantry, wrote by a man of distinction and reputation of the country, directed against a man of reputation lately arrived; that such {21} a piece, I say, cou'd not, by the utmost influence of King, Lords and Commons, by all the Authority Ecle'siastical, civil and military, be kept from finding its way to the Press. It was accordingly published in the S.ᵗ James's Chronicle; and a few days after I was very much surprised to find the following Piece in the same Chronicle.

M. Rousseau to the Printer of S.ᵗ James's Chronicle.
In Wootton, 7 April, 1766.

Sir, you have been wanting in that respect which every private person owes to crowned heads, in publickly ascribing to the King of Prussia, a letter full of baseness and extravagance, by which circumstance alone, you might be very well assured he could not be the author. You have even dared to subscribe his name, as if you had seen him write it with his own hand. I inform you, Sir, that this letter was fabricated at Paris, and, what rends and afflicts my heart, that the impostor hath his accomplices in England.

In justice to the King of Prussia, to truth, and to myself, you ought therefore to print the letter I am now {22} writing, and to which I set my name, by way of reparation for a fault, which you would undoubtedly reproach yourself for if you knew of what atrociousness you have been made the instrument. Sir, I make you my sincere salutations.

J. J. R.

I was sorry to see such extreme Rage on account of so unavoidable an Incident as the Publication of the King of Prussia's letter; but I shou'd have accused my-self of the blackest and most malevolent disposition if I had ever imagined, that M. Rousseau suspected me for the Publisher, and had in his intentions directed all this rage against me. Yet M. Rousseau now informs me, that this is the case. Just eight days before I had received a letter wrote in the most amicable terms imaginable.[11] I am surely the last Man in the world, who, in common sense, ought to be suspected; yet without even the pretence of the smallest proof or probability, I am, of a sudden, the first Man, not only suspected, but certainly concluded, to be the publisher. I am {23} without

---

11. That of the 29ᵗʰ of March

further Enquiry or Explication intentionally insulted in a public Paper; I am, from the dearest friend, converted into a treacherous and malignant Enemy; and all my present and past services are at one stroke very artfully cancelled. Were it not ridiculous to employ reasoning on such a subject and with such a man, I might ask of M. Rousseau, why, I am supposed to have any malignity against him? My Actions in a hundred instances had sufficiently demonstrated the contrary; and it is not usual for Favours conferred to beget Ill will in the Person who conferrs them. But supposing I had secretly entertained an animosity toward him, would I run the risque of a discovery by so silly a vengeance, and by sending this Piece to the Press; when I knew, from the usual avidity of the News Writers to find Articles of Intelligence, that it must necessarily, in a few days, be laid hold of?

But not imagining that I was the object of so black and ridiculous a Suspicion, I pursued my usual train, {24} by serving my friend in the least doubtfull manner. I renew my Application to General Conway, as soon as the state of that Gentleman's health permitted it: The General applies again to His Majesty. His Majesty's consent is renewed: The Marquiss of Rockingham, first Commissioner of the Treasury, is also applyed to: The whole Affair is happily finished; and full of Joy, I now convey the intelligence to my friend. M. Conway received from him the following letter in a few days.

M. Rousseau to General Conway
12 of May 1766.

Sir, affected with a most lively sense of the favour his Majesty hath honoured me with, and with that of your goodness, which procured it me, it affords me the most pleasing sensation to reflect, that the best of Kings, and the Minister most worthy of his confidence, are pleased to interest themselves in my fortune. This, Sir, is an advantage of which I am justly tenacious, and which I will never deserve to lose. {25} But it is necessary I should speak to you with that frankness you admire. After the many misfortunes that have befallen me, I thought myself armed against all possible events. There have happened to me some, however, which I did not foresee, and which indeed an ingenuous mind ought not to have foreseen: hence it is that they affect me by so much the more severely. The trouble in which they involve me, indeed, deprives me of the ease and presence of mind necessary to direct my conduct: all I can reasonably do, under so distressed a situation, is to suspend my resolutions about every affair of such importance as is that in agitation. So far from refusing the beneficence of the King from pride, as is imputed to me, I am proud of acknowledging it, and am only sorry I cannot do it more publicly. But when I actually receive it, I would be able to give up myself entirely to those sentiments which it would naturally inspire, and to have an heart replete with gratitude for his Majesty's goodness and yours. I am not at all afraid this manner of thinking will make any alteration in yours towards me. Deign, therefore, Sir, to preserve that goodness for me, till a more happy opportunity, {26} when you will be satisfied that I defer taking the advantage of it, only to render myself more worthy of it. I beg of you, Sir, to accept of my most humble and respectful salutations.

J. J. R.

This letter appeared both to General Conway and to me a plain refusal as long as the article of secrecy was insisted on; but as I knew, that M. Rousseau had been acquainted with that condition from the beginning, I was the less surprized at his silence towards me. I thought, that my friend, conscious of having treated me ill in this affair, was ashamed to write to me; and having prevailed on General Conway to keep the matter still open, I wrote a very friendly letter to M. Rousseau, exhorting him to return to his former way of thinking and to accept the Pension.

As to the deep distress which he mentions to General Conway and which he says deprives him even of the use of his reason, I was set very much at my ease on that head, by receiving a {27} letter from M. Davenport, who told me that his Guest was at that very time, extremely happy, chearful, and even sociable. I saw plainly, in this event, the usual infirmity of my friend, who wishes to interest the world, by passing for sickly and persecuted and distressed and unfortunate, beyond all measure, even while he is the most happy and contented. His pretences of an extreme sensibility had been too frequently repeated, to have any effect on a man who was so well acquainted with them.

I waited three weecks in vain for an answer; I thought this a little odd, and even wrote so to M. Davenport, but having to do with a very odd sort of man, and still accounting for his silence, by supposing him ashamed to write to me, I was resolved not to be discouraged, nor to lose an essential service on account of a vain ceremonial. I accordingly renewed my Applications to the Ministers, and was so happy as to be enabled to write the following letter to M. Rousseau, the {28} only one of so old a date, of which I have a Copy,

M. Hume to M. Rousseau
Lisle street Leicester-fields 19. of June, 1766.

As I have not received any answer from you, I conclude that you persevere in the same resolution of refusing all marks of His Majesty's Goodness, as long as they must remain a secret. I have therefore apply'd to General Conway to have this condition removed, and I was so fortunate as to obtain his promise, that he wou'd speak to the king for that purpose. It will only be requisite, said he, that we know previously from M. Rousseau, whether he wou'd accept of a Pension publickly granted him, that his Majesty may not be exposed to a second refusal. He gave me authority to write to you on that subject; and I beg to hear your resolution as soon as possible. If you give your consent, which I earnestly entreat you to do, I know, that I cou'd depend on the good Offices of the Duke {29} of Richmond, to second General Conway's application; so that I have no doubt of success. I am, my Dear Sir,

Yours with great sincerity,

D. H.

In five days I receiv'd that following Answer;

M. Rousseau to M. Hume
In Wootton 23 June 1766.

I imagined, Sir, that my silence, truly interpreted by your own conscience, had said enough; but since you have some design in not understanding me, I shall speak. You have but ill disguised yourself. I know you, and you are not ignorant of it. Before we had any personal connections, quarrels, or disputes; while we knew each other only by literary reputation, you affectionately made me the offer of the good offices of yourself and friends. Affected by this generosity, I threw myself into your arms; you brought me to England, apparently to procure me an asylum, but in fact to bring me to dishonour. You applied to this noble work, with a zeal worthy of your heart, and a success worthy of your abilities.

You needed not have taken so much pains: you live and converse with the world; I with myself in solitude. The public love to be deceived, and you were formed {30} to deceive them. I know one man, however, whom you can not deceive; I mean yourself. You know with what horror my heart rejected the first suspicion of your designs. You know I embraced you with tears in my eyes, and told you, if you were not the best of men, you must be the blackest of mankind. In reflecting on your private conduct, you must say to yourself sometimes, you are not the best of men: under which conviction, I doubt much if ever you will be the happiest.

I leave your friends and you to carry on your schemes as you please; giving up to you, without regret, my reputation during life; certain that, sooner or later, justice will be done to that of both. As to your good offices in matters of interest, which you have made use of as a mask, I thank you for them, and shall dispense with profiting by them. I ought not to hold a correspondence with you any longer, or to accept of it to my advantage in any affair in which you are to be the mediator. Adieu, Sir, I wish you the truest happiness; but as we ought not to have any thing to say to each other for the future, {31} this is the last letter you will receive from me.

J. J. R.

I immediately sent the following Reply:

M. Hume to M. Rousseau
June 26 1766.

As I am conscious of having ever acted towards you, the most friendly part, of having always given the most tender, the most active proofs of sincere affection; you may judge of my extreme surprize on perusing your Epistle: Such violent accusations, confined altogether to generals, it is as impossible to answer, as it is impossible to comprehend them. But affairs cannot, must not remain on that footing. I shall charitably suppose, that some infamous Calumniator has belyed me to you: But in that case, it is your duty, and I am persuaded it will be your inclination, to give me an opportunity of detecting him and of justifying my-self, which can only be done by your mentioning the particulars, of which I am accused. You say, that I {32} my-self know that I have been false to you; but I say it loudly, and will say it to the whole world, that

I know the contrary, that I know my friendship towards you has been unbounded and uninterrupted, and that tho' instances of it have been generally remarked both in France and England the smallest part of it only has as yet come to the knowledge of the public. I demand, that you will produce me the man who will assert the contrary; and above all, I demand, that he will mention any one particular in which I have been wanting to you; You owe this to me, you owe it to yourself, you owe it to truth and honour and justice, and to every thing that can be deemed sacred among men. As an innocent man, I will not say as your friend, I will not say as your Benefactor; but I repeat it, as an innocent man, I claim the Privilege of proving my innocence, and of refuting any scandalous lye which may have been invented against me. M. Davenport, to whom I have sent a Copy of your letter, and who will read this before he delivers it, I am confident will second my demand, and will tell you, that nothing possibly {33} can be more equitable. Happily, I have preserved the letter you wrote me after your arrival at Wotton; and you there express in the strongest terms, indeed in terms too strong, your satisfaction in my poor endeavours to serve you: The little epistolary intercourse which afterwards passed between us has been all employed on my side to the most friendly purposes; Tell me, what has since given you offence: Tell me of what I am accused: Tell me the man who accuses me. Even after you have fulfilled all these conditions to my satisfaction and to that of M. Davenport, you will have great difficulty to justify the employing such outrageous terms towards a Man, with whom you have been so intimately connected, and whom on many accounts you ought to have treated with some regard and decency.

M. Davenport knows the whole transaction about your Pension, because I thought it necessary, that the Person, who had undertaken your settlement shou'd be fully acquainted with your circumstances; lest he shoud be tempted {34} to perform towards you concealed acts of generosity, which if they accidentally came to your knowledge, might give you some grounds of Offence. I am, Sir,

D. H.

M. Davenport's Authority procured me in three weecks the following enormous letter; which however has this advantage, that it confirms all the material Circumstances of the foregoing Narrative.

{35} {36} {37}
Mr Rousseau to Mr Hume
In Wootton 10, July, 1766.

Sir, I am indisposed, and little in a situation to write; but you require an explanation, and it must be given you: it was your own fault you had it not long since,[12] but you did not desire it, and I was therefore silent: at present you do, and I have sent it. It will be a long one, for which I am very sorry; but I have much to say, and would put an end to the subject at once.

As I live retired from the world, I am ignorant of what passes in it. I have no party, no associates, no intrigues; I am told nothing, and I know only what I feel. But as care hath been taken to make me severely feel; that I well know. The first concern of those who engage in bad designs is to secure themselves from legal proofs of detection: it would not be very advisable to seek a remedy against them at law. The innate conviction of the heart admits of another kind of proof, which influences the sentiments of honest men. You well know the basis of mine.

You ask me, with great confidence, to name your accuser. That accuser, Sir, is the only man in the world whose testimony I should admit against you; it is yourself. I shall give myself up, without fear or reserve, {38} to the natural frankness of my disposition; being an enemy to every kind of artifice, I shall speak with the same freedom as if you were an indifferent person, on whom I placed all that confidence which I no longer have in you. I will give you a history of the emotions of my heart, and of what produced them; while speaking of Mr Hume in the third person, I shall make yourself the judge of what I ought to think of him. Notwithstanding the length of my letter, I shall pursue no other order than that of my ideas, beginning with the premises, and ending with the demonstration.

I quitted Switzerland, wearied out by the barbarous treatment I had undergone; but which affected only my personal security, while my honour

---

12. First Lye: Mr Rousseau never gave me an Opportunity of demanding an Explication. If he ever entertained any of those black and absurd Suspicions, of which this Letter is so full, he always kept them to himself, as long as we lived together.

was safe. I was going, as my heart directed me, to join my Lord Mareschal; when I received at Strasburg, a most affectionate invitation from Mr Hume, to go over with him to England, where he promised me the most agreeable reception, and more tranquillity than I have met with. I hesitated some time between my old friend and my new one; in this I was wrong. I preferred the latter, and in this was still more so. But the desire of visiting in person a celebrated nation, of which I had heard both so much good and so much ill, prevailed. Assured I could not lose George Keith, I was flattered with the acquisition of David Hume. His great merit, extraordinary abilities, and established probity of character, made me desirous of annexing his friendship to that with which I was honoured by his illustrious countrymen. {39} Besides, I gloried not a little in setting an example to men of letters, in a sincere union between two men so different in their principles.

Before I had received an invitation from the King of Prussia, and my Lord Mareschal, undetermined about the place of my retreat, I had desired, and obtained by the interest of my friends, a passport from the Court of France. I made use of this, and went to Paris to join Mr Hume. He saw, and perhaps saw too much of, the favourable reception I met with from a great Prince, and I will venture to say, of the public. I yielded, as it was my duty, though with reluctance, to that eclat; concluding how far it must excite the envy of my enemies. At the same time, I saw with pleasure, the regard which the public entertained for Mr Hume, sensibly increasing throughout Paris, on account of the good work he had undertaken with respect to me. Doubtless he was affected too; but I know not if it was in the same manner as I was.

We set out with one of my friends, who came to England almost entirely on my account. When we were landed at Dover, transported with the thoughts of having set foot in this land of liberty, under the conduct of so celebrated a person, I threw my arms round his neck, and pressed him to my heart, without speaking a syllable; bathing his cheeks, as I kissed them, with tears sufficiently expressive. This was not the only, nor the most remarkable instance I have given him of the {40} effusions of a heart full of sensibility. I know not what he does with the recollection of them, when that happens; but I have a notion they must be sometimes troublesome to him.

At our arrival in London, we were mightily caressed and entertained: all ranks of people eagerly pressing to give me marks of their benevolence and esteem. Mr Hume presented me politely to every body; and it was natural for me to ascribe to him, as I did, the best part of my good reception. My heart was full of him, I spoke in his praise to every one, I wrote to the same purpose to all my friends; my attachment to him gathering every day new strength, while his appeared the most af-fectionate to me, of which he frequently gave me instances that touched me extremely. That of causing my portrait to be painted, however, was not of the number. This seemed to me to carry with it too much the affectation of popularity, and had an air of ostentation which by no means pleased me. All this, however, might have been easily excusable, had Mr Hume been a man apt to throw away his money, or had a gallery of pictures with the portraits of his friends. After all, I freely confess, that, on this head, I may be in the wrong.[13]

But what appears to me an act of friendship and generosity the most undoubted and estimable, in a word, the most worthy of Mr {41} Hume, was the care he took to solicit for me, of his own accord, a pension from the King, to which most assuredly I had no right to aspire. As I was a witness to the zeal he exerted in that affair, I was greatly affected with it. Nothing could flatter me more than a piece of service of that nature; not merely for the sake of interest; for, too much attached, perhaps, to what I actually possess, I am not capable of desiring what I have not, and, as I am able to subsist on my labour, and the assistance of my friends, I covet nothing more. But the honour of receiving testimonies of the goodness, I will not say of so great a monarch, but of so good a father, so good a husband, so good a master, so good a friend, and, above all, so worthy a man, was sensibly affecting: and when I considered farther, that the minister who had obtained for me this favour, was a living instance of that probity which of all others is the most important to mankind, and at the same time

---

13. The Story was this: My Friend, Mr Ramsay, a Man of Merit, as well as a distinguished Painter, proposed to me to draw Mr Rousseau's Picture. After it was begun, he told me, that he intended it as a Present to me. So that neither did the first Idea come into my head, nor did the Picture cost me a farthing. Mr Rousseau was equally mistaken, when he payed me a Compliment on that Civility in his Letter of the 29' of March, and at present when he cavils at it.

hardly ever met with in the only character wherein it can be useful, I could not check the emotions of my pride, at having for my benefactors three men, who of all the world I could most desire to have my friends. Thus, so far from refusing the pension offered me, I only made one condition necessary for my acceptance; this was the consent of a person, whom I could not, without neglecting my duty, fail to consult.

Being honoured with the civilities of all the world, I endeavoured to make a proper return. In the mean time, my bad state of health, and being accustomed to live in the country, made my residence {42} in town very disagreeable. Immediately country houses presented themselves in plenty; I had my choice of all the counties of England. Mr Hume took the trouble to receive these proposals, and to represent them to me; accompanying me to two or three in the neighbouring counties. I hesitated a good while in my choice, and he increased the difficulty of determination. At length I fixed on this place, and immediately Mr Hume settled the affair; all difficulties vanished, and I departed; arriving presently at this solitary, convenient, and agreeable habitation, where the owner of the house provides every thing, and nothing is wanting. I became tranquil, independent; and this seemed to be the wished-for moment when all my misfortunes should have an end. On the contrary, it was now they began; misfortunes more cruel than any I had yet experienced.

Hitherto I have spoken in the fulness of my heart, and to do justice, with the greatest pleasure, to the good offices of Mr Hume. Would to Heaven that what remains for me to say were of the same nature! It would never give me pain to speak what would redound to his honour; nor is it proper to set a value on benefits till one is accused of ingratitude, which is the case at present. I will venture to make one observation, therefore, which renders it necessary. In estimating the services of Mr Hume, by the time and the pains they took him up, they were of an infinite value, and that still more from the good will displayed in their performance; but for the actual service they were of to me, it was much more in appearance than reality. I did not come over to beg my bread in England; {43} I brought the means of subsistence with me. I came merely to seek an asylum in a country which is open to every stranger without distinction. I was, besides, not so totally unknown as that, if I had arrived alone, I should have wanted either assistance or service. If some persons have sought my acquaintance for the sake of Mr Hume, others have sought it for my own. Thus, when Mr Davenport, for example, was so kind as to offer my present retreat, it was not for the sake of Mr Hume, whom he did not know, and whom he saw only in order to desire him to make me his obliging proposal; so that, when Mr Hume endeavours to alienate from me this worthy man, he takes that from me which he did not give me.[14] All the good that hath been done me, would have been done me nearly the same without him, and perhaps better; but the evil would not have been done me at all; for why should I have enemies in England? Why are those enemies all the friends of Mr Hume? Who could have excited their enmity against me? It certainly was not I, who knew nothing of them, nor ever saw them in my life. I should not have had a single enemy had I come to England alone.[15]

I have hitherto dwelt upon public and notorious facts, which, from their own nature, and my acknowledgment, have made the greatest eclat. Those which are to follow are particular and secret, at least in their cause; and all possible measures have been taken to keep the knowledge of them from the public; but as they are well known {44} to the person interested, they will not have the less influence toward his own conviction.

A very short time after our arrival in London, I observed an absurd change in the minds of the people regarding me, which soon became very apparent. Before I arrived in England, there was not a nation in Europe in which I had a greater reputation, I will venture to say, or was held in greater estimation. The public papers were full of encomiums on me, and a general outcry prevailed on my persecutors. This was the case at my arrival, which was published in the newspapers with triumph; England prided itself in affording me refuge, and justly gloried on that occasion in its laws and government; when all of a sudden, without the least assignable cause, the tone was changed, and that so speedily and totally, that, of all the caprices of the public, never was known any thing more surprising. The signal was given in a certain *Magazine*, equally full of follies and false-

---

14. Even since M Rousseau's Rupture with me, I have employed my good Offices with Mr Davenport to continue the same charitable Care of his unhappy Guest.
15. Such Effects of a diseased Imagination! For, as he confesses, that he has no Connexions nor Commerce with any body, all this comes from his own Imagination.

hoods, in which the author, being well informed, or pretending to be so, gives me out for the son of a musician. From this time I was constantly spoken of in print in a very equivocal or slighting manner.[d] Every thing that had been published concerning my misfortunes was misrepresented, altered, or placed in a wrong light, and always as much as possible to my disadvantage. So far was any body from speaking of the reception I met with at Paris, and which had made but too much noise, it was not generally supposed that I durst have appeared in that {45} city, even one of Mr Hume's friends being very much surprised when I told him I came through it.

Accustomed as I had been too much to the inconstancy of the public, to be affected by this instance of it, I could not help being astonished, however, at a change, so very sudden and general, that not one of those who had so much praised me in my absence, appeared, now I was present, to think even of my existence. I thought it something very odd that, immediately after the return of Mr Hume, who had so much credit in London, with so much influence over the booksellers and men of letters, and such great connections with them, his presence should produce an effect so contrary to what might have been expected; that among so many writers of every kind, not one of his friends should show himself to be mine; while it was easy to be seen, that those who spoke of him were not his enemies, since, in noticing his public character, they reported that I had come through France under his protection, and by favour of a passport which he had obtained of the court; nay, they almost went so far as to insinuate, that I came over in his retinue, and at his expense. All this was of little signification, and was only singular; but what was much more so, was, that his friends changed their tone with me as much as the public. {46} I shall always take a pleasure in saying that they were still equally solicitous to serve me, and that they exerted themselves greatly in my favour; but so far were they from showing me the same respect, particularly the gentleman at whose house we alighted on our arrival, that he accompanied all his actions with discourse so rude, and sometimes so insulting, that one would have thought he had taken an occasion to oblige me, merely to have a right to express his contempt.[16] His brother, who was

16. Second Lye, to be proved such from M. Rousseau himself, who wrote to Mr Stewart,

at first very polite and obliging, altered his behaviour with so little reserve, that he would hardly deign to speak a single word to me, even in their own house, in return to a civil salutation, or to pay any of those civilities which are usually paid in like circumstances to strangers.[17] Nothing new had happened, however, except the arrival of J. J. Rousseau and David Hume: and certainly the cause of these alterations did not come from me, unless, indeed, too great a portion of simplicity, discretion, and modesty, be the cause of offence in England. As to Mr Hume, he was so far from assuming such a disgusting tone, that he gave into the other extreme. I have always looked upon flatterers with an eye of suspicion: and he was so full of all kinds[18] of flattery, that he even {47} obliged me, when I could bear it no longer, to tell him my sentiments on that head.[19] His behaviour was such as to render few words necessary, yet I could have wished he had substituted, in the room of such gross encomiums, sometimes the language of a friend; but I never found any thing in his, which savoured of true friendship, not even in his manner of speaking of me to others in my presence. One would have thought that, in endeavouring to procure me patrons, he strove to deprive me of their good will; that he sought rather to have me assisted than loved; and I have been sometimes surprised at the rude turn he hath given to my behaviour before people who might not unreasonably have taken offence at it. I shall give an example of what I mean. Mr Pennick of the Museum, a friend of my Lord Mareschal's, and minister of a parish where I was solicited to reside, came to see me. Mr Hume made my excuses, while I myself was present, for not having paid him a visit. Doctor Matty, said he, invited us on Thursday to the Museum, where Mr Rousseau should have seen you; but he chose rather to go

---

the Person here meant, a Letter from the Country, full of the strongest and justest Acknowledgements of all his Civilities and Services.

17. Third Lye: The Person here meant is the most inoffensive Man in the World.

18. I shall mention only one, that made me smile; this was, his attention to have, every time I came to see him, a volume of *Eloisa* upon his table; as if I did not know enough of Mr Hume's taste for reading, as to be well assured, that of all books in the world, *Eloisa* must be one of the most tiresome to him.

19. Mr Rousseau's two first Letters, which I have inserted, on purpose, show on what Side the Compliments were most payed. This is also a Lye, which I shall throw into the dozen: He never objected to any Civilities, which I payed him; and he expressed indeed a general Satisfaction in every part of my Conduct.

with Mrs Garrick to the play: we could not do both the same day. You will confess, Sir, this was a strange method of recommending me to Mr Pennick.[20]

I know not what Mr Hume might say in private of me to his acquaintance, but nothing was more {48} extraordinary than their behaviour to me, even by his own confession, and even often through his own means. Although my purse was not empty, and I needed not that of any other person, which he very well knew, yet any one would have thought I was come over to subsist on the charity of the public, and that nothing more was to be done than to give me alms in such a manner as to save me a little confusion.[21] I must own, this constant and insolent piece of affectation was one of those things which made me averse to reside in London. This certainly was not the footing on which any man should have been introduced in England, had there been a design of procuring him ever so little respect. This display of charity, however, may admit of a more favourable interpretation, and I consent it should. To proceed.

At Paris was published a fictitious letter from the King of Prussia, addressed to me, and replete with the most cruel malignity. I learned with surprise that it was one Mr Walpole, a a friend of Mr Hume's who was the editor; I asked him if it were true; in answer to which question, he only asked me, of whom I had the information. A moment before he had given me a card for this same Mr Walpole, written to engage him to bring over such papers as related to me from Paris, and which I wanted to have by a safe hand.

I was informed that the son of that quack Tronchin, my most mortal enemy, was not only the friend {49} of Mr Hume, and under his protection, but that they both lodged in the same house together; and when Mr Hume found that I knew it, he imparted it in confidence; assuring me at the same time that the son was by no means like the father. I lodged a few nights myself, together with my governante, in the same house; and by the air

---

20. I do not remember any thing of this silly Story; but it must be false, because I remember, that we had chosen different days for going to the Museum and to the Comedy.
21. This alludes, I suppose, to two or three Dinners sent him from M Stewart's house, when he chose to dine at home: Which proceeded from the Accident that there was no Traiteur in the Neighbourhood.

and manner with which we were received by the landladies, who are his friends, I judged in what manner either Mr Hume, or that man, who, as he said, was by no means like his father, must have spoken to them both of her and me.[22]

All these facts put together, added to a certain appearance of things on the whole, insensibly gave me an uneasiness which I rejected with horror. In the mean time, I found the letters I wrote did not come to hand; those I received had often been opened; and all went through the hands of Mr Hume.[e] If at any time any one escaped him, he could not conceal his eagerness to see it. One evening, in particular, I remember a very remarkable circumstance of this kind that greatly struck me.[23]

As we were sitting one evening, after supper, silent by the fire-side, I caught his eyes intently fixed on mine, as indeed happened very often; and that in a manner of which it is very difficult to give an idea. At that time

---

22. What a black Mind! to entertain Suspicions against me, because I live in Friendship with Mr Walpole, or because the Son of his Enemy happens to take Lodgings in the same House with me, or because he fancies, that my Landladies, who cannot speak a Word of French, looked coldly on him one day. I only said, that young Tronchin did not entertain the same Prejudices as his Father against him.

23. It is necessary to explain this circumstance. I had been writing on Mr Hume's table, during his absence, an answer to a letter I had just received. He came in, very anxious to know what I had been writing, and hardly able to contain himself from desiring to read it. I closed my letter, however, without showing it him; when, as I was putting it into my pocket, he asked me for it eagerly, {50} saying he would send it away on the morrow, being post-day. The letter lay on the table. Lord Newnham came in. Mr Hume went out of the room for a moment, on which I took the letter up again, saying I should find time to send it the next day. Lord Newnham offered to get it inclosed in the French ambassador's packet, which I accepted. Mr Hume re-entered the moment his Lordship had inclosed it, and was pulling out his seal. Mr Hume officiously offered his own seal, and that with so much earnestness, that it could not well be refused. The bell was rung, and Lord Newnham gave the letter to Mr Hume's servant, to give it to his own, who waited below with the chariot, in order to have it sent to the ambassador. Mr Hume's servant was hardly got out of the room, but I said to myself, I'll lay a wager the master follows. He did not fail to do as I expected. Not knowing how to leave Lord Newnham alone, I staid some time before I followed Mr Hume. I said nothing; but he must perceive that I was uneasy. Thus, although I have received no answer to my letter, I doubt not of its going to hand; but I confess, I cannot help suspecting it was read first.[24]

24. These infamous and black Suspicions are built on such a silly Foundation, that every Circumstance of this Story may be either true or false without being of any Consequence.

he gave me a stedfast, piercing look, mixed with a sneer, which greatly disturbed me. To get rid of the embarrassment I lay under, I endeavoured to look full at him in my turn; but, in {50} fixing my eyes against his, I felt the most inexpressible terror, and was obliged soon to turn them away. The speech and physiognomy of the good David is that of an honest man; but where, great God! did this good man borrow those eyes he fixes so sternly and unaccountably on those of his friends?

The impression of this look remained with me, and gave me much uneasiness. My trouble increased even to a degree of fainting; and if I had not been relieved by an effusion of tears, I had been suffocated. Presently after this I was seized with the most violent remorse; I even despised myself; till at length, in a transport which I still remember with delight, I sprang on his neck, embraced him eagerly; while almost choked with sobbing, and bathed in tears, I cried out, in broken accents, *No, no, David Hume cannot be treacherous. If he be not the best of men, he must be the basest of mankind.*[25] David Hume politely returned my embraces, and, gently, tapping me on the back, repeated several times, in a good-natured and easy tone, *Why, what, my dear Sir! Nay, my dear Sir! Oh, my dear Sir!* He said nothing more. {51} I felt my heart yearn within me. We went to bed; and I set out the next day for the country.

Arrived at this agreeable asylum, to which I have travelled so far in search of repose, I ought to find it in a retired, convenient, and pleasant habitation; the master of which, a man of understanding and worth, spares for nothing to render it agreeable to me. But what repose can be tasted in life, when the heart is agitated? Afflicted with the most cruel uncertainty, and ignorant what to think of a man whom I ought to love and esteem, I endeavoured to get rid of that fatal doubt, in placing confidence in my benefactor. For, wherefore, from what unaccountable caprice should he display so much apparent zeal for my happiness, and at the same time entertain secret designs against my honour. Among the several observations that disturbed me, each fact was in itself of no great moment; it was their concurrence that was surprising; yet I thought, perhaps, that

---

25. This is a fourth Lye the most studied and most premeditated of the whole. See my subsequent Letter to Mr Rousseau page 74.

Mr Hume, informed of other facts, of which I was ignorant, could have given me a satisfactory solution of them, had we come to an explanation. The only thing that was inexplicable, was, that he refused to come to such an explanation; which both his honour and his friendship rendered equally necessary. I saw very well there was something in the affair which I did not comprehend, and which I earnestly wished to know. Before I came to an absolute determination, therefore, with regard to him, I was desirous of making another effort, and to try to recover him, if he had permitted himself to be seduced by my enemies, {52}{53} or, in short, to prevail on him to explain himself one way or other. Accordingly I wrote him a letter, which he ought to have found very natural,[26] if he were guilty; but very extraordinary, if he were innocent. For what could be more extraordinary than a letter full of gratitude for his services, and at the same time, of distrust of his sentiments; and in which, placing in a manner his actions on one side, and his sentiments on the other, instead of speaking of the proofs of friendship he had given me, I desired him to love me, for the good he had done me![27] I did not take the precaution to preserve a copy of this letter; but as he hath done it, let him produce it: and whoever shall read it, and see therein a man labouring under a secret trouble, which he is desirous of expressing, and is afraid to do it, will, I am persuaded, be curious to know what kind of éclaircissement it produced, especially after the preceding scene. None. Absolutely none at all. Mr Hume contented himself, in his answer, with only speaking of the obliging offices Mr Davenport proposed to do for me. As for the rest, he said not a word of the principal subject of my letter, nor of the situation of my heart, of whose distress he could not be ignorant. I was more struck with this silence, than I had been with his phlegm during our last conversation. In this I was wrong; this silence was very natural after the other, and was no more than I ought to have expected. For when one hath ventured to declare to a man's face, *I am tempted to believe you a traitor*, {54} and he hath not the curiosity to ask you *for what*,[28] it may be depended on he will

---

26. It appears from what he wrote to me afterwards, that he was very well satisfied with this letter, and that he thought of it very well.

27. A fifth Lye: See the Letter itself, dated the 22^d of March, page 13, where there is a most unreserved Cordiality; not the least Appearance of Suspicion.

28. A Repetition of the fourth Lye, and consequently equivalent to a sixth.

never have any such curiosity as long as he lives; and it is easy to judge of him from these slight indications.

After the receipt of his letter, which was long delayed, I determined at length to write to him no more. Soon after, every thing served to confirm me in the resolution to break off all farther correspondence with him. Curious to the last degree concerning the minutest circumstance of my affairs, he was not content to learn them of me, in our frequent conversations; but, as I learned, never let slip an opportunity of being alone with my governante,[29] to interrogate her even importunately concerning my occupations, my resources, my friends, acquaintances, their names, situations, place of abode, and all this after setting out with telling her he was well acquainted with the whole of my connections; nay, with the most jesuitical address, he would ask the same questions of us separately. One ought undoubtedly to interest one's self in the affairs of a friend; but one ought to be satisfied with what he thinks proper to let us know of them, particularly when people are so frank and ingenuous as I am. Indeed all this petty inquisitiveness is very little becoming a philosopher.

About the same time I received two other letters which had been opened. The one from Mr Boswell, the seal of which was so loose and disfigured, that Mr Davenport, when he received it, remarked the same to Mr Hume's servant. The other was from Mr d'Ivernois, {55} in Mr Hume's packet, and which had been sealed up again by means of a hot iron, which, awkwardly applied, had burnt the paper round the impression. On this I wrote to Mr Davenport to desire him to take charge of all the letters which might be sent for me, and to trust none of them in any body's hands, under any pretext whatever. I know not whether Mr Davenport, who certainly was far from thinking that precaution was to be observed with regard to Mr Hume, showed him my letter or not; but this I know, that the latter had all the reason in the world to think he had forfeited my confidence, and that he proceeded nevertheless in his usual manner, without troubling himself about the recovery of it.

---

29. Seventh Lye: I never had but one *tete a tete* with his Gouvernante. It was about half an hour on her first Arrival. It was not likely I cou'd have any other Subject of Conversation with her but about him.

But what was to become of me, when I saw, in the public papers, the pretended letter of the King of Prussia which I had never before seen, that fictitious letter, printed in French and English, given for genuine, even with the signature of the King, and in which I knew the pen of Mr d'Alembert as certainly as if I had seen him write it?

In a moment a ray of light discovered to me the secret cause of that touching and sudden change, which I had observed in the public respecting me; and I saw the plot which was put in execution at London, had been laid in Paris.

Mr d'Alembert, another intimate friend of Mr Hume's, had been long since my secret enemy, and lay in watch for opportunities to injure me without exposing himself. He was the only person, among the men {56} of letters, of my old acquaintance, who did not come to see me, or send their civilities during my last passage through Paris.[30] I knew his secret disposition, but I gave myself very little trouble about it, contenting myself with advising my friends of it occasionally. I remember that being asked about him one day by Mr Hume, who afterwards asked my governante the same question, I told him that Mr d'Alembert was a cunning, artful man. He contradicted me with a warmth that surprised me; not then knowing they stood so well with each other, and that it was his own cause he defended.

The perusal of the letter above mentioned alarmed me a good deal, when, perceiving that I had been brought over to England in consequence of a project which began to be put in execution, but of the end of which I was ignorant, I felt the danger without knowing what to guard against, or on whom to rely. I then recollected four terrifying words Mr Hume had made use of, and of which I shall speak hereafter.[31] What could be thought

---

30. [A note presented in French by Hume in the manuscript, as though written by D'Alembert himself:] Here is the truth. I [D'Alembert] knew that M. Rousseau had received in a very cold fashion one of my friends, M. Watelet; by the way I got from him something about me, from what I understand, without knowing why, that he did not like me. However, I begged M. Hume to ask him if he would accept to see me. After a few days, M. Hume told me that he had not be able to convince him, because M. Rousseau was such in a bad mood as he seemed unnerved by the visits he got. I did not do anything then, and I did not say anything to M. Rousseau. *Note de Mr. D'Alembert.*[f]

31. This is a Preparation to his twelfth Lye: But we shall be indulgent to him: We shall not

of a paper in which my misfortunes were imputed to me as a crime, which tended, in the midst of my distress, to deprive me of all compassion, and, to render its effects still more cruel, pretended to have been written by a Prince who had afforded me protection? What could I divine would be the consequence of such a beginning? The people in England read the public papers, and are in no wise prepossessed in favour of foreigners. {57} Even a coat, cut in a different fashion from their own, is sufficient to excite a prejudice against them. What then had not a poor stranger to expect in his rural walks, the only pleasures of his life, when the good people in the neighbourhood were once thoroughly persuaded he was fond of being persecuted and pelted? Doubtless they would be ready enough to contribute to his favourite amusement. But my concern, my profound and cruel concern, the bitterest indeed I ever felt, did not arise from the danger to which I was personally exposed. I have braved too many others to be much moved with that. The treachery of a false friend,[32] to which I had fallen a prey, was the circumstance that filled my too susceptible heart with deadly sorrow. In the impetuosity of its first emotions, of which I never yet was master, and of which my enemies have artfully taken the advantage, I wrote several letters full of disorder, in which I did not disguise either my anxiety or indignation.

I have, Sir, so many things to mention, that I forget half of them by the way. For instance, a certain narrative in form of a letter, concerning my manner of living at Montmorency, was given by the booksellers to Mr Hume, who showed it me. I agreed to its being printed, and Mr Hume undertook the care of its edition; but it never appeared. Again, I had brought over with me a copy of the letters of Mr du Peyrou, containing a relation of the treatment I had met with at Neufchâtel. I gave them into the hands of the same bookseller to have them translated and reprinted. {58} Mr Hume charged himself with the care of them; but they never appeared.[33] The supposititious letter of the King of Prussia, and

---

count it for a Lye apart.

32. How innocent I am of every thing that regards this feigned Letter of the King of Prussia appears from Mr Walpole's Letter annexed. The Publication of the King of Prussia's Letter was unavoidable after Copies had been dispersed in Paris and in London.

33. The booksellers have lately informed me that the edition is finished, and will shortly be published. This may be; but it is too late, and what is still worse, it is too opportune for the

its translation, had no sooner made their appearance, than I immediately apprehended why the other pieces had been suppressed,[34] and I wrote as much to the booksellers. I wrote several other letters also, which probably were handed about London; till at length I employed the credit of a man of quality and merit, to insert a declaration of the imposture in the public papers. In this declaration, I concealed no part of my extreme concern, nor did I in the least disguise the cause.

Hitherto Mr Hume seems to have walked in darkness. You will soon see him appear in open day, and act without disguise. Nothing more is necessary, in our behaviour towards cunning people, than to act ingenuously; sooner or later they will infallibly betray themselves.

When this pretended letter from the King of Prussia was first published in London, Mr Hume, who certainly knew that it was fictitious, as I had told him so, yet said nothing of the matter, did not write to me, but was totally silent; and did not even think of making any declaration of the truth, in favour of his absent friend.[35] It answered his purpose better to let the report take its course, as he did.

Mr Hume having been my conductor into England, he was of course in a manner my patron and protector. If it were but natural in him to undertake my defence, it was no less so that, {59} when I had a public protestation to make, I should have addressed myself to him. Having already ceased writing to him, however, I had no mind to renew our correspondence.[36] I addressed myself therefore to another person. The first slap on the face I gave my patron. He felt nothing of it.

In saying the letter was fabricated at Paris, it was of very little conse-

---

purpose intended to be served.

34. Eighth Lye: Mr Rousseau was told above two Months ago by Mr Becket, the Bookseller, that the Reason why this Publication was retarded, was the Sickness of the Translator. I never promised to have any Care or Inspection over this Edition, as is well known to Mr Becket. M. Rousseau is therefore here guilty of a ninth Lye.

35. The King of Prussia's Letter was known by all the World to be feigned and to be wrote by Mr Walpole.

36. Mr Rousseau had wrote me only eight days before a very cordial Letter, that of the 29' of March: But as this may only be a Defect of Memory, we shall not put it in the Class of his Lyes.

quence to me whether it was understood particularly of Mr d'Alembert, or of Mr Walpole,[37] whose name he borrowed on the occasion. But in adding that, what afflicted and tore my heart was, the impostor had got his accomplices in England; I expressed myself very clearly to their friend, who was in London, and was desirous of passing for mine. For certainly he was the only person in England, whose hatred could afflict and rend my heart. This was the second slap of the face I gave my patron. He did not feel, however, yet.

On the contrary, he maliciously pretended that my affliction arose solely from the publication of the above letter, in order to make me pass for a man who was excessively affected by satire. Whether I am vain or not, certain it is I was mortally afflicted; he knew it, and yet wrote me not a word. This affectionate friend, who had so much at heart the filling of my purse, gave himself no trouble to think my heart was bleeding with sorrow.

Another piece appeared soon after, in the same papers, by the author of the former, and still if possible more cruel, in which the writer could not disguise his rage at the reception I met with at Paris.[38] This however did not affect me; it told me nothing new. Mere libels may take their course without giving me any emotion; and {60} the inconstant public may amuse themselves as long as they please with the subject. It is not an affair of conspirators, who, bent on the destruction of my honest fame, are determined by some means or other to effect it. It was necessary to change the battery.

The affair of the pension was not determined. It was not difficult, however, for Mr Hume to obtain, from the humanity of the minister, and the generosity of the King, the favour of its determination. He was required to inform me of it, which he did. This, I must confess, was one of the critical moments of my life. How much did it cost me to do my duty! My preceding engagements, the necessity of showing a due respect for the goodness of the King, and for that of his minister, together with the desire of displaying how far I was sensible of both; add to these the advantage of being made

---

37. Mr Walpole assures me, that he never was more than once in Company with M Dalembert, and never exchanged three Words with him in his Life.

38. I never saw this pretended Libel in my Life.[g]

a little more easy in circumstances in the decline of life, surrounded as I was by enemies and evils; in fine, the embarrassment I was under to find a decent excuse for not accepting a benefit already half accepted; all these together made the necessity of that refusal very difficult and cruel: for necessary it was, or I should have been one of the meanest and basest of mankind to have voluntarily laid myself under an obligation to a man who had betrayed me.[39]

I did my duty, though not without reluctance. I wrote immediately to General Conway, and in the most civil and respectful manner possible, without giving an absolute refusal, excusing myself from accepting the pension for the present.

Now, Mr Hume had been the only {61} negociator of this affair, nay the only person who had spoke of it. Yet I not only did not give him any answer, though it was he who wrote to me on the subject, but did not even so much as mention him in my letter to General Conway. This was the third slap of the face I gave my patron, which if he does not feel, it is certainly his own fault, he can feel nothing.

My letter was not clear, nor could it be so to General Conway, who did not know the motives of my refusal; but it was very plain to Mr Hume, who knew them but too well. He pretended nevertheless to be deceived as well with regard to the cause of my discontent, as to that of my declining the pension; and, in a letter he wrote me on the occasion, gave me to understand that the King's goodness might be continued towards me, if I should reconsider the affair of the pension. In a word, he seemed determined, at all events, to remain still my patron, in spite of my teeth. You will imagine, Sir, he did not expect my answer; and he had none. Much about this time, for I do not know exactly the date, nor is such precision necessary, appeared a letter, from Mr de Voltaire to me, with an English translation, which still improved on the original. The noble object of this ingenious performance, was to draw on me the hatred and contempt of the people, among whom I was come to reside. I made not the least doubt that

---

39. It appears, however, that the only preceding Proofs of my Treachery, are my unlucky Countenance and the Publication of the King of Prussia's Letter by the Printer of the S[t] James's Chronicle.

my dear patron was one of the instruments of its publication; particularly when I saw that the writer, in endeavouring to alienate from me those who {62} might render my life agreeable, had omitted the name of him who brought me over. He doubtless knew that it was superfluous, and that with regard to him, nothing more was necessary to be said. The omission of his name, so impoliticly forgot in this letter, recalled to my mind what Tacitus says of the picture of Brutus, omitted in a funeral solemnity, viz. that every body took notice of it, particularly because it was not there.

Mr Hume was not mentioned; but he lives and converses with people that are mentioned. It is well known his friends are all my enemies; there are abroad such people as Tronchin, d'Alembert, and Voltaire; but it is much worse in London; for here I have no enemies but what are his friends. For why, indeed, should I have any other? Why should I have even them? What have I done to Lord Littleton, whom I don't even know?[40] What have I done to Mr Walpole, whom I know full as little? What do they know of me, except that I am unhappy, and a friend to their friend Hume? What can he have said to them, for it is only through him they know any thing of me? I can very well imagine, that, considering the part he has to play, he does not unmask himself to every body; for then he would be disguised to nobody. I can very well imagine that he does not speak of me to General Conway and the Duke of Richmond as he does in his private conversations with Mr Walpole, and his secret correspondence with Mr d'Alembert. But let any one discover the {63} clue that hath been unravelled since my arrival in London, and it will easily be seen whether Mr Hume does not hold the principal thread.

At length the moment arrived in which it was thought proper to strike the great blow, the effect of which was prepared for by a fresh satirical piece put in the papers.[41] Had there remained in me the least doubt, it

---

40. Mr Rousseau, seeing this Piece of Voltaire advertised in the News-Papers, wrote to Mr Davenport, who was then at London, desiring him to bring it down to him. I told Mr Davenport, that the printed Copy was very incorrect but that I cou'd procure him a correct manuscript Copy from Lord Lyttleton. This Incident suffices for Mr Rousseau to prove Lord Lyttleton his mortal Enemy and my intimate Friend; And that we are in a plot together against him. But he ought at least to infer that the incorrect printed Copy did not come from me.
41. I never saw this Piece either before or after its Publication. I am not sure that it ever

would have been impossible to have harboured it after perusing this piece, as it contained facts unknown to any body but Mr Hume; exaggerated, it is true, in order to render them odious to the public.

It is said in this paper that my door was opened to the rich, and shut to the poor. Pray, who knows when my door was open or shut, except Mr Hume, with whom I lived, and by whom every body was introduced that I saw? I will except one great personage, whom I gladly received without knowing him, and whom I should still have more gladly received if I had known him. It was Mr Hume who told me his name when he was gone; on which information, I was really chagrined, that, as he deigned to mount up two pair of stairs, he was not received in the first floor. As to the poor, I have nothing to say about the matter. I was constantly desirous of seeing less company; but as I was unwilling to displease any one, I suffered myself to be directed in this affair altogether by Mr Hume, and endeavoured to receive every body he introduced as well as I could, without distinction, whether rich or poor. It is said in the same piece that I received my {64} relations very coldly, *not to say any thing worse*. This general charge relates to my having once received, with some indifference, the only relation I have, out of Geneva, and that in the presence of Mr Hume.[42] It must necessarily be either Mr Hume or this relation who furnished that piece of intelligence. Now, my cousin, whom I have always known for a friendly relation and a worthy man, is incapable of furnishing materials for public satires against me. Add to this, that his situation in life confining him to the conversation of persons in trade, he has no connection with men of letters or paragraph writers, and still less with satirists and libellers; so that the article could not come from him. At the worst, can I help imagining that Mr Hume must have endeavoured to take advantage of what he said, and construed it in favour of his own purpose? It is not improper to add, that, after my rupture with Mr Hume, I wrote an account of it to my cousin.

In fine, it is said in the same paper that I am apt to change my friends. No great subtlety is necessary to comprehend what this reflection is preparative to.

---

existed. None of my Acquaintance who I have spoke to, ever saw it or heard of it.[h]

42. Tenth Lye: I was not present when Mr Rousseau received his Cousins. I afterwards saw them together, and only for a Moment, on the Terrace at Buckingham Street.

But let us distinguish facts. I have preserved some very valuable and solid friends for twenty-five to thirty years. I have others whose friendship is of a later date, but no less valuable, and which, if I live, I may preserve still longer. I have not found, indeed, the same security in general {65} among those friendships I have made with men of letters. I have for this reason sometimes changed them, and shall always change them when they appear suspicious; for I am determined never to have friends by way of ceremony; I have them only with a view to show them my affection.

If ever I was fully and clearly convinced of any thing, I am so convinced that Mr Hume furnished the materials for the above paper.

But what is still more, I have not only that absolute conviction, but it is very clear to me that Mr Hume intended I should: For how can it be supposed that a man of his subtlety should be so imprudent as to expose himself thus, if he had not intended it? What was his design in it? Nothing is more clear than this. It was to raise my resentment to the highest pitch, that he might strike the blow he was preparing to give me with greater eclat. He knew he had nothing more to do than put me in a passion, and I should be guilty of a number of absurdities. We are now arrived at the critical moment which is to show whether he reasoned well or ill.

It is necessary to have all the presence of mind, all the phlegm and resolution of Mr Hume, to be able to take the part he hath taken, after all that has passed between us. In the embarrassment I was under in writing to General Conway, I could make use only of obscure expressions, to which Mr Hume, in quality of my friend, gave what interpretation he pleased. Supposing, therefore, for he knew very well to the contrary, that it was the circumstance of {66} secrecy which gave me uneasiness, he obtained the promise of the General to endeavour to remove it; but before any thing was done, it was previously necessary to know whether I would accept of the pension without that condition, in order not to expose his Majesty to a second refusal.

This was the decisive moment, the end and object of all his labours. An answer was required: he would have it. To prevent effectually indeed my neglect of it, he sent to Mr Davenport a duplicate of his letter to me; and, not content with this precaution, wrote me word, in another billet, that he could not possibly stay any longer in London to serve me. I was giddy with amazement on reading this note. Never in my life did I meet with any thing so unaccountable.

At length he obtained from me the so much desired answer, and began presently to triumph. In writing to Mr Davenport, he treated me as a monster of brutality and ingratitude. But he wanted to do still more. He thinks his measures well taken; no proof can be made to appear against him. He demands an explanation: he shall have it, and here it is.

That last stroke was a masterpiece. He himself proves every thing, and that {67} beyond reply.

I will suppose, though by way of impossibility, that my complaints against Mr Hume never reached his ears; that he knew nothing of them; but was as perfectly ignorant as if he had held no cabal with those who are acquainted with them, but had resided all the while in China.[43] Yet the behaviour passing directly between us; the last striking words which I said to him in London; the letter which followed replete with fears and anxiety; my persevering silence still more expressive than words; my public and bitter complaints with regard to the letter of Mr d'Alembert; my letter to the Secretary of State, who did not write to me, in answer to that which Mr Hume wrote to me himself, and in which I did not mention him; and in fine my refusal, without deigning to address myself to him, to acquiesce in an affair which he had managed in my favour, with my own privity, and without any opposition on my part; all this must have spoken in a very forcible manner, I will not say to any person of the least sensibility, but to every man of common sense.

Strange that, after I had ceased to correspond with him for three months, when I had made no answer to any one of his letters, however important the subject of it, surrounded with both public and private marks of that affliction which his infidelity gave me; a man of so enlightened an understanding, {68} of so penetrating a genius by nature, and so dull by design, should see nothing, hear nothing, feel nothing, be moved at

---

43. How shoud I have known the least of these nonsensical Suspicions? Mʳ Davenport, the only person of my Acquaintance, who saw Mʳ Rousseau, assures me, that he was entirely ignorant of them.

nothing; but, without one word of complaint, justification, or explanation, continue to give me the most pressing marks of his good will to serve me, in spite of myself? He wrote to me affectionately, that he could not stay any longer in London to do me service, as if we had agreed that he should stay there for that purpose! This blindness, this insensibility, this perseverance, are not in nature; they must be accounted for, therefore, from other motives. Let us set this behaviour in a still clearer light; for this is the decisive point.

Mr Hume must necessarily have acted in this affair, either as one of the first or last of mankind. There is no medium. It remains to determine which of the two it hath been.

Could Mr Hume, after so many instances of disdain on my part, have still the astonishing generosity as to persevere sincerely to serve me? He knew it was impossible for me to accept his good offices, so long as I entertained for him such sentiments as I had conceived. He had himself avoided an explanation. So that to serve me without justifying himself,[44] would have been to render his services useless; this therefore was no generosity. If he supposed that in such circumstances I should have accepted his services, he must have supposed me to have been an infamous scoundrel. {69} It was then in behalf of a man whom he supposed to be a scoundrel, that he so warmly solicited a pension from his Majesty. Can any thing be supposed more extravagant?

But let it be supposed that Mr Hume, constantly pursuing his plan, should only have said to himself, This is the moment for its execution; for, by pressing Rousseau to accept the pension, he will be reduced either to accept or refuse it. If he accepts it, with the proofs I have in hand against him, I shall be able completely to disgrace him: if he refuses, after having accepted it, he will have no pretext, but must give a reason for such refusal. This is what I expect; if he accuses me, he is ruined.

If, I say, Mr Hume reasoned with himself in this manner, he did what was consistent with his plan, and in that case very natural; indeed this is the only way in which his conduct in this affair can be explained, for upon any other supposition it is inexplicable: if this be not demonstrable, nothing

---

44. Eleventh Lye, being a Repetition of the fourth.

ever was so. The critical situation to which he had now reduced me, re-recalled strongly to my mind the four words I mentioned above; and which I heard him say and repeat, at a time when I did not comprehend their full force. It was the first night after our departure from Paris. We slept in the same chamber, when, during the night, I heard him several times cry out {70} with great vehemence, in the French language, *Je tiens J. J. Rousseau.* I know not whether he was awake or asleep.[l]

The expression was remarkable, coming from a man who is too well acquainted with the French language, to be mistaken with regard to the force or choice of words. I took these words, however, and I could not then take them otherwise than in a favourable sense: notwithstanding the tone of voice in which they were spoken, was still less favourable than the expression. It is indeed impossible for me to give any idea of it; but it corresponds exactly with those terrible looks I have before mentioned. At every repetition of them I was seized with a shuddering, a kind of horror I could not resist, though a moment's recollection restored me, and made me smile at my terror.[45] The next day all this was so perfectly obliterated, that I did not even think of it during my stay in London, and its neighbourhood. It was not till my arrival in this place, that so many things have contributed to recall these words to my mind; and indeed recall them every moment.

These words, the tone of which dwells on my heart, as if I had but just heard them; those long and fatal looks so frequently cast on me; the patting me on the back, with the repetition of *O, my dear Sir,* in {71} answer to my suspicions of his being a traitor:[46] all this affects me to such a degree, after what preceded, that this recollection, had I no other, would be sufficient to prevent any reconciliation or return of confidence between us; not a night indeed passes over my head, but I think I hear, *Rousseau, I have you,* ring in my ears as if he had just pronounced them.

Yes, Mr Hume, I know you *have me;* but that only by mere externals:

---

45. Without Scruple, I may set down this as the twelfth Lye; and a swinging one it is.

46. A new Repetition of the fourth Lye; but we shall also give this to the dozen. Yet this Letter was sealed with Mr Rousseau's usual Motto, *Vitam impendere vero* [*Life devoted to the truth*]. Did ever any body yet know a Pretender to superior Virtue, that had common Honesty?

you have me in the public opinion and judgment of mankind. You have my reputation, and perhaps my security, to do with as you will. The general prepossession is in your favour; it will be very easy for you to make me pass for the monster you have begun to represent me; and I already see the barbarous exultation of my implacable enemies. The public will no longer spare me. Without any farther examination, every body is on the side of those who have conferred favours; because each is desirous to attract the same good offices, by displaying a sensibility of the obligation. I foresee readily the consequences of all this, particularly in the country to which you have conducted me; and where, being without friends, and an utter stranger to every body, I lie almost entirely at your mercy. The sensible part of mankind, however, will comprehend that I must be so far from seeking {72} this affair, that nothing more disagreeable or terrible could possibly have happened to me in my present situation. They will perceive that nothing but my invincible aversion to all kind of falsehood, and the possibility of my professing a regard for a person who had forfeited it, could have prevented my dissimulation, at a time when it was on so many accounts my interest. But the sensible part of mankind are few, nor do they make the greatest noise in the world.

Yes, Mr Hume, you *have me* by all the ties of this life; but you have no power over my probity or my fortitude, which, being independent either of you or of mankind, I will preserve in spite of you. Think not to frighten me with the fortune that awaits me. I know the opinions of mankind; I am accustomed to their injustice, and have learned to care little about it. If you have taken your resolution, as I have reason to believe you have, be assured mine is taken also. I am feeble indeed in body, but never possessed greater strength of mind.

Mankind may say and do what they will, it is of little consequence to me. What is of consequence, however, is, that I should end as I have {73} begun; that I should continue to preserve my ingenuousness and integrity to the end, whatever may happen; and that I should have no cause to reproach myself either with meanness in adversity, or insolence in prosperity. Whatever disgrace attends, or misfortune threatens me, I am ready to meet them. Though I am to be pitied, I am much less so than you, and all the revenge I shall take on you is, to leave you the tormenting consciousness of being obliged, in spite of yourself, to have a respect for the unfortunate person you have oppressed.

In closing this letter, I am surprised at my having been able to write it. If it were possible to die with grief, every line was sufficient to kill me with sorrow. Every circumstance of the affair is equally incomprehensible. Such conduct as yours hath been, is not in nature: it is contradictory to itself, and yet it is demonstrable to me that it has been such as I conceive. On each side of me there is a bottomless abyss! and I am lost in one or the other.

If you are guilty, I am the most unfortunate of mankind; if you are innocent, I am the most culpable. You even make me desire to be that contemptible object. Yes, the situation to which you see me reduced, prostrate at your feet, crying out for mercy, and doing every thing to obtain it; {74} publishing aloud my own unworthiness, and paying the most explicit homage to your virtues, would be a state of joy and cordial effusion, after the grievous state of restraint and mortification into which you have plunged me. I have but a word more to say. If you are guilty, write to me no more; it would be superfluous, for certainly you could not deceive me. If you are innocent, justify yourself. I know my duty; I love, and shall always love it, however difficult and severe. There is no state of abjection that a heart, not formed for it, may not recover from. Once again, I say, if you are innocent, deign to justify yourself; if you are not, adieu for ever.

J. J. R.

I hesitated sometime whether I should make any reply at all. But at last I wrote to M. Rousseau the following concise letter,

M. Hume to M. Rousseau
Lisle street Leicester-fields 22. July, 1766

Sir, I shall only answer one Article of your {75} long letter: It is that which regards the conversation between us the evening before your departure. M. Davenport had imagined a good natured Artifice, to make you believe that a Retour Chaise had cast up for Wootton, and I believe he made an advertisement to that purpose be put into the Papers, in order the better to deceive you. His intention was to save you some expences in the journey, which I thought a laudable project, tho' I had no hand, either in contriving or conducting it. You entertained however, suspicions of his design, while we were sitting alone by my fireside; and you reproched me with concurring in it. I endeavour'd to pacify you, and to divert the discourse, but to no purpose. You sat sullen, and was either silent or made me very peevish answers. At last you rose up, and took a turn or two about the room; when all of a sudden and to my great surprise, you claped yourself on my knee, threw your arms about my neck, kissed me with seeming ardour, and bedew'd my face with tears. You exclaimed, "My dear Friend, can you ever pardon this folly? After all the pains you {76} have taken to serve me, after the numberless instances of friendship you have given me, here I reward you with this ill humour and sullenness: But your forgiveness of me will be a new instance of your friendship, and I hope you will find at bottom that my heart is not unworthy of it." I was very much affected; and I believe there passed a very tender scene between us. You added, by way of compliment, that, tho' I had many better tittles to recommend me to Posterity yet perhaps my uncommon attachement and friendship to a poor unhappy persecuted man would not altogether be overlooked.

This incident, Sir, was somewhat remarkable; and it is impossible that either you or I could so soon have forgot it. But you have had the Assurance to tell me the Story twice in a manner so different or rather so opposite, that when I persist, as I do, in this account, it necessarily follows, that either you or I are a lyar. You imagine perhaps, that, because the incident passed {77} privately, without a witness, the Question will lie between the credibility of your assertion or of mine. But you shall not have this advantage or disadvantage, which ever you are pleased to term it. I shall produce against you other proofs, which will put the matter beyond controversy.

First: You are not aware, that I have a letter under your hand, which is totally irreconciliable with your account and confirms mine.[47]

---

47. That of the 22 of March; which is entirely cordial; and proves, that M. Rousseau had never expressed any of those black Suspicions of Treachery, on which he now insists: This letter also contains a peevish Paragraph about the hire of his Chaise.

Secondly: I told the Story, next day or the day after, to M. Davenport, with a friendly view of preventing any such good natured Artifices for the future: He surely remembers it.

Thirdly: As I thought the Story much to your honour, I told it to several of my friends here: I even wrote it to M.^{de} de Boufflers at Paris. I believe, no one will imagine, that I was at that time preparing before hand an Apology, in case of a rupture with you; which of all human events, I should then have {78} thought the most incredible, especially as we were separated almost for ever; and I still continued to render you the most essential services.

Fourthly: The Story, as I tell it, is consistent and rational: There is not common sense in your account. What! because sometimes when absent in thought, I have fixed a look or stare, you suspect me to be a traytor, and you have the assurance to tell me of such black and ridiculous suspicions! Are not most studious Men (and many of them more than I) subject to such reveries or fits of absence, without being exposed to such suspicions? You do not even pretend, that before you left London, you had any other solid grounds of suspicion against me.

I shall enter into no detail with regard to your letter: The other Articles of it are as much without foundation as you yourself know this to be. I shall only add in general, that I enjoy'd about a month ago, an uncommon pleasure, when I reflected, that, thro' many difficulties, and by most assiduous care and pains, I had, {79} beyond my most sanguine expectations, provided for your Repose, Honour, and Fortune. But I soon felt a very sensible uneasiness, when I found that you had, wantonly and voluntarily, thrown away all these advantages, and was become the declared Enemy of your own repose, fortune, and honour: I can not be surprized after this; that you are my enemy. Adieu and for ever.

D. H.

To all these papers I need only subjoin the following letter of M. Walpole to me, which proves how ignorant and innocent I am of this whole affair of the king of Prussia's Letter.

M. Walpole to M. Hume

Arlington street, July, 26 1766.

I can not be precise as to the time of my writting the King of Prussia's letter, but I do assure you with the utmost truth that it was several days before you left Paris, and before Rousseau's arrival there, of which I can give you a strong proof: {80} for I not only suppressed the letter while you staid there, out of delicacy to you; but it was the reason why, out of delicacy to my-self, I did not go to see him, as you often proposed to me; thinking it wrong to go and make a cordial visit to a man, with a letter in my pocket to laugh at him. You are at full liberty, Dear Sir, to make use of what I say in your Justification, either to Rousseau, or any body else. I shou'd be very sorry to have you blamed on my account; I have a hearty contempt of Rousseau, and am perfectly indifferent what any body thinks of the matter. If there is any fault, which I am far from thinking, let it lie on me. No parts can hinder my laughing at their possessor, if he is a Mountebank. If he has a bad and most ungratefull heart, as Rousseau has shown in your case, into the bargain, he will have my scorn likewise, as he will of all good and sensible men. You may trust your Sentence to such, who are as respectable Judges, as any that have pored over ten thousand and more volumes

Y.^{rs} most sincerely

H. W.

{81} Thus, I have given a narrative, as concise as possible, of this extraordinary Affair, which I am told, has much attracted the attention of the public, and which contains more unexpected incidents than any other, in which I was ever engaged. The persons to whom I have shown these original papers, which authenticate the whole, have differed very much in their opinion, as well of the use I should make of them as of M. Rousseau's present sentiments as state of mind. Some of them have maintained, that he is altogether insincere in his quarrel with me and his opinion of my guilt, and that the whole proceeds from that excessive pride, which forms the basis of his character, and which leads him both to seek the Eclat of refusing the king of England's bounty and to shake off the intolerable burthen of an obligation to me, by every sacrifice of honour, truth and friendship, as well as of interest.

They found their sentiments on the absurdity of that first supposition on which he grounds his anger, viz, that M. Walpole's letter, which he knew had been every where dispersed both in Paris and London, was given to the Press by me; and {82} as this supposition is contrary to common sense on the one hand, and not supported even by the pretence of the smallest probability on the other, they conclude, that it never had any weight even with the person himself who lays hold of it. They confirm their sentiments by the number of fictions and lyes which he employs to justify his anger; Fictions with regard to points, in which it is impossible for him to be mistaken. They also remark his real chearfulness and gaiety, amidst the deep melancholy, with which he pretended to be oppressed. Not to mention, the absurd reasoning which runs thro' the whole and on which it is impossible for any man to rest his conviction; and tho' a very important interest is here abandoned, yet money is not universally the chief object with mankind; Vanity weighs further with some men, particularly with this philosopher; and the very ostentation of refusing a pension from the king of England, an ostentation which with regard to other Princes he has often sought, were alone a sufficient motive for his present criminal conduct.

There are others of my Friends who regard {83} the whole affair in a more compassionate light, and consider M. Rousseau as an object rather of pity than of anger. They suppose the same domineering pride and ingratitude to be the basis of his character; but they are also willing to believe, that his brain has received a sensible shake, and that his judgement, set afloat, is carryed to every side, as it is pushed by the current of his humours and of his passions. The absurdity of his belief is no proof of its insincerity: He imagines himself the sole important being in the Universe: He fancies all mankind to be in a combination against him: His greatest benefactor, as hurting him most, is the chief object of his animosity: and tho' he supports all his Whimsies by lyes and fictions, this is so frequent a case with such wicked men, as are in that middle state between sober reason and total frenzy, that it needs give no surprize to any body.

I own, that I am somewhat inclined to this latter opinion; tho' at the same time, I much question, whether, in any period of his life, M. Rousseau was ever more in his {84} senses than he is at present. The former brilliancy of his genius and his great talent for writing are no proof of the contrary. It is an old remark, that great Wits are near allyed to madness; and even in those frantic letters, which he has wrote to me, there are evidently strong traces of his wonted genius and eloquence. He has frequently told me, that he was composing his Memoirs, in which Justice shou'd be done to his own character, to that of his friends and to that of his enemies; and as M. Davenport informs me, that, since his retreat into the Country, he has been much employed in writing, I have reason to conclude, that he is at present finishing that undertaking. Nothing could be more unexpected to me than my passing so suddenly from the class of his friends to that of his enemies; but his transition being made, I must expect to be treated accordingly; and I own, that this reflection gave me some Anxiety. A Work of this nature, both from the celebrity of the person and the strokes of eloquence interspersed, would certainly attract the attention of the public; and it might be published either after my death or after that of the author. In the former case, there wou'd be nobody who {85} could tell the story or justify my memory. In the latter, my Apology, wrote in opposition to a dead person, wou'd lose a great deal of its authenticity. For this reason, I have at present collected the whole story into one narrative, that I may show it to my friends and at any time have it in my power to make whatever use of it, they and I should think proper. I am and always have been such a lover of peace, that nothing but necessity or strong reasons shall oblige me to give it to the public.[i]

Editors' notes

[a]. "Advertisement of the French Editors" appears in *Concise and Genuine Account* prior to Hume's voice. Hume did want that included in *Concise and Genuine Account*.

[b]. In the *Concise and Genuine Account*, the makers of the pamphlet in London introduced into the narrative the names of both the Comtesse de Boufflers and the Marquise de Verdelin, contrary to Hume's instructions to suppress their names. Hume was incensed, as expressed in his letter to William Strahan of 25 November 1766.

[c]. In his December 1766 letter to Thomas Becket about changes to make to *Concise and Genuine Account*, should there be a second edition, Hume says that the second line of Latin here should read instead *Hic domus, hac patria est*.

[d]. Hume provided Strahan with a note to be inserted here. Instead it was given as an erratum at the end of *Concise and Genuine Account*. It is not of consequence.

[e]. Here, Hume successfully had inserted into *Concise and Genuine Account* (p. 51) a footnote in which he explains why he combed a load of Rousseau's mail he carried to Rousseau. Rousseau paid fees for receiving incoming mail, most of which was from

admirers, abusers, and so on. When Hume presented the load of mail to him, he told Hume to return the whole load and recover the postage fees. But what of letters from friends and associates trying to reach him? Rousseau responded that he would send them instructions about how to reach him. Hume explains: "But till his instructions for that purpose could arrive, what could I do more friendly, than to save, at my own expence, his letters from the curiosity and indiscretion of the clerks of the post-office?" (p. 51 n. of *Concise and Genuine Account*).

[f]. The English translation of this note is by Luc Marest, of the manuscript text as transcribed by Raymond Troussons (1994), "Querelles de philosophes: Rousseau et d'Alembert," *Romanische Forschungen* 106(1–4), p. 156 n.23.

[g]. The true author of the two subsequent articles in *St. James's Chronicle*, George de Yverdum, came forward when he heard about Rousseau accusing Hume of having produced them.

[h]. Rousseau was presumably referring to one of the two articles in *St. James's Chronicle* soon discovered to have been written by George de Yverdum.

[i]. Regarding "*Je tiens J. J. Rousseau*": The French editors fabricated a note as though it were Hume's, and it is translated and included in *Concise and Genuine Account* (p. 79). When Hume, in December 1766, wrote out a few corrections and additions in the event of a second edition, which never happened, he provided an insertion to be added to that fabricated note. Hume's would-be insertion alludes to Themistocles in Persia, and is treated in the article by Daniel Klein that appears in this volume.

[j]. Following Hume's final words, *Concise and Genuine Account* has two items (plus an erratum), both used in the French version and both of which Hume wanted retained. The first is a motto in Latin by Seneca; the second is "Declaration of Mr. D'Alembert, relating to Mr. Walpole's Letter."

References

Damrosch, Leo. 2005. *Jean-Jacques Rousseau: Restless Genius*. Boston: Houghton Mifflin Company.

Edmonds, David, and John Eidinow. 2006. *Rousseau's Dog: Two Great Thinkers at War in the Age of Enlightenment*. New York: Harper Perennial.

Goodman, Dena. 1991. The Hume-Rousseau Affair: From Private *Querelle* to Public *Procès*. *Eighteenth-Century Studies* 25(2): 171–201.

Harris, James. 2015. *Hume: An Intellectual Biography*. Cambridge, UK: University of Cambridge Press.

Hume, David. 1766a. *Exposé succinct de la contestation qui s'est élevée entre M. Hume et M. Rousseau, avec les pièces justificatives*, trans. J. Suard. Paris.

Hume, David. 1766b (*CGA*). *A Concise and Genuine Account of the Dispute between Mr. Hume and Mr. Rousseau: With the Letters That Passed Between Them During Their Controversy; As Also, the Letters of the Hon. Mr. Walpole, and Mr. D'Alembert, Relative to This Extraordinary Affair;*

Translated from the French. London: T. Becket and P. A. De Hondt.

Hume, David. 1932. *The Letters of David Hume,* ed. J. Y. T. Greig. Oxford: Oxford University Press.

Hume, David. 2021 [1766]. *Hume's Manuscript Account of the Extraordinary Affair Between Him and Rousseau,* eds. Daniel B. Klein, Jason Briggeman, and Jacob R. Hall. *Econ Journal Watch* 18(2): 278–326.

Klein, Daniel B. 2021. To Tolerant England and a Pension from the King: Did Hume Subconsciously Aim to Subvert Rousseau's Legacy? *Econ Journal Watch* 18(2): 327–350.

Meyer, Paul H. 1952. The Manuscript of Hume's Account of His Dispute with Rousseau. *Comparative Literature* 4(4): 341–350.

Mossner, Ernest Campbell. 2001. *The Life of David Hume,* 2nd ed. Oxford: Clarendon Press.

Rasmussen, Dennis C. 2017. *The Infidel and the Professor: David Hume, Adam Smith, and the Friendship That Shaped Modern Thought.* Princeton, N.J.: Princeton University Press.

Zaretsky, Robert, and John T. Scott. 2009. *The Philosophers' Quarrel: Rousseau, Hume, and the Limits of Human Understanding.* New Haven, Conn.: Yale University Press.

To Tolerant England and a Pension from the King: Did Hume Subconsciously Aim to Subvert Rousseau's Legacy?

Daniel B. Klein[1]

> *You have but ill disguised yourself. I know you, and you are not ignorant of it... [Y]ou brought me to England, apparently to procure me an asylum, but in fact to bring me to dishonour. You applied to this noble work, with a zeal worthy of your heart, and a success worthy of your abilities... The public love to be deceived, and you were formed to deceive them. I know one man, however, whom you can not deceive; I mean yourself.*
> —Jean-Jacques Rousseau to David Hume, 23 June 1766
> (quoted in Hume 2021/1766, 297–298)

> *Son* Contract social *pourroit bien le venger dans un tems des persécution qu'il a éprouvées.*[2]
> —Adam Smith in conversation, 1784, as reported by
> Barthélemy Faujas de Saint-Fond (1797, 2:279)

It seems to me that practically all scholarship, even historiography, can be viewed as explanatory, in that certain things are treated as objects to be explained, and explanations are offered. Also, explanation may be seen as the spine of theorizing. Thus, even in historiography, we can find theorizing. I suggest three questions to bear in mind when theorizing (Klein 2014b):

1. Theory of what?
2. Why should we care?
3. What merit in your explanation?

---

1. I am grateful for help and feedback from Jacob Hall, Luc Marest, Erik Matson, Nelson Lund, Dennis Rasmussen, Marcus Shera, and José L. Tasset.
2. The translation in Saint-Fond (1907, 2:246) is: "His *Social Contract* will in time avenge him for all the persecutions he suffered."

Here, I theorize about David Hume's motivations in the Hume-Rousseau affair—that is, the causes of Hume's eagerness, zeal, and dogged perseverance, in the face of a train of Jean-Jacques Rousseau's oddities, improprieties, and derelictions, and indeed in the face of unmitigated uncertainty about Rousseau's intentions, "to settle the celebrated Rousseau" (I:527)[3] in England and to procure for Rousseau a pension from the king. The causes of Hume's actions, therefore, are the answer to *Theory of what?*

The explanation explored here is that Hume subconsciously aimed to diminish Rousseau's legacy. Settling down in England, in arrangements crafted by Hume, and enjoying a royal pension would have undermined Rousseau's persona as an audacious radical critic of refinement, of modern commercial society, of established aristocracies, and of England in particular. He would be seen—or portrayed—as accepting and assimilating to that which he scorned and pretended to expose. That explanation is not suggested in discussions of the affair with which I am acquainted.[4]

As for *Why should we care?*, a number of responses come to mind: (a) Hume and Rousseau were fascinating human beings, they have been and continue to be important figures, and plumbing their motivations deepens our feeling for them, for their writings, and for their significance; (b) thinking about the counterfactual of Hume successfully settling Rousseau in England with a royal pension provides a historical perspective and may deepen our understanding of history; (c) plumbing the depths of Hume's motivations teaches us about our ways of interpreting the conduct of historical figures.

As for *What merit in your explanation?*, my response must be made in rivalry with competing explanations of Hume's conduct, including:

- The praise and praiseworthiness of coming to Rousseau's aid;
- the notoriety and celebrity, especially in France, of being Rousseau's protector;

---

3. The citation "(I:527)" means volume 1, page 527 of *The Letters of David Hume* (1932) edited by J. Y. T. Greig. The quoted snippet is Hume explaining one of the reasons he returns to London, in a letter to Hugh Blair 28 December 1765.

4. I do not know whether any French-language literature suggests the hypothesis explored here. English-language literature on the Hume-Rousseau affair includes Goodman 1991; Mossner 2001, 512–532; Damrosch 2005, 403–433; Edmonds and Eidenow 2006; Zaretsky and Scott 2009; Harris 2015, 416–421; Rasmussen 2017, 133–145.

- the praise and praiseworthiness in demonstrating a freedom-oriented solidarity among persecuted persons;
- the praise and praiseworthiness in demonstrating generosity towards intellectual adversaries; and
- the praise and praiseworthiness in serving Britain and the British establishment, including the King, George III, from whom the royal pension was procured.

Are those explanations not adequate? Is there not ample evidence for them? Is my explanation, the aim to diminish Rousseau's legacy, meritorious in ways that the others are not? And what evidence can I give for my explanation? This article labors under the rubric of the third question, *What merit in your explanation?*

Rousseau accused Hume of taking actions against him, particular actions deemed damaging, insulting, or incriminating.[5] Whether there is anything really to any of Rousseau's accusations does not much matter to the present interpretation. The accusations, in the concrete, concern trivialities; I have sifted the English-language evidence about them pretty thoroughly.[6] My sense of the matter is that on every count Hume is probably innocent, basically innocent, or 'guilty' of a non-offense. The burden of proof is on Rousseau, and he never meets it. The allegations are almost always absurd or unintelligible, and often deceitful. Rousseau was a very morally irresponsible person, prone to lying, getting into quarrels, and making enemies. His behavior in England after the blowup tends to confirm his guilt throughout (Zaretsky and Scott 2009, 194–197). Dennis Rasmussen (2017, 140) speaks of "the groundless nature of Rousseau's allegations."

But, if the whole effort was undertaken to subvert Rousseau's legacy, does Hume still enjoy an aura of innocence? If the whole effort was undertaken to subvert Rousseau's legacy, would that make the basic deed a dirty one?

---

5. The 1766 French version of the account is the Hume 1766a item in the reference list here. The 1766 English version is the Hume 1766b item. The new presentation of the account, appearing alongside the present article, is listed as Hume 2021/1766.
6. I do not read French. I wish I could read Hume's French correspondence, Rousseau's correspondence (51 volumes), and French commentary and scholarship on the matter.

TABLE 1. Timeline of Hume-Rousseau affair

2 July 1762	Hume's first letter to Rousseau
4–5 January 1766	"Je tiens J. J. Rousseau" would have occurred in Senlis, France[7]
10–11 January 1766	Crossing the Channel together from Calais to Dover
22 March 1766	Rousseau arrives and moves into Wootton in Staffordshire, a little-used residence owned by Richard Davenport
12 May 1766	Rousseau's equivocal letter to Conway, not accepting (nor conclusively refusing) the pension
23 June 1766	Rousseau's first open declaration to Hume of enmity
10 July 1766	Rousseau's mammoth memorial/letter, the last to Hume
15 July 1766	Hume encourages Davenport to continue his accommodating of Rousseau
22 July 1766	Hume's last letter to Rousseau
2 September 1766	Hume reiterates to Davenport to continue his accommodating of Rousseau
21 October 1766	*Exposé succinct* published in Paris
November 1766	*Concise and Genuine Account* published in London
1 May 1767	Rousseau vacates Wootton
21–22 May 1767	Rousseau crosses from England to Calais
February–July 1767	Hume advises officials (successfully) to sustain/rehabilitate the offer of the pension

In reading Hume's account of the affair one is struck at two moments in Rousseau's mammoth 10 July 1766 letter, which refers to Hume in the third person as though testifying before a public audience. As Dena Goodman (1991, 184) puts it, "Rousseau the narrator took upon himself the multiple roles of victim, witness, judge, accused, and prosecutor." The two moments that are by far most curious and arresting are Hume's alleged "stedfast, piercing look, mixed with a sneer" and his alleged repeated terrible nocturnal utterance, "*Je tiens J. J. Rousseau*"—"I've got J. J. Rousseau," or, "I have J. J. Rousseau" (see Hume 2021/1766, 307, 318). In the letter, these two moments

---

7. In the 10 July letter, Rousseau writes of "*Je tiens*" having happened "the first night after our departure from Paris" (see Hume 2021/1766, 318), which would be Senlis, but elsewhere he says, twice, Roye, France. Evidently, as Mossner (2001, 516 n.2) explains, it could not have happened there because they did not sleep in the same chamber.

are dramatized and linked. Rousseau's account prompts the reader to doubt Hume's declared motives. Such intuition, if it exists, might stem from a sense that Hume might have aimed to subvert Rousseau's legacy.

Did Rousseau suspect that Hume's aim was to subvert his legacy? To my knowledge, Rousseau never came out and said that was Hume's aim. If Rousseau had felt that it was, would Rousseau have accused him of it, explicitly and publicly? Maybe not, because he might then be in a position of needing to explain why settling in England and accepting a royal pension would, at least in Hume's imagination, have tended to subvert his legacy.

We need to clarify the sort of outcome Hume hoped for. For us, it is counterfactual. The counterfactual is a changed history from sometime after they land in Dover 11 January 1766. Suppose that the 'English Settlement,' if you will—that is, accommodation in England and the royal pension—were accepted by Rousseau. Suppose that he settled in England for many years or even to 1778, the year he died. Perhaps Rousseau would have produced works like:

1. *Dictionary of Music* (1767)

Published after Rousseau's death in 1778:

2. *Confessions* (written 1765–1770)
3. *Considerations on the Government of Poland* (written 1772)
4. *Dialogues: Rousseau, Judge of Jean-Jacques* (written 1772–1776)
5. *Reveries of the Solitary Walker* (written 1777)

As a set of activities and as a single, protracted decision, Hume's arranging of things for Rousseau gets started July 1762. Going into the decision, Hume surely knew the following four works:

- *Discourse on the Arts and Sciences*, 1750
- *Discourse on the Origin and Foundations of Inequality Among Men*, 1754
- *Discourse on Political Economy*, 1755
- *Julie; or, The New Heloise*, 1761

As for the following three works, Hume surely came to know them shortly after publication:

- *The Social Contract, or Principles of Political Right*, 15 May 1762[8]
- *Emile, or On Education*, 22 May 1762
- *Letters Written from the Mountain*, 1764

The three Discourses would have been quite sufficient to lead Hume to regard Rousseau as profoundly wrongheaded in morals and politics. Rasmussen writes:

> Hume's thoroughgoing defense of the modern, liberal, commercial order was matched by Rousseau's blistering attack on that order. Hume believed, more strongly than even Smith, that civilization, refinement, and commerce brought in their wake an indissoluble chain of industry, knowledge, and humanity, while Rousseau insisted that they led to little more than inequality, dependence, and corruption. Where Hume was moderate and pragmatic, Rousseau was radical—radical in both his critique of the existing order and in the various prescriptions he offered to fix it. (Rasmussen 2017, 134–136)

I believe if someone asked Hume in 1765, 'Do you think that, irrespective of Rousseau's personal well-being, the world would be better off from his settling in England with a royal pension?,' he would have said yes. He would sense that the English Settlement would reduce the sway of the wrongheadedness of Rousseau's works through 1762, as well as any future works. As for how the English Settlement would affect Rousseau's activities going forward, that too is something that Hume might have had hopes for. Hume might have, firstly, hoped that the pension and peaceful settlement in English would have subdued Rousseau. In Volume 3 of his *History of England* (1983, 3:135–136), Hume had highlighted the social benefits of putting the leaders of otherwise enthusiastic and troublesome religious sects on state salaries "to bribe their indolence." Second, the English Settlement might help to bring Rousseau around to better thinking; it is possible that Hume hoped for Rousseau to become improved and produce less pernicious ideas. These possibilities might be summarized as taming Rousseau, and that, too, is something I include in 'subverting Rousseau's legacy'—I mean a legacy *and a Rousseau* like those

---

8. The day of publication of *The Social Contract* and *Émile* are given in Gourevitch's chronology, provided in both of his Rousseau Cambridge Texts volumes (Rousseau 1997a; b).

of our history. But even apart from the either turning Rousseau into 'dead wood' or improving his ideas, the English Settlement would have significantly deflated his legacy, I think, and I think Hume sensed that.

If there is merit in my explanation, that merit need not exist over against the other explanations. It can be but an element within a bevy of explanations. My explanation, or *strand* of explanation, would be quite dependent on the other strands for cover. Were my strand true, even if Hume were conscious of it he could hardly reveal it plainly to Rousseau: 'Jean-Jacques, I wish to fix things for you in England so as to mitigate the sway of your pernicious writings.' Nor, on the improvement angle, could he say: 'Dear Jean-Jacques, I wish to fix things for you in England so as to cure your wrongheadedness.' Instead, Hume would play up the agreeable explanations.

We all know that motives that need to be kept underground on some occasions typically therefore also need to be kept underground on other occasions as well, or even all occasions, because occasions cannot reliably be kept separate. ('But *Le Bon David* told me his *real* aim is…'). That is, people talk, word gets around. One needs to habitualize his story, both to ensure that he performs it accurately on needful occasions and to make it convincing, as flowing naturally from frankness and openness. In a course of action of such sort, when one first commences, the articulated motive will usually be of the public-story sort, and, once set out, one's subconscious is chary to ever reveal that some other impetus was at work all along ('Fooled ya!'). The unsaid impetus may remain hidden, and inarticulate or subconscious. Scholars say that consciousness accounts for no more than five percent of brain activity, and perhaps as little as one percent (McGilchrist 2009, 187); there's a lot that your consciousness is not privy to.

One might be so habitualized to his public story that he might deny the unsaid impetus *even to himself* ('in denial'), though real. There is no necessary scandal in any of this, contrary to how Rousseau painted it. It's the way things are once society and language get beyond the primeval band, and post-band existence is not something to scandalize.

For these reasons, lack of direct evidence is not necessarily conclusive. We would not particularly expect to find direct evidence for my explanation, even if real. Maybe there was a dog in the night that didn't bark. One line of evidence is that Hume continued to work to salvage the plan, or parts of it, as much as a year after mutual enmity had become common knowledge, though

Hume may have had other reasons to salvage what could be salvaged of the plan.

Throughout our rumination, we should bear in mind that Hume's motivations might have been not only multiple but shifting in balance over time. Certain motivations may have waxed and waned as things went on.

Hindsight bias

After making a start on the present paper in the summer of 2021, I experienced a progression of sentiment, from greater confidence in my explanation to lesser confidence. A cause of that progression had been a growing awareness of the 1765 Hume not having known certain things that I know. I felt that the advantage of hindsight had distorted my impressions. Two aspects of our post-January 1766 history stand out.

First, Rousseau rejected the English Settlement, and, moreover, from all we know about Rousseau's 66 years (1712–1778), accepting the English Settlement would have been highly out of character. If one ascribes to Hume such impressions of a scarcely-tamable Rousseau, then one wonders: Why undergo such difficulties if the chance of success is close to zero? Hume's declared motives begin to seem inadequate and dubious. When I first immersed myself in the account of the affair, I kept asking myself: *What was Hume thinking?* His actions seem vain and foolish, as Adam Smith seemed to indicate when he wrote: "I am thoroughly convinced that Rousseau is as great a Rascal as you, and as every man here believes him to be" (Smith 1986, 112). Hume's copious epistolary remarks on the affair often have a frenetic air, as though he is confused and afraid that perhaps the warnings of Baron d'Holbach—"you're warming a viper in your bosom" (Mossner 2001, 515)—might be right. Writing to his friends, Hume's estimations of Rousseau are variably complimentary and depreciating. To smooth the path for Rousseau, Hume (2021/1766, 290) practices small manipulative guiles, such as his effort to secretly subsidize production of a recent work of his and to fix lodging and secretly pay more for it than he would tell Rousseau he paid.[9] And sometimes Hume's letters to his friends have an air of false

---

9. Edmonds and Eidinow (2006, 268–270) offer a listing of recriminations against Hume, highly unreliable and biased, I feel. Some of Hume's other small fibs include: In his 22 Oc-

confidence. In hindsight, it all seems to drive inexorably toward mutual hatred and disgust. Rasmussen says "the break between them was all but inevitable" (2017, 137).

I've come to realize, however, that, while the break may have been inevitable, hindsight was distorting my view, that Hume might not have realized how improbable the English Settlement was; he might have been far off in his estimate of chance of success. If Hume had thought that settling Rousseau in England would be simple, that increases the plausibility of his motives having been primarily of the simpler sort, notably the doing of a good turn, like holding the door for someone.

Second, there is Rousseau's influence or legacy. This has two dimensions. One is magnitude, which has been enormous. But did Hume foresee its full extent? Almost certainly not. But if he anticipated half, even a quarter, that might be enough to give life to my explanation. Another is its value, positive or negative. I think it negative. Hume did as well, as I'll show, but again hindsight might make me more confirmed in that valence than Hume could have been. In her excellent article, Goodman quotes Friedrich Melchior Grimm about Rousseau having come 200 years after his time, namely the 16th-century age of religious factions organized around a charismatic personality. Goodman exclaims, "How wrong he was!," and shows the pro-Rousseau public reaction in France that quickly emerged after Grimm had made his

---

tober 1765 letter to Rousseau, Hume should not have told of "the Respect, which every one there [England] bears to your Character" (as translated by Mossner 2001, 510; Hume's original French is at I:526). Hume knew, but said otherwise to Rousseau, that Davenport arranged a chaise for Rousseau for a journey he was to make, arranged under some false pretenses of it being available just coincidentally (II:29–30, 33). Hume's diminishing of the derisiveness of Horace Walpole's spoof Frederick the Great letter seems forced.

Also, though not fibs *to Rousseau*, Hume seems to overlook several of his friends when he says that his friends came round to supporting his publishing his account of the affair, as noted by Rasmussen (2017, 143; see also Mossner 2001, 529).

And I would not say, as Hume does, that Rousseau's letter to him of March 29 was written "in the most amicable terms imaginable" (Hume 2021/1766, 295) and was "very cordial" (ibid., 312 n.29), nor that in that of March 22 "there is a most unreserved Cordiality; not the least Appearance of Suspicion" (308 n.20) and was "entirely cordial" (322 n.40). Indeed, in retrospect, Rousseau's words take on a definite antagonistic meaning, for example the following from the March 22 letter: "To make another happy, is to deserve to be happy one's self. May you therefore find in yourself the reward of all you have done for me!" (291). Such double-entendre recurs in those two letters, and I find it inconceivable that Hume did not sense a deep enmity in them, if only subconsciously.

remark (Goodman 1991, 198). "[T]hey responded rather in a Rousseauian fashion," writes Goodman (ibid., 199), though the reaction was otherwise among Rousseau's dwindling associates in France (Damrosch 2005, 428). In a budding age of proto-social-media, Hume, like Grimm, simply might not have seen how irresponsible people—the public—are, and hence how large Rousseau's influence would be.

I came to recognize that, if we can reasonably imagine a 1765 Hume who:

a. thinks the English Settlement will be easy; or
b. does not expect Rousseau to ever have much future influence, regardless; or
c. does not sense the value of that influence to be particularly negative,

then my explanation suffers. I have put the premises (a), (b), and (c) rather starkly. Indeed, if either (b) or (c) is strongly the case, then my explanation simply dies.

By the time I completed this article, however, I had experienced yet another progression of sentiment, recovering much of the original confidence I had had for some time and up to when I made a start on writing the article. The theorized Hume is somewhere between the Hume of those stark assumptions and the Hume I had thought up to then. My own sense of the theorized Hume now has moved a little toward the starkly-stated Hume, but only a little. An anxiety about possible hindsight bias induced me to think more carefully about these considerations.

Rousseau's legacy, had the English Settlement succeeded

Would Hume have sensed that the English Settlement would greatly diminish Rousseau's legacy? The "greatly" refers not to the magnitude of Rousseau's legacy, but to the reduction in it, as if multiplying by a scalar like 0.3. I think Hume would recognize that Rousseau's legacy would be reduced substantially. Let us look at some of Rousseau's words, to 1762, and ponder how the English Settlement would have affected their legacy.

Near the beginning of the *Discourse on the Arts and Sciences*, Rousseau describes modern enslavement:

> While the Government and the Laws see to the safety and the well-being of
> men assembled, the Sciences, Letters, and Arts, less despotic and perhaps more
> powerful, spread garlands of flowers over the iron chains with which they are
> laden, throttle in them the sentiment of that original freedom for which they
> seemed born, make them love their slavery, and fashion them into what is called
> civilized Peoples. Need raised up Thrones; the Sciences and Arts have made
> them strong. Earthly Powers, love talents and protect those who cultivate them!
> Civilized peoples, cultivate them: Happy slaves, you owe them the delicate and
> refined taste on which you pride yourselves; the sweet character and urbane
> morals which make for such engaging and easy relations among you; in a word,
> the appearances of all the virtues without having a single one. (Rousseau 1997a,
> 7)

Rousseau is rich, but think how much richer this becomes on the English
Settlement. He ironically advises Earthly Powers: "love talents and protect
those who cultivate them!" That's how Earthly Powers enslave us! Meanwhile,
Rousseau flies to "iron chains," contrived by none other than David Hume,
the most illustrious exponent of slavery's devices, "the Sciences, Letters, and
Arts."

In a footnote to the passage just quoted, Rousseau explains: "Princes
always view with pleasure the dissemination among their subjects of a taste
for the agreeable Arts... For besides thus nurturing in them that pettiness of
soul so suited to servitude, they well know that all the needs which a People
imposes on itself are so many chains which it assumes" (1997a, 7 n.). On
the English Settlement, people might wonder: Does that princely pension
likewise work a pettiness of soul so suited to servitude? Rousseau concludes
the footnote: "the Savages of America who go about altogether naked and
live entirely off the products of their hunt have proved impossible to tame.
Indeed, what yoke could be imposed upon men who need nothing?" How
would this sound when spoken by a man in a royal yoke?

Imagine how the following would sound from a Rousseau who had
embraced the English Settlement, from *The Social Contract* (1762): "As for you,
modern peoples, you have no slaves, but are yourselves slaves; you pay for
their freedom with your own. Well may you boast of this preference; I find in
it more cowardice than humanity" (1997b, 115).

Thusly did Rousseau explain modern enslavement. Turn now to the life
of virtue, from the *Discourse on Political Economy*, which appeared in 1755 in
volume V of Diderot and d'Alembert's *Encyclopedia.*

Certain it is that the greatest marvels of virtue have been produced by love of fatherland... It is patriotism that produced the many immortal actions whose brilliance dazzles our weak eyes, and the many great men whose antique virtues are treated as fables ever since patriotism has been turned into derision. That should not surprise us; the transports of tender hearts look like so many chimeras to anyone who has not felt them; love of fatherland, a hundred times more lively and delightful than the love of a mistress, can also be conceived only experiencing it; but it is easy to recognize in all the hearts it excites, in all the actions it inspires, this seething and sublime ardor which even the purest virtue does not radiate when separated from love of fatherland. (1997b, 16)

Undeceive yourself, he urges, by knowing from experience love of fatherland; only then will you radiate that sublime ardor a hundred times more lively than the love of a mistress (a thousand times that of your children, no doubt), from his home in a country where he cannot speak the language, on the English Settlement.

Perhaps Rousseau would, however, have learned the language and love of his adopted fatherland—England! How would the following remarks strike a reader, given that Rousseau had accepted the English Settlement?:

[From *Essay on the Origins of Languages*, probably written before 1762:]
At Homer's feast an ox is slaughtered to regale one's guests, as one might nowadays slaughter a suckling pig... To get a notion of the meals of the ancients one need only consider the meals of present-day Savages; I almost said of Englishmen. (1997a, 270)

[From *Émile*, 1762:]
The English are noted for their cruelty [footnote: I am aware that the English make a boast of their humanity and of the kindly disposition of their race, which they call 'good-natured people;' but in vain do they proclaim this fact; no one else says it of them.] (Rousseau 1911, 118, n.1)

[From *The Social Contract*, 1762:]
Any law which the People has not ratified in person is null; it is not a law. The English people thinks it is free; it is greatly mistaken, it is free only during the election of Members of Parliament; as soon as they are elected, it is enslaved, it is nothing. The use it makes of its freedom during the brief moments it has it fully warrants its losing it. (1997b, 114)

[From *Considerations on the Government of Poland*, written 1772:]
The Lawgiver as a body is impossible to corrupt, but easy to deceive. Its rep-

resentatives are difficult to deceive, but easily corrupted, and it rarely happens
that they are not corrupted. You have before your eyes the example of the
English Parliament... (1997b, 201)

These four passages on England (only two of which could have been known
to Hume at the time) help us understand how England in particular, as a place
for settling, would have subverted Rousseau's legacy. They also speak to why
a pension from the English Crown would have been rather different from the
support he received from others.[10]

Someone like Rousseau can appeal to people with literary politics, but the
seduction would falter when it is common knowledge that the author enjoyed
a royal pension and caretaking by Hume and the British establishment. It
is hard to imagine that Hume would not have sensed the huge hit that
Rousseau's persona, and legacy, would take. After the blowup, Hume wrote
to Smith (August 1766) that exposing Rousseau's conduct "would blast him
for ever; and blast his Writings at the same time: For as these have been
exalted much above their Merit, when his personal Character falls, they would
of Course fall below their Merit" (II:83).

Accepting the English Settlement would have subverted Rousseau's legacy
partly in the way it would have served the English Crown and Britain's
reputation as a tolerant and liberal nation—as a refuge for persecuted intellectuals. As early as 1 July 1762, Hume wrote to the Comtesse de Boufflers,
"as I have some connexions with men of rank in London, I shall instantly
write to them, and endeavour to make them sensible of the honour M.
Rousseau has done us in choosing an asylum in England" (I:363). On 5 July
1762, he wrote to Gilbert Elliot:

> Our present King and present Minister [Lord Bute] are desirous of being
> thought encouragers of learning: can they have a more proper opportunity of
> showing to the whole world that they are in earnest? Monsieur Rousseau is now
> thrown out of his ordinary course of livelihood; and tho he rejects presents
> from private persons, he may not think himself degraded by a pension from

---

10. Regarding offers of monetary support that Rousseau accepted, it is not something I have
researched thoroughly. Damrosch (2005, 419) indicates that circa 1765 Rousseau enjoyed a
guaranteed annual income of 600 livres (about 30 pounds) from George Keith Earl Marischal,
who, it seems cut off Rousseau after the blowup (ibid., 428), 300 livres from Marc-Michel Rey,
and 300 livres from publisher Pierre Guy. Other forms of support—protection, hospitality,
lodging, etc.—Rousseau received from numerous other individuals, over the years.

a great monarch: and it would be a singular victory over the French, worth a hundred of our Mindens,[11] to protect and encourage a man of genius whom they had persecuted. (I:367)

In a 19 January 1766 letter to the Comtesse de Boufflers, Hume reported how General Conway "seemed to embrace with zeal the motion of giving him [Rousseau] a pension, as honourable both to the King and nation. I shall suggest the same idea to other men in power whom I may meet with, and I do not despair of succeeding" (II:3). Rousseau, then, would be helping the British in a victory over the French. The optics of falling in with—or becoming a pet of— the British establishment would not have enhanced his appeal with would-be enthusiasts.

That the English Settlement would have hurt Rousseau's legacy is something of which readers are vaguely aware. Such vague awareness gives an unaccountable pungency to "*Je tiens J. J. Rousseau.*" Rousseau cannot come out and accuse Hume of aiming to subvert his legacy. But nonetheless Rousseau could have used aspects of the subversion idea to suggest ulterior motivation and to embellish his victimization. In his 10 July 1766 letter, he writes: "I saw very well there was something in the affair which I did not comprehend" (quoted in Hume 2021/1766, 308). And he explains that a reason for his taking up Hume's invitation was to set "an example to men of letters, in a sincere union between two men so different in their principles" (ibid., 301). Rousseau highlights Hume's initial "good offices" to him, including "the zeal" Hume exerted in soliciting the royal pension and the trouble he took to find suitable accommodation (302, 303, 308, 314). Rousseau explains to Hume that, to confirm his suspicions of Hume, he embarked on a determined plan of disdaining Hume, enumerating a first, second, and third "slap of the face" dealt to Hume (312–313). Rousseau's 10 July letter opens by addressing Hume in the second person but soon shifts to the third person: "Could Mr. Hume, after so many instances of disdain on my part, have still the astonishing generosity as to persevere sincerely to serve me?... [H]e must have supposed me to have been an infamous scoundrel. It was then in behalf of a man whom he supposed to be a scoundrel, that he so warmly solicited[12] a pension from

---

11. On 1 August 1759, at Minden, during the Seven Years War, Britain and allies defeated France and allies.

12. Where Rousseau writes "solicited a pension," think: *labored to maintain* the plan of a royal

his Majesty" (318). Rousseau drives home that Hume had to have an ulterior motive.

And what, according to Rousseau, was it? What sense, after all, did Rousseau propose that *we make* of "*Je tiens J. J. Rousseau*"?

Rousseau tells us, in effect, that Hume, motivated perhaps by envy,[13] plotted, since Paris,[14] to draw Rousseau to England and then proceed to deceive, torment and humiliate him by conspiring with associates to deride, slight, and ignore Rousseau, by tampering with his mail, by suppressing publication of two pieces Rousseau sought to be published (see Hume 2021/1766, 306, 311), and by plotting to disgrace Rousseau over the royal pension, somehow (cf. Rasmussen 2017, 140).[15] The ulterior motive for this most marvelous plot of petty torments, according to Rousseau, is completely unsatisfying; it lacks substance and coherence. Far from wanting to trouble himself with tending Rousseau's comforts, and even farther from wanting to torment Rousseau, Hume wanted to realize the English Settlement, maintain an awkward yet peaceful cordiality with Rousseau, and otherwise be over with it.

My point is: That the English Settlement would subvert Rousseau's legacy lurked in the shadows of some people's minds, but no one could come out and say it.

---

pension.

13. "He [Hume] saw [in Paris], and perhaps saw too much of, the favourable reception I met with from a great Prince, and I will venture to say, of the public. I yielded, as it was my duty, though with reluctance, to that eclat; concluding how far it must excite the envy of my enemies" (quoted in Hume 2021/1766, 301).

14. "I saw the plot which was put in execution at London, had been laid in Paris" (quoted in Hume 2021/1766, 310).

15. Rousseau's explanation of how Hume would "disgrace" him over the pension is unintelligible to me (quoted in Hume 2021/1766, 318).

Further on Hume's motives

Subverting Rousseau's legacy an impetus?

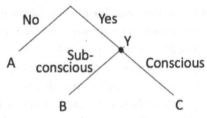

Figure 1. Subverting an impetus? Conscious?

Figure 1 is not a sequence of Hume's thoughts or decisions. Rather it helps us analyze *our* questions about Hume's impetus. I suggest that subverting Rousseau's legacy was an impetus, which would put us to node Y. As for whether Hume was conscious of that impetus, I think basically no, which would put us at B. My feeling is that Hume may have been a little bit conscious of it, putting him between B and C, but closer to B.

Again, Hume must have seen how the English Settlement would have diminished Rousseau's would-be legacy, whatever its magnitude, like multiplying by 0.3, and that he thought that legacy bad. Here I elaborate on these matters, and on Hume's consciousness of the conjectured impetus.

By the time the business starts in early July 1762, it was plain to everyone that Rousseau spoke to something in people, and the world responded, as he was very famous. Hume shows awareness of that from the start. In Paris in 1765, Hume marveled at the reception of Rousseau: "It is impossible to express or imagine the Enthusiasm of this Nation in his favour… Voltaire and every body else, are quite eclipsd by him" (I:529). Enjoying his role as Rousseau's designated conductor and protector, Hume elaborates colorfully on Rousseau's fame and popularity. He remarks on it frequently in his letters, for example in letter of 22 March 1766: "[O]f all the Writers that are or ever were in Europe, he is the man who has acquird the most enthusiastic and most passionate Admirers" (II:27). I recognize that witnessing the mania for Rousseau in the 1760s does not convince one that Rousseau will have a powerful influence for decades and centuries to come. After the blowup and the publication of Hume's *Concise and Genuine Account* of the affair, Hume says that Rousseau's popularity has been punctured and deflated, even "consign'd to perpetual Neglect and Oblivion," because Rousseau's rascality has been exposed (II:166; see also 168).

As for Hume's assessment of Rousseau's works and their influence, prior to the blowup it is ambivalent. First, we highlight the negative. Hume did not write anything of Rousseau until early July 1762, in correspondence with the Comtesse de Boufflers, who, importantly, is both highly sympathetic (at that time, but not later) to Rousseau and is becoming romantically entangled with Hume.[16] Hume eagerly responds to the idea of helping to settle Rousseau in Britain, writing back to Boufflers and writing to Rousseau. He also writes, 5 July 1762, to Gilbert Elliot and comments on Rousseau's works: "For my part, tho I see some tincture of extravagance in all of them, I also think I see so much eloquence and force of imagination, such an energy of expression, and such a boldness of conception, as entitles him to a place among the first writers of the age" (I:366). In this passage, written to a friend and fellow Scot, we see an ambivalence from the outset: The praise is about technique and style, not character and substance; he sees "some tincture of extravagance in all of them." In a letter of early 1765, he ventures to remark to the Comtesse on *Letters Written from the Mountain*, in which Rousseau sought vengeance on the rulers of Geneva after the city censored and burned *The Social Contract* and *Émile*:

> I have read a great part of Les Lettres de la Montagne. The book in my humble opinion will not do credit to M. Rousseau, though it might to another. I disapprove particularly of the seditious purpose of the last letters, which have succeeded but too well at Geneva: for the magistrates of that city, which the author had formerly celebrated with reason as one of the best governed in the world, are in mortal fear every hour of being massacred by the populace. (I:493)

Hume does not endorse censorship, of course, but duty and justice call also upon Rousseau, who wields his own powers. Hume is quite right that *Letters Written from the Mountain* is incendiary. It says that "if one remarked an inclination toward violence in a Government" then "there would remain a

---

16. Edmonds and Eidinow (2006, 266) suggest that perhaps Hume wanted to please the Comtesse de Boufflers. I have not much explored the idea (their correspondence is mostly in French, which I cannot read). I incline toward thinking that it may have initially prompted Hume to help Rousseau as she desired, but that other motives quickly became the dominant ones.

sad but legal remedy, which in this extreme case could be employed as one employs the hand of a Surgeon when gangrene breaks out" (Rousseau 2001/ 1764, 305). The final paragraph urges the people to "come together" against Geneva's ruling council, for united makes right:

> But above all come together. You are ruined without resource if you remain divided. And why would you be divided when such great common interests unite you? How do base jealousy and petty passions dare to make themselves heard in such danger? Are they worth being satisfied at such a high price, and will it be necessary for your children to say someday while weeping over their chains: here is the fruit of our fathers' dissentions? In a word, it is less a question of deliberation here than of concord; the choice of which course you will take is not the greatest question: Were it bad in itself, take it all together; *by that alone it will become the best*, and you will always do what needs to be done provided that you do so in concert. There is my advice, Sir, and I end where I began. By obeying you I have fulfilled my final duty toward the Fatherland [Geneva]. (Rousseau 2001/1764, 306)

In a letter to Hugh Blair, 28 December 1765, Hume tells of Rousseau's recent travels through Switzerland on the road to Paris: "The Council of Berne, frightend for his Neighbourhood, on account of his democratical, more than his religious Principles, orderd him immediately to withdraw from their State" (I:528). Leo Damrosch (2005, 424) notes, "the British government was certainly alarmed by the inflammatory politics of *Letters Written from the Mountain.*"

Perhaps Hume did not foresee the influence that Rousseau's moral and political writings would have. Still, we should ask: What did he think of the political works? He wrote Blair in a letter of 25 March 1766: "I think this Work [*Heloise*] his Master-piece; tho' he himself told me, that he valu'd most his *Contract sociale*; which is as preposterous a Judgement as that of Milton, who preferd the Paradise regaind to all his other Performances" (II:28). In the letter of 25 March 1766, to Blair, Hume reports that Rousseau himself had told him, "I still dread, that my Writings are good for nothing at the bottom, and that all my Theories are full of Extravagance" (II, 31).

After the blowup, Hume expresses—so quickly—a damning assessment of Rousseau's work, without ever denying Rousseau's eloquence. He would repeat the story about Rousseau confessing disgust at his own attempts at thought (see II:103–104). He writes 15 July 1766 to the Comtesse that Rousseau is "a man who has but too long deceived a great part of mankind" (II:62). In late Sept 1766, to Turgot, he suggests that, of course, he had always thought Rousseau's works sophistical and dangerous: "You know, that I always esteemed his Writings for their Eloquence alone and that I looked on them, at the bottom, as full of Extravagance and Sophystry... Is there any Harm that the Public in general shou'd adopt the same Sentiments, and shou'd appreciate at their just Value Compositions *whose general Tendency is sure rather to do hurt than Service to Mankind?*' (II:91, italics added). Writing to Blair in May 1767, anticipating Rousseau's memoirs, Hume predicts that they "will be full of Eloquence & Extravagance; tho' perhaps as reasonable as any of his past Productions. For I do not imagine he was ever much more in his Senses than at present" (II:141).

Hume's ambivalence about Rousseau pertains both to whether he might see danger in Rousseau's influence and whether he was conscious of an impetus within himself to reduce that danger. Similarly, we should reflect on the respect that Hume had for Rousseau, as a man.

Hume's trail of remarks about Rousseau begins with his initial and enthusiastic response (1 July 1762) to the Comtesse about "asylum in England," saying, "I revere his greatness of mind" (I:363). The next day (2 July 1762), Hume writes his first communication to Rousseau, including:

> I have long coveted, the Pleasure of your Acquaintance; and in time, as I wou'd fain flatter myself, the Honour of your Friendship. For I will use the Freedom of telling you bluntly, without affecting the Finesse of a well-turnd Compliment, that, of all men of Letters in Europe, since the Death of President Montesquieu, you are the Person whom I most revere, both for the Force of your Genius and Greatness of your Mind. ... Permit me also some Liberty of boasting on this Occasion while I pretend, that my Conduct & Character entitle me a Sympathy with Yours; at least, in my Love of philosophical Retreat, in my Neglect of vulgar Prejudices, and in my Disdain of all Dependence: And if these Circumstances had happily prov'd the Foundation of an amicable Connexion between us; I shou'd have entertain'd the Project of engaging you to honour this part of the World with your Company... (I:364–365)

Hume's praises are frequent, but always followed by 'buts,' sometimes a considerable list of 'buts,' such as in his February 1766 letter to the Marquise de Barbentane (II:14).

But the lack of respect is also looming before the acrimony begins to surface. For example, to Blair, 28 December 1765, Hume writes: "I am well assur'd, that at times he believes he has Inspirations from an Immediate Communication with the Divinity: He falls sometimes into Ecstacies which retain him in the same Posture for Hours together" (I:530). To the Comtesse in January 1766, he says of Rousseau, "I believe at the same time that nobody knows himself less" (II:2).

Consider the start of Hume's short letter to Smith of January 1766:

> Dear Smith
>
> I can write as seldom and as Short as you—I am sorry I did not see you before I left Paris. I am also sorry I shall not see you there soon. **I shall not be able to fix Rousseau to his Mind for some Weeks yet**: He is a little variable & fanciful, tho' very agreeable. (II:5–6, boldface added)

Hume tells Smith that he will fix Rousseau "to his Mind." The remark is striking in its terseness and confidence, as though counting down to saying 'mission accomplished!' Although I think Smith disliked Rousseau and thought his influence was bad,[17] I rather doubt that Smith ever encouraged the mission or ever expected it to succeed.

After the blowup, which happens June–July 1766, the ambivalence is gone entirely; afterward there is only enmity, often mixed with pity. To Blair, 1 July, he writes that Rousseau "is surely the blackest and most atrocious Villain, beyond comparison, that now exists in the World; and I am heartily asham'd of any thing I ever wrote in his Favour" (II:57). Later that month, Hume reflects on Rousseau's abusiveness: "I do not however find, that, in other Respects he is madder than usual; nor is his Conduct towards me much worse than toward M. Diderot about seven Years ago" (II:70). To Turgot in September 1766 he writes: "The Life of such a Man is to be regarded as one contu'd Lye and Imposture" (II:90)

Salvage efforts even after the blowup

After the blowup in July 1766, it is a full ten months before Rousseau departs England, on 21 May 1767, never to return (see Zaretsky and Scott

---

17. I treat Smith's attitude toward Rousseau in Klein 2014a and Klein 2021. Lund (2022) argues that Smith repeatedly twisted Rousseau's words and arguments.

2009, 194–197). Hume tells Blair of Rousseau's departure from Wootton, Davenport's extra house: "You may perhaps have heard, that Rousseau has elop'd from Mr Davenport without any Warning; leaving all his Baggage except Mad^{lle} [Marie-Thérèse La Vasseur], about thirty pounds in Davenport's hands, and a Letter on the Table abusing him in the most violent Terms, insinuating that he was in a Conspiracy with me to ruin him" (II:135; cf. Edmonds and Eidinow 2006, 241, 251). The last piece of correspondence between Hume and Rousseau was 22 July 1766. Yet Hume's efforts to salvage what he could of the English Settlement continued to at least July 1767, *a full year after open mutual enmity*.

After Hume has received the hateful letter of 10 July 1766, he writes to Davenport on 15 July: "if I may venture to give my Advice, it is, that you wou'd continue the charitable Work you have begun, till he be shut up altogether in Bedlam, or till he quarrel with you and run away from you" (II:65). Hume reiterates to him the same advice on 2 September 1766: "I shall use the Freedom to repeat my Exhortations to you, that you continue, as long as possible, the same good Offices towards him, which you have so charitably begun" (II:87). And Hume says in the Account: "Even since M. Rousseau's Rupture with me, I have employed my good Offices with Mr. Davenport to continue the same charitable care of his unhappy guest" (2021/1766, 303 n.7).

As for the pension, the possibility of which Rousseau himself continued to inquire after with the King's agents, Hume reports to Blair on 24 February 1767:

> General Conway told me on my Arrival, that Rousseau had made an Application to him, thro' the Canal of Mr Davenport, to have his Pension granted to him. The General's Answer was, that I was to be in town in a few days; and without my Consent and even full Approbation he would take no Step in that Affair. You may believe, that I exhorted him to do so charitable an Action. (II:121)

On 19 March 1767, Hume writes to William Robertson:

> When the matter was proposed to me, I exhorted the General to do this act of charity to a man of genius, however wild and extravagant. The King, when applied to, said, that since the pension had once been promised, it should be granted, notwithstanding all that had passed in the interval. And *thus the affair is happily finished*, unless some new extravagance come across the philosopher, and

engage him to reject what he has anew applied for. (II:131, italics added)

The italicized bit is curious: "thus the affair is happily finished." Does Hume mean that this finish to the affair, that is, Rousseau receiving the pension, is a happy one? Or simply that we are happy to be finished with the affair?

In the 1 July 1767 letter to Davenport, Hume writes: "I know not, what can be done with regard to his Pension: It has pass'd all the Forms in the Treasury; but unless he appoint some Person to receive it, it never can be pay'd. Be so good as to mention that Matter to him, and desire him to write a Letter to Charles Lowndes Esqr Secretary to the Treasury, appointing him to pay the Money to some Person, whom he, Rousseau, shall chuse" (II:147).

Rousseau never received any pension payments.[18] A final snippet about the pension from Hume's correspondence is of note. He writes to the Comtesse on 26 April 1768: "I think that this philosopher [Rousseau] now speaks less of his return to this country; which indeed does not well suit him, as he would here be neither courted nor persecuted. *He does well to enjoy his pension at a distance from us*" (II:176, italics added). I suppose Hume means, *if* there is still life in the pension possibility, Rousseau would do well to enjoy it at a distance from Britain.

Why did Hume try to salvage what he could of the English Settlement? Maybe to display that he was not embittered against Rousseau, to show that he was bigger than the personal acrimony, and maybe to burnish the reputation of England as a tolerant nation and to serve British elites. I confess that those are reasonable enough. Still, another possible reason is that he continued to sense that the royal pension and settling in England would tend to subvert Rousseau's legacy.

"I have Themistocles, I have Themistocles"

In December 1766, Hume wrote to the London bookseller Thomas Becket, who had worked with Strahan in publishing *A Concise and Genuine Account*. In the letter Hume gives a dozen revisions, mostly very minor, to be made, in the event of a second edition, which never happened. One revision

---

18. I asked around with several Rousseau scholars, and the responses were all to the effect: No, not as far as we know. Edmonds and Eidinow (2006, 253) indicate that as of 1770 Rousseau had not received any payments of the pension.

is an insertion about Themistocles. So far as I know, it has not been noted in any of the treatments of the affair.

The Themistocles insertion pertains to *"Je tiens J. J. Rousseau."* The insertion is an addition to the footnote given when Rousseau reports Hume saying *"Je tiens J. J. Rousseau,"* a footnote supposedly by Hume. It appears, however, that that footnote was one of those that was entirely the creation of the editors in France. With the insertion, then, Hume is adding something to something he did not write but which he could not simply undo or disavow as not of his composing. The footnote reads:

> I cannot answer for every thing I may say in my sleep, and much less am I conscious whether or not I dream in French. But pray, as Mr Rousseau did not know whether I was asleep or awake when I pronounced those terrible words, with such a terrible voice, how is he certain that he himself was well awake when he heard them? (Hume 1766b, 79)

To that, Hume, in his December 1766 letter to Becket, instructs the following addition for a never-realized second edition:

> If M. Rousseau consult his Plutarch, he will find, that when Themistocles fled to Persia, Xerxes was so pleas'd with this Event, that he was heard to exclaim several times in his sleep, I have Themistocles, I have Themistocles. Why will not M. Rousseau understand my Exclamation in the same Sense? (II:117)

Hume's allusion conforms to the text of Plutarch's *Lives of the Noble Grecians and Romans*. Themistocles had been run out of Athens and fled to Persia. Plutarch (1975, 150) says that accounts differ as to whether the Persian king in the story was Xerxes or his son, as Xerxes died about that time, so Plutarch proceeds to speak simply of "the king." Prior to encountering the king, Themistocles applied to a Persian commander to approach the king with the following message: "I, that come hither to increase the power and glory of the king, will not only submit myself to his laws, since so it hath pleased the god who exalteth the Persian empire to this greatness, but will also cause many more to be worshippers and adorers of the king" (ibid.). Themistocles afterwards encounters the king and says: "If you save me, you will save your suppliant; if otherwise, will destroy an enemy of the Greeks" (ibid., 151). Plutarch continues:

The king heard him attentively, and, though he admired his temper and courage, gave him no answer at that time; but, when he was with his intimate friends, rejoiced in his great good fortune, and esteemed himself very happy in this, and prayed to his god Arimanius, that all his enemies might be ever of the same mind with the Greeks, to abuse and expel the bravest men amongst them. Then he sacrificed to the gods, and presently fell to drinking, and was so well pleased, that in the night, in middle of his sleep, he cried out for joy three times, '*I have Themistocles the Athenian.*' (Plutarch 1975, 151, italics added)

Themistocles the Athenian was well treated by the Persian king. Once they could converse in the Persian language, "the king invited him to partake of his own pastimes and recreations both at home and abroad, carrying him with him a-hunting, and made him his intimate so far that he permitted him to see the queen-mother, and converse frequently with her." The king assimilated Themistocles to Persian customs: "[T]he favours shown to other strangers were nothing in comparison with the honours conferred on him" (152).

The Themistocles would-be insertion regarding "*Je tiens J. J. Rousseau*" is significant. Hume casts Rousseau as Themistocles, who migrates in attitudinal space across empires to settle down in peace with a pension from the king. On the notion that Hume's Persia is worth fortifying, everyone is better off, including the good soul of J. J. Rousseau. On that notion, Hume is helping Rousseau to become, in spite of himself, a better person.

Concluding remarks

In 1767 there appeared a pseudonymous squib titled, "Heads of an Indictment Laid by J. J. Rousseau, Philosopher, Against D. Hume, Esq." (reprinted in II:446–448). Its author, "Freebody," lays out twelve indictments. Here are words from the first indictment:

1. That the said David Hume, to the great scandal of philosophy, and not having the fitness of things before his eyes, did concert a plan...to ruin the said J. J. Rousseau for ever, by bringing him over to England, and there settling him to his heart's content.

Those words fit my suggested explanation for Hume's puzzling and perseverant endeavor to settle Rousseau in England with a royal pension. If Rousseau had embraced the settlement and royal pension in England, his legacy would have been diminished, maybe much diminished.

I think Hume strove to do things that would make the world better off, and with more scruple than most. I daresay the world would have been much better off if Hume had gotten Rousseau to settle in England with a royal pension. I believe that Hume never had any interest or inclination to torment Rousseau. On my speculation, Hume was manipulative, but it was a manipulation that, if successful, Rousseau would have consented to and participated in. It would have been, in a sense, the assisting of Rousseau in his own effort to manipulate himself. It would be Hume and Rousseau cooperating in the manipulation of Rousseau. Hume endeavored to bring Rousseau, with his own consensual participation, to a better state of being.

People are always somewhat confused about their personal affairs. But the period July 1762 to July 1766 was especially disorienting for Hume. He was appointed in 1763 secretary of the embassy in France, and in Paris he enjoyed a tremendous cultural celebrity wholly new to him. He was confused about his relationship with the Comtesse de Boufflers, and, relatedly, about where to live out his remaining years, and whether he would ever again write works that enhanced his *oeuvres* and legacy. Hume was flustered by various trends and machinations in English politics, including a hostility toward the influence of Scots in government office.

Amid all these commotions within Hume's selfhood was the affair with Rousseau. That an impetus works subconsciously gains plausibility if the person is in a state of novelty, distraction, and perplexity. Sometimes we don't know what we're doing.

Psychologizing the terrestrial transactions of an important person in history, occurring more than 250 years ago, is a novelty for me. I share my ponderings to the extent of my knowledge. I encourage others to tell me what I've missed and to criticize this essay, not least as concerns French-language materials.

References

Damrosch, Leo. 2005. *Jean-Jacques Rousseau: Restless Genius*. Boston: Houghton Mifflin Company.

Edmonds, David, and John Eidinow. 2006. *Rousseau's Dog: Two Great Thinkers at War in the Age of Enlightenment*. New York: Harper Perennial.

Goodman, Dena. 1991. The Hume-Rousseau Affair: From Private *Querelle* to Public *Procès*. *Eighteenth-Century Studies* 25(2): 171–201.

Harris, James. 2015. *Hume: An Intellectual Biography.* Cambridge, UK: University of Cambridge Press.

Hume, David. 1766a. *Exposé succinct de la contestation qui s'est élevée entre M. Hume et M. Rousseau, avec les pièces justificatives,* trans. J. Suard. Paris.

Hume, David. 1766b. *A Concise and Genuine Account of the Dispute between Mr. Hume and Mr. Rousseau: With the Letters That Passed Between Them During Their Controversy; As Also, the Letters of the Hon. Mr. Walpole, and Mr. D'Alembert, Relative to This Extraordinary Affair; Translated from the French.* London: T. Becket and P. A. De Hondt.

Hume, David. 1932. *The Letters of David Hume,* ed. J. Y. T. Greig. Oxford: Oxford University Press.

Hume, David. 1983. *The History of England from the Invasion of Julius Caesar to the Revolution in 1688,* ed. W. B. Todd, 6 vols. Indianapolis: Liberty Fund.

Hume, David. 2021 [1766]. *Hume's Manuscript Account of the Extraordinary Affair Between Him and Rousseau,* eds. Daniel B. Klein, Jason Briggeman, and Jacob R. Hall. *Econ Journal Watch* 18(2): 278–326.

Klein, Daniel B. 2014a. Review of Dennis Rasmussen, The Problems and Promise of Commercial Society: Adam Smith's Response to Rousseau. *Adam Smith Review* 7: 323–329.

Klein, Daniel B. 2014b. Three Frank Questions to Discipline Your Theorizing. In *Theorizing in Social Science: The Context of Discovery,* ed. Richard Swedberg, 106–130. Stanford, Calif.: Stanford University Press.

Klein, Daniel B. 2021. Smith on Rousseau. *Adam Smith Works* (Liberty Fund, Carmel, Ind.), May 3.

Lund, Nelson. 2022. Adam Smith on Rousseau and the Origin of Languages. *Interpretation: A Journal of Political Philosophy* 48(2): 209–238.

McGilchrist, Iain. 2009. *The Master and His Emissary: The Divided Brain and the Making of the Western World.* New Haven, Conn.: Yale University Press.

Mossner, Ernest Campbell. 2001. *The Life of David Hume,* 2nd ed. Oxford: Clarendon Press.

Plutarch. 1975. *The Lives of the Noble Grecians and Romans,* ed. A. H. Clough, trans. J. Dryden. New York: Modern Library.

Rasmussen, Dennis C. 2017. *The Infidel and the Professor: David Hume, Adam Smith, and the Friendship That Shaped Modern Thought.* Princeton, N.J.: Princeton University Press.

Rousseau, Jean-Jacques. 1911 [1762]. *Émile,* trans. B. Foxley. London: Dent and Sons.

Rousseau, Jean-Jacques. 1997a. *The Discourses and Other Early Political Writings,* ed. V. Gourevitch. Cambridge, UK: Cambridge University Press.

Rousseau, Jean-Jacques. 1997b. *The Social Contract and Other Later Political Writings,* ed. V. Gourevitch. Cambridge, UK: Cambridge University Press.

Rousseau, Jean-Jacques. 2001. *Letter to Beaumont, Letters Written from the Mountain, and Related Writings,* eds. C. Kelly and J. R. Bush, trans. C. Kelly and E. Grace. Hanover, Vt.: Dartmouth College Press.

Saint-Fond, Barthélemy Faujas de. 1797. *Voyage En Angleterre, En Ecosse et Aux Iles Hébrides.* Paris: Chez H. J. Jansen.

Saint-Fond, Barthélemy Faujas de. 1907. *A Journey Through England and Scotland to the Hebrides in 1784*. Glasgow: Hugh Hopkins.

Smith, Adam. 1986. *The Correspondence of Adam Smith*, eds. Ernest C. Mossner and Ian S. Ross. Indianapolis: Liberty Fund.

Zaretsky, Robert, and John T. Scott. 2009. *The Philosophers' Quarrel: Rousseau, Hume, and the Limits of Human Understanding*. New Haven, Conn.: Yale University Press.

Glimpses of David Hume

Here collected are anecdotes and miscellanea about David Hume. Most of the 25 items presented here may also be found in James Fieser's marvelous 10-volume compilation *Early Responses to Hume* (Thoemmes Press, 2nd revised edition 2005), volumes 9 and 10 containing material about Hume's life and reputation. We are grateful for Professor Fieser's useful and agreeable work.

Only three of the items are not contained in the Fieser volumes. Two of them are from Hume himself. The item numbered XXIII is Hume's disavowal of *A Treatise of Human Nature*, which, I think, sometimes receives less consideration than it deserves (though I do not mean to suggest that taking the disavowal seriously would imply not taking the *Treatise* seriously and regarding it reverentially). The other Hume passage constitutes the final item, a portion of Hume's personal drama in the Conclusion of Book I of the *Treatise*. A textual case has been made that it is intimately paralleled by Adam Smith's parable of the poor man's son (Matson and Doran 2017).

In reproducing material, we have sometimes inserted information in brackets to provide context. Most notably, into the excerpt from Hume's Conclusion we have inserted four bracketed comments, to show how we think that that vital passage should be understood. When, in introducing an item, we have given some words to frame it, words immediately following the Roman numeral that enumerates the item, those words of ours are not in brackets. We also caught and corrected a few minor errors.

A reference list including all the original sources appears at the end of this document, whereas the citations to sources of the 25 items follow immediately below here.

Sourcing of the 25 items:

- I. Burton 1846, 452; Fieser 2005b, 288
- II. Burton 1846, 451; Fieser 2005b, 288
- III. Chambers 1832, 95–96; Fieser 2005b, 275
- IV. Diderot 1938, 77; Mossner, trans., 2001, 483; Fieser 2005b, 301
- V. Stewart 1802, 213; Fieser 2005b, 296
- VI. Mackenzie 1822, 24–25; Fieser 2005b, 261–262
- VII. Burton 1846, 456; Fieser 2005b, 289
- VIII. Mackenzie 1822, 22–23; Fieser 2005b, 261
- IX. Chambers 1832, 32; Fieser 2005b, 275
- X. Chambers 1832, 73; Fieser 2005b, 276
- XI. Burton 1846, 450; Fieser 2005b, 287
- XII. Chambers 1832, 184; Fieser 2005b, 276–277
- XIII. Boswell 1970/1776, 12–13; Fieser 2005a, 289
- XIV. Heathcote 1767; Fieser 2005a, 159–160
- XV. Boswell 1874, 263; Fieser 2005b, 147
- XVI. Burdy 1792, 100; Fieser 2005b, 302–303
- XVII. Mackenzie 1927, 171; Fieser 2005b, 266–267
- XVIII. *English Review* 1787; Fieser 2005b, 303
- XIX. Lady Anne Lindsay, quoted in Hunter 1960, 135 n.15; Fieser 2005b, 186
- XX. Mackenzie 1822, 21–22; Fieser 2005b, 260
- XXI. Mackenzie 1927, 169; Fieser 2005b, 265
- XXII. Stewart 1802, 76; Fieser 2005b, 296
- XXIII. Hume 1777
- XXIV. Beauchamp 2000, xvi
- XXV. Hume 1978, 268–271

I.

He seems…to have been occasionally absent in his habits; but there is no such collection of practical illustrations of this failing, as we possess in the case of Smith and others. I only remember having heard of one trifling instance, of which I had an account from an eyewitness. Hume had been dining with Dr. [John] Jardine, and there had been much conversation about "internal light." In descending the stair leading from the Doctor's "flat," when he left the party, Hume failed to observe that after so many flights which reached the street door, there was, according to a not uncommon practice, another flight of stairs leading to the cellars. He continued his descent, accordingly, till the very end, where some time afterwards he was found in extreme darkness and perplexity, wondering how it was that he could find no outlet. The circumstance bore rather curiously on some opinions he had been maintaining, and Jardine said, shaking his head, "Oh David! Where is your internal light?"

II.

The tone of his thoughts sometimes rose to enthusiasm. Thus the son of his valued friend [Adam] Ferguson, remembers his father saying, that, one clear and beautiful night, when they were walking home together, Hume suddenly stopped, looked up to the starry sky, and said, more after the manner of "Hervey's Meditations" than the "Treatise of Human Nature," "Oh, Adam, can any one contemplate the wonders of that firmament, and not believe that there is a God!"

III.

This distinguished philosopher was one day passing along a narrow footpath which formerly winded through a boggy piece of ground at the back of Edinburgh Castle, when he had the misfortune to tumble in, and stick fast in the mud. Observing a woman approaching, he civilly requested her to lend him a helping hand out of his disagreeable situation; but she, casting one hurried glance at his abbreviated figure, passed on, without regarding his request. He then shouted lustily after her; and she was at last prevailed upon by his cries to approach. "Are na ye Hume the Deist?" inquired she, in a tone which implied that an answer in the affirmative would decide her against lending him her assistance. "Well, well," said Mr Hume, "no matter: you know, good woman, Christian charity commands you to do good, even to your enemies." "Christian charity here, Christian charity there," replied the woman, "I'll do naething for ye till ye turn a Christian yoursell: ye maun first repeat baith the Lord's Prayer and the Creed, or faith I'll let ye groffle there as I faund ye." The sceptic was actually obliged to accede to the woman's terms, ere she would give him her help. He himself used to tell the story with great relish.

IV.

The first time that M. Hume found himself at the table of the Baron [D'Holbach], he was seated beside him. I don't know for what purpose the English philosopher took it into his head to remark to the Baron that he did not believe in atheists, that he had never seen any. The Baron said to him: "Count how many we are here." We are eighteen. The Baron added: "It isn't too bad a showing to be able to point out to you fifteen at once: the three others haven't made up their minds."

V.

Among the most distinguished speakers in the Select Society were Sir Gilbert Elliott, Mr. Wedderburn, Mr. Andrew Pringle, Lord Kames, Mr. Walter Stewart, Lord Elibank, and Dr. Robertson. The Honourable Charles Townshend spoke once. David Hume and Adam Smith never opened their lips.

VI.

About this time (1755) was produced a periodical publication, which attracted less notice at the time than it has since excited, when its principal authors had attained such celebrity as to make the world anxious to know the smallest of their productions,—I mean the Original *Edinburgh Review*, of which only two numbers were published; the article by Adam Smith, a Criticism on

Johnson's Dictionary, was very conspicuous.

David Hume was not among the number of the writers of the Review, though we should have thought he would have been the first person whose cooperation they would have sought. But I think I have heard that they were afraid both of his extreme good nature, and his extreme artlessness; that, from the one, their criticisms would have been weakened, or suppressed, and, from the other, their secret discovered. The merits of the work strongly attracted his attention, and he expressed his surprise, to some of the gentlemen concerned in it, with whom he was daily in the habit of meeting, at the excellence of a performance written, as he presumed, from his ignorance on the subject, by some persons out of their own literary circle. It was agreed to communicate the secret to him at a dinner, which was shortly after given by one of their number. At that dinner he repeated his wonder on the subject of the *Edinburgh Review*. One of the company said he knew the authors, and would tell them to Mr Hume upon his giving an oath of secrecy. "How is the oath to be taken," said David, with his usual pleasantry, "of a man accused of so much scepticism as I am? You would not trust my Bible Oath; but I swear by the το καλον and the το πρεπον [the beautiful and the becoming] never to reveal your secret." He was then told the names of the authors and the plan of the work, but it was not continued long enough to allow of his contributing any articles.

VII.

The Poker Club...seems to have had no other direct and Specific object but the consumption of claret. The duty laid on that national wine, by "the English statesman," so pathetically commemorated by John Home, was a heavy blow and great discouragement to the club; but it rallied, and returned to its old esteemed beverage; and, indeed, it is a somewhat curious circumstance, that the national taste, created by the early intercourse with France and the consequent cheapness of French wines, still lingers in Scotland, where claret is much more generally consumed than in England. The club met in Fortune's tavern every Friday. It was the practice, at each meeting, to name two to be, what were called, "attendant members;" an arrangement, probably, designed to form a nucleus round those whose attendance was uncertain, but who might drop in occasionally in the course of the evening, could form themselves; and to prevent any general desertion of the club, or, what might be, perhaps, more calamitous, the accident of any individual finding himself, for the night, its sole and solitary representative. We find Hume duly taking his turn in these attendances, and keeping the minutes according to rotation. On the 20th January, 1775, there is this emphatic entry, in his handwriting, "As Mr. Nairne was one of the attendant members, and neglected his duty, the club sent him the bill."

VIII.

Such was the free and cordial communication of sentiments, the natural play of fancy and good humour, which prevailed among the circle of [Scottish] men whom I have described. It was very different from that display of learning—that prize-fighting of wit, which distinguished a literary circle of our sister country, of which we have some authentic and curious records. There all ease of intercourse was changed for the pride of victory; and the victors, like some savage combatants, gave no quarter to the vanquished. This may, perhaps, be accounted for more from the situation than the dispositions of the principal members of that society. The literary circle of London was a sort of sect, a *caste* separate from the ordinary professions and habits of common life. They were traders in talent and learning, and brought, like other traders, samples of their goods into company, with a jealousy of competition which prevented their enjoying, as much as otherwise they might, any excellence in their competitors.

IX.

Hume, Smith, and other literati of the last century, used to frequent a tavern in a low street in Edinburgh called the Potterrow; where, if their accommodations were not of the first order, they had at least no cause to complain of the scantiness of their victuals. One day, as the landlady was bringing in a *third* supply of some particularly good dish, she thus addressed them: – "They ca' ye the *literawti*, I believe; od, if they were to ca' ye the *eaterawti*, they would be nearer the mark."

X.

David Hume and Lady Wallace once passed the Firth from Kinghorn to Leith together, when a violent storm rendered the passengers apprehensive of a salt-water death; and her ladyship's terrors induced her to seek consolation from her friend, who, with infinite *sang froid*, assured her he thought there was great probability of their becoming food for fishes. "And pray, my dear friend," said Lady Wallace, "which do you think they will eat first?" "Those that are gluttons," replied Hume, "will undoubtedly fall foul of me, but the epicures will attack your ladyship."

XI.

One occasionally meets with venerable persons who remember having been dandled on Hume's knee, and the number of these reminiscences indicates that he was fond of children. ... In one instance, a vivid recollection was preserved of the difficulty, from his fatness, of getting sufficient room on his knee, and the necessity of keeping fast hold of the corner of his laced waistcoat.

XII.

A certain person, to shew his detestation of Hume's infidel opinions, always left any company where he happened to be, if Hume joined it. The latter, observing this, took occasion one day to reprehend it as follows:— "Friend," said he, "I am surprised to find you display such a pointed aversion to me; I would wish to be upon good terms with you here, as, upon your own system, it seems very probable we shall be doomed to the same place hereafter. You hope I shall be damned for want of faith, and I fear you will have the same fate for want of charity."

XIII.

I [James Boswell] asked him if the thought of annihilation never gave him any uneasiness. He said not the least; no more than the thought that he had not been, as Lucretius observes. "Well," said I, "Mr. Hume, I hope to triumph over you when I meet you in a future state; and remember you are not to pretend that you was joking with all this infidelity." "No, no," said he. "But I shall have been so long there before you come that it will be nothing new." In this style of good humour and levity did I conduct the conversation. Perhaps it was wrong on so awful a subject. But as nobody was present, I thought it could have no bad effect. I however felt a degree of horror, mixed with a sort of wild, strange, hurrying recollection of my excellent mother's pious instructions, of Dr. Johnson's noble lessons, and of my religious sentiments and affections during the course of my life. I was like a man in sudden danger eagerly seeking his defensive arms; and I could not but be assailed by momentary doubts while I had actually before me a man of such strong abilities and extensive inquiry dying in the persuasion of being annihilated. But I maintained my faith. I told him that I believed the Christian religion as I believed history. Said he: "You do not believe it as you believe the Revolution." "Yes," said I; "but the difference is that I am not so much interested in the truth of the Revolution; otherwise I should have anxious doubts concerning it. A man who is in love has doubts of the affection of his mistress, without cause."

XIV.

He [Jean-Jacques Rousseau] was never perhaps in a situation before, where he was so little liable to be molested; where he was so unnoticed, so altogether left to his own will and humor. For the good people of England, after the first stare was over, had (as their way is) entirely done with him. Far from continuing to admire, they had ceased to mention him; and, if they had not totally forgot, they cared no more about him, than if he had been in Swisserland. His misery increased: your letter appeared: it became extreme. He fell into a paroxysm: he raged: and, in short, as sometimes happeneth among wild beasts, he fell upon his Keeper. To speak without a figure, he quarreled with his greatest friend and benefactor *Mr. Hume*, by all accounts the most quiet, the most humane, the most amiable of men; and who in the present case seems only faulty, in having condescended to humor a man, whom it is not possible to oblige: and nothing doubtless but the exceeding humanity of *Mr. Hume*, and his prejudices for *Mr. Rousseau*, could hinder one of his vast penetration from discerning somewhat earlier, than he seems to have done, that *Rousseau* was a savage, whom no offices of kindness could civilize and tame.

XV.

David Hume used to say that he did not find it an irksome task to him to go through a great many dull books when writing history. "I then read," said he, "not for pleasure, but in order to find out facts." He compared it to a sportsman seeking hares, who does not mind what sort of ground it is that he goes over farther than as he may find hares in it.

XVI.

Upon Mr. Skelton's arrival in London, he brought his manuscript to Andrew Millar the Bookseller, to know if he would purchase it, and have it printed at his own expense. The Bookseller desired him, as is usual, to leave it with him for a day or two, until he would get a certain gentleman of great abilities to examine it, who could judge, if the sale would quit the cost of printing. These gentlemen who examine manuscripts, in the Bookseller's cant, are called *triers*. "Can you guess (he [i.e., Skelton] said to me) who this gentleman was, that tried my *Deism Revealed*." "No, I cannot." "Hume the infidel." He came it seems to Andrew Millar's, took the manuscript to a room adjoining the shop, examined it here and there for about an hour, and then said to Andrew, *print*.

XVII.

He [David Hume] wanted a book out of the Advocates Library, of which the learned antiquarian [Walter] Goodall, author of the first Vindication of Queen Mary [of Scotland], was then acting Librarian. He was sitting in his elbow-chair so fast asleep, that neither David nor a friend who accompanied him could wake Goodall by any of the usual means. At last David said, "I think I have a method of waking him," and bawled into his ear, "Queen Mary was a strumpet and a murtherer." – "It's a damned lie," said Goodall, starting out of his sleep, and David obtained the book he sought.

XVIII.

The celebrated Mr. Hume used to call Dr. Franklin "the first fruits of America." The American revolution has given elasticity and energy to the minds of the inhabitants, has called forth talents and abilities of every kind, and produced a more copious harvest than the solitary "first fruits" observed by Mr. Hume seemed to indicate.

XIX.

of Hume at age 16

You know the Truthfulness of his Honest Nature…as a Boy he was a fat, stupid, lumbering Clown, but full of sensibility and Justice,—one day at my house, when he was about 16 a most unpleasant odour offended the Company before dinner…"O the Dog…the Dog," cried out everyone "put out the Dog; 'tis that vile Beast Pod, kick him down stairs pray…pray."—

Hume stood abashed, his heart smote him…"Oh do not hurt the Beast" he said…"It is not Pod, it is Me!" …

How very few people would take the evil odour of a stinking Conduct from a guiltless Pod to wear it on their own rightful Shoulders.

XX.

Once, I have been told, he was in a small degree ruffled by a witticism of Mr John Home's, who, though always pleasant, and often lively, seldom produced what might be termed or repeated as wit. The clerk of an eminent banker in Edinburgh, a young man of irreproachable conduct, and much in the confidence of his master, eloped with a considerable sum with which he had been entrusted. The circumstance was mentioned at a dinner where the two Humes, the historian and the poet, and several of their usual friendly circle, were present. David Hume spoke of it as a kind of moral problem, and wondered what could induce a man of such character and habits as this clerk was said to possess, thus to incur, for an inconsiderable sum, the guilt and the infamy of such a transaction. "I can easily account for it," said his friend John Home, "from the nature of his studies, and the kinds of books which he was in the habit of reading." "What were they?" said the philosopher. "Boston's

Fourfold State" rejoined the poet, "and Hume's Essays." David was more hurt by the joke than was usual with him, probably from the singular conjunction of the two works, which formed, according to his friend's account, the library of the unfortunate young man.

XXI.

David Hume was not at all the Jacobite or Tory which he was sometimes accused of being, and as his History was supposed to evince. He had an indolent gentleness in his nature which was averse to enthusiasm and perhaps unfriendly to bold ideas and bold expression. He loved the moderate, the temperate in everything, and from that disposition as well as his propensity to disbelief he had an aversion to the fanatics and *Cromwellian* partisans of the Commonwealth. From this inclination to mildness and moderation he was perhaps not so much an admirer of Shakespeare as he ought to have been, and rather cautioned his friend John Home against an over-admiration of that great dramatist, and desired him to read constantly Corneille and Racine.

XXII.

Dr. [William] Robertson used frequently to say, that in Mr. Hume's gaiety there was something which approached to *infantine*; and that he had found the same thing so often exemplified in the circle of his other friends, that he was almost disposed to consider it as characteristical of genius.

XXIII.

In 1775 Hume wrote a brief Advertisement, which, after his death in 1776, was placed at the start of the 1777 volume containing the two enquiries, the dissertation on the passions, and the natural history of religion. Here is the Advertisement in full.

Most of the principles, and reasonings, contained in this volume, were published in a work in three volumes, called *A Treatise of Human Nature*: A work which the Author had projected before he left College, and which he wrote and published not long after. But not finding it successful, he was sensible of his error in going to the press too early, and he cast the whole anew in the following pieces, where some negligences in his former reasoning and more in the expression, are, he hopes, corrected. Yet several writers, who have honoured the Author's Philosophy with answers, have taken care to direct all their batteries against that juvenile work, which the Author never acknowledged, and have affected to triumph in any advantages, which, they imagined, they had obtained over it: A practice very contrary to all rules of candour and fair-dealing, and a strong instance of those polemical artifices, which a bigotted zeal thinks itself authorised to employ. Henceforth, the Author desires, that the following Pieces may alone be regarded as containing his philosophical sentiments and principles.

XXIV.

The full set of Hume's reasons for the disavowal of *THN* may not be recoverable, but it is probable that his 'repenting' of his early work was unfeigned...

XXV.
from the Conclusion of Book I of A Treatise of Human Nature

The *intense* view of these manifold contradictions and imperfections in human reason has so wrought upon me, and heated my brain, that I am ready to reject all belief and reasoning, and can look upon no opinion even as more probable or likely than another. Where am I, or what? From what causes do I derive my existence, and to what condition shall I return? Whose favour shall I court, and whose anger must I dread? What beings surround me? and on whom have I any influence, or who have any influence on me? I am confounded with all these questions, and begin to fancy myself in the most deplorable condition imaginable, inviron'd with the deepest darkness, and utterly depriv'd of the use of every member and faculty.

Most fortunately it happens, that since reason is incapable of dispelling these clouds, nature herself suffices to that purpose, and cures me of this philosophical melancholy and delirium, either by relaxing this bent of mind, or by some avocation, and lively impression of my senses, which obliterate all these chimeras. I dine, I play a game of back-gammon, I converse, and am merry with my friends; and when after three or four hours' amusement, I wou'd return to these speculations, they appear so cold, and strain'd, and ridiculous, that I cannot find in my heart to enter into them any farther.

Here then I find myself absolutely and necessarily determin'd to live, and talk, and act like other people in the common affairs of life. But notwithstanding that my natural propensity, and the course of my animal spirits and passions reduce me to this indolent belief in the general maxims of the world, I still feel such remains of my former disposition, that I am ready to throw all my books and papers into the fire, and resolve never more to renounce the pleasures of life for the sake of reasoning and philosophy. For those are my sentiments in that splenetic humour, which governs me at present. I may, nay I must yield to the current of nature, in submitting to my senses and understanding; and in this blind submission I show most perfectly my sceptical disposition and principles. But does it follow, that [we suggest that the preceding five words be read as: But, following such impulse to submission, I then find that] I must strive against the current of nature, which leads me to indolence and pleasure; that I must seclude myself, in some measure, from the commerce and society of men, which is so agreeable; and that I must torture my brain with subtilities and sophistries [for example, Hume's subsequent writings on morals, culture, politics, and history], at the very time that I cannot satisfy myself concerning the reasonableness of so painful an application, nor have any tolerable prospect of arriving by its means at truth and certainty. Under what obligation do I lie of making such an abuse of time? And to what end can it serve either for the service of mankind, or for my own private interest? No: If I must be a fool, as all those who reason or believe any thing *certainly* are, my follies [again, for example, Hume's subsequent writings on morals, culture, politics, and history] shall at least be natural and agreeable. Where I strive against my inclination, I shall have a good reason for my resistance; and will no more be led a wandering into such dreary solitudes, and rough passages, as I have hitherto met with [that is, the material in Book I preceding the Conclusion].

These are the sentiments of my spleen and indolence; and indeed I must confess, that philosophy has nothing to oppose to them, and expects a victory more from the returns of a serious good-humour'd disposition, than from the force of reason and conviction. In all the incidents of life we ought still to preserve our scepticism. If we believe, that fire warms, or water refreshes, 'tis only because it costs us too much pains to think otherwise. Nay if we are philosophers, it ought only to be upon sceptical principles, and from an inclination, which we feel to the employing ourselves after that manner. Where reason is lively, and mixes itself with some propensity, it ought to be assented to. Where it does not, it never can have any title to operate upon us.

At the time, therefore, that I am tir'd with amusement and company, and have indulg'd a *reverie* in my chamber, or in a solitary walk by a river-side, I feel my mind all collected within itself, and am naturally *inclin'd* to carry my view into all those subjects, about which I have met with so many disputes in the course of my reading and conversation. I cannot forbear having a curiosity to be acquainted with the principles of moral good and evil, the nature and foundation of government, and the cause of those several passions and inclinations, which actuate and govern me. I am uneasy to think I approve of one object, and disapprove of another; call one thing beautiful, and another deform'd; decide concerning truth and falshood, reason and folly, without knowing upon what principles I proceed. I am concern'd for the condition of the learned world, which lies under such a deplorable ignorance in all these particulars. I feel an ambition to arise in me of contributing to the instruction of mankind, and of acquiring a name by my inventions and discoveries. These sentiments spring up naturally in my present disposition; and shou'd I endeavour to banish them, by attaching myself to any other business or diversion, I *feel* I shou'd be a loser in point of pleasure; and this is the origin of my philosophy.

References

[Adam, William]. 1839. *Sequel to the Gift of a Grandfather*. Edinburgh.

Beauchamp, Tom L. 2000. Introduction to *An Enquiry Concerning Human Understanding* by David Hume, ed. Tom L. Beauchamp, xi–ciii. Oxford: Oxford University Press.

Boswell, James. 1874. *Boswelliana: The Commonplace Book of James Boswell*, ed. Charles Rogers. London: Grampian Club.

Boswell, James. 1970 [1776]. An Account of My Last Interview with David Hume, Esq., July 7, 1776. In *Boswell in Extremes 1776–1778*, eds. Charles McC. Weis and Frederick A. Pottle, 11–15. New York: McGraw-Hill.

Burdy, Samuel. 1792. *The Life of the Late Rev. Philip Skelton*. Dublin: W. Jones.

Burton, John Hill. 1846. *Life and Correspondence of David Hume: From the Papers Bequeathed by His Nephew to the Royal Society of Edinburgh, and Other Original Sources*, vol. 2. Edinburgh: W. Tait.

[Chambers, Robert]. 1832. *Scottish Jests and Anecdotes*. Edinburgh: W. Paterson.

Diderot, Denis. 1938. *Lettres à Sophie Volland*, vol. 2. Paris.

English Review. 1787. Review of *A Defence of the Constitutions of Government of the United States of America* by John Adams. *English Review* 10: 321–329.

Fieser, James, ed. 2005a. *Early Responses to Hume's Life and Reputation*, vol. 1 (*Early Responses to Hume*, vol. 9), 2nd ed. Bristol, UK: Thoemmes Press.

Fieser, James, ed. 2005b. *Early Responses to Hume's Life and Reputation*, vol. 2 (*Early Responses to Hume*, vol. 10), 2nd ed. Bristol, UK: Thoemmes Press.

Green, Thomas. 1834. *Diary of a Lover of Literature* [entry for November 8, 1801]. *Gentleman's Magazine* 1 (n.s.): 137–144.

[Heathcote, Ralph]. 1767. *A Letter to the Honorable Mr. Horace Walpole, Concerning the Dispute between Mr. Hume and Mr. Rousseau*. London: B. White.

Hume, David. 1777. *Essays and Treatises on Several Subjects*, vol. II. London: Cadell.

Hume, David. 1978. *A Treatise of Human Nature*, 2nd ed., eds. L. A. Selby-Bigge and P. H. Nidditch. Oxford: Oxford University Press.

Hunter, Geoffrey, ed. 1960. David Hume: Some Unpublished Letters 1771–1776. *Texas Studies in Literature and Language* 2(2): 127–150.

Kemp Smith, Norman. 2005. *The Philosophy of David Hume*. 2nd ed. New York: Palgrave Macmillan.

Mackenzie, Henry. 1822. *An Account of the Life and Writings of John Home, Esq.* Edinburgh: A. Constable.

Mackenzie, Henry. 1927. *The Anecdotes and Egotisms of Henry Mackenzie, 1745–1831*. London: Oxford University Press.

Matson, Erik W., and Colin Doran. 2017. The Elevated Imagination: Contemplation and Action in David Hume and Adam Smith. *Journal of Scottish Philosophy* 15(1): 27–45.

Mossner, E. C. 2001. *The Life of David Hume*, 2nd ed. Oxford: Oxford University Press.

Ross, Ian Simpson. 2016. Glimpses of Adam Smith. *Econ Journal Watch* 13(1): 168–191.

Stewart, Dugald. 1802. *Account of the Life and Writings of William Robertson*, 2nd ed. London: A. Strahan.

From Hume to Smith on the Common Law and English Liberty: A Comment on Paul Sagar

Jacob R. Hall[1]

In a *Political Theory* article, "On the Liberty of the English: Adam Smith's Reply to Montesquieu and Hume," Paul Sagar (2021) treats Smith in relation to Montesquieu and David Hume on the origins, development, and robustness of English liberty. In doing so he fashions something of a divide between Smith and Hume with respect to their views on the development of liberty in England. Sagar suggests a difference between Smith and Hume on the importance of the common law, that "Smith took more seriously than Hume the idea that liberty required not just an appropriate constitution but quotidian security as realized via law" (2021, 18). Sagar goes further to say that Hume would underestimate, or miss entirely, the idea "that liberty must be understood not just in terms of the form of constitution and wider political order, but also regarding the security of citizens as achieved via the legal system, and especially the operation of fair trials" (ibid., 14).

Upon reading and reflecting on Sagar's paper, I felt that Sagar had failed to do justice to Hume. I drafted a comment along the lines of the present article and submitted it to *Political Theory*, where Sagar's paper appears, but it was turned down without explanation.

Sagar on Smith and Hume

According to Sagar, Montesquieu, in a manner like Tacitus, traces English

1. I am grateful for feedback from Erik Matson, two anonymous referees, and the attendants of the Invisible Hand Seminar at George Mason University.

liberty back to the ancient customs of the Germans, rooted in bottom-up way in local practice and judgment. But in Montesquieu's estimation, English liberty was fragile. In Sagar's article, Hume is cast as counterpart to the Frenchman. Hume, according to Sagar, dated the origins of English liberty to the Glorious Revolution when Parliament secured its supremacy over the king. In Hume's estimation, English liberty was robust.

Sagar does not define what he means by liberty. Nor does he wade into interpreting how Montesquieu, Hume, and Smith use the word themselves. I do not fault him for that. In this paper I myself will avoid wading into debating the many meanings of liberty. But it is worth remembering that there are many meanings of liberty. Hume talks of liberty with many different modifiers. At times, Hume seems to see liberty as synonymous with general rules that are consistently and equitably applied. But other times, Hume's liberty is more akin to a particular constitutional order, particularly the post-revolution British constitution. Daniel Klein and Erik Matson (2020) argue that a central meaning of liberty in Hume is "others not messing with one stuff," which they dub "mere-liberty." Keeping these different senses of liberty in mind, even if in the background, is important.

Sagar then turns to Smith, arguing that we should situate the Scotsman "as intervening in the debate between Montesquieu and Hume on the origins, age, and robustness of English liberty" (2021, 2). He argues that Smith agreed with Hume on the importance of the Glorious Revolution for securing English liberty, but unlike Hume, Smith recognized that the reforms of the Revolution were "grafted onto, and…greatly enhanced by, a wider preexisting legal framework," namely the common law (ibid., 15). For Sagar's Smith, the common law, particularly the legal and administrative reforms of king Edward I (r. 1272–1307), constituted a major development in the story of English liberty, a development that Sagar supposes Hume underappreciated or missed entirely. In the course of making his argument about the importance of the common law in Smith's historical narrative in *Lectures on Jurisprudence*, Sagar overlooks Hume's discussions of the common law in *The History of England*.

Sagar (2021, 14) argues that Hume was "comparably inattentive," relative to Smith, on the importance of English common law for the development of liberty. *Comparably* inattentive—perhaps. But throughout his article Sagar regularly portrays Hume as *highly* inattentive to such historical developments. According to Sagar, Hume's narrative is "focused on the high politics of court and parliament and not the day-to-day affairs of legal administration," and, as a result, Hume supposedly misses the importance of the common law as an element of English liberty (ibid.). Instead, Hume's theory of English liberty supposedly turns merely on the serendipities of 1688. Sagar faults Hume for his supposed oversights: "Core aspects of English liberty long predated the Glorious Revolution in ways Hume had not appreciated" (ibid., 2).

Sagar is right to highlight Hume's emphasis on the Glorious Revolution for the development of English liberty. But he is wrong to conclude that Hume failed to recognize earlier elements of liberty prior to 1688. In volume 2 of the *History*, Hume discusses arbitrary measures Edward I took to secure funds for his war with France in 1296. The English barons mount a dissent and subsequently forced Edward I to cease and desist and to renew his oath to uphold Magna Carta. They even empowered knights in each county to investigate and punish royal officials for violating Magna Carta. Hume, reacting to the baronial response, writes:

> A precaution, which, though it was soon disused, as encroaching too much on royal prerogative, proves the attachment, which the English in that age bore to liberty, and their well-grounded jealousy of the arbitrary disposition of Edward. (*H*, 2:119–121)[2]

Nearly 400 years before the Glorious Revolution, Hume seems to believe the English bore an attachment to liberty. Liberty may not have been solidified, and the medieval institutions often worked against it, but its spirit inhabited the island.

Sagar (2021, 8) quotes volume six of the *History* in support of his claim that Hume felt it was "only in 1688 that English liberty was finally established and secured":

> The revolution alone...put an end to all these disputes: By means of it, a more uniform edifice was at last erected: The monstrous incoherence, so visible between the ancient Gothic parts of the fabric and the recent plans of liberty, was fully corrected: And to their mutual felicity, king and people were finally taught to know their proper bounds (*H*, 6:475–476; quoted in Sagar 2021, 8).

---

2. The notation "*H*, 3:76" means page 76 in the third volume of the Liberty Fund edition of Hume's *History of England*. I adopt such notation throughout. For Adam Smith's *Wealth of Nations* I adopt the abbreviation *WN* and for his *Lectures on Jurisprudence* I use *LJ*.

Sagar follows Hume's quotation by saying: "Against Montesquieu, Hume's verdict was that English liberty was not old but very new indeed" (2021, 8). But Hume is not saying here that only in 1688 did liberty spring forth. Hume's use of "fully corrected" does not preclude the development of elements prior to the revolution and partial corrections along the way. Earlier in the volume 5, Hume again speaks of elements of liberty that existed well before 1688:

> The grievances, under which the English laboured, when considered in them-selves, without regard to the constitution, scarcely deserve the name; nor were they either burthensome on the people's properties, or anywise shocking to the natural humanity of mankind... [Under Charles I's administration] all ecclesi-astical affairs were settled by law and uninterrupted precedent; and the church was become a considerable barrier to the power, both legal and illegal, of the crown. Peace too, industry, commerce, opulence; nay, even justice and lenity of administration, notwithstanding some very few exceptions: All these were enjoyed by the people; and every other blessing of government, except liberty, *or rather the present exercise of liberty*, and its proper security. (H, 5:249–250, my emphasis)

In Hume's estimation, and, as Sagar argues, Smith's, something meaningful did happen in 1688, but that did not mean that elements of liberty did not exist or were not upheld prior to 1688.

Sagar admits that Hume discusses habeas corpus a few times in his *History*, but correctly points out that Hume "tended to do so only incidentally" (2021, 14). Sagar then concludes that "there is no sustained effort by Hume to tell a story in which the liberty he believed was only secured by the 1688 revolution was itself augmented and buttressed by a wider legal culture that was by that point centuries old." He goes on to detail Smith's account of the English com-mon law and the legal reforms of Edward I. But Sagar overlooks Volume 1 and 2 of Hume's *History* where his discussions of the common law can be found, which dovetail with Smith's narrative.

As I see it, the divide between Smith and Hume is less than Sagar suggests, if it exists at all. Hume did in fact recognize the English common law as an element of English liberty. Rather than replying to Hume, Smith should be seen as developing on Hume's ideas and disseminating the results.

Sagar provides a fine summary of Smith's story given in the *Wealth of Nations* and the *Lectures on Jurisprudence* concerning the medieval barons' em-brace of luxury goods and commerce over retainers, retinues, and other instruments of war and plunder. Smith's narrative serves as a great example of his tendency to take the ideas of his friend, Hume, and refine and improve them. Hume's historical account of the civilizing of the barons occurs over two and a half volumes in a disjointed fashion. Hume only once comes out and identifies the phenomenon clearly (*H*, 3:76). Smith's *WN* account is a concise and straightforward 44 paragraphs. Notice how Smith condenses time in his famous "diamond buckles" passage:

> But what all the violence of the feudal institutions could never have effected, the silent and insensible operation of foreign commerce and manufactures gradually brought about. ... For a pair of diamond buckles perhaps, or for something as frivolous and useless, they [the barons] exchanged the maintenance, or what is the same thing, the price of the maintenance of a thousand men for a year, and with it the whole weight and authority which it could give them. (*WN*, 418–419.10)

We might ask, "How gradually did the civilizing process unfold?" Hume would say 450 years, give or take, and it was by no means monotonic. Smith was synthesizing and reformulating the arguments of Hume to make it coherent and understandable to his audience. By drawing out one distinct process taken up in Hume's *History*, Smith made the civilizing process of commerce more concrete and graspable.

But we should not say that Hume did not understand the importance of that civilizing process for English political development. He did. He even discusses mechanisms unmentioned in Smith's account, such as Henry VII's prohibition on baronial military retainers (*H*, 3:75) and his allowance of the barons to alienate their estates (*H*, 3:77). Nor would we say that Smith disagreed with Hume on the importance of that civilizing process for English liberty. Smith cites Hume favorably as "the only writer who, so far as I know, has hitherto taken notice of it" (*WN*, 412.4).

Sagar does not paint a divide between the two Scots on the dynamic by which the barons became gentlemen. He rightfully notes that Smith built upon Hume (Sagar 2021, 12). But on the importance of the common law, and England's legal system more generally, he does make a separation between Smith and Hume. That separation strikes me as inappropriate. Hume does not have a chapter on the common law in the *History*, nor is it discussed at length in an appendix. Also, there is no "Of the Common Law" in Hume's *Essays*. We are impoverished because of that. Hume does, however, take up the common law at many key moments in its development in his *History*. The common law is one example of his larger theme of jural integration and its importance for the development of English liberty.

Just as he builds upon, clarifies, and refines Hume's account of the barons becoming gentlemen, Smith takes up the common law in the *Lectures on Jurisprudence*. Hume spends two volumes giving his readers a rich display of examples of just how violent and licentious the barons were and how the common law (among other things), backed by the increasing authority of the king, suppressed their local authority. Smith distills Hume and combines him with the work of other scholars and his own knowledge to tell a coherent story about the development of the common law and its importance for English liberty. We will never know the extent to which Hume grasped the importance of the common law for development of English liberty, an importance that Smith teaches in his lectures. Hume had more to do than time allowed for, and he understood more than he passed down to us in essays. Hume certainly had much more than an inkling of the narrative that Smith would come to flesh out with greater detail.

Jural integration in England

Hume's *History of England* is situated between two grand arrivals to Britain: those of Julius Caesar in 55 BCE and William of Orange in 1688. Between those two men, Hume spends six volumes detailing England's high politics and the slow development of the English constitution. And like another great six-part epic saga that began 200 years after his death, Hume produced the *History* out of order. Nowhere in it does Hume have a sweeping analysis of the English common law. In fact, searching the text for "common law" yields only trivialities.

But that does not mean Hume neglects the development of England's legal system. In a sense, that development is a major theme of Hume's *History*. From Arthur to Henry VIII, England was ruled by multiple, competing powers. In volumes 1 and 2 Hume shows us, often in bloody detail, that the quantum of authority and legitimacy of the average medieval king was built on shifting sands (*H*, 2:283–284). In addition to the king, England was home to a number of powerful actors such as the towns, independent barons, and the Roman Church and its affiliate ecclesiastical bodies, not to mention the potential influence of the Welsh, Scottish, and French aristocracies. Each separate authority had its own jurisdiction, source of power and influence, and instruments for making their voice heard.

The existence of multiple powers capable of violence made medieval England a dangerous place to live. Hume characterizes the ancient constitution as one of minimal economic growth plagued by violence and political instability:

> The towns were situated either within the demesnes of the king, or the lands of the great barons, and were almost entirely subjected to the absolute will of their master. The languishing state of commerce kept the inhabitants poor and contemptible; and the political institutions were calculated to render that poverty perpetual. The barons and gentry, living in rustic plenty and hospitality, gave no encouragement to the arts, and had no demand for any of the more elaborate manufactures: Every profession was held in contempt but that of arms: And if any merchant or manufacturer rose by industry and frugality to a degree of opulence, he found himself but the more exposed to injuries, from the envy and avidity of the military nobles. (*H*, 1:463)

In addition to plundering their societal inferiors, the barons engaged in private warfare against each other, leaving the countryside in a continual state of chaos and lawlessness (*H*, 1:231, 237, 250, 284, 288, 350–351, 371–372, 400, 463, 2:11, 143, 189, 279). Even during periods of relative peace between the bigger political players, "men were never secure in their houses" and bands of robbers, often supported by encastellated barons, were known to plunder entire villages (*H*, 1:69, 288).

A main theme of Hume's *History* is the integration of the separate powers into a single unified government (Forbes 1975, 263; Whelan 2004, 256; Sabl 2012, 65). Dan Klein and I have produced a lengthy compendium that gives 142 quotations from Hume's *History* touching upon jural pluralism or jural integration (Hall and Klein 2020). Barry Weingast (2015; 2016; 2017) identifies similar themes in Smith's *Wealth of Nations* and *Lectures on Jurisprudence*. Integration went hand-in-hand with the increasing power and authority of the king. It was a slow process. Two steps forward, one step back. The personal characters of kings were of great importance, as evidenced by both Hume's historical narrative and his lengthy character portraits. The strongest and most respectable of kings always seemed to sire the weakest and least respectable heirs. Henry II begets John, and Edward I begets Edward II.

But through the centuries, the authority of the king increased in scale and in scope. Individual kings may have been weak, but the crown was growing stronger. The medieval era eventually gave way to what is now called the early modern period. Dating the achievement of establishing an integrated nation-state is not an exact science. If we wish to be poetic, perhaps that transition occurred at Bosworth when Henry Tudor crushed Richard III and his Yorkist supporters. Henry VII and his successor Henry VIII crafted reforms that led to demilitarization of the English aristocracy on a grand scale (*H*, 3:75, 77). By the time Hume discusses the reign of Elizabeth I in volume 4 the competing powers of the medieval era have fallen away and he speaks of *the* government. The Tudors and Stuarts still faced various political challenges, but the section header "Discontent of the Barons," used five times by Hume in the first two volumes, is absent from the early modern volumes, that is, volumes 3, 4, 5, and 6.

Hume on the common law

Hume hailed from a family of common-law lawyers.[3] Both his father and his two grandfathers were trained formerly in the law and were practiced barristers. He attended school in Edinburgh at an early age, which he abandoned at 14 without receiving his degree. But upon returning Hume took up studying the law, guided partly by Henry Home, Lord Kames (Mossner 2001, 53–54). Ernest Campbell Mossner has praised Hume's legal knowledge:

> In the end, Hume's legal knowledge, both theoretical and practical, was not inconsiderable. The theoretical, forming an integral part of moral philosophy, appears so frequently in his published works as to require no special comment. Of theoretical jurisprudence, Hume was a master. (Mossner 2001, 55)

Hume also would have had the entirety of the Advocates' Library collection at his disposal while working on the *History*. Post-Norman England experienced an explosion of administrative documentation, and it is reflected in Hume's

---

3. I thank an anonymous referee for bringing these biographical facts about Hume to my attention.

citations in the early volumes.

In medieval England, the rules enforced in the King's court were in competition with the other courts of the realm. An aggrieved man could seek justice in the county courts which administered local customary law or he could go to the ecclesiastical courts which administered canon law. A town merchant could take his case to a borough court to be judged by the rules of the *Lex mercatoria*. One might even go to one's feudal lord to make his case under the rules of feudal custom. The royal law, however, was common throughout the realm and was the origination point of what has come to be known as the common law (Hogue 1986/1966).

Arthur Hogue defined common law as "the body of rules prescribing social conduct and justiciable in the royal courts of England" (1986/1966, 5), and I use the phrase *common law* along those lines. At a more abstract level, common law is simply law held in common throughout the polity. A third sense of common law is law worked out through precedent. The three senses of common law are all rooted in the historical development of English common law. The royal law applied to all Englishmen, no matter where the crime was committed or who the perpetrator may have been. As royal judges travelled the kingdom hearing cases they learned and refined their legal judgments. By travelling, they made the royal law common throughout the realm. Through their travels they amassed a bank of precedent that they could call upon in subsequent cases.

Over time, the common law, enforced by the royal courts, subsumed or marginalized its competitors. As the authority and power of the king grew the "justice done in the king's name by men who [were] the king's servants became the most important kind of justice" (Pollock and Maitland 2010/1895, 91). The success of the common law went hand in hand with the centralization of power around the king. Hume said as much:

> It [the people's freedom] required the authority almost absolute of the sovereigns, which took place in the subsequent period, to pull down those disorderly and licentious tyrants, who were equally averse from peace and from freedom, and to establish that regular execution of the laws which, in a following age, enabled the people to erect a regular and equitable plan of liberty. (*H*, 2:525)

As the king's power and authority grew, so did the impact of his laws. Frederick Pollock and Frederic Maitland (1895), Arthur Hogue (1966), Harold Berman (1983), and John Baker (1995), all scholars of the common law, attest to that fact.

Another reason for the rise of the common law cited by Hume was the rediscovery of Justinian's Pandects, a compendium of juristic writings on Roman law (*H*, 2:520). For Hume, the rediscovery in 1130 of Justinian's Pandects was a glimmer of light from a more civilized era that would begin to illuminate a dark world. No other event "tended further to the improvement of the age" (ibid.).

With Justinian's Pandects in their hands, the clergy took up legal studies with great zeal. Less than ten years later, according to Hume, lectures in civil law were being given in Oxford. Although Roman civil law never rose to the same level of prominence in England as it did on the continent due to "the jealousy [of] the laity," and perhaps England's island geography, it left a permanent mark on English law (*H*, 2:520–521). The English jurists imitated their civil law equivalents, "rais[ing] their own law from its original state of rudeness and imperfection" (*H*, 2:521). Here Hume complements Larry Siedentop's *Inventing the Individual* (2014) on the importance of Christianity and the Catholic Church for the development of western liberalism. In chapter 16 of his book, Siedentop discusses the re-discovery of Justinian's Pandects, tracing its effects on both ecclesiastical and lay law over the subsequent chapters.

To find Hume's discussions of concrete legal development, we need to look at his coverage of the strongest medieval English kings: Henry II and Edward I. Only these men were able to extend their authority and carry out reform without having their political coalitions turn on them.

The reign of King Stephen (r. 1135–1154) was marked by "The Anarchy," a succession crisis that led to the complete breakdown of civil order in England (*H*, 1:279–295). Henry II (r. 1154–1189), upon winning the war and ascending to the throne, was tasked with cleaning up the mess and restoring order and justice to the kingdom. Hume depicts Henry II as a good and strong king who led England with a steady hand and an "equitable administration" (*H*, 1:359, 301, 370). He was a politically savvy man, as shown by his swift actions to demolish the castles illegally built by the local barons during The Anarchy (*H*, 1:360). He had his share of dark days (*H*, 1:310–338, 348–358), as all medieval kings did, but he was responsible for increasing the power of

147

the monarchy over the licentious barons and executing long-lasting reforms to England's legal system. In 1176, Henry II partitioned England into four divisions and appointed itinerant justices to travel along a circuit to hear and decide on the cases brought before them in the counties (H, 1:359–360). The general eyre, as the law circuit was called, furthered the mission of making the king's law common throughout the realm. The eyre increased the geographical influence of the king's laws and regularized Englishmen to its enforcement. It protected the lower gentry and the peasants from the arbitrary violence and corruption of the barons, and, albeit slowly, acted to curb baronial power (H, 1:360). This is all Hume's narrative, not mine, and it is a narrative of the common law.

But the expansion of royal justice and the common law was not a matter of force. Royal justice passed the market test and came to be the preferred court of law because it administered better justice. The justices in eyre were notable men of honor, in contrast to the local courts, thus the respectability of the common law was bolstered by their character (H, 1:360). They were also better trained and less corrupt than their local counterparts. Additionally, the common law possessed what no other court in England did—the weight of the monarchy.

After looking at the common law reforms under Henry II, Hume drops common law until his discussion of Edward I (r. 1272–1307). That is under-standable. What occupies Hume during the reigns of Richard I (r. 1189–1199), John (r. 1199–1215), and Henry III (r. 1216–1272) is tracing out the events that led to John's capitulation at Runnymede and the solidification of Magna Carta into the English political ethos. Like Henry II, Edward I inherited a mess. Edward's father, Henry III, was a relatively weak king who bumbled his way into a civil war against a group of discontented barons led by Simon de Montfort. Upon inheriting the crown, Edward "immediately applied himself to the re-establishment of his kingdom, and to the correcting of those disorders" introduced by Henry III's weak administration (H, 2:75).

Edward I was a strong king. A weak king would never have earned the nickname "Hammer of the Scots," which is reminiscent of the great Frankish king Charles Martel (688–741 CE), as *martel* in old French means 'hammer.' As recognized by Smith and discussed by Sagar, Edward I was a great legal reformer. Smith puts Edward I alongside Henry II as one of the greats in terms of his legislative capacity (LJ(A), v.34).

Hume's account of Edward I's legal reforms is similar to Smith's as recounted by Sagar, but not once does Sagar's article cite volumes 1 or 2 of the *History*. To diminish the power of the great barons, Edward offered his protection to the gentry, merchants, and serfs by instituting "an exact distribution of justice" and by "a rigid execution of the laws" (*H*, 2:75). He did so by insisting that, as he obeyed Magna Carta with respect to the barons, they too should extend and uphold Magna Carta with respect to their own vassals. He replaced judges that had grown corrupt under the former administration, and he provided the justice system as a whole with force sufficient to execute the law properly (*H*, 2:75). Hume says that by Edward's actions "the face of the kingdom was soon changed; and order and justice took place of violence and oppression" (*H*, 2:75–76). In fact, Hume argues that Edward's legal reforms were the chief advantage which the English attained from his reign—and even more importantly, that Englishmen "still continue to reap" the benefits of Edward's vigor in Hume's day (*H*, 2:141).

From Hume to Smith on English history

Samuel Pufendorf wrote in the preface to *An Introduction to the History of the Principal Kingdoms of States of Europe*:

> I hope therefor, that the Discreet Reader will look favourably upon this Work, not as a Piece design'd for Men of great Learning, but adapted to the Apprehensions and Capacities of young Men, whom I was willing to shew the Way, and, as it were, to give them a tast[e], whereby they might be encouraged to make a further search into this Study. (Pufendorf 2013/1695, 7)

Smith's *Lectures on Jurisprudence* can be read as engaging in the same mission, to impart the history and practice of jurisprudence to his young students. In crafting each lecture, Smith would have distilled the works of a number of writers, to deliver a coherent presentation of the subject matter. Reviewing the course material and preparing a lecture forces the mind to explore multiple potential angles, to see connections between seemingly disjointed phenomena, and to make concrete the abstract. As a result, Smith improved and refined the arguments of a number of great writers, not least Hume.

If a student approached Smith after his lecture to inquire about further reading on feudalism and medieval history, Smith may have pointed him towards the first two volumes of Hume's *History*. Smith cribs from Hume on multiple occasions over the course of his lectures, synthesizing Hume and folding in other bits of information from other sources to round out the lecture's topic. The influence of Hume and his *History* on Smith is clear. The editors of the Liberty Fund edition of the *Lectures* write in their introduction that "Smith's use of Montesquieu is clear from LJ(B), his dependence on Hume's *History* and *Essays* is more pronounced in LJ(A)" (*LJ*, 32). Simply searching on "Hume" in the body of the text of *LJ* yields 53 results, mostly contained in footnotes by the editors showing likeness between what Smith says and things Hume had said previously.

Smith's long discussions of feudal history and law place him in the camp of Hume, Henry Spelman, Matthew Hale, and Robert Brady in their efforts to debunk the idea of the ancient constitution of Edward Coke and the common-law lawyers. By teaching his students about the origins of feudalism and its implications for English legal developments, Smith educated his students against Coke's ideas. Simply by situating the origins of the common law with the Plantagenets kings, he stakes out a position, alongside Hume, against the idea of the ancient constitution.

As Sagar (2021, 17) discusses, Smith gives some importance to juries in his story of English liberty. Hume had a similar appreciation for the jury. He writes in volume I of his *History* that the jury is the best institution "calculated for the preservation of liberty and the administration of justice" (*H*, 1:77). He attributes the innovative legal practice to Alfred the Great's (r. 886–889) "popular and liberal plan" of the administration of justice (*H*, 1:77).

We moderns think of juries as an obvious form of adjudication. But the main competitor of the jury, trial by ordeal, or trial by combat if the dispute involved multiple parties, was a hardy weed. Hume saw trials by ordeal or combat as a mark of barbarism and backwards superstition (*H*, 1:181, 359, 486). Throughout the *History*, Hume uses the existence of ordeals and trial by combat as a way to gauge England's degree of civilization. When trial by ordeal was outlawed in England during the reign of Henry III, Hume wrote that it was "a faint mark of improvement in the age" (*H*, 2:72). Trial by combat would not ever be officially outlawed, but the legal reforms of Henry II brought about its gradual decline (*H*, 1:486). Hume clearly appreciated the importance of trial by jury and its role in developing a legal system that respected liberty.

Another common theme shared by the Smith and Hume is the importance of island geography for the development of British politics. In Hume's *History*, Britain's island geography protects it from would-be military invaders and provides a buffer from continental politics and foreign influence (*H*, 1:11–12, 207, 229, 299–300, 2:362, 522, 3:51, 88, 146, 348, 4:55). Smith extends Hume by explaining how Britain's island geography explains Britain's long tradition of not having a standing army, which Smith argues was the reason Britain did not fall prey to an authoritarian monarch like the French or the Spanish (*LJ(A)* iv.168–169).

Securing liberty or elements of a system of liberty?

I argue above that Hume recognized common law as an important element of English liberty. Elements come together to form compounds, and compounds are in a sense more than the sum of their parts. That brings me to a final point about Sagar's article: I find his grouping of Montesquieu, Hume, and Smith into a two-by-two matrix unsatisfactory. Sagar's Montesquieu thinks English liberty is old and fragile. Sagar's Hume thinks English liberty is new and robust. But after learning of Smith's discussions of the common law, how does Sagar want us to think about Smith?

At points in his article, Sagar seems to suggest that Smith fits into the two-by-two matrix. After discussing Smith's Humean affirmation of the Glorious Reformation, Sagar writes: "But this did not mean that English liberty was only as old as 1688, as Hume concluded" (2021, 15). After his account of Smith on the common law, Sagar suggests that Smith thought liberty to be new, but not as new as Hume: "But as a result, English liberty was much older in its core elements than the reforms effected by the Glorious Revolution alone" (ibid., 19). Does Sagar mean to suggest that Smith thought English liberty was mostly secured in 1307?

At other points, Sagar seems to suggest that Smith does not fit neatly into one of the cells of the two-by-two matrix. Instead, Sagar suggests that Smith saw the common law as an element of English liberty, much as I say that Hume did. Sagar (2021, 15) writes that although Smith understands the importance of the Glorious Revolution, Smith believes the 17th-century reforms stuck because they were "grafted onto, and [were] greatly enhanced by, a wider preexisting legal framework."

In the conclusion of his paper, Sagar poses a puzzle to the reader:

> [T]here remains obscurity in Smith's account as to how exactly his Humean story of England's constitutional liberty being secured in 1688 meshes with his jurisprudential account of liberty in terms of the security delivered by the common law as already being largely in place before the late seventeenth century, and which (if either) he considers most important. (Sagar 2021, 19)

Reading Smith and Hume as articulating important elements of English liberty helps to resolve Sagar's puzzle. The common law did not secure liberty in England; rather it was a single element in liberty's development.

After recognizing that Smith and Hume thought of the common law as an important element, it does not necessarily follow that they felt English liberty was robust. If it was so robust, why would Smith need to mount an extensive case for liberty in *The Wealth of Nations?* Why outline and argue for his vision of a liberal England if liberty were robustly secured by the Glorious Revolution and its aftermath?

Conclusion

On a careful reading of Hume's *History*, and from an awareness of Smith's pervasive cribbing from Hume, Sagar (2021) may wish to reconsider the gap he sees between Smith and Hume on the importance of English common law for the development of liberty. Smith should be seen as distilling, developing, and even disseminating Hume's interpretations. Smith's treatment of the Edwardian common-law reforms is similar to Hume's in terms of both the factual account and its importance for the English constitution. The development of the English common law can be read in Hume as a byproduct of the increasing power of the crown at the expense of the violent and licentious barons. With the local authority of the barons suppressed, and finally put to rest sometime between the Battle of Bosworth and the reign of Elizabeth I, England's stability was enhanced, allowing a more regular plan of liberty to take root and grow into a salient characteristic feature of the British state.

References

Baker, John H. 1995. Personal Liberty Under the Common Law of England, 1200–1600. In *The Origins of Modern Freedom in the West*, ed. R. W. Davis, 178–202. Stanford, Cal.: Stanford University Press.

Berman, Harold J. 1983. *The Formation of the Western Legal Tradition*. Cambridge, Mass.: Harvard University Press.

Forbes, Duncan. 1985. *Hume's Philosophical Politics*. London: Cambridge University Press.

Hall, Jacob R., and Daniel B. Klein. 2020. Jural Pluralism and Jural Integration in David Hume's *History of England*: A Compendium of 142 Quotes. *GMU Working Paper in Economics* (George Mason University, Fairfax, Va.) 20-36.

Hogue, Arthur. 1986 [1966]. *Origins of the Common Law*. Indianapolis: Liberty Fund.

Hume, David. 1983 (*H*). *The History of England from the Invasion of Julius Caesar to the Revolution in 1688*, ed. W. B. Todd, 6 vols. Indianapolis: Liberty Fund.

Hume, David. 1994. *Essays, Moral, Political, and Literary*, ed. Eugene F. Miller. Indianapolis: Liberty Fund.

Klein, Daniel B., and Erik W. Matson. 2020. Mere-Liberty in David Hume. In *A Companion to David Hume*, ed. Moris Polanco, 125–160. Guatemala City: Universidad Francisco Marroquin.

Mossner, Ernest C. 2001. *The Life of David Hume*. Oxford, UK: Oxford University Press.

Pollock, Frederick, and Frederic Maitland. 2010 [1895]. *The History of English Law before the Time of Edward I*, 2 vols. Indianapolis: Liberty Fund.

Pufendorf, Samuel. 2013 [1695]. *An Introduction to the History of the Principal Kingdoms and States of Europe*, ed. Michael J. Seidler, trans. Jodocus Crull. Indianapolis: Liberty Fund.

Sabl, Andrew. 2012. *Hume's Politics*. Princeton, N.J.: Princeton University Press.

Sagar, Paul. 2021. On the Liberty of the English: Adam Smith's Reply to Montesquieu and Hume. *Political Theory* 50(3): 381–404.

Siedentop, Larry. 2014. *Inventing the Individual*. Cambridge, Mass.: Harvard University Press.

Smith, Adam. 1976 [1776] (*WN*). *The Wealth of Nations*, ed. R. H. Campbell and A. S. Skinner, 2 vols. Oxford, UK: Oxford University Press.

Smith, Adam. 1982 (*LJ*). *Lectures on Jurisprudence*, ed. R. L. Meek, D. D. Raphael, and P. G. Stein. Oxford, UK: Oxford University Press.

Weingast, Barry R. 2015. Adam Smith's Industrial Organization of Religion: Explaining the Medieval Church's Monopoly and Its Breakdown in the Reformation. Working paper, October 18.

Weingast, Barry R. 2016. The Medieval Expansion of Long-Distance Trade: Adam Smith on the Town's Escape from the Violent and Low-Growth Feudal Equilibrium. *Stanford Law and Economics Olin Working Paper* (Stanford University, Stanford, Cal.) 492.

Weingast, Barry R. 2017. Adam Smith's Theory of Violence and the Political Economics of Development. In *Organizations, Civil Society, and the Roots of Development*, ed. Naomi R. Lamoreaux and John Joseph Wallis, 51–82. Chicago: University of Chicago Press.

Whelan, Frederick G. 2004. *Hume and Machiavelli: Political Realism and Liberal Thought*. Lanham, Md.: Lexington Books.

Adam Smith in Love

F. E. *Guerra-Pujol*[1]

> *Is any resentment so keen as what follows the quarrels of lovers, or any love so passionate as what attends their reconcilement?*
> —Adam Smith (1980a/1795, 36)

Was Adam Smith speaking from personal experience when he posed those questions?[2] Here I report on my investigations into the matter.

An investigation into someone's love life is not the sort of endeavor that Smith would have ever undertaken. At the same time, if someone had ever produced such a report on, say, Montaigne or Grotius, we can imagine Smith glancing at it. The authors we most admire and learn from are human beings, and their character, personality, and private lives often figure into our understandings of their works. In the present report on Smith's love life, I do not turn to interpreting Smith's works, notably *The Theory of Moral Sentiments*, which contains several substantive passages about romantic love and about lust and licentiousness.[3] Instead, I presuppose that the reader has a natural and

---

1. I thank Alain Alcouffe and three anonymous reviewers for their comments, clarifications, and suggestions.
2. This quotation appears in Section 1 of Smith's essay on "The History of Astronomy." Although "The History of Astronomy" was first published in 1795 along with some other writings of Smith, it is more likely than not that Smith first wrote this particular essay during his young adult years prior to his appointment at the University of Glasgow in 1751 (see Luna 1996, 133, 150 n.3).
3. Smith's discussion of romantic love appears in Book 1, Section 2, Chapters 1 and 2 of *The Theory of Moral Sentiments*, while his rebuke of lust and licentiousness appears in his critique of the ideas of Bernard Mandeville in Book 7, Section 2, Chapter 4. It is also worth noting that Smith's philosophical analysis of romantic love has generated significant scholarly commentary. See, for example, Den Uyl and Griswold 1996; Dawson 2013; Harkin 2013b; Tegos 2019. No evidence exists to indicate whether any of these passages are autobiographical in nature; nevertheless, Smith's treatment of romantic love in *The Theory of Moral Sentiments* seems consistent with a man who may have himself once fallen in love.

healthy curiosity about Smith's personal life, including his love life.

To begin with, previous scholars have adopted different stances when writing about Smith's love life. Some (Heilbroner 1999; Muller 1993; Ginzberg 1934; Mackay 1896; Haldane 1887) simply avoid the subject altogether. Others (Fay 2011, 144; Phillipson 2010, 136; Ross 2010, 227–228; Weinstein 2001, 8–10) entertain the possibility of love affairs, but do so reluctantly, either relegating their romantic speculations to a footnote (Stewart 1980/1811, 349–350) or merely alluding in passing to the possibility of Smith falling in love during his days as a travelling tutor in France (Ross 2010, 227–228; Buchan 2006, 77–78; Scott 1936, 404; Rae 1895, 212–213). By way of example, Edith Kuiper (2013, 69–70) devotes time and attention to "Smith's romantic relationships" and concludes that information about his love life is "scarce." Gavin Kennedy (2005, 4–5) addresses the possibility of numerous "love interests" in the opening pages of his intellectual biography of Smith—but calls the possibility "speculation." Dennis Rasmussen (2017, 131) refers to reports of Smith's dalliances as "rumors," while Nicholas Phillipson (2010, 136) refers to these reports as "gossip."

I do not fault Smith biographers for treating the gossip, rumors, and speculations lightly. But gossip and rumors might be true, and a careful look at all of the evidence is in order. Although his lifelong devotion to his intellectual life and to his widowed mother Margaret Douglas may have prevented him from getting married and forming his own household, the evidence shows that it is more likely than not that Smith fell in love on multiple occasions.

With a view toward systematizing the available evidence and extending the work of previous scholars, I will first put Smith's love life in historical context by describing the strict ecclesiastical regulation of sex in the Scotland of his youth. Next, I will reassemble the available evidence. Specifically, I shall present the following five pieces of primary evidence regarding Smith's loves:

- an obscure but intriguing end note that was first published in the second edition of Dugald Stewart's biography of Smith's life and writings;
- a private letter dated July 14, 1784, addressed to Stewart;
- a brief anecdote by Henry Mackenzie, a prominent Scottish lawyer and writer and a co-founder (along with Stewart) of the Royal Society of Edinburgh;

- a personal letter dated September 18, 1766, written by one of Smith's closest friends and confidants, containing details about Smith's love life; and
- a letter of introduction dated sometime in October 1766 authored in the hand of a possible love interest, Madame Marie-Jeanne Riccoboni.

In addition to the presentation of this body of evidence, I draw reasonable inferences, make several conjectures, and consider a few hypotheses concerning Smith's sexuality and romantic attachments. I then conclude by speculating about Smith's desire to have his papers destroyed and about the possibility of a lost travel diary from his Grand Tour.

The ecclesiastical regulation of sex in the Scotland of Smith's youth

One of the most regulated aspects of Scottish life during Smith's lifetime was sex (Hardy 1978; Mitchison and Leneman 2001). Smith's world was one in which intellectual life and sexual activity were strictly monitored by Church elders, and nowhere was the regulation of sexual morality more oppressive than in Scotland.[4] During Smith's lifetime, every parish in Scotland had its own ecclesiastic or church court. These parish courts or 'kirk sessions' had jurisdiction over every parishioner's private and public conduct, including over all matters of sexual morality. According to historians Rosalind Mitchison and Leah Leneman (2001), during Smith's lifetime the great majority of these church cases consisted of sexual matters.[5] Mitchison and Leneman have also painted a detailed picture of the repressive nature of Smith's world and of the roving jurisdiction of these parish courts or kirk sessions over sex:

> In the early modern period every parish in Scotland had its own church court (the kirk session) dealing with matters of conduct and morality. Drunkenness,

---

4. See generally Mitchison and Leneman 2001; Leneman and Mitchison 1987; 1988. For an overview of the legal and ecclesiastical regulation of sex in Scotland prior to the birth of Smith, see Hardy 1978.
5. Mitchison and Leneman (2001) survey over 8,000 church court records spread across 78 Scottish parishes from the mid-seventeenth to mid-eighteenth centuries.

sabbath breaking, slander, riotous behavior—all these came under the aegis of the session. However, partly through a sharper defining line between the roles of lay and of ecclesiastical jurisdictions, by the mid-eighteenth century the great majority of cases were of a sexual nature.... (Leneman and Mitchison 1988, 483)

Leneman and Mitchison (1988, 483) also emphasize "[t]he thoroughness with which these cases were pursued." By way of example:

The usual train of events was for an unmarried girl to be reported as 'with child' at a meeting of the kirk session and to be cited to appear at the next meeting. At that time she would be asked to name the man who had been guilty with her, and that man would in turn be cited to appear at a forthcoming meeting. Unless a case were in some way unusual, for instance if the man denied fornication with the woman, further enquiry would not normally be made into the circumstances surrounding the act. However, for some unknown reason, certain parishes in the Western Highlands and certain parishes in Fife often went on to ask where, when and how often intercourse had taken place. (Leneman and Mitchison 1988, 483)

Moreover, even marital sex in anticipation of marriage or 'ante-nuptial fornication' was a sin, though there was a disconnect between official Church doctrine and informal social norms on the matter of pre-marital sex.[6]

Thus, the sex lives of parishioners in the Scotland of Smith's youth were strictly monitored by Church elders, and the penalties for fornication, adultery, and other such moral offenses consisted of shaming penalties, or "penance on the pillar" (Leneman and Mitchison 1988, 495). Although Smith's theism and views of religion are unclear,[7] a cautious and careful scholar of Smith's stature would most likely not have wanted to incur such penalties as they would have derailed his prestigious academic career and lucrative private tutoring opportunities. These general observations must thus be kept in mind when exploring the question: Who were Smith's loves?

---

6. For ordinary people, betrothal was a part of marriage, and as such it made sexual intercourse permissible. Church elders, however, generally did not approve of such 'irregular' marriage. For the Church, a marriage required the public exchange of promises in the presence of the parish minister (Gillis 1985, 52–54; see also Hardy 1978, chs. 4 and 5).
7. Or in the words of Margaret Jacob (2019, 128, 126), "Adam Smith kept his religious beliefs very private" and "[his] private religious beliefs will probably never be known."

The evidence

Rasmussen (2017, 131) reports of "occasional rumors, throughout Smith's life, of potential romantic connections" but concludes that "none of them amounted to much."[8] Similarly, Ian Simpson Ross (1995; 2010), the scholar who has painted the most comprehensive picture to date of Smith's possible amorous interludes (2010, 227–228), concludes that "the biographer can do little more with the topic of Smith's sex life than contribute a footnote to the history of sublimation." Information about Smith's romantic encounters is admittedly "scarce" (Kuiper 2013, 62), but it is not non-existent. At least five separate pieces of primary evidence mention or refer to Smith's love life.[9]

Dugald Stewart's "Note (H.)"

The earliest published reference to Smith's love life appears in 1811, 21 years after Smith's death, in the very last endnote—"Note (H.)"—of the third and fourth editions of Dugald Stewart's biographical essay "An Account of the Life and Writings of Adam Smith" (Stewart 1811a, 150; 1811b, 552).[10] Stewart's enigmatic note reads in full as follows:

> In the early part of Mr Smith's life *it is well known to his friends*, that he was for several years attached to a young lady of great beauty and accomplishment. How far his addresses were favourably received, or what the circumstances

---

8. It is unclear whether the "them" in this passage refers to the rumors of Smith's romantic connections or to Smith's possible romances themselves. Harkin (2013a, 502) notes a "complete dearth of information" about Smith's love life, while Weinstein (2001, 10) describes Smith's romantic life as "virtually non-existent."

9. More significantly, the authors of these five separate sources of information—these five historical witnesses, so to speak—all knew Smith personally or knew people who travelled in Smith's social circles.

10. An historical aside is in order. Dugald Stewart had originally written his biography of Smith in the early 1790s and had read his "Account of the Life and Writings of Adam Smith" to members of the Royal Society of Edinburgh on January 21 and March 18 of the year 1793. He then published his biographical essay in 1794 in Volume 3 of the *Transactions of the Royal Society of Edinburgh*. A second edition of this essay was then published in 1795 in a book titled *Essays on Philosophical Subjects*. Neither the 1794 edition of Stewart's essay nor the 1795 one, however, contain any notes or any reference to Smith's love life. As a further aside, "Note (H.)" subsequently became "Note (K.)" when additional end notes were added to the 1858 edition of Stewart's biographical essay (see Ross 1980, 265–268, who provides a complete list of the first five editions of Stewart's biography of Smith).

were which prevented their union, I have not been able to learn; but I believe it is pretty certain that, after this disappointment, he laid aside all thoughts of marriage. The lady to whom I allude died also unmarried. She survived Mr Smith for a considerable number of years, and was alive long after the publication of the first edition of this Memoir. I had the pleasure of seeing her when she was turned of eighty, and when she still retained evident traces of her former beauty. The powers of her understanding and the gaiety of her temper seemed to have suffered nothing from the hand of time. (Stewart 1980/1811, 349–350, my emphasis)

Ian Simpson Ross (2010, 227) describes this early love interest as "a Fife lady whom he [Smith] had loved very much," but neither Ross nor Stewart provides any additional evidence about the geographical location of this love affair; nor do they identify this woman by name.[11] Nevertheless, if this love affair occurred in the Kirkcaldy of Smith's youth, a small parish with a population around 1500 at the time (Heilbroner 1999, 46), it should not be impossible to identify the lady. I explore this matter further in the next part of this paper.[12]

Regardless of the question of geographical location, Stewart is a credible witness to an attachment "well known" to Smith's friends. Stewart knew Smith and many of Smith's acquaintances.[13] Also, to give the reader some idea of Stewart's stature and sterling reputation, he co-founded—along with Henry Mackenzie, a Scottish lawyer, novelist, and writer whom we shall re-encounter soon—the Royal Society of Edinburgh in 1783 and held the chair of moral philosophy at the University of Edinburgh for thirty-five years, from 1785 until 1820.[14] Why would Stewart risk sullying his own reputation (and that of his friend Smith) by reporting mere gossip or an unfounded rumor?

---

11. Fay (2011/1956, 144) refers to her as the "Maid of Fife."

12. For what it is worth, Alain Alcouffe and Andrew Moore (2018, 15 n.18) identify Smith's "lady of Fife" as Lady Janet Anstruther, who "was renowned for her beauty and for her reputation as a flirt." Dugald Stewart's original "Note (H.)," however, refers to a lost love "in the early part of Mr. Smith's life," while Alcouffe and Moore are referring to "a famous lady of Fife in the 1760's," when Smith would have been in his late 30s and early-to-mid 40s. Also, Lady Janet is said by one source to have died at the age of 76 in 1802, so she may not have lived to see her 80th birthday.

13. Or in the words of Alain Alcouffe and Philippe Massot-Bordenave (2020, x): "Dugald Stewart...had the advantage of having been close to both Smith and witnesses to his life."

14. For more information about Stewart's contributions to the Scottish Enlightenment, see Haakonssen 1984; Rashid 1985; Wood 2000.

James Currie's letter to Stewart in 1794 about a French connection

A next relevant item is a letter dated July 14, 1794, addressed to Stewart (Currie 1831, 317–320). This personal correspondence is signed by one James Currie (1756–1805), a medical doctor who was then residing in Liverpool, and is addressed to "Dugald Stewart, Esq." This letter is important because it contains a second-hand account of a second Smith love affair.

Before proceeding any further, however, why did Currie write this letter to Stewart? Since Dugald Stewart's biography of Smith was read to the members of the Royal Society of Edinburgh in January and March of 1793 and then appeared in published form a year later (1794), it is possible that Currie himself may have obtained a copy of this first edition of Stewart's biography of Smith. Or, Currie may have heard about Stewart's biography from someone who, in turn, had either heard or read Stewart's account.[15] Currie writes to Stewart with the intention of providing further proof of an affair involving Smith. Although this evidence consists of a second-hand report, Currie states that his source of information, a "Captain Lloyd," spent considerable time with Smith and with Smith's student Henry Scott, the Third Duke of Buccleuch,[16] during their three-year Grand Tour in the mid-1760s.[17] Currie writes:

Another source from which I have heard much of Dr. Smith, was the infor-

---

15. The first edition of Stewart's biography of Smith was published in the third volume of *The Transactions of the Royal Society of Edinburgh* in 1794.

16. For an in-depth biography of the Third Duke of Buccleuch, as well as a portrait and family tree, see Alcouffe and Massot-Bordenave (2020, 28–34); for a short biography of Duke Henry, see Valentine 1970, 2:773.

17. For a summary of Smith's travels in France see generally Ross 2010, ch. 13, as well as Rae 1895, chs. 12–14. (For a map and detailed timeline of Smith's extensive travels in the South of France, see also Alcouffe and Massot-Bordenave 2020, xiii–xiv, xviii–xix.) In summary, Duke Henry's stepfather, Charles Townsend, had appointed Smith to be the future Duke's private tutor and chaperone, and Smith personally supervised Duke Henry's Grand Tour from early 1764 through the fall of 1766. Duke Henry, a direct descendant of King Charles II of England and King Henry IV of France, was born into one of the wealthiest and most prestigious families in Scotland, and upon coming of age in September of 1767, Smith's pupil would become one of Scotland's largest landowners (see generally Alcouffe and Massot-Bordenave 2020, 28–34; Valentine 1970, 2:773). For a description of Duke Henry's landholdings and his lifelong friendship with Smith, see Bonnyman 2014.

mation of a Captain Lloyd, who was much in [Smith's] intimacy in France; and who passed the whole time that he spent at Abbeville with the Duke of [Buccleuch], in his society. Captain Lloyd was bred a soldier, but left the army early. He is one of the most interesting and most accomplished men I ever knew. (Currie 1831, 317–318)[18]

Currie says further: "I could perceive from many circumstances [that Smith and Lloyd] were on a footing of great intimacy; and many curious particulars of the Doctor's [Smith's] conduct he has related" (Currie 1831, 318). Among these "curious particulars" are the allegations that Smith "was deeply in love with an English lady" during his sojourn in Abbeville.[19] Currie's report reads as follows:

Dr. Smith, it seems, while at Abbeville, was deeply in love with an English lady there. What seems more singular, a French Marquise, a woman of talents and *esprit*, was smitten, or thought herself smitten, with the Doctor, and made violent attempts to obtain his friendship. She was just come from Paris, ... [and she] was determined to obtain his friendship; but after various attempts was obliged to give the matter up. Dr. Smith had not the easy and natural manner of Mr. Hume.... He [Smith] was abstracted and inattentive. He could not endure this French woman, and was, besides, *dying for another*. (Currie 1831, 318–319, my emphasis)

---

18. Hirst (1904, 131) speculates that Captain Lloyd was "doubtless on a patriotic visit to the field of Crecy" when he reportedly met Smith and Duke Henry in Abbeville.

19. The precise date of Smith's stay in Abbeville and his reasons for visiting there are unclear. In an unpublished paper, I speculate that Smith may have travelled to Abbeville to witness the execution of the Chevalier de La Barre, who became the last man in Europe to be put to death for the crime of blasphemy. For detailed histories of this case, see Claverie 1992; 1994; Chassaigne 1920. At the time, "l'affaire du Chevalier de La Barre" attracted attention across France—even attracting the sustained notice of the celebrated atheist and free-thinker Voltaire, who wrote not one but two accounts of the young de La Barre's prosecution and sentence (see Voltaire 2000/1766; 2000/1775. (Voltaire's first essay about this case is dated 15 July 1766, but some scholars believe this essay was actually written in 1767 or 1768.) For a summary of Voltaire's involvement in this notorious case, see Claverie 1994; see also Braden 1965, 58–65. Also, this case has become so central to the identity and history of modern France that many streets are named after the Chevalier de La Barre and many monuments were subsequently erected in his honor, including a statue standing at the gates of the famous Sacred Heart Cathedral in the Montmarte neighborhood of Paris. A picture of this particular monument to de La Barre is available online. Alas, this monument was taken down during the Second World War on orders of Marshal Philippe Pétain and melted down (Caulcutt 2020).

Currie then concludes his July 1794 letter by offering to put Stewart in touch with Captain Lloyd. Alas, no evidence exists of further communication between Lloyd and Stewart or between Stewart and Currie.

Henry Mackenzie's recollections of Miss Campbell

The next piece of primary evidence comes from Henry Mackenzie (1745–1831), a distinguished Scottish lawyer and popular novelist who, as I mentioned previously, co-founded, along with Stewart, the Royal Society of Edinburgh.[20] According to Ross (2010, 227), Mackenzie knew Smith personally and "was much in Smith's company when he [Smith] lived in Edinburgh in the last twelve years of his life."

Toward the end of his long and remarkable life, Mackenzie jotted down a series of personal recollections, hoping to have these memories published in a book of "anecdotes and egotisms," as Mackenzie himself referred to them (Fieser 2003, 251). Mackenzie's wide-ranging collection of anecdotes was eventually assembled by Harold William Thompson and published by Oxford University Press in 1927.[21] Among other things, Mackenzie's collection of anecdotes includes an entry with the title of "Smith and Hume in Love." The first part of Mackenzie's brief recollection about Smith is quoted in full below:

> Adam Smith [was] seriously in love with Miss Campbell of _____ (the name is so numerous that to use it cannot be thought personal), a woman of as different dispositions and habits from him as possible. (Mackenzie 1927, 176; reprinted in Fieser 2003, 255, omission and parenthetical remark both appear in the original)[22]

Who was "Miss Campbell of _____"? When exactly did Smith fall

---

20. For a sketch of Mackenzie's life as well as his contributions to Scottish letters, see Scott 1834; Drescher 2004; see also Fay 2011, 2; Valentine 1970, 2:567–568.
21. Thompson wrote his dissertation on Mackenzie. For an overview of Thompson's life and work, see Caplan, French, and Mineka 1964.
22. About David Hume, Mackenzie goes on to write (1927, 176; reprinted in Fieser 2003, 255): "His friend, David Hume, was deeply smitten with a very amiable young lady, a great friend of mine, Miss Nancy Ord, but the disparity of age prevented his proposing to her, which he once intended. She was a great admirer of his, and he was a frequent guest at her father's, where I met him, and made one of his whist party with the young lady and some other person. I played well at the time and so did she. D. Hume was vain of his playing whist. That game has much of observation in it, and such games best suit a thinking man."

in love with her? And what, if anything, became of this romance? In a parenthetical remark, Mackenzie implies that "Campbell" was a common last name—a "name so numerous that to use it cannot be thought personal"—so that he is not giving anything way by identifying "Miss Campbell" as the object of Smith's affections. That said, could Mackenzie's Miss Campbell nevertheless be the same "young lady of great beauty and accomplishment" that Stewart refers to in Note (H.)—now Note (K.)—of his biography of Smith? Or could Mackenzie perhaps be referring to Lady Frances Scott (1750–1817), the daughter of Caroline Campbell Scott and Duke Henry's younger sister? This conjecture is not far-fetched, especially considering Mackenzie's observation that the woman was "of as different dispositions and habits from him as possible"—she being the daughter of a wealthy aristocratic family and he an absent-minded professor. Smith corresponded with Lady Frances on multiple occasions, and both lived at Dalkeith House during the fall of 1767.[23] Further below, however, I explain why it seems unlikely that the Miss Campbell in Mackenzie's anecdote is the young Lady Frances.

Colbert's letter of September 1766: a smoking arrow?

There is a fourth piece of primary evidence, a long French-language letter addressed to Smith and to his teenage pupil, Henry Scott, the Third Duke of Buccleuch.[24] The identity of the letter's author is disguised under an abbreviated and jocular pseudonym: "Le Gr. Vic. Eccossois," which stands for Grand Viccaire Eccossois (Smith 1987, 165). Nevertheless, it is most likely that this French-speaking "Great Scottish Vicar" was none other than Seignelay Colbert de Castle-Hill, also known as Abbé Colbert, a fellow Scotsman and Smith's "chief guide and friend" during his extended 18-month sojourn in the South of France (Rae 1895, 176).[25] In one passage of this

---

23. At least three letters by Smith addressed to Lady Frances survive: nos. 97, 98, and 225 in Smith 1987. For details regarding Smith's stay at Dalkeith, see Bonnyman 2014, 58–59.
24. At the time this contemporaneous letter was composed, Smith was serving as a private tutor and chaperone for Duke Henry—and for his younger brother Hew Campbell Scott as well, who had joined them in Toulouse subsequently (see Alcouffe and Massot-Bordenave 2020, chs. 1 and 2; Bonnyman 2014, ch. 2; Ross 2010, ch. 13).
25. It is also worth noting that Colbert would eventually be appointed the Bishop of Rodez (Alcouffe and Massot-Bordenave 2020, 63–64), but at the time of Smith's travels in France, Colbert had been appointed as one of the vicars general of the diocese of Toulouse in the South of France. For an overview of Abbé Colbert's life and career as well as an illuminating

intimate letter, dated September 18, 1766,[26] the author refers in jest to some of Smith's romantic attachments, including one by name:

> Et tu, Adam Smith, philosophe de Glasgow, heros et idole des high-broad Ladys, que fais tu, mon cher ami? Comment gouvernes tu La duchesse d'Anville et Mad. de Boufflers, ou ton coeur est il toujours epris des charms de Mad. Nicol et des apparent apparens que laches de cette autre dame de Fife, que vous aimees tant? (letter dated 18 September 1766, National Archives of Scotland, GD224/2040/62/3, quoted in Alcouffe and Moore 2018)

Translated, the passage is:

> And you, Adam Smith, Glasgow philosopher, high-broad Ladies' hero and idol, what are you doing my dear friend? How do you govern the Duchess of Anville and Madame de Boufflers, where your heart is always in love with Madame Nicol and with the attractions as apparent as hidden of this lady of Fife that you loved. (as translated in Alcouffe and Massot-Bordenave 2020, 260)[27]

This letter of 1766 is a crucial piece of evidence for two reasons. First of all, it is the first primary source to mention Smith's love interest in France by name, and secondly, it is the first source to pinpoint the geographical location in Scotland of Smith's first love. Does "this hidden lady of Fife" refer to the same woman mentioned in Note (H.) of Stewart's biography of Smith? Does "Madame Nicol" refer to the love interest in Abbeville mentioned in James Currie's hearsay report?[28] Either way, Colbert's testimony is a highly credible source by any measure. He became Smith's closest friend and confidant during Smith's sojourn in Toulouse (March 1764 to November 1765), and he even travelled with Smith and Duke Henry to Bordeaux and

---

summary of his relationship to Smith, see Alcouffe and Massot-Bordenave 2020, 54–66.

26. Private correspondence dated September 18, 1766, located in the National Archives of Scotland, GD224/2040/62/3. The letter is reprinted in full in Alcouffe and Massot-Bordenave 2020, 260–261. The *Correspondence of Adam Smith* edited by Ernest Campbell Mossner and Ian Simpson Ross incorrectly dates the letter as "February 18, 1766" (letter 91 in Smith 1987). As a result, at least two scholarly sources (Buchan 2006, 77; Kuiper 2013, 76 n.11) incorrectly identify the date of this letter as February 18, 1766, instead of September 18, 1766. Also, Kuiper (2013, 76 n.11) incorrectly attributes the authorship of this letter to David Hume.

27. For slightly different translations of Abbé Colbert's letter of September 18, 1766, see Ross 2010, 227; Buchan 2006, 77; Smith 1987, 111).

28. Ross (2010, 227) reads the two letters in this way.

to other places in the South of France during this 18-month period (Alcouffe and Massot-Bordenave 2020, 216–217; see also Rae 1895, 179). Colbert got to know Smith the man, for the jocular and intimate tone of his letter suggests camaraderie and close connections, or in the words of Alain Alcouffe and Philippe Massot-Bordenave (2020, 217), the letter "is probably a private correspondence between friends who have established trust."

Riccoboni's letter of October 1766

The last piece of primary evidence is a letter from Madame Marie-Jeanne Riccoboni dated sometime in October of 1766.[29] Although Riccoboni is little remembered today, she was a highly accomplished actress in the Théâtre-Italien, located in the Hôtel de Bourgogne of Paris,[30] and an illustrious *femme de lettres*, one of the best-selling novelists of her day (Darnton 1998, 255). Riccoboni became acquainted with Smith during his extended residency in Paris in 1766.

Recall that Smith, along with Duke Henry and the Duke's younger brother Hew Campbell Scott, had returned to Paris in late 1765 or early 1766. At some point thereafter, perhaps in the Parisian salon of the Baron d'Holbach,[31] did Smith and Riccoboni become acquainted (Nicholls 1976, 16). Riccoboni described the impression Smith had made during their first meeting in a private letter dated May 21, 1766:

> Two Englishmen have arrived here. One [David Hume] is a friend of Garrick's; the other is Scottish; my God what a Scot! He speaks with difficulty through big teeth, and he's ugly as the devil. He's Mr. Smith, author of a book I haven't read. I speak to him about Scotland, and especially about mountains. (quoted in Dawson 2018, 6)

Whatever Smith lacked in looks or vocal refinement, however, he must have made up with his intellect and personality, for Riccoboni quickly devel-

---

29. I wish to thank Alain Alcouffe for bringing this correspondence to my attention.
30. For a history of this celebrated theater, see Roy 1995.
31. Baron d'Holbach (Paul-Henri Thiry) was a philosopher, translator, and devotee of the French Enlightenment who played a prominent role in Parisian intellectual circles through his salon. The guest list of his salon included many of the most prominent intellectual and political figures in Europe (see LeBuffe 2020). For an introduction to the institution of the Parisian salon, see Goodman 1994.

oped "a schoolgirl crush on the Scot" (Leddy 2013, 11). In a subsequent letter addressed to fellow actor David Garrick and dated sometime in October 1766, she reveals her feelings for Smith thus:

> I am very pleased with myself, my dear Garrick, to offer you that which I miss very sharply: the pleasure of Mr. Smith's company. I am like a foolish young girl who listens to her lover without ever thinking of loss, which always accompanies pleasure. Scold me, beat me, kill me! But I adore Mr. Smith, I adore him greatly. I wish the devil would take all our philosophes, as long as he returns Mr. Smith to me. (quoted in Leddy 2013, 11; Dawson 2018, 10)

Riccoboni's exuberant confession, however, may very well be an example of unrequited love or simply fondness and affection, as we have no further evidence of any affair between the two. Also, the month of October 1766— the month in which Riccoboni wrote the second letter quoted above—was a fateful moment for the Smith party in Paris, for that was the month that Duke Henry's younger brother died of fever in Paris and Smith and Duke Henry decided to cut short their Grand Tour. It thus seems possible that Riccoboni, writing immediately upon Smith's departure, might have been exaggerating her feelings.

As for Smith's words about Riccoboni, he mentions her in a 1766 letter to Hume (Smith 1987, 113), but, more significantly, Smith ranks her as a novelist among illustrious company in material he introduced in the sixth edition of *The Theory of Moral Sentiments*: "The poets and romance writers, who best paint the refinements and delicacies of love and friendship, and of all other private and domestic affections, Racine and Voltaire, Richardson, Marivaux, and Riccoboni, are, in such cases, much better instructors than Zeno, Chrysippus, or Epictetus" (Smith 1976/1790, 143.14).

To sum up, the evidence presented thus far—Stewart's own testimony in his 1811 "Note (H.)"; Mackenzie's brief 1831 anecdote; and Colbert's intimate 1766 letter—all suggest that Smith had fallen in love on at least two or perhaps three occasions during his life, while additional evidence—Riccoboni's letter of October 1766 as well as Currie's secondhand report in his July 1794 letter to Stewart—indicate that Smith was not lacking in admirers during his sojourn overseas. But who were these ladies?

Inferences and conjectures

I will now draw the most reasonable inferences from the evidence presented above and propose several new concrete conjectures. Given my background in law—I graduated Yale Law School (Class of '93) and teach law and ethics at the University of Central Florida—I will borrow the common law's 'more likely than not' or 'preponderance of the evidence' standard used to try facts in civil cases. I argue that it is more likely than not that Smith did, in fact, fall in love on several occasions in his life.

Smith's first love?: The hidden lady of Fife

Stewart, the only biographer who knew Smith when he was alive, reports from his personal knowledge that it was "well-known to [Smith's] friends that he was for several years attached to a young lady of great beauty and accomplishment," that this attachment occurred "in the early part of Mr Smith's life," and that he (meaning Stewart) had once met the lady in person "when she was turned of eighty" (Stewart 1980/1811, 349, 350). Stewart's *Account* is a professional and circumspect work, choosing its words carefully. Given these facts and their reputable source, I conjecture that this love, Smith's first romantic attachment, would most likely have occurred or begun during the years 1746 to 1748, when the young Smith returned to his hometown, the small coastal community of Kirkcaldy, and lived with his mother for two years after having completed his formal studies at Oxford.[32] Smith would have been between 23 and 25 years old at that stage in his life.

Further, given the small population in Kirkcaldy during Smith's lifetime as well as the existence of detailed Church records for this small parish, it

---

32. In the alternative, it is also possible—but in my view less likely—that Smith's first love may have been a Glaswegian, a resident of the port city of Glasgow, where Smith lived for over 15 years—first from 1737 to 1740, when he was a student at the University of Glasgow, and then from 1751 to 1763, when he held a prestigious professorship there. (For a visual outline of Smith's biography, see that produced by Liberty Fund; see also Wight 2002, App. A, 267–269.) I say, however, "less likely" because Smith would have been very young during his first residency at the University of Glasgow (1737–1740). During the extended period of his second residency in Glasgow (1751–1763), Smith would have been financially independent and thus less dependent on his mother, so we cannot rule out the remote possibility of a lost love in Glasgow. Towards the end of his life, Smith himself once referred to his years in Glasgow "as by far the happiest and most honourable period of my life" (see letter 274 in Smith 1987, dated November 16, 1787; see also Alcouffe and Massot-Bordenave 2020, 4, 12).

is my belief that historians should be able to identify the woman with some confidence.[33] For their part, Alain Alcouffe and Andrew Moore (2018, 15 n.18) have recently identified a reference to "this hidden lady of Fife" in Colbert's September 1766 letter as Lady Janet Anstruther (1725–1802), who "was renowned for her beauty and for her reputation as a flirt."[34] Is this the same lady referred to by Stewart (1980/1811, 349–350) in "Note (H.)," now "Note (K.)," in his first-hand account of Smith's life? Alcouffe and Moore (2018, 15 n.18) speak of "a famous lady of Fife in 1760's." Stewart's "Note (H.)," however, dates this love to "the early part of Mr Smith's life." Also, Stewart mentions in "Note (H.)" that he himself had the pleasure of meeting the lady "when she was turned of eighty," but when exactly did this meeting occur? "Note (H.)" did not appear in published form until 1811, and Stewart states in "Note (H.)" that this lady "survived Mr Smith for a considerable number of years, and was alive long after the publication of the first edition of this Memoir," so the meeting between Stewart and the Smith's first love could have occurred as late as 1810. If she were 80 years old in 1810, then she would have been born in 1730, seven years after Smith's birth in 1723.[35]

For my part, I wonder whether Smith's mother, Margaret Douglas Smith, who was by all accounts a strong-willed and dominating mother (Kuiper 2013),[36] may have objected to any proposed union between her son and this first love. Of course, Smith and the woman may, themselves, one or both, have seen a union as impractical or unwelcome for any number of reasons. But I wish to explore now the specific conjecture of a maternal veto, more or less against the inclinations of the son. Such a conjecture is relevant given what we know about early modern Scottish society as well as Smith's lifelong devotion to his mother.[37]

---

33. According to Heilbroner (1999, 46), Kirkcaldy boasted a population of only 1500 souls at the time of Smith's birth in 1723. See also Jacob (2019, 124), who notes that Edinburgh, the largest city in Scotland during Smith's lifetime, had only about 40,000 residents.

34. There is a 1761 portrait of Lady Anstruther by Sir Joshua Reynolds. I thank Alain Alcouffe for bringing the existence of this beautiful portrait to my attention.

35. Given that Lady Janet Anstruther was reportedly born in 1725, Alcouffe and Moore's conjecture about her might be correct, after all. On the other hand, Stewart writes in his Note (H.) of 1811 that he "had the pleasure of seeing her [Lady Janet?] when she was turned of eighty," but as mentioned previously, Lady Janet is said to have died in 1802, aged 76.

36. There is at least one existing portrait of Margaret Douglas.

37. Or in the words of John Rae (1895, 4): "His mother herself was from the first to last

Margaret Douglas Smith belonged to the landed gentry, descending from a respected landowning family on her mother's side.[38] Adam Smith's complete financial dependence on his mother during this stage of his life must also be noted.[39] Smith was most likely largely financially dependent on the support of his widowed mother until his initial appointment in 1751, at the age of 27, as the Chair of Logic at the University of Glasgow.[40]

Although parental consent was not a legal requirement in early modern Scotland (Leneman 1999, 673; Leneman and Mitchison 1993, 845, 847), it was generally expected that "children should have the consent of their parents, or those 'in loco parentis', to their marriage" (Hardy 1978, 531). The parental consent norm was so pervasive that it "could vary from marriages arranged by parents without consideration being given to the personal wishes of their children to marriages where the child made the selection of marriage partner and the parents were expected to accede to their choice" (ibid.). This parental consent norm makes all the more sense given the economic structure of Scottish society during Smith's lifetime, a neo-feudal and religious society in which property, especially property in land, was held on a family basis.[41]

Smith's second love?: Madame Nicol

Next, I conjecture that Smith may have fallen in love yet again at some

---

the heart of Smith's life." Smith's first biographer, Dugald Stewart (1980), also confirms the central role Margaret Douglas played in Smith's life.

38. *See* Özler 2012, 346–347; Kuiper 2013, 64. For his part, Smith's father—also named Adam Smith—had died a few months before his son Adam was born and had accumulated some wealth during his lifetime, having served as "Judge Advocate for Scotland and Comptroller of the Customs in Kirkcaldy" (Rae 1895, 1). By all accounts, Smith's father left a large income and considerable property to his young widow, Margaret Douglas Smith (see Özler 2012, 346; Kuiper 2013, 64).

39. By way of example, one of Smith's own cousins, Lydia Marianne Douglas, found herself in dire financial straits after she married a man against the will of her parents (see Ross 1995, 401).

40. A year or two after this initial appointment, Smith subsequently accepted the Chair of Moral Philosophy at the University of Glasgow (Heilbroner 1999, 46), a position he held until early 1764, when he departed on his Grand Tour with Duke Henry.

41. *Cf.* Leneman (1999, 675), explaining why some Scottish couples resorted to clandestine marriages: "usually because the man was (or said he was) financially dependent on relations who would not approve of marrying at that stage in his life, or of his choice of wife."

point during his Grand Tour (1764–1766) alongside Duke Henry (Henry Scott Campbell), the Duke of Buccleuch.[42] In 1764 Smith was no advanced senior—he was 41 years old—and one of our primary sources—Colbert's letter of 1766—identifies a Madame Nicol as a possible love interest during Smith's travels in France.[43] More recently, Alain Alcouffe and Philippe Massot-Bordenave (2020, 262) have identified this potential love interest as a resident of Toulouse: "Madame Nicol, the wife of Capitoul Nicol."[44] Was this the same woman with whom Smith is reported to have fallen in love in Abbeville in 1766? Is it possible that Smith had already fallen in love with her during his 18-month stay in the south of France?

The main outline of Smith's travels in France is well known (Ross 2010, Ch. 13; Rae 1895, chs. 12–14). After arriving in Paris on February 13, 1764, Smith and his pupil Duke Henry travelled to the south of France and established a base in the tranquil town of Toulouse, where they lived for many months.[45] They arrived in Toulouse in March of 1764, travelled across the South of France during the summer and autumn of 1764, and returned to Toulouse a second time in January of 1765.[46] At some point upon his return to Toulouse in early 1765, Smith wrote a letter to Charles Townsend, Duke Henry's stepfather and the man who was financing their Grand Tour,

---

42. In setting off for France, the father of modern economics and the young duke were following an elite and well-established tradition, for the Grand Tour was a rite of passage of the sons of elite British families as well as the "'crown' of [their] education" (Cohen 2001, 129; Brodsky-Porges 1981, 178). Michèle Cohen (1992; 2001) has explored the educational and cultural ideals of the Grand Tour and has identified many deep "contradictions and ambiguities" of these tours. In addition, the sexual aspect of Grand Tours by young British aristocrats (and their tutors?) during this era should also not go unnoticed (see, e.g., Chapter 5 of Black 2011/1985, which is titled "Love, Sex, Gambling, and Drinking;" see also Black 1981, 660, 666 n.7; Black 1984, 413–414; Cohen 1992, 255–256).

43. In the alternative, could this Madame Nicol refer to the Marie-Louise-Nicole Elizabeth (1716–1794), the duchesse d'Anville? According to Mossner and Ross (in Smith 1987, 111 n.3), Marie-Louise-Nicole—with her son, the young Duc de La Rochefoucauld—met Smith in Geneva at the end of 1765.

44. Although Alcouffe and Massot-Bordenave (2020, 262) provide additional details about Madame Nicol's husband, Jacques Nicol de Montblanc, a wealthy Anglophile Frenchman who presided over the Mont Blanc Estate in the present Croix Daurade district of Toulouse, they do not provide any further details about Madame Nicol.

45. Smith and Duke Henry were subsequently joined by the Duke's younger brother, Hew Campbell Scott.

46. See the timeline in Bonnyman 2014, xiii–xiv; see also chs. 4 and 5.

requesting permission to relocate to Paris.[47] Was Smith hoping to leave Toulouse to avoid public scrutiny or to arrange a *rendezvous* with Madame Nicol, i.e., away from her husband, Capitoul Nicol?

Either way, Charles Townsend granted Smith's request in a letter dated April 22, 1765,[48] but two points are worth noting. First, Smith and Duke Henry did not leave the South of France for good until the fall of 1765,[49] so for some unknown reason Smith was apparently in no hurry to leave Toulouse, after all (Alcouffe and Massot-Bordenave 2020, 285). Did this change of itinerary have anything to with the aforementioned Madame Nicol?

Secondly, Townsend warns his stepson in his April 22, 1765 letter "against any female attachment" (Ross 1974, 184). The relevant part of Townsend's April 22 letter reads as follows:

> If you go much into mixed company, as I suppose you will, let me warn you against any female attachment. Your rank & fortune will put women of subtle characters upon projects which you should not be the dupe of, for such connexions make a young man both ridiculous & unhappy. Gallantry is one thing; attachment is another; a young man should manifest spirit & decorum even in this part of his character, & preserve his mind entire & free in lesser as well as greater things. (Ross 1974, 184)

Townsend's warning to his stepson Duke Henry was not an academic or abstract admonition, for a fellow contemporary with personal knowledge of Townsend's habits and dispositions, Lady Louisa Stuart (1985/1827, 38), describes Duke Henry's stepfather as "a man of pleasure, a libertine." In any case, could Townsend's warning "against any female attachment" have been meant for Smith as well?

---

47. According to Alcouffe and Massot-Bordenave (2020, 283), it was Smith—not his pupils Henry and Hew—who wanted to relocate from Toulouse to Paris. Alcouffe and Massot-Bordenave even speculate that Smith was becoming "impatient."
48. This letter is reprinted in full in Ross (1974, 182–184) and in Alcouffe and Massot-Bordenave (2020, 284–285).
49. Smith and Duke Henry, along with the Duke's younger brother Hew Campbell Scott, eventually returned to the City of Lights sometime during the month of February of 1766 (see Guerra-Pujol 2022), where they resided until the month of October of that same year, until Hew's tragic and untimely death. *Cf.* Ross (1995, 209): "it has been assumed that Smith and his pupils [Hew and Henry] travelled to Paris from Geneva in December 1765." See also the timeline in Alcouffe and Massot-Bordenave 2020, xiii–xiv.

Sex in the City of Light: The Paris theater scene

Previously, we presented evidence regarding Madame Riccoboni. It is worth mentioning that Riccoboni, an accomplished actress and novelist, and Smith, an admirer of the stage, were by all accounts avid theater and opera fans, especially during Smith's stay in the City of Lights.[50] Indeed, "it is very likely Smith took recommendations from Riccoboni as to which theatrical performances to attend" (Dawson 2018, 8), and so it is not far-fetched to imagine to them attending a play or opera or concert together.

Many Smith scholars have failed to mention that these theatrical venues were the center of an elite Parisian sexual marketplace, the famed *dames entretenues* or "kept women" of French high society (Kushner 2013). Famous for their talent, glamour, and beauty, these *femmes galantes* were the most highly sought-after women of pleasure in all Europe, models and actresses who "earned their living by engaging in long-term sexual and often companionate relationships with men from the financial, political, and social elites, known as *le monde* (high society)" (ibid., 3). This sultry scene overlapped directly with the world of the theater.[51] Although not all theater women were kept mistresses or *femmes galantes*, "[i]t was widely understood that any woman in the Opéra, and to a lesser degree the other theater companies, was a *dame entretenue*, or at least wanted to be" (ibid., 31). The world of theater was the center of this high-end sex market because "being on the stage greatly increased...'sexual capital,' the desirability of a mistress and hence the prices she could command for her services" (ibid., 5), and the theater district of the French capital was teeming with high-end brothels and places of ill repute.[52] But there is no evidence to indicate that Smith himself partook of any such transactions.

---

50. By way of example, John Rae (1895, ch. 14) and Ian Simpson Ross (2010, ch. 13), scholars who have produced two of the most comprehensive biographies of Smith, both commented on Smith's fondness for the opera during his second sojourn in Paris.
51. Kushner (2013, 4–5): "About a fifth of the kept women under police surveillance at midcentury worked in the theater. Most were in the Opéra or its school, as dancers and singers."
52. In the words of Kushner (2013, 110), "Many brothels were in the center of town, on the rue St. Honoré or nearby, making them convenient for men leaving the Opéra."

"Miss Campbell" is probably not Lady Frances Scott Campbell

The most tenuously conjectured love affair would be one during Smith's extended stay at Dalkeith House in late 1767. On this theory Smith may have carried out a short-lived love affair with the younger sister of his former pupil Henry Scott,[53] Lady Frances Douglas (1750–1817), née Campbell Scott, whose mother's maiden name was Campbell and whose other brother, Hew, was referred to as Hew Campbell Scott.[54] Lady Frances would have been 17 years old at the time (Stuart 1985/1827, 54); as a result, such an affair, if it really occurred, would be one between a man of 44 and young woman of 17. Lady Frances did not wed until 1783.[55]

Also worth noting is that Smith may have first met Lady Frances nine years earlier, when Duke Henry's stepfather Charles Townsend "visited Scotland in the summer of 1759 with Lady Dalkeith [Caroline Campbell Scott] and her daughter [Lady Frances]" (Ross 1974, 179). Among other places on his Scottish itinerary, Townsend went to Glasgow "to make the necessary arrangements for the period five years ahead when the duke would...complete his studies by travelling on the Continent with his tutor" (Ross 1974, 179).

Of particular relevance to this conjecture is Mackenzie's recollection about "Smith and Hume in Love," in which he partially identifies by name a "Miss Campbell of _____ " as the object of Smith's romantic affections. Could this "Miss Campbell" be a veiled or indirect reference to Lady Frances, whose mother's maiden name was also Campbell? If so, her prominence

---

53. Recall that Smith was Duke Henry's private tutor during their Grand Tour from February 1764 to October 1766. As a further aside, Edith Kuiper (2013, 70) incorrectly identifies Lady Frances as Duke Henry's elder sister. In fact, Lady Frances was four years younger than her brother (see Alcouffe and Massot-Bordenave 2020, 32–33; Bonnyman 2014, 1).

54. The mother of Lady Frances and her brothers Henry and Hew was Caroline Campbell Scott, Lady Dalkeith (Ross 1974, 178). For more details about Caroline Campbell and her family background, see Bonnyman 2014, 9, 12–19.

55. See Alcouffe and Massot-Bordenave 2020, 290. When she married in 1783, at the age of 33, Lady Frances became Lord Archibald Douglas' second wife (see Jill Rubenstein's biography of Lady Frances in Stuart 1985/1827, 11). For a short biography of Lord Douglas, see Valentine 1970, 1:258. As a further aside, Lady Frances, upon reaching the age of 21, was entitled to an income from her family of £600 per year (see Stuart 1985/1827, 59). To put this monetary amount in perspective, Smith's compensation for serving as the Duke's private tutor during their Grand Tour from 1764 to 1766 consisted of an annual salary of £500, plus travel expenses, and a pension of £300 a year thereafter (see Mackay 1896, 237; Heilbroner 1999, 48; Bonnyman 2020, 41).

and subsequent marriage in 1783 to Lord Archibald Douglas might explain Mackenzie's reluctance to identify her by name.[56]

Duke Henry, along with his sister Lady Frances and other members of the Buccleuch family, returned to the Buccleuch estates in Scotland and took up residency at Dalkeith House in September of 1767 upon Duke Henry's coming of age.[57] According to one scholarly source (Bonnyman 2014, 59–60), Smith resided at Dalkeith House in the fall of 1767, a stay that coincides with Lady Frances's residency there.[58] Moreover, Smith's stay at Dalkeith House lasted at least two months, from mid-September to mid-November 1767.[59] Thus the possibility of a love affair between Smith and the young Lady Frances during this time, though unlikely, is not altogether inconceivable.[60]

56. Recall that Mackenzie did not jot down this particular passage about "Miss Campbell" until the end of his life—the late 1820s or early 1830s. Also, as an aside, in the very same passage in which Mackenzie mentions "Miss Campbell" as the object of Smith's affections, Mackenzie also writes about David Hume's love life, but instead of partially disclosing or withholding the identity of Hume's romantic attachment, as he does with Adam Smith, Mackenzie fully identifies Hume's love interest by name as "Miss Nancy Ord" (Mackenzie 1927, 176; reprinted in Fieser 2003, 255).

57. Dalkeith House (or Dalkeith Palace) was the Buccleuch family's principal residence in Scotland and is located only four miles south of Edinburgh, where Smith lived the last 12 years of his life. This neo-classical palace was commissioned and built in the early eighteenth century and then refurbished in preparation for Duke Henry's first visit to Scotland in honor of his reaching the age of majority (see Bonnyman 2014, 10, 57–58). There exists an engraving of this palace as it appeared in the early eighteenth century.

58. In her memoir of her cousin and close friend Lady Frances, Lady Louisa Stuart (1985/1827) confirms that Lady Frances had been growing up in London under the watchful eye of her stepfather Charles Townsend. Lady Stuart (1985/1827, 48–50) also describes the circumstances surrounding Lady Frances's return to Scotland.

59. For further details regarding Smith's stay at Dalkeith, see Bonnyman 2014, 58–59. According to Ross (1974, 180), Heilbroner (1999, 50), and Kuiper (2013, 76, n.14), Smith may have also visited Dalkeith House and the Buccleuch estates on several subsequent occasions. None of these sources, however, provide any actual evidence in support of this proposition, so it is unclear whether Smith, in fact, ever returned to or stayed at Dalkeith House following his initial two-month stay in late 1767.

60. For a biography of Lady Frances written by a contemporary of hers, see Stuart 1985/1827. Among other things, Lady Louisa Stuart's intimate memoir of Lady Frances's life and circle of family and friends paints a very unflattering picture of Lady Frances's mother; in addition, Stuart (1985/1827, 45–49) describes Lady Frances's stepfather Charles Townsend as extremely possessive: "unwilling ever to have her out of his sight." Stuart's intimate memoir also highlights Lady Frances's worldliness and awareness of adult double standards (see especially ibid., 54, 58). Given these facts, along with her stepfather's (Charles Townsend)

This conjecture, however, is doubtful. In his brief recollection, Mackenzie says that "Miss Campbell" was "a woman of as different dispositions and habits from him as possible." That he would make such a remark without also remarking on other extraordinary aspects of an affair with Lady Frances would be odd, unless he purposely wanted to disguise her identity. In that case, however, why identify her as "Miss Campbell" at all? In a parenthetical remark immediately following the words "Miss Campbell of _____" (see quoted text in Mackenzie 1927, 176, reprinted in Fieser 2003, 255), Mackenzie says that "the name is so numerous that to use it cannot be thought personal." This comment further suggests that "Campbell" tells little or nothing about the woman's identity. Also worth noting here is the reference to "*Miss* Campbell" instead of *Lady* or *Dame* or some other signifier of aristocratic distinction. Perhaps this reference to "Miss" points us away from Lady Frances.

That said, however, two additional points are worth making regarding the relationship between Lady Frances and Smith. Firstly, among the letters of Smith that were not lost or destroyed are three addressed directly to Lady Frances, dated October 15, 1766, October 19, 1766, and March 17, 1783 (Smith 1987, letters 97, 98, and 225). The two of 1766 precede Smith's visit to Dalkeith, and concern the melancholy news of the death, in France, of Campbell Scott, brother of both Lady Frances and the Duke of Buccleuch. The third letter, of 1783, is brief and somewhat curious. It is thought to be authored by Smith, but it refers to Smith in the third person. Specifically, it thanks Lady Frances for having sent to Smith "his paper on upon Italian and English verse" and promises "to send her a more perfect copy as soon as he has compleated his plan" (Smith 1987, 265). It would seem that Smith had shared his essay on Italian and English verse, which is contained in the modern edition of *Essays on Philosophical Subjects*.

Secondly, Lady Louisa Stuart (1985/1827, 90–93)—who wrote an intimate memoir of her cousin and best friend, Lady Frances—mentions toward the end of her memoir that she (Lady Frances) may have had a mysterious lost love of her own. Or in the melodramatic words of Lady Louisa herself: Lady

---

sudden death in August of 1767, perhaps it is not far-fetched to imagine a romance or fling between her and Smith. There exists a portrait of Lady Frances by Sir Joshua Reynolds when she was still a child. As a further aside, Lady Frances was an accomplished artist in her own right; a collection of her works is available from Tate.

Frances had at one time in her life fallen "prey [to] one of those fixed, deep-rooted torturing passions" (ibid., 90). Could this lost love have been Smith?

For context, at this point in her Lady Frances memoir, Lady Louisa is writing about Frances Scott's decision to marry a widower, Lord Archibald Douglas.[61] According to Lady Louisa, Lady Frances confided to her:

> ...at one time I could not doubt that he was extremely inclined to make me his proposals, and would have done so on a very little encouragement. But no—Oh no!—I had just—only just enough reason left to see that this must not be—that we must never marry—it would have been madness to think of it—And I withstood the temptation like a famished wretch refraining from the food he knows to be mingled with poison. (Stuart 1985/1827, 91)

Who is the "he" to whom Lady Frances is referring to here? Could it be none other than Adam Smith? Alas, not only did Lady Frances fail to reveal the identity of this lost love to Lady Louisa; she explicitly forbade Lady Louisa "to guess who it was" (Stuart 1985/1827, 93).[62] Nevertheless, although Lady Louisa reports that Lady Frances never gave her "the least clue to discover who this person was" (ibid., 92), Lady Louisa does identify three possible clues in her memoir of Lady Frances, none of which rule Smith out.

The first clue is a temporal one. Writing from the vantage point of 1781 or 1783,[63] Lady Louisa (1985/1827, 90) says that this love affair originated many years ago but "not less than twelve or fourteen" years. In other words, Lady Frances' mysterious love affair occurred in the late 1760s or early 1770s, right after Smith's stay at Dalkeith house in the fall of 1767.

The next clue involves the wavering religious beliefs of Lady Frances' lost love. According to Lady Louisa (Stuart 1985/1827, 91), this lover was "an unbeliever, almost to the extent of atheism."[64] Although Smith's private

---

61. Lord Archibald and Lady Frances wed on May 1, 1783 (see Stuart 1985/1827, 95). Lady Frances was Lord Archibald's second wife.

62. Lady Louisa further states: "I confess I had an eager desire to know [the identity of Lady Frances' lost love]; but so far from gratifying my curiosity, [Lady Frances] besought me...to repress it, desist from enquiring, and forbear to even form a conjecture" (Stuart 1985/1827, 92).

63. Although this part of the memoir deals with "the momentous year 1783" (Stuart 1985/ 1827, 85), the year Lady Frances wed Lord Archibald Douglas, Lady Louisa also mentions an anecdote from the year 1781 involving Lady Portarlington (ibid., 92).

64. For the reader's reference, here is the complete passage in which this clue appears

religious beliefs are unknown, since he was careful during his life to keep his views about religion to himself, it is not inconceivable that Smith confided his private views to someone he was romantically attached to. (Indeed, perhaps it was Smith's secularism—especially in an age of religious conformity—that prevented his love interests from going any further.)

The last clue approaches closest to Smith. According to Lady Louisa:

> The only thing [Lady Frances] ever let fall which might have led to [a conjecture] was a circumstance mentioned by chance in speaking of Mr. Townshend [Lady Frances's stepfather]. She had told him, she said, that she felt quite sure she should never be in love—the persuasion of most sensible young people before their hour is come—"Yes, you will" answered he gazing at her pensively—"Your brother [Duke Henry] will come from abroad, and amongst his young friends your eye will single out some man destined to be master of your fate"—"Good heavens!" added she with energy, putting her hand to her forehead—"One would actually suppose he had been endowed with the spirit of prophecy." (Stuart 1985/1827, 92–93)

Although Smith could not be considered one of Duke Henry's "young friends," Smith did return with Duke Henry from abroad, resided at Dalkeith House with Duke Henry and Lady Frances in the fall of 1767, and was by all accounts (Bonnyman 2014; Alcouffe and Massot-Bordenave 2020) Duke Henry's closest friend and confidante at the time.

To sum up our conjectures thus far: all the available pieces of evidence, scarce as they are, as well as the most reasonable inferences that can be drawn from these sources, point to the existence of two or perhaps three love interests. One is Stewart's mysterious maiden of Smith's youth, a time and place in which people's love lives were strictly monitored by Church elders and in which parental consent for marriage was the norm. Another is Colbert's Madame Nicol in Old Regime France, the France of Louis XV, literary salons, and the *demimonde*. A third is "Miss Campbell," though that could be anyone, including possibly the Lady of Fife.

(Stuart 1985/1827, 91): "One particular [Lady Frances] mentioned [to Lady Louisa], that in conversation which passed between them [between Lady Frances and her lover], he had frankly avowed himself an unbeliever, almost to the extent of atheism."

Additional conjectures

For thoroughness, we may also consider two additional conjectures about Smith's sexuality and love life. One is that Smith was romantically involved with his unmarried cousin Janet Douglas. Miss Douglas had moved into Smith's household as early as 1754 (Özler 2012, 348) and lived under the same roof with Smith and Smith's mother—Douglas's aunt, Margaret Douglas Smith—until her death in 1788 (Kennedy 2005, 5).[65] Given the decades that they lived in the same household, this thought is something that a nosy sleuth must ponder,[66] though there is no evidence in support of the speculation beyond these circumstantial facts. Indeed, the lack of evidence for what would be such a protracted and proximate intimacy constitutes strong evidence against the idea.

A final hypothesis is that Smith was not attracted to women.[67] Daniel Klein has pointed out to me in conversation how some of the surviving correspondence between Smith and Hume (see especially Smith 1987, letters 70, 88, 92, and 121), as well as the remarkable frequency in Smith's works of subtle, playful, inside-joke-like textual connections to Hume's works, suggests a 'bromance' and brotherly tenderness between them, although Klein clarifies to me that he does not mean to suggest a sexual relationship. In a letter dated February 22, 1763, Smith invites Hume to visit him in Glasgow thus: "Tho you have resisted all my Sollicitations, I hope you will not resist this" (Smith 1987, 139). And in a letter dated September 1765, Smith writes to Hume:

---

65. Alas, scholars have been unable to confirm Janet Douglas's year of birth (Kuiper 2013, 62).

66. Weinstein (2001, 10) says that Miss Douglas and Smith were "quite close." Weinstein, however, does not suggest that Janet Douglas and Smith were romantically involved—only that Smith "seemed to have good relationships with women as his time and stature would have allowed." For what it is worth, Voltaire, who Smith admired, is alleged to have had an affair with his niece, Madame Denis, during their younger years (see, for example, Alcouffe and Massot-Bordenave 2020, 171 n.8). Nevertheless, such types of incestuous relationships were strictly forbidden by the Church of Scotland (Hardy 1978), and during most of Smith's lifetime the sex lives of Scots were strictly monitored by the local 'kirk sessions' or ecclesiastical courts of each parish (Mitchison and Leneman 1998).

67. Regarding speculation that Smith may have been gay, both Edith Kuiper (2013, 70) and Gavin Kennedy (2005, 4) conclude that it is unfounded; see, also, a fascinating and thoughtful discussion on the Reddit website r/AskHistorians.

In short I have a very great interest in your settling at London, where, after many firm resolutions to return to Scotland, I think it is most likely I shall settle myself. Let us make short excursions together sometimes to see our friends in France and sometimes to see our friends in Scotland, but let London be the place of our ordinary residence. (Smith 1987, 161)

Absence of evidence or evidence of absence? Smith's lost diary and the destruction of his private papers

Smith's letters

Is there any evidence of a love affair written in Smith's own hand? In an early essay Smith wrote on the "Imitative Arts" (1980b/1795, 190), Smith states: "It is a lover who complains, or hopes, or fears, or despairs." Also, some references to romantic love appear in various places in *The Theory of Moral Sentiments*, but on his deathbed Smith specifically instructed his literary executors, Joseph Black and James Hutton, to destroy his unpublished manuscripts, correspondence, and other private papers (Ross 2010, 404–405). In fact, Smith may have insisted on the destruction of his private papers and letters as early as 1773 (Phillipson 2010, 279), when he had made his first will and had appointed his friend David Hume his executor. Nevertheless, despite Smith's desire to have his private papers and personal letters destroyed upon his death, a small sample of Smith's correspondence still survives, including three letters addressed to Lady Frances. According to Alcouffe and Massot-Bordenave (2020, x), in all "only 193 letters written by [Smith] and 129 addressed to him remain."[68]

The key question is, Why did Smith want to destroy his private letters and papers as early as 1773, only a few years removed after his extended sojourn in the South of France (1764–1765), his ten-month residency in the City of Lights (1766), and his two-month stay at Dalkeith House (1767)? Most

---

68. Most of these remaining 322 letters (304 to be exact) are reprinted in Smith 1987. Also, according to W. R. Scott (1940, App. II 272, 273): "there is just a possibility that a large body of documents relating to Smith may still be in existence" and "there remain opportunities, even at this late date, for remedying the present meagre knowledge of Adam Smith's life." Tracking down any new Smith letters addressed to Lady Frances, however, will be a daunting task. Lady Frances, for example, eventually married Archibald Douglas in 1783, and the couple had six children (see Jill Rubenstein's biography of Lady Frances, in Stuart 1985/1827).

scholars, like Ross (2010, 405), point to "Smith's prudence" and "his concern for his literary reputation" as the motivating factors.[69] Alcouffe and Massot-Bordenave (2020, 133) write: "it is important to underline also that the place ascribed to the judgement of posterity is found in the arrangements which he [Smith] to make prior to his death; to make his personal papers disappear and thus to control the image which posterity would later preserve of him."

The lost travel diary

It has been reported that Smith brought back no less than three trunks of documents from his extended travels in France (Alcouffe and Massot-Bordenave 2020, 204). Also, according to Jeremy Black (1981, 657), the custom of "keeping a travel diary of some form" among the British during their Grand Tours was "relatively widespread." In addition, Smith scholar W. R. Scott (1940, App. II 273) has speculated that Smith or his pupil (or both?) may have kept a travel diary during their extended travels in the South of France and Paris in the mid-1760s (see also Ross 2010, 248 n.2; Rasmussen 2017, 286 n.61). In an unfinished appendix to his survey article titled "Studies Relating to Adam Smith during the Last Fifty Years," Scott (1940) specifically refers to the existence of this lost diary,[70] which was sold in the 1920s to an unknown buyer from an Edinburgh bookshop owned by one Mr Orr:

> Contrary to the report of Dugald Stewart, Mr. Orr, a bookseller of George Street, Edinburgh, maintained that Adam Smith did keep a diary when he was in France, and that he had had it in his possession and had sold it for cash to an unknown customer who was believed to be from one of the Dominions, or perhaps from the United States. (Scott 1940, App. II 273)

Scott (1940, 273) further reports in his survey article that he was personally able to interview the employee who had made the actual sale and that this employee "was clear as to the…particulars": the fact that Mr Orr's bookshop

---

69. Likewise, a reviewer has suggested to me that Smith simply wanted to avoid any airing or public scrutiny of his private views about "religion, politics, his correspondence with Hume, etc."

70. W. R. Scott (1868–1940), the Professor of Political Economy at the University of Glasgow, was a prolific writer and an authority on the life and works of Smith (see Coase 1993, 355). Given these impeccable credentials and his record of scholarship, Scott is a credible source of information.

had at one time a copy of Smith's travel diary and had sold it for cash to an unknown buyer.[71] Scott further speculates about the identity of this unknown buyer:

> It may be guessed that the purchaser cannot have been an economist, else he would surely have printed extracts from a manuscript of such interest. It may be he was a collector of autographs, in which case the tracing of the diary must be largely a matter of chance. (Scott 1940, App. II 274)

Perhaps this lost diary, if it exists at all, would contain details of Smith's personal life during his travels in France.

Given the absence of strong evidence, Ross (2010, 228) famously concluded that "the biographer can do little more with the topic of Smith's sex life than contribute a footnote to the history of sublimation." But is this sparse record evidence of absence? The little available evidence shows that most likely Smith fell in love at least twice, if not three times: that he had a romantic bond with the Lady of Fife and quite possibly one with Madame Nicol. That Mackenzie's "Miss Campbell" accounts for an actual and separate affair is less likely. Beyond that, who knows! Or, as Smith himself is once reported to have asked, "Am I beau to no one but my books?"[72]

References

Alcouffe, Alain, and Andrew Moore. 2018. Smith's Networks in Occitania—March 1764–October 1765. Presented at the 31st Annual Conference of Eighteenth-Century Scottish Studies Society, July 17–21, 2018 (Glasgow).

Alcouffe, Alain, and Philippe Massot-Bordenave. 2020. *Adam Smith in Toulouse and Occitania: The Unknown Years*. London: Palgrave Macmillan.

Black, Jeremy. 1981. British Travellers in Europe in the Early Eighteenth Century. *Dalhousie Review* 61(4): 655–667.

Black, Jeremy. 1984. France and the Grand Tour in the Early Eighteenth Century. *Francia* 11: 407–416.

---

71. Alas, this employee's memory as to the date of the sale was foggy. Specifically, Scott (1940, 273) reports the employee "was doubtful about the date of the transaction. In 1935 he thought it was over ten years earlier, and last year [1939] he put it back to 'nearly twenty years ago.'"

72. Quoted in Wight 2002, 292. For a slightly different formulation of this possibly apocryphal quotation, see Smellie 1800, 297 (quoted in Rae 1895, 329; Heilbroner 1999, 45): "I am a beau in nothing but my books."

Black, Jeremy. 2011 [1985]. *The British and the Grand Tour*. London: Routledge.

Bonnyman, Brian. 2014. *The Third Duke of Buccleuch and Adam Smith: Estate Management and Improvement in Enlightenment Scotland*. Edinburgh: Edinburgh University Press.

Braden, Irene. 1965. *Voltaire and Injustice*. Master's thesis, Kansas State University, Manhattan, Kan.

Brodsky-Porges, Edward. 1981. The Grand Tour: Travel as an Educational Device, 1600–1800. *Annals of Tourism Research* 8(2): 171–186.

Buchan, James. 2006. *The Authentic Adam Smith: His Life and Ideas*. New York: Norton.

Caplan, Harry, Walter H. French, and Francis E. Mineka. 1964. Harold William Thompson, June 5, 1891–February 21, 1964. Cornell University (Ithaca, N.Y.).

Caulcutt, Clea. 2010. French Free-Thinking Knight Still a Controversial Figure. RFI.fr (France Médias Monde, Paris), December 16.

Chassaigne, Marc. 1920. *Le procès du Chevalier de la Barre*. Paris: Librairie Victor Lecoffre.

Claverie, Elisabeth. 1992. Sainte indignation contre indignation éclairée: L'affaire du Chevalier de La Barre. *Ethnologie Française* 22(n.s., 3): 271–290.

Claverie, Elisabeth. 1994. Procès, affaire, cause: Voltaire et l'innovation critique. *Politix* 7(26): 76–85.

Coase, Ronald H. 1993. Duncan Black, 1908–1991. *Proceedings of the British Academy* 82: 353–365.

Cohen, Michèle. 1992. The Grand Tour: Constructing the English Gentleman in Eighteenth-Century France. *History of Education* 21(3): 241–257.

Cohen, Michèle. 2001. The Grand Tour: Language, National Identity, and Masculinity. *Changing English: Studies in Culture and Education* 8(2): 129–141.

Colbert, Abbé. 1766. Letter dated 18 September 1766. *National Archives of Scotland*, GD224/2040/62/3.

Currie, James. 1831. Letter 87 ("To Dugald Stewart, Esq., Edinburgh, July 14, '94, Respecting Dr. Adam Smith"). In *Memoir of the Life, Writings, and Correspondence of James Currie, M.D. F.R.S., of Liverpool*, ed. William Wallace Currie, vol. 2, 317–320. London: Longman, Rees, Orme, Brown, & Green.

Darnton, Robert. 1998. Two Paths Through the Social History of Ideas. *Studies on Voltaire and the Eighteenth Century* 359: 251–294.

Dawson, Deidre. 2013. Love, Marriage and Virtue: Mary Wollstonecraft and Sophie de Grouchy, Marquise de Condorcet, Respond to The Theory of Moral Sentiments. *Adam Smith Review* 7: 24–46.

Den Uyl, Douglas J., and Charles L. Griswold Jr. 1996. Adam Smith on Friendship and Love. *Review of Metaphysics* 49(3): 609–637.

Drescher, H. W. 2004. Mackenzie, Henry (1745–1831). In *Oxford Dictionary of National Biography*, ed. David Cannadine. Oxford: Oxford University Press.

Fay, C. R. 2011 [1956]. *Adam Smith and the Scotland of his Day*, reissue ed. Cambridge, UK: Cambridge University Press.

Fieser, James. 2003. *Early Responses to Hume*, vol. 10. London and New York: Thoemmes Press.

Gillis, John R. 1985. *For Better, for Worse: British Marriages, 1600 to the Present*. Oxford: Oxford

University Press.

Ginzberg, Eli. 1934. *The House of Adam Smith*. New York: Columbia University Press.

Goodman, Dena. 1994. *The Republic of Letters: A Cultural History of the French Enlightenment*. Ithaca, N.Y.: Cornell University Press.

Guerra-Pujol, F. E. 2022. Adam Smith in the City of Lights. Working paper.

Haakonssen, Knud. 1984. From Moral Philosophy to Political Economy: The Contribution of Dugald Stewart. In *Philosophers of the Scottish Enlightenment*, ed. Vincent Hope, 211–232. Edinburgh: Edinburgh University Press.

Haldane, R. B. 1887. *Life of Adam Smith*. London: Walter Scott.

Hardy, John R. 1978. *The Attitude of the Church and State in Scotland to Sex and Marriage: 1560–1707*. M. Phil. thesis, University of Edinburgh.

Harkin, Maureen. 2013a. Adam Smith on Women. In *The Oxford Handbook of Adam Smith*, eds. Christopher J. Berry, Maria Pia Paganelli, and Craig Smith, 501–520. Oxford: Oxford University Press.

Harkin, Maureen. 2013b. Adam Smith on Women: Introduction. *Adam Smith Review* 7: 3–7.

Heilbroner, Robert L. 1999. *The Worldly Philosophers: The Lives, Times, and Ideas of Great Economic Thinkers*, 7th rev. ed. New York: Touchstone.

Hirst, Francis Wrigley. 1904. *Adam Smith*. London: Macmillan.

Jacob, Margaret C. 2019. *The Secular Enlightenment*. Princeton, N.J.: Princeton University Press.

Kennedy, Gavin. 2005. *Adam Smith's Lost Legacy*. Basingstoke, UK: Palgrave Macmillan.

Kuiper, Edith. 2013. The Invisible Hands: Adam Smith and the Women in his Life. *Adam Smith Review* 7: 62–78.

Kushner, Nina. 2013. *Erotic Exchanges: The World of Elite Prostitution in Eighteenth-Century Paris*. Ithaca, N.Y.: Cornell University Press.

LeBuffe, Michael. 2020. Paul-Henri Thiry (Baron) d'Holbach. In *The Stanford Encyclopedia of Philosophy*, ed. Edward N. Zalta. Metaphysics Research Lab, Stanford University (Stanford, Calif.).

Leddy, N. B. 2013. Grave, Philosophical, and Cool Reasoner: Mary Wollstonecraft on the Use of Gender in Adam Smith. *Adam Smith Review* 7: 8–17.

Leneman, Leah. 1999. Wives and Mistresses in Eighteenth-Century Scotland. *Women's History Review* 8(4): 671–692.

Leneman, Leah, and Rosalind Mitchison. 1987. Scottish Illegitimacy Ratios in the Early Modern Period. *Economic History Review* 40(1): 41–63.

Leneman, Leah, and Rosalind Mitchison. 1988. Girls in Trouble: The Social and Geographical Setting of Illegitimacy in Early Modern Scotland. *Journal of Social History* 21(3): 483–497.

Leneman, Leah, and Rosalind Mitchison. 1993. Clandestine Marriage in the Scottish Cities, 1660–1780. *Journal of Social History* 26(4): 845–861.

Luna, Francesco. 1996. From the *History of Astronomy* to the *Wealth of Nations*: Wonderful Wheels and Invisible Hands in Adam Smith's Major Works. In *Inflation, Institutions and Information: Essays in Honour of Axel Leijonhufvud*, eds. Daniel Vaz and Kumaraswamy Velupillai, 131–153. London: Macmillan.

Mackay, A. J. G. 1896. *A History of Fife and Kinross*. Edinburgh and London: William Blackwood and Sons.

Mackenzie, Henry. 1927 [1831]. Smith and Hume in Love. In *The Anecdotes and Egotisms of Henry Mackenzie, 1745–1831*, ed. Harold W. Thompson, 176. Oxford: Oxford University Press.

Mitchison, Rosalind, and Leah Leneman. 2001. *Girls in Trouble: Sexuality and Social Control in Early Modern Scotland, 1670–1780*, 2nd ed. Dalkeith, UK: Scottish Cultural Press.

Muller, Jerry Z. 1993. *Adam Smith: In His Time and Ours*. Princeton, N.J.: Princeton University Press.

Nicholls, James C. 1976. Introduction to *Mme Riccoboni's Letters to David Hume, David Garrick and Sir Robert Liston, 1764–1783*, by Marie-Jeanne Riccoboni, ed. James C. Nicholls. Oxford: Voltaire Foundation at the Taylor Institution.

Özler, Şule. 2012. Adam Smith and Dependency. *Psychoanalytic Review* 99(3): 333–358.

Phillipson, Nicholas. 2010. *Adam Smith: An Enlightened Life*. New Haven, Conn.: Yale University Press.

Rae, John. 1895. *Life of Adam Smith*. London: Macmillan.

Rashid, Salim. 1985. Dugald Stewart, "Baconian" Methodology, and Political Economy. *Journal of the History of Ideas* 46(2): 245–257.

Rasmussen, Dennis C. 2017. *The Infidel and the Professor: David Hume, Adam Smith, and the Friendship That Shaped Modern Thought*. Princeton, N.J.: Princeton University Press.

Ross, Ian Simpson. 1974. Educating an Eighteenth-Century Duke. In *The Scottish Tradition: Essays in Honour of Ronald Gordon Cant*, ed. G. W. S. Barrow, 178–197. Edinburgh: Scottish Academic Press.

Ross, Ian Simpson. 1980. Introduction to *Account of the Life and Writings of Adam Smith, LL.D.* by Dugald Stewart. In *Essays on Philosophical Subjects*, by Adam Smith, eds. W. P. D. Wightman and J. C. Bryce, 265–268. Oxford: Oxford University Press.

Ross, Ian Simpson. 1995. *The Life of Adam Smith*. Oxford: Clarendon Press.

Ross, Ian Simpson. 2010. *The Life of Adam Smith*, 2nd ed. Oxford: Oxford University Press.

Roy, Donald. 1995. Comédie-Italienne. In *The Cambridge Guide to the Theatre*, ed. Martin Banham, 233–234. Cambridge, UK: Cambridge University Press.

Scott, Walter. 1834. Henry Mackenzie. In *Miscellaneous Prose Works of Sir Walter Scott*, ed. Walter Scott, vol. 4, 1–19. Edinburgh: Cadell.

Scott, W. R. 1936. New Light on Adam Smith. *Economic Journal* 46(183): 401–411.

Scott, W. R. 1940. Studies Relating to Adam Smith During the Last Fifty Years. *Proceedings of the British Academy* 26: 249–274.

Smellie, William. 1800. *Literary and Characteristical Lives of John Gregory, M.D.; Henry Home, Lord Kames; David Hume, Esq.; and Adam Smith, LL.D.* Edinburgh: Alex. Smellie.

Smith, Adam. 1976 [1790]. *The Theory of Moral Sentiments*, eds. D. D. Raphael and A. L. Macfie. Oxford: Oxford University Press.

Smith, Adam. 1980a [1795]. The History of Astronomy. In *Essays on Philosophical Subjects*, ed. W. P. D. Wightman and J. C. Bryce, 33–105. Oxford: Oxford University Press.

Smith, Adam. 1980b [1795]. Of the Nature of That Imitation Which Takes Place in What Are Called the Imitative Arts. In *Essays on Philosophical Subjects*, ed. W. P. D. Wightman and J. C. Bryce, 176–209. Oxford: Oxford University Press.

Smith, Adam. 1987. *The Correspondence of Adam Smith*, 2nd ed., eds. Ernest C. Mossner and Ian Simpson Ross. Oxford: Oxford University Press.

Stewart, Dugald. 1811a. *Account of the Life and Writings of Adam Smith, LL.D.* In *Biographical Memoirs of Adam Smith, LL.D., of William Robertson, D.D., and of Thomas Reid, D.D.,* 3–152. Edinburgh: George Ramsay and Company.

Stewart, Dugald. 1811b. *Account of the Life and Writings of Adam Smith, LL.D.* In *The Works of Adam Smith, LL.D. and F.R.S. of London and Edinburgh,* ed. Dugald Stewart, vol. 5, 403–552. London: T. Cadell and W. Davies.

Stewart, Dugald. 1980 [1811]. *Account of the Life and Writings of Adam Smith, LL.D.,* ed. Ian Simpson Ross. In *Essays on Philosophical Subjects,* by Adam Smith, eds. W. P. D. Wightman and J. C. Bryce, 269–351. Oxford: Oxford University Press.

Stuart, Lady Louisa. 1985 [1827]. *Memoire of Frances, Lady Douglas,* ed. Jill Rubenstein. Edinburgh: Scottish Academic Press.

Tegos, Spyridon. 2019. Is Love Ridiculous??? *Adam Smith Works* (Liberty Fund, Inc., Carmel, Ind.), February 11.

Valentine, Alan. 1970. *The British Establishment, 1760–1784: An Eighteenth-Century Biographical Dictionary,* vols. 1 and 2. Norman, Okla.: University of Oklahoma Press.

Voltaire. 2000 [1766]. An Account of the Death of the Chevalier de La Barre. In *Treatise on Tolerance and Other Writings,* ed. Simon Harvey, 139–148. Cambridge, UK: Cambridge University Press.

Voltaire. 2000 [1775]. Cry of Innocent Blood. In *Treatise on Tolerance and Other Writings,* ed. Simon Harvey, 151–156. Cambridge, UK: Cambridge University Press.

Weinstein, Jack Russell. 2001. *On Adam Smith.* Belmont, Calif.: Wadsworth Publishing Co.

Wight, Jonathan B. 2002. *Saving Adam Smith: A Tale of Wealth, Transformation, and Virtue.* Upper Saddle River, N.J.: Prentice Hall.

Wight, Jonathan B. 2020. Email correspondence with the author, November 8.

Wood, Paul. 2000. Dugald Stewart and the Invention of "The Scottish Enlightenment." In *The Scottish Enlightenment: Essays in Reinterpretation,* ed. Paul Wood, 1–35. Rochester, N.Y.: University of Rochester Press.

Professional Scholarship from 1893 to 2020 on Adam Smith's Views on School Funding: A Heterodox Examination

Scott Drylie

"Adam Smith is difficult to apprehend in his totality for the perverse reason that he is in parts so regrettably well known." So wrote Alexander Gray (1931, 124–125) in his work *The Development of Economic Doctrine*. The statement might well apply to Smith's position on who should fund the education of youth. It takes little effort to deduce that there exists an orthodoxy of sorts that Smith supported government-subsidized education through taxation. Scholars regularly assert that Smith "advocated for" (Baum 1992, 152), "pleaded for" (Reisman 1976, 225), "urged for" (Wilson 1989, 60), "insisted upon" (Fleischacker 2004, 235), or "demanded" (Skinner 1996, 192) such subsidization. If true, education ranks as one of the most significant exceptions to Smith's presumption against government involvement in the production of goods and services outside of nightwatchman-state functions. Yet an important passage may suggest that the totality of Smith's views on school funding is complex. Using this passage as a lens, the current study inspects the scholarship on this issue.

In previous work (notably Drylie 2020), I have offered an alternative reading of Smith. I propose that Smith is not decidedly favorable to taxpayer funding of education, that he certainly is not favorable to full funding, and that it is reasonable to read him as leaning against any taxpayer funding at all. I am, therefore, suspicious of common claims made about Smith's position and curious as to how those claims have come about and persisted. My reading is based on the full "Article" entitled "Of the Expence of the Institutions for the Education of Youth," located in Book 5, Chapter 1 of *The Wealth of*

Nations (Smith 1976/1776, hereafter WN). It is also based on the passage in question, found in the "Conclusion of the Chapter," which summarizes each of his positions from Book 5, Chapter 1.

Smith's final sentence of his summary on education in "Conclusion of the Chapter" presents a grave problem to the orthodox characterization. The complete summary reads:

> The expence of the institutions for education and religious instruction, is likewise, no doubt, beneficial to the whole society, and may, therefore, without injustice, be defrayed by the general contribution of the whole society. This expence, however, might perhaps with equal propriety, and even with some advantage, be defrayed altogether by those who receive the immediate benefit of such education and instruction, or by the voluntary contribution of those who think they have occasion for either the one or the other. (WN, V.i.i.5)

Those are Smith's final words on the subject. What should be clear is that Smith does not convey any certain or strong support for taxpayer-funded public education. Rather, Smith coolly acknowledges that state provision may be justifiable, and then immediately pivots away to express that it may be better to pursue solutions through voluntarily financed schools and the networks of charity schools in his time. There is no obvious final recommendation, and the passage resists being further reduced. Whether it conveys ambivalence, uncertainty, equivocation, or disinclination toward the state, it is inconvenient for any interpretation that associates Smith with public education.

The seeming incongruence between this passage and some familiar interpretations raises several questions. To what degree has this passage made its way into the scholarship? How have its complex sentiments been treated? How should we judge of the methods and results of the scholarship on the subject? In seeking answers to these questions, I aim to contribute to the tradition of scrutinizing scholarly methods, to bring to light disparate views, to spur further exploration of the passage, and to identify a future research agenda for a topic already frequently commented on. Smith is both a key figure in the history of thought and an authority figure for political persuasions. Smith's position on an issue as profound as school funding has, then, widespread implications for discussions of the role of the state.

Analysis of patterns

To assess the presence and treatment of this passage in scholarship, I took the approach of creating as large a sample as possible. Research was conducted from 2015 to 2020 through several university library consortiums and by way of online resources. The disciplines predominantly surveyed were the history of thought, economics, public policy, law, education, and history. Within Smithian literature, topics generally examined were education, justice, charity, beneficence, the division of labor, alienation, the theory of history, the role of the state, liberalism, egalitarianism, democracy, and French influence. A wide variety of search terms were employed to account for these themes, as well as to account for the varying language of 'schooling' and 'education' across time and place (e.g., public, popular, liberal, universal, elementary, primary, parish, charity, and compulsory). Phrase searches from Smith's writing were also used within Google search engines. To overcomes some of the quirks of Google's algorithms, searches were conducted from different computers (i.e., IP addresses) and different geographical locations (i.e., servers).

The result of the search is a set of 191 unique English-language publications from 177 different authors, each specifically addressing Smith's position on school funding. Of the 191, a subset of 54 from 52 different authors cited the key passage in some way. The interpretations range in scope from extensive to passing.

Several exclusions are important to note. First, I have tried to exclude all items for which one has to infer the author's position based on the spirit of the text or on the author's other writings. Second, I exclude reprints of the same article. Third, I exclude blogs and online-only discussions. I do, however, include items outside of formal publication sources in the few cases where I found a working paper, thesis, or dissertation which cited the passage. Lastly, commentary prior to 1893 has been excluded. That date is chosen as the publication year of the first editions of James Bonar's *Philosophy and Political Economy in Some of Their Historical Relations* and Edward Cannan's *History of Theories of Production and Distribution*—two important works signifying the start of the English-speaking world's adoption of an academic form of Smithian scholarship (Tribe 2008).[1] Commentary on Smith's views on

---

1. Montes (2003) and Tribe (2008) make a convincing case that Henry Thomas Buckle's seri-

education prior to the date of 1893 is infrequent and mostly from politicians, social leaders, philosophers, and clergy as opposed to what we might call professional academics (and is addressed in Drylie 2020).

The specific questions I first wish to answer will be done largely with quantitative analysis: (1) How prominent are the various views of Smith's position? (2) Does the passage in question occur randomly in the sample set, or does its occurrence *predict* the nature of the interpretation which the author wishes to convey? (3) Has the treatment of the passage changed over time? (4) Does a scholar's academic discipline predict the treatment of the passage? (5) Can the treatment of the passage begin to provide an indication of the quality of the scholarship?

To these ends, I first organized the examples according to the nature of the interpretation of Smith's position. The interpretations range from full taxpayer funding to none. However, owing to each interpretation's unique tone, rhetoric and context, it was not possible to reliably place each along a precise continuum. They thus had to be binned into categories. I decided on two broad categories, which for simplicity I will call 'state' and 'dissenting' interpretations. The first contains variants that emphasize a concrete and substantial financial role for taxpayer funding; the second contains those which significantly diminish that role, push back against it, or outright reject it.

Two dimensions were looked at to confidently place each interpretation into the categories of 'state' and 'dissenting': the extent of taxpayer funding, and the nature of Smith's commitment to government responsibility. For the state category, the extent of taxpayer funding ranges from full to moderate, and the nature of Smith's commitment ranges from inspired to accepting. The state category includes three common interpretative patterns: (1) It includes those who believe Smith wholeheartedly insisted upon a comprehensive and extensive funding scheme resembling the variants of today's universal public education. (2) The state category also includes most who identify his proposal as mixed-mode, relying on both taxes and user fees. Although mixed-mode can mean anything from nearly complete taxpayer support to almost none, those included here are interpretations in which Smith accepts taxpayer

---

ous effort in *History of Civilization in England* in 1857 and 1861 was not representative of a growing interest in Britain, and that it was poorly received.

support of an amount at least equal to other funding (that is, notionally, 50 percent). (3) Finally, the state category includes nearly all of those who explain Smith's acceptance of government as based on a market failure theory. Although 'market failure' is a precondition which could represent either a high or low standard, those included here have treated the precondition as an easily applied, obvious rationale rather than an unsettling decision of when, how much, and how long to intervene.[2] In the end, what all those in the state category have in common is a portrayal of Smith as granting with moderate to significant conviction a moderate to significant role for government, and thus of setting out education as a major exception to his liberty principle.

The second category is 'dissenting.' The extent of taxpayer funding in these interpretations ranges from, as it were, 49 percent to none, and Smith's commitment to government responsibility ranges from unsure to principally resistant. Like the state category, the dissenting category includes three common interpretative patterns: (1) It includes those who believe Smith is uncertain of any role for government. (2) The dissenting category also includes those who emphasize in Smith a different preference and recommendation than state funding—for instance, user fees or charity. (3) Finally, the dissenting category includes those who admit there is a possible role for taxes in a mixed-model concept—but only a minority one marked by a strong limit or principle. What they all convey to me is something distinctly *otherly*—a reluctance toward state involvement, or merely a fine tolerance for timely, cautious, and highly conditioned state involvement.[3]

I then assessed the data based on how each author 'handled' the passage. Authors took one of four approaches. They may have: (1) cited nothing of the passage nor made reference to it, (2) cited it in whole, (3) cited just the first part, which conveys support for taxpayer funding, or (4) cited just the second part, which contains the sentiment at odds with taxpayer funding. Table 1 organizes the results based on the nature of the interpretation and the

---

2. Keep in mind that Smith in *The Theory of Moral Sentiments* cautions against forcing beneficence: "Of all the duties of a law-giver, however, this, perhaps, is that which it requires the greatest delicacy and reserve to execute with propriety and judgment...to push it too far is destructive of all liberty, security and justice" (Smith 1976/1790, II.ii.I.8).

3. Reliable categorizing was of highest concern. In my deciding whether to categorize an item 'state' or 'dissenting,' I believe that only a few examples, which present mixed-modes or uncertainty, were subject to possible categorization error.

handling of the passage. The publications contributing to each cell count are provided in Appendix A.

TABLE 1. Nature of the interpretation vs. handling of the passage

	No citation	Full citation	1st part only	2nd part only	Total
State	117	14	20	0	151
Dissenting	20	15	1	4	40
Total	137	29	21	4	191

A few simple calculations provide the initial findings. Seventy-nine percent (151/191) of publications present a state interpretation, and 21 percent (40/191) present a dissenting interpretation. There appears, then, to indeed be a dominant interpretation of Smith as an advocate of substantive taxpayer support. As for the prevalence of Smith's final words on the matter, 71 percent (137/191) omit the passage entirely. Surprisingly, another 10 percent (20/191) elect to *truncate* the passage and omit those heterodox sentiments in the second part. Thus, of the 191 articles in the survey, just 19 percent cite the heterodox part which motivates the current study—and that figure likely is upwardly biased in my sample, the result of a search technique specifically intent on finding instances of citations. In short, Smith's final words, especially the compelling heterodox part, have been broadly excluded from scholarship.

Why has this passage been cited so infrequently? The joint frequencies from Table 1 reveal a pattern which suggests an answer. The table shows that 79 percent (151/191) hold a state view, of which only 23 percent (34/151) cite the passage in any way. Twenty-one percent (40/191) hold a dissenting view, of which 50 percent (20/40) cite the passage. The passage is rare among those holding a state view, and it figures prominently among those proposing a dissenting view. The odds ratio puts into perspective the imbalance. Those with a state interpretation are only 29 percent as likely to cite the passage as those with a dissenting interpretation.[4] The strength of this pattern suggests that authors' decisions to look to this passage for value is highly determined by

---

4. Contingency tables and odds ratios are frequently used in medical research. The odds ratio calculation is $(34/117)/(20/20)$. The Pearson chi-squared test confirms that the decision to cite the passage is related to the choice to offer a state interpretation ($\chi^2 = 11.78$, $p < .0005$).

the message they wish to convey. With the preponderance of scholars holding an overall state view of the article, this passage has not provided any marginal benefit to their case or its nuance has not been appealing.

How should one judge of this pattern? One could fault orthodoxy, claiming that due diligence requires citing such an important passage regardless of the message one wishes to convey. But it is also possible that the tensions of the article have been resolved through other textual means. And if the state interpretation is unimpeachable, perhaps some authorial discretion as to what to cite can be tolerated. Therefore, the strong association between a state interpretation and omission—though provocative—is not conclusive evidence of deficiency. How one should judge of this pattern in the orthodox publications will require qualitative assessment, which I will provide in the literature review. Similarly, how to judge of dissenting views' extensive use of the passage will depend upon the case they make.

Upon closer inspection, however, there is a takeaway from this pattern which does reflect poorly on the scholarship, specifically on the body of state interpretations. Table 2 reframes the data, looking only at the 54 who cited the passage in any capacity. It relates each publication's interpretation to whether it omitted or cited the heterodox part.

TABLE 2. Treatment of the heterodox sentiment
by those who acknowledge the passage

	Omitted	Cited	Total
State	20	14	34
Dissenting	1	19	20
Total	21	33	54

Of the 34 publications which put forward a state interpretation, 59 percent (20/34) truncated the passage, omitting the heterodox sentiments. This sort of omission cannot be viewed as acceptable authorial discretion. Nor can it be discounted as simple ignorance of the passage's existence. To omit part of what is arguably an indivisible whole reveals either exceptionally inattentive reading or a willingness *to suppress* that which is ill-suited to the author's intended message. The odds ratio shows that among scholars who saw some appeal in this passage, those with a state interpretation were only about 4 percent as likely as those with a dissenting interpretation to reveal its heterodox part. Or the inverse, those with a dissenting interpretation were 27 times more likely to show it.[5] There is a profound asymmetry in method here, with the state interpretations avoiding complexity and the dissenting interpretations admitting of it. Among those who acknowledge the existence of the passage, the heterodox part has been treated either as a skeleton to be kept in the closet or as a skeleton key. The pattern raises the question—one which cannot be answered—as to how many of the other 117 with a state interpretation actively concealed this passage entirely to avoid having to address its complexity.[6]

A closer reading reveals another shortcoming of the orthodox literature. Of the 151 publications which offer a state view, I have found only one case which responds to a main dissenting argument—and even this case is evasive on the specific dissenting argument of school funding. The case is from Mark Blaug (1975, 572 n.12) who is appreciative of E. G. West's body of work and grants him authority on many fine points on the history of education, referencing him 14 times. Nonetheless, Blaug claims Smith supported public education and, in doing so, he entirely avoids West's assertion that Smith favored private funding. Blaug only confronts West on the more elementary argument that Smith insisted upon freedom of choice.[7] Proponents of the state interpretation thus have almost universally ignored the dissenting inter- pretations—and here it is worth noting that they have also ignored the *initial* commentary, i.e., that from the 18th and 19th centuries, which was particularly drawn to Smith's resistance to the idea of subsidization (Drylie 2020). This pattern of failing to address dissenting views foreshadows what a closer literature review might be able to confirm: that the orthodox interpretation has not won an argument but rather assumed the victory.

Have these patterns changed over time? I considered several possible historical demarcations to use for splitting the publications into eras, and

---

5. The odds ratio calculation is $(14/20)/(19/1)$. The Pearson chi-squared test confirms that the decision to suppress is highly likely to be related to the choice to offer a state interpretation ($\chi^2 = 15.35$, p < .0001).

6. 'Turnabout is fair play' has not been adopted by dissenting literature. The four who cited just the heterodox part paraphrased the state sentiments of the first part. There is no case in which the dissenting literature simply ignores evidence of state sentiments in Smith's writing.

7. Others reference West as an authority of Smith's views of education or take issue with other aspects of his work, but steer even further from his position on school funding (e.g., Leathers and Raines 2003, 55).

chose the year 1976; as the bicentennial of the publication of *The Wealth of Nations*, 1976 coincides with expanded interest in Smith (especially outside of economics) and roughly with a rediscovery of Smith's other work, *The Theory of Moral Sentiments*, which has elsewhere tended to change the nature of Smithian discourse on the role of the state (Labio 2006; C. Smith 2014). Table 3 in Appendix B shows the contingency table using the 1976 demarcation. There does not appear to be a relationship between the nature of the interpretation and era. Dissenting interpretations constituted 18 percent of the sample before 1976, and 22 percent from 1976 onward, a statistically insignificant difference.[8] Also, although there has been an uptick in the presence of the passage in the literature (as seen in Table 4 in Appendix B),[9] there remains an unwillingness to fully reveal or engage with the heterodox sentiments.

I also explored whether the academic discipline of the author was related to the decision to cite or suppress the heterodox part of the passage. Fifty-four cited the passage in any capacity. Forty-two of those were economists or historians of economic thought, of whom 31 (74 percent) cited the heterodox part. Eleven were non-economists, of whom only two (18 percent) cited the heterodox part.[10] Thus, once it was determined to mine this passage for meaning, the heterodox part has almost exclusively been brought forth into the scholarship by economists and historians of economic thought (31/33). The decision to use the first part of the passage but to suppress the second can be associated with the non-economics disciplines in the sample (e.g., education, law, sociology, public affairs, and philosophy with no known focus on economics).[11] Table 5 in the Appendix B shows the contingency table.[12]

In summary, there is a dominant position that Smith advocated taxpayer funding, and there has been no discernable movement away from that position. Despite Smith providing a summary that stands in tension with that position, only a small portion of the scholarship has cited it. Despite that sum-

---

8. The Pearson Chi-squared test fails to reject the null, thus the era appears unrelated to the nature of the interpretation ($\chi^2 = .26$, p = .61). Robustness checks using different demarcation dates came to the same result. For instance, year 2000 ($\chi^2 = .08$, p = .77).

9. $\chi^2 = 11.87$, p = .0005.

10. One example was removed as that it was published by an organization with no disclosure of the authors.

11. But it should be noted that a great many economists and historians of economic thought fail to cite it at all.

12. $\chi^2 = 11.48$, p = .0007.

mary being in a distinct section called the "Conclusion of the Chapter" *which has as its solitary function to summarize his recommended roles of the state,* many have cherry-picked from it. Smith's writings have attracted many disciplines but very few outside of economics and the history of economic thought have cited the summary in whole. The tendency to suppress or avoid complexity begins to hint at the possibility that authorial discretion may have to be challenged, and due diligence insisted upon.

Literature review

The literature review seeks to answer the following questions: (1) What is it about Smith's article on education which creates such a strong adherence to the state interpretation and leads to a decision to omit the key passage? (2) What, in contrast, comes into service for the dissenter other than the key passage? (3) Has the key passage moderated the state view in any way? (4) How should we recognize credibility on this matter?

The logic of state interpretations

Two passages are frequently cited to serve state interpretations of Smith: "The publick can facilitate this acquisition [of the most essential parts of education] by establishing in every parish or district a little school" (WN, V.i.f.55); and "Though the state was to derive no advantage from the instruction of the inferior ranks of people, it would still deserve its attention that they should not be altogether uninstructed" (V.i.f.61).

Many find it clear that Smith proposed extensive reliance on taxes and government control. Mike Hill and Warren Montag (2015, 75): "What Smith has in mind here...is nothing less than public education." Patricia Werhane (1991, 19): Smith had in mind "the ideal of universal public education." Sandy Baum (1992, 152): "Smith advocated universal education with the expenses to be paid out of general public revenues." And Ellwood Cubberly (1920, 621): "The State has every right, not only to take over elementary education as a state function and a public charge, but also to make it free and compulsory."

Smith's plan would be a major change. Ryan Hanley (2009, 59–60): "Smith makes clear precisely what he has in mind...an expansive and unprecedented proposal for public education at state expense." Gertrude Himmelfarb (1984,

59): "He urged the establishment of a state-administered, state-supported, state-enforced system of education with only token fees to be paid by the parents... He now advanced a scheme requiring a greater measure of government involvement than anything that had ever existed before." Gavin Kennedy (2005, 226): Smith's proposal "represented a substantial intervention by the state in the economic mode of his narrative of perfect liberty." Emma Rothschild (1992, 91): Education contains "some of his boldest proposals." Dennis Rasmussen (2008, 107) calls Smith a radical, naming public education the "most important" of his recommendations to aid the poor. And Samuel Fleischacker (2004, 234–235) goes further, believing that Smith's extensive recommendation in education demonstrates that his concept of sovereign is thus "broad enough to include practically all the tasks that modern welfare liberals, as opposed to libertarians, would put under government purview."

Yet there appears to be a limit imposed upon his would-be proposal. Smith warns, "The master being partly but not wholly paid by the publick; because if he was wholly, *or even principally* paid by it, he would soon learn to neglect his business" (WN, V.i.f.55, my emphasis).

This passage has lent to a different pattern of responses: the mixed-mode interpretation whereby Smith is said to have sought only partial funding through taxation. Jessie Norman (2018): "The remedy Smith advanced is for government to establish a widespread system of local schools...paid for partly at public expense and partly through very moderate fees."[13] This mixed-mode interpretation is widespread and gains credence with scholars based on the fact that Smith provides an example (and one close to home): the Scottish parish system. Ian Ross (1984, 183): "Smith advocates a system of limited universal education, something like that of the parochial schools of Scotland." Charles Fay (1930, 32): "He extols the parish schools of Scotland." As for the right mix of taxes and user fees, Smith is silent. Those whom I have categorized as offering a state interpretation seem to suggest this example is determinant of a request for a large proportion for taxes. Dissenting literature does not.[14]

---

13. See also Anderson 1995, 27; Muller 1993, 151; Buchan 2006, 113; Skinner 1996, 193; Weinstein 2013, 204; Norman 2018; C. Winch 1998, 371; Hanley 2016, 505.

14. Missing on both sides is attention to the historical record which could shed light on the financial arrangements that Smith may have been aware of and possibly found exemplary. Contrast this oversight to the great attention given to identifying his source for the pin-factory

What motivates Smith to cede responsibility to a state apparatus? A common answer in the state literature is that expanding education through the state could relieve suffering and provide private and public benefits. Smith has much to say on these matters. Of suffering, Smith provides a compelling depiction of the poor laborer, which includes moving comments such as: "He naturally loses...the habit of such exertion, and generally becomes as stupid and ignorant as it is possible for a human creature to become. The torpor of his mind renders him, not only incapable of relishing or bearing a part in any rational conversation, but of conceiving any generous, noble, or tender sentiment" (V.i.f.50).

Many have noted the passion with which Smith describes that suffering, and they imply that these passions motivate him in his endorsement of government intervention. Smith's words are "harrowing" (Muller 1993, 150), "disturbing" (Young 1997, 200), "uncharacteristically animated' (L. Hill 2007, 343), "damning" (Himmelfarb 2012, 14), the "harshest denunciation of commercial society," and "a diatribe against the effects of the division of labor" (Rasmussen 2008, 108–110).[15]

As for benefits, Smith writes, "The more they are instructed, the less liable they are to the delusions of enthusiasm and superstition, which, among ignorant nations, frequently occasion the most dreadful disorders." Educated people are "more decent and orderly," "more respectable" as well as respectful of superiors, "more disposed to examine, and more capable of seeing through, the interested complaints of faction and sedition," and "less apt to be misled into any wanton or unnecessary opposition to the measures of government" (V.i.f.61).

This vigorous treatment of benefits has perhaps attracted the greatest attention. There seems to be universal agreement among those in my survey that Smith saw social and/or private value in the poor having education. The state and dissenting literature differ largely in specifying what kinds of actions such potential benefits mandate for Smith. The state literature has generally chosen to elaborate on these benefits as evidence of the strength of his commitment

---

analysis.

15. It should be noted that some judgments such as these are shaded with delight at the notion that Smith is belatedly recognizing the irony of his beneficial system having deleterious side effects, and that some others feel these negative effects were exaggerated by Smith for rhetorical purposes.

to education and derived from this commitment a willingness to involve government to ensure its access. The dissenting literature has resisted deriving such an implication.

The state literature richly discusses the benefits. Jacob Viner (1927, 227): "Smith supports the participation of the government in the general education of the people, because it will help prepare them for industry, will make them better citizens and better soldiers, and happier and healthier men in mind and body." Rothschild (1998, 210–220): Smith wants people to be able to "speculate about the origins of the universe, or go to performances of tragedies, or to have conversations about their moral sentiments." Ross (1984, 182–183): "He is led to interest himself in the vertical penetration of the Enlightenment"—meaning, the transmission of a "homogeneity of knowledge that animated the enterprise of *Encyclopédie*." Jack Russell Weinstein (2007, 64): "His education comments are concerned with political as well as moral stability… Class barriers, in a commercial society, are great barriers to mutual sympathy." Weinstein (ibid., 65), again: "A society only has perfect liberty if its members are actually capable of changing their trade when it pleases them." James Alvey (1998, 4): "Moderation, a type of self-command (which is integral to Smith's moral theory) is a sort of public good requiring government support."

Irrespective of how compelling the case for expanded educational access is, a great many recognize that Smith does set a *precondition* for state provision. In the prelude to his public works analysis, Smith considers it appropriate for the sovereign to provide only those goods and services "which it can never be for the interest of any individual, or small number of individuals, to erect and maintain; because the profit could never repay the expence…though it may frequently do much more than repay it to a great society" (IV.ix.51). For Smith, private parties would need to reveal a current and future inability to provide the socially beneficial product.

Some specifically note this precondition. Kevin Quinn (2013, 121) writes, "As with any other good, then, the case for government involvement in its provision or financing will depend, for the economist, on identifying a market failure of some sort."[16] Others seem implicitly to recognize it, and

---

16. See also Sen 2013; Lawson and Silver 1973, 253; Spengler 1977, 33; Kennedy 2008, 235; Rauhut 2005, 30; Weinstein 2013, 202.

others to give it no attention. Regardless, for those whom I have classified as having a state interpretation, this precondition has been met in Smith's time or would inevitably be met in any society built upon liberal commerce. Jerry Muller (1993, 148, 150): Smith was "writing at a time when there was no general education. … As an antidote to the mental degradation caused by the division of labour, Smith recommended universal public schooling, largely at government expense." Quinn (2013, 121): "There did not seem to be a market for educating the poor." Alvey (1998, 4): "Education is not sufficiently provided to the public by the private sector." Dogan Göçmen (2012, 62): "As a solution to alienation…Smith proposes universal education." Paul McNulty (1973, 361): "His real purpose was to point out that the deleterious effects of division of labor could be overcome or eliminated by governmental programs supporting educational or cultural programs in which the laboring poor could participate." Public funding of education was necessary if Smith's liberal project for commerce was to be considered virtuous.

Scholars have consistently focused on these passages to make the case for Smith as an advocate of taxpayer funding. Such a focus, however, is tight, and that potentially comes with the cost of excluding other material that arguably alters the context and the reading of these passages. And it happens that all of the passages occur *in the last quarter* of Smith's article. In the first three-quarters of the article there is a remarkably different tone, as there is in the "Conclusion of the Chapter."

The logic of state interpretations which cite the passage

Some advocates of the state interpretation have let the "Conclusion of the Chapter" passage appear in their articles. Has doing so caused some moderation of the state view that has not been captured by my broad categorization scheme? Is there something to learn about the passage from their readings of it?

Unsurprisingly, those citing just the first part add no new perspective. Brian Lund (2002): "The economists, [Smith in particular], who promoted the market as the most efficient distributive mechanism agreed that education was the most important exception to the general prohibition against state intervention." Edmund Phelps (1997): "The public sector was to serve economic development—to expand opportunity." Irene Gordon and Lawrence Boland

(1998, 1235): "Adam Smith clearly acknowledges that there is a necessary social role for government [in defense, justice, roads, and education]…. Market failures exist." Elise Brezis (2006, 21): "Adam Smith was aware of the positive externalities of education on the society, and therefore thought that educational institutions should be financed in some part by the state."

Rather than showing any particular attenuation of state sentiment, there was even a tendency toward didactic and dubious fiddling with state sentiments. Janice McClung Holtkamp (1994, 3), for example, places the truncated first part in the position of an epigraph—therein, summoning Smith as a definitive and authoritative voice introducing a study which will claim to show "that investment in higher education by society is a necessary and beneficial endeavor." D. Naismith (1988, 28) includes the first part in artificial block quote which creates a highly deterministic characterization of Smith. He cites the third duty of the sovereign as "erecting and maintaining certain public works and certain public institutions." But he removes all the conditions, and instead appends to it "Education…may, *therefore*, without injustice, be defrayed by the general contribution of the whole society" (ibid., my emphasis). The "therefore" takes on a far different association than in Smith's original. And Frank Solomon (2013, 158) uses an artificial block quotation to the same effect: He conjoins Smith's "The publick can facilitate" clause to the *final* paragraph of the "Conclusion of the Chapter" instead of to the key education paragraph I have focused on which is adjacent to it.[17] The final paragraph merely restates the *general* principle of market failure, therein permitting Solomon to avoid the *hedged* comment about its applicability to education.

Perhaps surprisingly, those who cited the whole passage also did not attenuate their interpretations in any way. Joseph Spengler (1975), Elehanan Cohn (1979), Claire Palley (1991), Brendan Walsch (1998), Orhan Kayaalp (2004), and Wilfried ver Eeck (2013) may have cited the whole passage, but they provide no interpretation of the whole. Instead, they appear to have cited it merely for the apparent drift of its first part.

Only a few authors cite the whole passage *and* sense the contrary drift of the second part. Andrew Skinner, for example, writes of the conclusion, "The modern reader has to make a considerable effort to understand Smith's intentions" (2012, 168). Skinner also writes that "Smith's position was thus

---

17. Solomon (2013) has not been included in the dataset as he did not cite the passage.

somewhat ambiguous" (1995, 88). Murray Milgate and Shannon Stimson (2009, 114) find that the duality of the passage shows Smith was "less than whole-hearted." Charles Leathers and Patrick Raines (2003, 54–69) pause at it as well. However, none of these authors maintain these dissenting tacks. They each resolve the passage by adopting a dual-policy interpretation which is common in the literature.

This dual-policy interpretation states that Smith had two views of subsidization, one for the rich attending universities and one for the poor needing elementary education. Smith addresses both types of students within his article "Education of Youth." The argument goes that Smith cannot recommend subsidies as a financial structure for universities because they tend to corrupt quality, but he nonetheless recommends expanding them as a solution for the poor. Reisman (1998, 376) writes, "In respect to Oxford, Smith was a libertarian... In respect to secondary education for the lower classes, however, he was visibly more interventionist." Richard Stone (2005, 69–71): Smith is "curiously negative" regarding the "educational arrangements of his day" for higher education; but Smith is an "optimist" regarding "the children of the common people." Rothschild (1998, 209): "He finds no good reason that the public should pay for educational endowments, or for the great ecclesiastical corporations...but he is strongly in favour, by contrast, of public support for the education of the 'common people.'" Jerry Evensky (2005, 228): "Although Smith wants government to finance education for the working class children, he is very much against government financing of that institution which provides the instruction of people of all ages: religion." Clyde Dankert (1974, 164): "It should be added that our author was thinking here [on the disincentives of endowments] primarily of education for the well-to-do classes. He supported a somewhat different arrangement for the education of the masses."[18] Finally, Pierre Tu (1966, 10) and George Fallis (2007, 91), who cite Smith's final words, assert this dual-policy perspective as well.

The question is: on what basis has this dual-policy account been established? It is unclear. There is no particular citation which establishes it, and the authors do not explain themselves. My inference is that the two distinct policies either appear so self-evident to these authors that they feel it requires

---

18. For more examples see Morrow 1927, 326; Robbins 1965, 90; A. Brown 1975, 267; Himmelfarb 1984, 58; Rothschild 1998, 210; Ortman 1999, 303; Birch 1998, 34.

no elaboration, or that they arrive at two policies as a logical necessity to make sense of an article which is at first highly critical of subsidization and then seemingly receptive to it. Only those who cite Smith's final words and sense its duality seem to wrestle overtly with the dual-policy idea.

For instance, Skinner provides varying interpretations. In one instance, he resolves the tension in the passage in support of the mixed-mode model (Skinner 1995). In others, he wants to address the passage as only applicable to university students and ignore that it applies, as written, to elementary education as well (Skinner 1988; 2012). Skinner leans toward the dual-policy interpretation, stating that Smith "protested against" university subsidization (Skinner 1988, 12–13) but recommended elementary subsidization even as it "infringe[s] the natural liberty of the subject" (1988, 10). Similarly, Milgate and Stimson (2009) and Leathers and Raines (1992; 1999) want to discuss the passage only in relationship to *religious* education. Milgate and Stimson (2009, 114) assert that Smith "sharply distinguished" his views of elementary education from religious education, rejecting endowments for religion but "unambiguously" recommending taxes for elementary education. It is important to note that to maintain this interpretation, Milgate and Stimson tinker with Smith's final words which pertain to "education and religious instruction" alike, and they drop the word "education." These efforts by Skinner (1988) and Milgate and Stimson (2009) seem to imply that Smith's message requires some rewriting or downplaying in order to align it with their impression from the article itself. But again on what basis is that impression formed?

As far as I can tell, it is only Leathers and Raines (2003) who provide a stated *reasoning* to adopt a dual-policy interpretation. Leathers and Raines state that "the entire discussion of the education of youth devoted more attention to university education for the sons of 'gentlemen and men of fortune' than to the basic education of the 'common people'" (2003, 54). In addition, they too seem to be governed by another premise—namely, that Smith's writing tends toward "incompleteness, weaknesses and contradictions" (ibid., 69). My reading of their approach is that Smith's final words—which make no distinction between the rich and the poor—should have done so if they were to be consistent with Smith's treatment of endowments. Predominantly derived from observations of universities, his study of endowments produces only weak implications for what to do about elementary education. Smith had no intention for the lessons of endowments to be broadly applicable.[19]

If there are other rationales by which to establish a dual-policy perspective, I am unaware of them. Another that I sense but cannot attribute to any particular author is that Smith, in facing whether to commence a public work, contemplated the issue in terms of likelihood *and* magnitude of effects. Smith's article might make clear that he views positive effects as unlikely, but perhaps Smith finds that the upside potential for the poor renders public financing a worthwhile experiment, i.e., worth the risk of wasted expenses and further marginal degeneration. None have written anything so formal. However, this narrative perhaps fits with the spirit and narrative of many interpretations: Smith is embarrassed by the strength or excessively broad application of his argument for commerce in WN, and now he must concede to a different perspective and make amends for the damages done to the poor. That is, Smith's cool calculations and excessive prudence must give way to a compassion. The problem with this rationale, however, is that it certainly goes too far if Smith's final words represent his views. Namely, the only effect of this transformation of thought in his final adjudication is that, instead of rejecting government outright, he cautiously includes it as an option in a solution set, and a disadvantaged option at that.

To conclude, very few of those who cite Smith's final words note the contrary drift, and those who do nonetheless recast it in favor of a state interpretation. As such, moderation of the state views has not occurred. In this process, some curious liberties have certainly been taken with Smith's final words, but in doing so these authors elevate the challenge for anyone who would place value in them. Perhaps the conclusion poorly represents Smith's views, and must be reinterpreted through the greater lens of the article. And indeed, one wouldn't want to abandon an entire article in favor of a single citation if that citation is not representative of the rest.

But is it the case that Smith's final words do not match the article? The dissenting literature relies on both, suggesting there are harmonies between them. The dissenting literature also takes some pride in recognizing these harmonies and has accused the orthodox literature of inattentive reading. For instance, they state that much of the article, especially his criticism of

---

19. Leathers and Raines (2003, 55), interestingly, reference E. G. West to dispute his position regarding economic gains, but they do not acknowledge that West had a different reading of the key passage.

endowments, has been "neglected" (West n.d., 2) and treated as "mere curiosum" (Rosenberg 1960, 568). I draw a similar conclusion about the state literature. I find little attention being dedicated to the first three-quarters of the article. I also identify a great many authors who sense the article is "contradictory," "vague," "awkward," "unspecific," "muddled," "odd," "deficient," "ambiguous," "wandering" and "unformulated,"[20] and yet who have not pursued these internal tensions and peculiarities for alternative meanings. Different levels of attentiveness to much of the article may account for the disparate views.

The logic of dissenting interpretations

The survey identified 40 interpretations which hold a dissenting view of Smith's favored role for government in education. They take great inspiration from the first three-quarters of the article, from which none of the prior quotes come. There Smith maintains that endowments are disincentives to quality instruction because they provide guaranteed salaries to teachers irrespective of performance. For dissenting scholars, his depiction of the ill effects confidently answers the primary question of his study: Are endowments a good model which validates establishing government schools based on a tax fund (V.i.f.2–4)? The dissenting scholars answer with varying degrees of confidence that endowments provide no such validation for taxes. They do not directly address the possibility of a dual-policy interpretation. They instead treat his argument as uniformly condemnatory. As that their accounts are usually relatively terse, I must infer why they do not consider the dual-policy view. They either find the specifics of college and university endowments as unessential to his argument; or they reject the factual basis of Leathers and Raines's premise that Smith is predominantly focused on colleges and education. I will first identify some of the passages that inform their reading. Then, I will outline what I believe steers dissenting scholars away from a dual-policy perspective.

Some of the most highly critical passages of endowments occur, indeed, in regards to colleges and universities. Smith writes of the fully salaried university teacher: "His interest is, in this case, set as directly in opposition to his duty

---

20. Leathers and Raines 2003, 69; Weinstein 2013, 186, 202; Berry 1997, 145; Stanfield 2005, 1; Macdonald 2019, 144; Small 1907; Blaug 1975, 572.

as it is possible to set" (V.i.f.7). Of partially salaried teachers, he writes of partial effort, and explains that effort is "always more or less diminished" accordingly (6). Authorities cannot improve this causal relationship. "In the university of Oxford, the greater part of the publick professors have, for these many years, given up altogether even the pretence of teaching" (8). Authorities often worsen the causal relationship, rendering the teacher "obsequious" to the arbitrary goals and "one of the meanest and most contemptible persons in the society" (9). Of natural will toward excellence and personal reward, Smith is suspicious (4).

In each case, Smith's explanation is clear and rhetorically charged. Guaranteed salaries and limits on student choice of college teachers will "extinguish all emulation" (V.i.f.13), "blunt the edge of all those incitements to diligence" in teachers (14), and cause a teacher to operate with interests as "in opposition to his duty as it is possible to set" (7). The college tutor or teacher may "commonly teach very negligently and superficially" (33), may "flatter himself that he is giving a lecture" (14), may "neglect his duty" (8), even "altogether" (9). Endowments, at least, in colleges and universities, fail to achieve quality because of their primary function of subsidizing the teachers' salaries.

Endowments also fail to produce meaningful curricula. With teachers and administrators receiving guaranteed salaries, students have no means to command change. As a result, over time the curricula fail to render the education "proper" for "the education of gentlemen or men of the world, or more likely either to improve the understanding, or to mend the heart" (V.i.f.32). They become full of "exploded systems and obsolete prejudices" (34). Some fields may even be a "useless and pedantick heap of sophistry and nonsense" (46). Regardless of intent, a lecture devolves into a "sham-lecture" full of "nonsense" (14).

Does this negative assessment of colleges amount to a condemnation of a specific college form of endowment or, instead, does it contribute to condemnation of all endowments? I believe dissenting scholars generally recognize that Smith does not set up his study to find a variegated set of cause-and-effect relationships, nor does he find them. He asserts that performance pay is integral to effort "in every profession" (V.i.f.4)—even in teaching, about which he hypothesizes that endowments "have necessarily diminished more or less the necessity of application in the teacher" (5). Here is not a partial or particular hypothesis about colleges. In fact, he believes his hypothesis to be true in both "*schools* and colleges" (ibid., my emphasis). In the ensuing test of his hypothesis, in no case does his commendation of them depend upon any variable unique to colleges.

Dissenting scholars may note that Smith also addresses non-college examples and his message is consistent. Endowed colleges and universities are without merit, but England's privately funded "publick schools" for grammar and language (by which he means schools outside the home), are "much less corrupted than the universities" because they are based on user fees. In another comparison, in *endowed* riding schools, "good effects" are "not commonly so evident"—but in *privately funded* schools of fencing and dancing, a student "seldom fails of learning to fence or to dance" (V.i.f.16). The distinguishing characteristic of these comparisons is solely whether endowments exist—not whether a certain kind of endowment exists or whether a certain kind of student is involved. The comparisons make the point that endowed schools differ from private schools; endowed schools do not differ from each other in ways that require him to modify his judgment.

Dissenting scholars may also note that Smith is consistently critical across a *large* sample set. Unsatisfied with the limited variety in his contemporaneous examples, he turns to the historical records of ancient societies to determine if endowments have ever had a positive outcome. Smith examines the ancients' schools of gymnastics and music; reading, writing, and accounting; philosophy and rhetorick; and civil law. He cannot find a single example where subsidization was a cause of the success of the school. Moreover, he makes clear that a better direction of focus for governments may be the stimulation of demand for education rather than the supply. Counting these schools amongst his examples may render Leathers and Raines's premise false. Smith dedicates more time to colleges and universities, but those examples constitute a minority set in his entire study.

Still, why address colleges and universities at all in a study dedicated to understanding the "Institutions for the Education of Youth?" And then why so much attention? Does this not inevitably confuse the reader as to the proper scope of his condemnation? To the first question, to provide a thorough study would require attention to them, as that the concept of the "education of youth" contained within its domain college and university students. This can be established by legal accounts (e.g., Pickering 1762), as well as through common parlance and other education writing (e.g., Denning

1763). To the second question, there are two natural reasons for the magnified attention. First, endowed colleges predominate among the potential contemporaneous examples. Endowments, as a means of funding, are strongly intertwined with the history of colleges from their 13th century inception (Wood 1792) and thus they represent the bulk of contemporaneous examples at his disposal. Second, they are the examples which his audience had experience with and could relate to. Smith is using familiar college and university examples in the same manner that a parent would use known and poignant examples of car crashes to advise their rash child how to avoid the same end.

But one might argue that these answers are insufficient to explain Smith's lengthy and well-known *history* of colleges and universities, which spans approximately a quarter of the article. I cannot speculate as to what dissenting scholars think of this history, but in my own work I have offered some additional context which explains its length. Namely, his history does not occur arbitrarily as a digression (or a fixation). It is prompted by a specific challenge from a rhetorical interlocutor: a warm-hearted and well-intended sentiment which argues that despite endowments' problems, something is better than nothing (V.i.f.18).[21] Smith's history is a carefully chosen response to this sentiment, a case study or morality tale for the audience unmoved by his methodology thus far. His history goes on to show that endowments are greatly to blame for the intellectual, moral, and social destruction occurring across Europe. A series of ironic counter-responses to the challenge wraps up his history: a portrayal of wealth turning to poverty, legacies degrading into feebleness, science devolving into nonsense, and good intentions ending in social ruin (V.i.f.34–37, 46–47). The history of colleges and universities provides the correct lens to make these points, as worries of moral decay and poor quality in British colleges was a frequent point of conversation at the time. Smith utilizes those anxieties to his advantage. That he again rebukes the challenging sentiment of something-is-better-than-nothing later in the article reveals how much the sentiment worries him for its ability to persuade people to retain some faith in the rotten institution of endowments.[22]

---

21. In Drylie (2020), I more fully show the presence of a dialogic structure used by Smith to further his argument, and I characterize this paragraph as an interjection of incredulity. Leathers and Raines (2003, 56) attribute this warm-hearted sentiment to Smith himself, calling it his "most revealing comment." I find no merit to that reading based on the context.
22. He concludes his overall assessment of endowments, "Were there no publick institutions

Finally, I suspect that some scholars are attentive to the tone and manner in which he concludes his analysis of endowments. He writes of the ancients: "The demand for such instruction produced, what it *always* produces, the talent for giving it; and the emulation which an unrestrained competition *never* fails to excite, appears to have brought that talent to a very high degree of perfection" (V.i.f.45, my emphasis). He finds that the ancients, unburdened by endowments, were superior to modern teachers. He also introduces the language of markets for the first time in the article. He writes of "competition," "trade," "sale," "goods," "price," "profit," "demand," and "bankruptcy" (45). Therein, he situates the market for education back into his general view that freely functioning markets can naturally arrive at superior ends for society. Education is unexceptional. It may need encouragement and protection, but it is not so distinct that it requires government production.

Dissenting literature pulls from these citations and impressions to various degrees and arrives at a range of portrayals of Smith. Smith is either unsure, restrained in his invitation to government, principally resistant to government, or advocating alternatives to government. I shall now provide examples of their commentary.

Given his earlier criticism of endowments, some scholars react to the tone, ambiguity, and under-defined qualities of his would-be recommendations for government, and they derive uncertainty. Arthur Lynn (1976, 371): "No final solutions and little practical guidance are to be found here. Given the *intractability of such problems*, his uncertainty is understandable; one has the impression that he really favored market-like price equivalents in most cases but recognized the pragmatic reality" (my emphasis). Christopher Lucas (1972, 363–364): "Whether the government was to help support the system also is uncertain." Among those who cite the passage, Peter Browning (1983, 70) writes, "Smith's long—and delightful—discourse on education does not, however, lead him to any firm conclusion on who should pay." Tom Stonier (1985, 14–15): Smith "equivocated on the question of whether the expense of education should be borne by public or private funds."

---

for education, no system, no science would be taught for which there was not some demand" (V.i.f.46). This statement has frequently been misattributed to the statist idea that a society cannot rely on the preferences of society, but rather must provide what legislators know to be of importance. But an honest assessment of the context shows that it is his second and very pointed rebuke of the idea that any action is better than none.

Others grant there is a role for government but believe there is no textual basis for anything more than a minimal one. Milton Friedman (1976): "Smith himself did not regard his third duty as providing extensive scope for governmental activity." Jeffrey Young (1997, 200): "Government must take 'some pains,' but there is no indication that this requires anything more than a marginal infringement of a natural liberty...It does not necessarily mean government operated schools, much less the demise of capitalism." James Otteson (2011, 166–167): "This intrusion on the free market that Smith endorses is quite a weak one." P. J. O'Rourke (2007, 141): "Adam Smith was only a tepid advocate of public education." West (1964, 466): "Adam Smith was especially careful to avoid a state system which would reproduce the errors of endowed schools." West (1980, 998), again: "Close textual examination reveals the tamest of Smithian programs...This is surely not a program of social control via coercive *state* education." Alexandra Hyard (2007, 76) concludes that Smith's proposal was "a minor proposition" and "mainly...a private matter."

Occasionally, the reasons for Smith's resistance are elaborated upon. Milton Friedman (1976): "Despite Smith's acceptance of the appropriateness of governmental establishment and maintenance of such institutions, he devotes most of his discussion to a *scathing attack* on the effects of governmental or church control of institutions of learning" (my emphasis). Fay (1930, 187): "The sacredness of liberty to him explains why, unless there be no other way, he is disinclined to the provision of education by an external body." Charles Griswold (1999, 254) finds approval for government only "as long of course, as the means chosen are carefully thought through so as to prevent the evils that always accompany the creation of state-enforced standards (e.g., the creation of administrators of those standards, in this case teachers, whose income is assured)." And West (1964, 475) reminds the reader that "suggested improvements must be envisaged in the realm of the politically possible. The state is not a disembodied abstraction and its officials are presumably just as fallible as other human beings." In large part, these scholars have reacted to Smith's criticism of endowments and understood his displeasure through a broader understanding of his relationship to liberty.

Those who cite the passage convey a similar message of disapproval, and often characterize it as his pointed, conclusive *warning* against the state. Steve Bradley and Jim Taylor (2004, 2): "In spite of the warnings delivered by Smith in the 18th century, and the recent interventions by Friedman and other right-wing academics, the trend until very recently has been towards increasing government intervention in education by the state." David Friedman (1997): "It is often said that Adam Smith, despite his general belief in Laissez-faire, made an exception for education. That is not entirely true. In the course of a lengthy and interesting discussion, Smith argues both that education is a legitimate government function, at least in some societies, and that it is a function which governments perform very badly." Robert Wright (2017, 126): "Smith, after all, was a keen observer of government. He realized that although the government could occasionally run a successful business, like the loan office in Pennsylvania, the public pawnshop in Hamburg, and the various postal systems, government businesses often failed because of 'slothful and negligent' provision, and 'thoughtless extravagance.'" And George Montgomery (1949), introducing the whole "Conclusion of the Chapter" writes, "Were Smith's treatment of government spending and borrowing to have come to the attention of certain politicians and liberal economists of the past two decades, they should have refrained from making some of the flagrantly immature declarations as to the significance of the economy of the state and particularly public debts." Smith's final words, then, permit these authors to heavily weight Smith's overall suspicion of the state. Education is not an exception.

Some scholars conclude that Smith's faith in private action was discernible in the article and constitutes his preference. Milton Friedman (1976): "[Smith] favored financing [institutions for the education of youth] largely by specific fees." Edward Ryan (1990, 152): "Smith gave his support to this method [of user fees] in such areas as education and the use of turnpikes." West (1964, 465–467): Smith preferred to "remove all obstacles to competition" and rely on "market forces in providing education." Eamonn Butler (2007, 69): "He remains unclear on just how much government should pay towards this basic education, though he expresses high regards for the private schools for the skills like fencing or dancing, where the students pay the whole amount."

Those citing the passage agree. David Friedman (1997): "His conclusion is that while it is legitimate for government to subsidize education, it may be more prudent to leave education entirely private." Wright (2017, 126): "Most public services, therefore, were best left to the private sector, including, where appropriate, non-profit corporations." Kerry King (2005b, 357): "Although the debate over school choice has just recently become a major topic in education reform, implementing choice and competition in education was first discussed by Adam Smith." Arthur Taylor (1972, 47): Education, "being of benefit to society as a whole, could legitimately be made a public charge...[but] Adam Smith offered [the free market] a modicum of encouragement when he expressed a preference for a system in which the expense of education was 'defrayed altogether by those who receive the immediate benefit.'"

Aside from user fees, the phrase "voluntary contribution" in the passage conveys to some authors that Smith also held faith in charity. Walter Clark (1903, 230) concluded succinctly that Smith approved of "education of common people in charity schools." Jack High (1985, 317), paraphrasing Smith: "If we do in fact benefit from the additional education of others, voluntary contributions enable us to capture these benefits without the necessity of government action." Robert Heilbroner (1986, 312) comments in his condensed version of WN that education "may also be defrayed by general contribution, but better by fees and voluntary contribution." West (1994), adopting the persona of Smith in a mock interview with the Minneapolis Federal Reserve, states: "I always wanted the parents, even poor parents, to pay fees covering some significant part of the costs, and if there was to be some non-parent support, I recommended voluntary contributions from the immediate neighbors. This was not therefore an argument in favor of state education as so many writers tend to believe." Finally, my own work aims to rehabilitate the place of charity in his thoughts on education (Drylie 2016; 2020).

The thought of charity has crossed the mind of a few who offer a state interpretation, but they sell Smith short. Daniel Rauhut (2005, 29–30) implies that Smith missed the fact that "private agents can provide several of the things Smith lists as government duties." Reisman (1998, 371): "The State is in and the market is out—or perhaps Smith simply threw in his cards without appreciating just how much the automaticity of interest could rise to the challenge." And Gaston Rimlinger (1976, 230) claims Smith had "little faith in private charity." Overall, few have noted or have taken Smith's phrase "voluntary contributions" as a meaningful proposal. However, Smith does in fact identify charity as an option in the article, which he attributes to the English solution to the problem (V.i.f.55). A close reading will reveal that he in no way dismisses the option.

A pattern that emerges in the dissenting literature is that Smith, indeed, contemplated a role for government but constrained or denied it. These scholars turn to the abundance of criticism of endowments as evidence that Smith's true message to the reader is to proceed warily and to resist the seduction of any apparent easy solution. Because of public benefits, government action may be looked at as just; however, government action will likely disappoint and end up being unjust.

Three distinguished dissenting interpretations

It is important to note that the dissenting literature has not strongly argued the points I make above, nor heavily substantiated them. My above citations of Smith far exceed evidence provided by any one of them. And while those who cite the passage tend to make the argument more forcefully, there remains a tendency toward terseness. In only three cases do scholars provide elaborate interpretations. Each makes contributions beyond points in my foregoing discussion.

Knud Haakonssen (2006, 20–21), who does not cite the passage, writes that government is part of the solution to "replace the moral community of spectators that is lost when people move away from the dependency relationships of traditional society to the 'anonymity' of the wage economy in commercial society." But then he importantly defines Smith's notion of governance as encompassing "the great number of public offices which were certainly of a civic nature but which were not offices of the state." Here is a notion of governance which opens up a much more indeterminate solution set of possibilities than the set of mixed-mode options which have presented themselves so far. Haakonssen concludes that the funding for education will come "in part by society, and by the multiplicity of confessional groups that tend to arise from freedom of religion." The politics to such ends should crucially be driven by "a wide variety of leadership roles in local communities."

The other two distinguished interpretations do cite the passage and apply a similar historical perspective. First, E. G. West, who has investigated this subject more than any other has, wrote:

Smith was ultimately so heavily critical of the way in which any element of "subsidy" was in danger of being squandered, that one often gets the impression he believed they were typically non-productive, if not counterproductive. The penultimate paragraph of his long section on public works [the key passage discussed in this paper] deserves more attention than it usually receives. It shows Smith's final balance of all the arguments reviewed earlier in the same chapter... It is relevant that Smith relies on voluntary contributions from the "neighbours." These neighbors would recognize benefits to themselves of the prospects of the poor in near proximity to them having an education. With a free-rider problem partially resolved through proximity, education can therefore be left to these neighbors to provide subsidies to augment family education and expenditure. (West 1977, 15–16)

West is particularly keen on Smith's "voluntary contribution" phrase because he believes Smith's concept of the sovereign was not equivalent with today's government, but rather represented a range of government and quasi-government roles. The sovereign was generally cast first as a "stage manager" and not a "leading actor," a protector of property and markets, not a producer (West 1977, 18). The sovereign's role would involve, then, the active enabling of both private and charitable markets, which at the time did require enabling (Drylie 2020).

The last example is from Craig Smith:

Without this local responsibility there is a real danger that the providers will become unaccountable and inefficient. The sort of government action that Smith is endorsing here is clearly not that of a remote eighteenth-century national government, but rather that of a local association accountable to its residents. Moreover, even in this case the service is to be organised in such a way that the individuals involved have direct relationships unmediated by a state apparatus. Those who "receive the immediate benefit of such education and instruction" are reasonably to be expected to meet the expense, just as those who make use of the legal system will support the expense involved through court fees. It would seem that Smith thought that most of the activities covered by his heading of police would be maintained at a sub-national level and quite separately from the institutions concerning justice. (C. Smith 2012, 795)

These interpretations by Haakonssen, West, and Craig Smith have similar qualities. They eschew the cloying framework which is so common in the literature and which states that *even* this icon of the free market could admit its shortcomings when it came to important things like education. Instead, they reveal that a close reading of the text in historical context allows the article to be both internally coherent as well as coherent to the principles that run through WN. They cast Smith as a writer who is gifted, disciplined, and tending toward consistency in his thinking. They elaborate on the logical possibilities of the text—like those sensed by, say, a William Boyd (1932, 324), who only speculated that Smith's choice to name the agent as "the public" is one that "leaves open the possibility of other educational authorities." They resist the temptation to conceal complexities, and over-define the solution for the modern reader, as did Eli Ginzberg (2002, 102) who simply replaced the word "public" with "state" in the phrase, "The public can facilitate, encourage, and impose." They resist the misdeeds of, say, an Albion Small (1907), who misquoted Smith's subject of criticism throughout the first three quarters of the article as "private endowments," when Smith in fact makes no distinction and used the phrase "publick endowments" (V.i.f.3). Regardless of one's ilk, these well-known scholars' efforts on this topic deserve as much attention as their efforts elsewhere have received.

Conclusion

There are many aspects of Smith's article which could bring public education to mind. Smith recognizes the challenge of educational access and describes the problems of the poor; he identifies many private and social benefits which would derive from more widespread access; he specifies a market-failure rationale for government to intervene; and he makes a call to action. But Smith also provides a theory that public subsidization, *as a specific kind of action*, will be corrupting; and as one of his first French translators noted, Smith lays out "incontestable examples" of that corruption (Garnier 1843/1802, xxx).

The challenge for the reader has been to determine how to characterize Smith's call to action, given his misgivings about endowments. The majority since 1893 have either lightly weighted or dismissed his anxieties about endowments and have read the text as providing a clear prescription of subsidization. Those who have dissented have been moved by the vigor of his criticism and have characterized his call to action as vague or constrained by his criticism.

The observed pattern in the literature suggests that that literature does not constitute a body of knowledge that makes a strong case for either interpretative choice. The state view almost universally suffers, at a minimum, from omissions. Those who perpetuate the state view have rarely cited Smith's final adjudication of the funding options, and have even regularly suppressed, ignored, and deflected the part which is inconvenient for the state view. A strong refutation of the inconvenient part is absent, and a recognition that others have dissenting views has almost never been put to paper. The state interpretation hangs a great deal on the claim that Smith's views of endowments are irrelevant. On the other side, the dissenting view suffers from lack of voice. They have not recognized that the prevalence of state view in the literature necessitates that they provide more evidence and a stronger case. They have not cried out that there may be an injustice occurring in the manner in which many scholars position Smith within a political discourse. The result is that debatable points remain undebated, and unresolved elements of the text remain unexplored.

I will conclude with an attempt to stimulate the debate which I feel is missing. I provide a series of additional inconveniences for the state inter-pretation. The dismissal of three-quarters of the article has allowed for the avoidance of these inconveniences. They also have not been substantively put forward, or addressed at all, by dissenting authors. Each elevates what I would expect to be a reasonable burden-of-proof to make the state case. I have elaborated on each of these in prior work (notably Drylie 2020).[23]

- In the most famous of his purported advocacy quotations, Smith writes "*The publick* can facilitate this acquisition by establishing in every parish or district a little school" (V.i.f.55, my emphasis). Could Smith's use of the term "the public" instead of "government" matter? A concept of the public as being distinct from the state did exist in Smith's time. Moreover, Smith's use of the term regularly reflects that distinction. Considering that immediately after this

---

23. I borrow this burden-of-proof phrase from Charles Griswold (1999, 295), who writes, "A burden-of-proof argument suffuses Smith's writing in political economy; the state may intervene in all sorts of ways, but those who would have it do so are required to show why it should in this particular instance, for how long, and in precisely what fashion, and how its intervention will escape the usual dangers of creating entrenched interest groups and self-perpetuating monopolies."

statement he identifies two ways to establish a school—the Scottish quasi-government model and the English charity model—a different interpretation is possible. Namely, Smith takes advantage of the ambiguity of the term *the public* and uses it as an expedient to broadly summon agents, both governmental and civilian, to consider this option.

- The Scottish quasi-government education system in Smith's time was not on a strong foundation, but the extant charity system was thriving, broadly supported by those in the rising ranks, and well-known. Thus, his readers would need convincing to abandon charity for government. Smith makes no such compelling case. He never adjudicates clearly in favor of the state system over the merits of charity, but rather places them in close equipoise as the introduces them. In the "Conclusion of the Chapter" he even tends to favor charity, as the term "voluntary contribution" would have clearly conveyed charity in his time.

- Smith repeatedly portrays endowed schools as "corrupt" (e.g., V.i.f.17, 20, 30, 33, 45, 49). But he also specifically denies government any claim to success throughout his assessment of ancient schools, and he chastises historians who have given governments too much credit (V.i.f.39–45). He accuses them of fabricating "ingenious reasons," being "predisposed" to see wisdom in ancient governance (40), and tending to "over rate" the role of the legislator (45). Therein, he asserts that there is a distinct bias or prejudice of thought on the matter—one which he cannot be cajoled to adopt (45). If Smith still wanted to recommend tax-financed endowments, Smith sets a high bar for himself to explain why society should replace extant options for the poor with one that is theoretically flawed, historically unproven, widely corrupt, and supported by prejudicial thinking. He does not, and likely had no intention to, make such a case.

- The idea of widespread schooling based on a tax fund was afoot in Britain when Smith wrote. It had been recently posed by the popular moralist John Brown (1765) and was passionately critiqued by the famous scientist and educational thinker Joseph Priestley (1765) as well as by the popular, outspoken reverend Samuel Parr (1828/

1780). However, none had done justice to the topic, relying on theoretical arguments rather than comprehensive evaluations of endowments' potential merit. Smith is almost certainly aware of these famous debates, and his article's rigorous approach may serve to rectify their deficiencies. Perhaps most important to note, however, is that Brown's inspiration for his provocative work was Montesquieu, who asserted in his 1748 *The Spirit of the Laws* that government should take a role in providing education (2001, 53–56). Montesquieu is generally treated as insignificant in the historiographies on education, but he had an important temporary impact in Britain through Brown's work. Smith mentions Montesquieu in his article (V.i.f.40) and rebukes him along with other historians for their romanticism of government. In doing so, Smith most definitely has entered into this contemporaneous debate, and taken a side against government.

- In a few brief paragraphs, Smith's possible solutions contain at least 13 examples of restraints and limits (V.i.f.54–56). The defining quality of his solutions is their smallness. Even the idea of a school-per-parish is restrained, as that such a model had already been shown to be insufficient in providing widespread access in most Scottish parishes. Smith did not make a push for an elaborate, complete, or expensive solution.

- Smith never specifies that small schools, small incentive rewards, and mandatory capability testing should *all* happen. They could be three independent options. Additionally, the multiple calls for the state and the public to "give attention" to education also never specify *which* option. Given that Smith shows an appreciation for demand-side encouragements instead of supply-side provisions in the article (V.i.f.41, 42, 44, 45) and elsewhere in Book V, Chapter 1 (V.i.e.26, V.i.g.3, V.i.g.14), it is credible to think that he may prefer incentive rewards and capability testing. These demand-side alternatives to subsidized schools, however, are almost never discussed in the scholarship.

- Smith shows a glowing appreciation for *patience* on the topic of education (V.i.f.45, V.i.g.14, V.i.g.3). He shows the same appreciation throughout Book 5, Chapter 1 (V.i.d.9, V.i.e.26). His standard for market failure is that a private solution shows itself to *never* be possible. This pattern, and his failure to cite urgency on the topic of the poor, suggest that an unfortunate situation for the poor would not easily sway him to seek immediate or dramatic change.

- In Smith's time the primary goal of philanthropists was to convince social, political, and academic leaders that the poor should have education at all, many of whom saw widespread access as a threat to the natural order of Britain. For a person of his place and rank, Smith takes a radical position in support of the poor having education. But an argument for education is not an argument for government provision of this education. Historical context would suggest that today's reader should resist the urge to lightly treat this distinction.

- In Smith's time, numerous writers juxtaposed the 'dead' giving which had established endowments with the 'living' giving of charity. Despite both being a form of subsidization, endowments fail because of a lack of ongoing scrutiny for quality and purpose, whereas charity succeeds through great attention to these. The strength of this juxtaposition can be surmised by its longevity into the late 19th century. In Smith's final adjudication, he employs a juxtaposition as well—between "general contribution" and "voluntary contribution." This juxtaposition benefits from the contemporaneous one, and, I would argue, efficiently aligns Smith with the larger thinking about how endowments differ from charity. Without Smith having to elaborate why he finds charity superior, his preference for charity be understandable to his audience. And, indeed, the initial responses indicate that his immediate audience saw him as a supporter of charity for schooling.

Quentin Skinner warns that "we can only classify the unfamiliar in terms of the familiar." In doing so, we may end up with "conceptual muddles and mistaken empirical claims" (1969, 4–6). On the topic of education, today's public-school models are familiar to writers. It is hard not to think that this familiarity makes certain passages appear as if Smith was prescient—and, if one favors the public-school model, worthy of praise. But a closer textual examination reveals there is much weighing against such an interpretation.

That which has been presented as supportive of orthodoxy is not unequivocally so. As Smith was writing, there was an array of government reform initiatives being discussed surrounding the regulation of endowments and charity, and even, nascently, the possible provision by government. Smith enters into that discussion, providing an important study that was received by his immediate audience as providing cautionary lessons (Drylie 2020). Nathan Rosenberg (1960, 570) suggested that the result of giving too little credit to Smith's interest in exact institutional details in Book V, Chapter 1 "has been a neglect of some of the most fruitful and suggestive aspects of Smith's analysis and a distortion of the broader implications of his argument." I second that view. And on reflecting on Alexander Gray's comments at the start of this study, I am inclined to believe that on the topic of education, the familiar and the partial may have, indeed, displaced the unfamiliar and whole.

Appendix A: List of publications addressing Smith's position on school funding

State interpretation

Did not cite the passage: Bonar (1893), Sadler (1897), Holman (1898), Small (1907), Graves (1913), Cubberly (1920), Curoe (1921), Morrow (1927), Viner (1927), Butts (1947), Curtis (1948), Jarman (1951), Pollard (1957), Mulhern (1959), Fulton (1963), West (1964); Robbins (1965), Silver (1965), Pike (1965), Brubacher (1966), Miller (1966), Barnard (1969), R. Freeman (1969), Lamb (1973), Lindgren (1973), Lawson and Silver (1973), Hollander (1973), McNulty (1973), Dankert (1974), Blaug (1975), A. Brown (1975), Peacock (1975), Rimlinger (1976), Spiegel (1976), Spengler (1977), D. Winch (1978), Ginzberg (1979), Arrow (1979), Paul (1979), Campbell & Ross (1981), Davis (1981), Robertson (1983), Ross (1984), Harpham (1984), Himmelfarb (1984), Raphael (1985), Rabushka (1985), Lissner (1986), M. Brown (1988), Wilson (1989), Haakonssen (1989), Werhane (1991), D. Winch (1991), Pack (1991), Baum (1992), Rothschild (1992), Muller (1993), Hollander (1993), Minowitz (1993), Bassiry & Jones (1993), Malloy (1994a), Malloy (1994b), Fitzgibbons (1995), Anderson (1995), D. Winch (1996), Drosos (1996), Skinner (1996), Donald (1997), Fitzgibbons (1997), Berry (1997), Stabile (1997), Rothschild (1998), C. Winch (1998), Reisman (1998), Alvey (1998), Rashid (1998), Ortman (1999), Tribe (1999), Fiori & Pesciarelli (1999), Alvey (2001), Ginzberg (2002), Chandra (2004), Fleischacker (2004), Kayaalp (2004), Kennedy (2005), Rothschild (2005), Evensky (2005), Stone (2005), C. Smith (2006), Pocock (2006), Buchan (2006), Rothschild & Sen (2006), Weinstein (2006), Holler (2006), Hill (2007), Weinstein (2007), Rasmussen (2008), Kennedy (2008), Hanley (2009), Peterson (2009), Sen (2009), Perelman

(2010), Klump & Woersdoerfer (2010), Göçmen (2012), Quinn (2013), Weinstein (2013), Pack (2013), Labio (2013), Sen (2013), Aspromourgos (2013), Hall (2014), Alexander, Salmon and Alexander (2014), Hill & Montag (2015), Lee (2017), Wolcott (2018), Norman (2018), MacDonald (2019).

Full citation: Tu (1966)*, Spengler (1975), Cohn (1979), Skinner (1988)^, Palley (1991), Leathers and Raines (1992)^, Skinner (1995), Walsh (1998), Leathers and Raines (1999)^, Kayaalp (2004), Fallis (2007), Milgate & Stimson (2009), Skinner (2012)^, ver Eecke (2013).

First part only: Clay (1968)**, Bates (1973)**, Reisman (1976), Eze (1983), Novak (1986), Naismith (1988), National Development and Security (1994), Holtkamp* (1994), Phelps (1997), Gordon & Boland (1998), Lund (2002), Leathers & Raines (2003)^, Hungerford & Wassmer (2004)~, Brezis (2006) Bogotch (2011), S. Freeman (2011), Buschman (2013), Fagbamiye (2015), Akinleye & Ogunmakin (2016), Lee (2017).

Second part only: (none).

Dissenting interpretation

Did not cite the passage: Clark (1903)*, Fay (1930), Boyd (1932), West, (1964b), West (1967), Lucas (1972), Lynn (1976), M. Friedman (1776), Haakonssen (1989), Ryan (1990), West (1991), Young (1997), Griswold (1999), Rauhut (2005), Butler (2007), Hyard (2007), O'Rourke (2007), Otteson (2011), Phillipson (2012), Hanley (2016).

Full citation: Montgomery (1949)~, West (1977), Browning (1983), High (1985), Heilbroner (1986), Stonier (1988), West (1994), D. Friedman (1997), Dougherty (2002)~, Bradley & Taylor (2004), King (2005a)*, King (2005b), Thomas (2017), Wright (2017), Drylie (2020).

First part only: Billet (1978).

Second part only: Taylor (1972), West (1980), West (1990), C. Smith (2012).

Notes. * dissertation; ** master's thesis; ~ readily inferable; ^ applied only to universities or religious institutions, but view of elementary expressed as taxpayer funded elsewhere.

Appendix B

TABLE 3. Contingency table of era vs. nature of the interpretation

	Before 1976	1976 and since	Total
State	36	115	151
Dissenting	8	32	40
Total	44	147	191

TABLE 4. Contingency table of era vs. decision to cite the passage at all

	Before 1976	1976 and since	Total
Omit	44	93	137
Cite	6	48	54
Total	50	141	191

TABLE 5. Contingency table of discipline vs. decision to cite or suppress 2nd part

	Economics	Other	Total
Cite	31	2	33
Suppress	11	9	20
Total	42	11	53

References

Akinleye, Gideon, and Adeduro Ogunmakin. 2016. The Effect of Tax Avoidance on Government Budget Implementation in Southwest Nigeria. *International Journal of Accounting and Taxation* 4(1): 53–68.

Alexander, Kern, Richard Salmon, and F. King Alexander. 2014. *Financing Public Schools*. London: Routledge.

Alvey, James. 1998. Adam Smith's Higher Vision of Capitalism. *Journal of Economic Issues* 32(2): 441–448.

Alvey, James. 2001. Moral Education as a Means to Human Perfection and Social Order: Adam Smith's View of Education in a Commercial Society. *History of the Human Sciences* 14(2): 1–18.

Anderson, Robert. 1995. *Education and the Scottish People: 1750–1918*. Oxford: Clarendon Press.

Arrow, Kenneth. 1979. Division of Labor in the Economy, the Polity, and Society. In *Adam Smith and Modern Political Economy*, ed. Gerald O'Driscoll, 152–164. Ames, Iowa: Iowa

State University Press.

Aspromourgos, Tony. 2013. Adam Smith on Labor and Capital. In *The Oxford Handbook of Adam Smith*, ed. Christopher Berry, Maria Pia Paganelli, and Craig Smith, 267–289. Oxford: Oxford University Press.

Barnard, Howard. 1969. *Education and the French Revolution*. Cambridge, UK: Cambridge University Press.

Baron, Reuben, and David Kenny. 1986. The Moderator-Mediator Variable Distinction in Social Psychological Research: Conceptual, Strategic, and Statistical Considerations. *Journal of Personality and Social Psychology* 51(6): 1173–1182.

Bassiry, G. R., and Marc Jones. 1993. Adam Smith and the Ethics of Contemporary Capitalism. *Journal of Business Ethics* 12(8): 621–627.

Bates, T. 1973. *Aspects of the Theory of Human Capital and Its Applications to South African Economic Development*. Master's thesis, Rhodes University (Grahamstown, South Africa).

Baum, Sandy. 1992. Poverty, Inequality, and the Role of Government: What Would Adam Smith Say? *Eastern Economic Journal* 18(2): 143–156.

Berry, Christopher. 1997. *Social Theory and the Scottish Enlightenment*. Edinburgh: Edinburgh University Press.

Billet, Leonard. 1978. Justice, Liberty and Economy. In *Adam Smith and the Wealth of Nations: Bicentennial Essays*, ed. Fred Glahe, 83–109. Boulder, Colo.: Colorado Associate University Press.

Birch, Thomas. 1998. An Analysis of Adam Smith's Theory of Charity and the Problems of the Poor. *Eastern Economic Journal* 24(1): 25–41.

Blaug, Mark. 1975. The Economics of Education in English Classical Political Economy: A Reexamination. In *Essays on Adam Smith*, ed. Andrew Skinner and Thomas Wilson, 568–599. Oxford: Clarendon Press.

Bodkin, Ronald. 1976. A Retrospective Look at Adam Smith's Views on University Education. *Eastern Economics Journal* 32(2): 64–71.

Bogotch, Ira. 2011. International Handbook of Leadership for Learning, 25, Part 1. In *US Cultural History: Visible and Invisible Influences on Leadership for Learning*, ed. Tony Townsend and John MacBeath. 29–49. London: Springer.

Bonar, James. 1893. *Philosophy and Political Economy in Some of Their Historical Relations*. New Work: Swan Sonnenschein.

Boyd, William. 1932 [1921]. *The History of Western Education*. London: A & C Black, Ltd.

Bradley, Steve and Jim Taylor. 2004. The Economics of Secondary Schooling. In *International Handbook on the Economics of Education*, eds. Geraint Johnes and Jill Johnes, 368–483. Cheltenham, UK: Edward Elgar.

Brezis, Elise. 2006. Education, Inequality and Economic Growth. Working paper.

Brown, Archie. 1975. Adam Smith's First Russian Followers. In *Essays on Adam Smith*, eds. Andrew Skinner and Thomas Wilson, 247–273. Oxford: Oxford University Press.

Brown, John. 1757. *Thoughts on Civil Liberty, on Licentiousness and Faction*. London: L. Davis and C. Reymers.

Brown, Maurice. 1988. *Adam Smith's Economics*. London: Croon Helm.

Browning, Peter. 1983. *Economic Images: Current Economic Controversies*. New York: Addison-

Wesley Longman.

Brubacher, John. 1966. *A History of the Problems of Education*. New York: McGraw Hill.

Buchan, James. 2006. *The Authentic Adam Smith*. New York: W. W. Norton and Company.

Buschman, John. 2013. Democracy, Market Solutions, and Educative Institutions: A Perspective on Neoliberalism. *Progressive Librarian* (Progressive Librarians Guild, St. Paul, Minn.) 41: 5–17.

Butler, Eamonn. 2007. *Adam Smith—A Primer*. London: Institute of Economic Affairs.

Butts, Freeman. 1947. *A Cultural History of Education: Reassessing out Educational Traditions*. New York: McGraw-Hill Book Company.

Campbell, T. D., and I. S. Ross. 1981. The Utilitarianism of Adam Smith's Policy Advice. *Journal of the History of Ideas* 42(1): 73–92.

Cannan, Edward. 1903. *History of Theories of Production and Distribution, Second Edition*. London: P.S. King and Son.

Chandra, Ramesh. 2004. Adam Smith, Allyn Young, and the Division of Labor. *Journal of Economic Issues* 38(3): 787–805.

Clark, Walter. 1903. *Josiah Tucker, Economist*. Dissertation, Columbia University.

Clay, James. 1968. *Human Capital: A Review of the Literature*. Master's thesis, University of Colorado.

Cohn, Elehanan. 1979. *The Economics of Education*. Cambridge, Mass.: Ballinger Publishing Company.

Cubberly, Ellwood. 1920. *The History of Education*. Boston: Houghton Mifflin.

Curoe, Philip. 1921. *The History of Education*. New York: Globe Company Book.

Curtis, Stanley. 1948. *The History of Education in Great Britain*. London: University Tutorial Press.

Dankert, Clyde. 1974. *Adam Smith: Man of Letters*. Hicksville, N.Y.: Exposition Press.

Darwall, Stephen. 1999. Sympathetic Liberalism: Recent Work of Adam Smith. *Philosophy and Public Affairs* 28(2): 139–164.

Davis, Denis. 1981. Back to the Beginnings: Credentialism, Productivity, and Adam Smith's Division of Labor. *Higher Education* 10(6): 649–661.

Demsetz, Harold. 1969. Information and Efficiency: Another Viewpoint. *Journal of Law and Economics* 12(1): 1–22.

Denning, Daniel. 1763. *The Royal English Dictionary*. London: R. Baldwin, J. Richardson, S. Crowder.

Dougherty, Peter. 2002. *Who's Afraid of Adam Smith? How the Market Got its Soul*. Hoboken, N.J.: John Wiley and Sons.

Drosos, Dionysios. 1996. Adam Smith and Karl Marx: Alienation in Market Society. *History of Economic Ideas* 4(1–2): 325–351.

Drylie, Scott. 2016. *Interpreting Adam Smith's Views on the Education of the Poor in the Age of Benevolence*. Ph.D. dissertation, George Mason University (Fairfax, Va.).

Drylie, Scott. 2020 (forthcoming). Adam Smith on Schooling: A Classical Liberal Rereading. *Journal of Economic Behavior and Organization*.

Evensky, Jerry. 2005. *Adam Smith's Moral Philosophy: A Historical and Contemporary Perspective on Markets, Law, Ethics, and Culture*. Cambridge, UK: Cambridge University Press.

Eze, Agom. 1983. *Economics of Education: The Nigerian Experience*. Somerset West, South Africa: New Africa Publication Company.

Fagbamiye, Emmanuel. 2015. ICT and Teacher Education in East Africa. In *Teacher Education Systems in Africa in the Digital Era*, ed. Bade Adegoke and Adesoji Oni, 153–162. Oxford: African Books Collective.

Fallis, George. 2007. *Multiversities, Ideas, and Democracy*. Toronto: University of Toronto Press.

Fay, Charles Ryle. 1930. Adam Smith and the Dynamic State. *Economic Journal* 40(157): 25–34.

Fiori, Stefano, and Enzo Pesciarelli. 1999. Adam Smith on Relations of Subordination, Personal Incentives and the Division of Labour. *Scottish Journal of Political Economy* 46(1): 91–106.

Fitzgibbons, Athol. 1995. *Adam Smith's System of Liberty, Wealth and Virtue: The Moral and Political Foundations of the Wealth of Nations*. Oxford: Oxford University Press.

Fitzgibbons, Athol. 1997. The Moral Foundations of the Wealth of Nations. *International Journal of Social Economics* 24(1–3): 91–104.

Fleischacker, Samuel. 2004. *On Adam Smith's Wealth of Nations: A Philosophical Companion*. Princeton, N.J.: Princeton University Press.

Freeman, R. D. 1969. Adam Smith, Education and Laissez-faire. *History of Political Economy* 1(1): 173–186.

Freeman, Samuel. 2011. Capitalism in the Classical and High Liberal Tradition. *Social Philosophy and Policy Foundation* 28(2): 19–55.

Friedman, David. 1997. The Weak Case for Government Schools. *Liberty* (Port Townsend, Wash.) 11(1).

Friedman, Milton. 1976. Adam Smith's Relevance for 1976. Presentation to the Mont Pelerin Society, St. Andrews, UK.

Fulton, Robert. 1963. *Adam Smith Speaks to Our Times*. Boston: Christopher Publishing House.

Garnier, Germain. 1843. Short View of the Doctrine of Smith, Compared with tTat of the French Economists. In *An Inquiry into the Nature and Causes of the Wealth of Nations* by Adam Smith, ed. T. Nelson. Edinburgh: Thomas Nelson and Sons.

Graves, Frank. 1913. *A History of Education in Modern Times*. New York: Macmillan.

Ginzberg, Eli. 1979. An Economy Formed by Men. In *Adam Smith and Modern Political Economy*, ed. G. O'Driscoll. Ames, Iowa: Iowa State University Press.

Ginzberg, Eli. 2002. *Adam Smith and the Founding of Market Economics*. London: Routledge.

Göçmen, Dogan. 2012. The Adam Smith Problem and Adam Smith's Utopia. In *New Essays on Adam Smith's Moral Philosophy*, eds. W. Robison and D. Suits. New York: RIT Press.

Gordon, Irene, and Lawrence Boland. 1998. The Accounting-Economics Interface: Where the Market Fails. *International Journal of Social Economics* 25: 1233–1243.

Gray, Alexander. 1931. *The Development of Economic Doctrine*. Gateshead on Tyne, UK: Northumberland Press Limits.

Griswold, Charles. 1999. *Adam Smith and the Virtues of Enlightenment*. Cambridge, UK: Cambridge University Press.

Haakonssen, Knud. 2006. Introduction: The Coherence of Smith's Thoughts. In *The*

Cambridge Companion to Adam Smith, ed. Knud Haakonssen, 1–21. Cambridge, UK: Cambridge University Press.

Haakonssen, Knud. 1989. *The Science of the Legislator: The Natural Jurisprudence of David Hume and Adam Smith*. Cambridge, UK: Cambridge University Press.

Hall, Lauren. 2014. Two Invisible Hands: Family, Markets, and the Adam Smith Problem. In *Propriety and Prosperity: New Studies on the Philosophy of Adam Smith*, ed. David Hardwick and Leslie Marsh, 240–253. London: Palgrave Macmillan.

Hanley, Ryan. 2009. *Adam Smith and the Character of Virtue*. Cambridge, UK: Cambridge University Press.

Hanley, Ryan. 2016. *Adam Smith: His Life, Thought, and Legacy*. Princeton, N.J.: Princeton University Press.

Harpham, Edward. 1984. Liberalism, Civic Humanism, and the Case of Adam Smith. *American Political Science Review* 78(3): 764–774.

Heilbroner, Robert. 1973. The Paradox of Progress: Decline and Decay in the Wealth of Nations. *Journal of the History of Ideas* 34(2): 243–262.

Heilbroner, Robert. 1986. *The Essential Adam Smith*. New York: Norton.

High, Jack. 1985. State Education: Have Economists Made a Case? *Cato Journal* (Cato Institute, Washington, D.C.) 5(1): 305–323.

Hill, Lisa. 2007. Adam Smith, Adam Ferguson, and Karl Marx on the Division of Labor. *Journal of Classical Sociology* 7(3): 339–368.

Hill, Mike, and Warren Montag. 2015. *The Other Adam Smith*. Stanford, Cal.: Stanford University Press.

Himmelfarb, Gertrude. 1984. *The Idea of Poverty: England in the Early Industrial Age*. New York: Vintage Books.

Himmelfarb, Gertrude. 2012. *The Moral Imagination: From Adam Smith to Lionel Trilling*. Lanham, Md.: Rowman and Littlefield Publishers.

Hollander, Samuel. 1973. *The Economy of Adam Smith*. Toronto: University of Toronto Press.

Holler, Manfred. 2006. Adam Smith's Model of Man and Some of its Consequences. *Homo Oeconomicus* 23(3–4): 467–488.

Holman, Henry. 1898. *English National Education*. London: Blackie.

Holtkamp, Janice McClung. 1994. *States' Support of Higher Education: A Theoretical and Empirical Analysis*. Ph.D. dissertation, Iowa State University.

Hungerford, Thomas L., and Robert W. Wassmer. 2004. K–12 Education in the U.S. Economy. April. National Education Association (Washington, D.C.).

Hutchison, T. 1990. Adam Smith and the Wealth of Nations. In *The Scottish Contribution to Modern Economic Thought*, ed. Douglas Mair. Aberdeen: Aberdeen University Press.

Hyard, Alexandra. 2007. Adam Smith and French Ideas on Education. *Adam Smith Review* 3: 75–95.

Jarman, Thomas. 1951. *Landmarks in the History of Education*. John Murray: London.

Kayaalp, Orhan. 2004. *The National Element in the Development of Fiscal Theory*. Hampshire, UK: Palgrave Macmillan.

Kennedy, Gavin. 2005. *Adam Smith's Lost Legacy*. New York: Palgrave Macmillan.

Kennedy, Gavin. 2008. *Adam Smith: A Moral Philosopher and His Political Economy*. New York:

Palgrave Macmillan.

King, Kerry. 2005a. *Essays on the Publicness of Education and the Effects of School Choice on Student Achievement*. Ph.D. dissertation, West Virginia University.

King, Kerry. 2005b. The Impacts of School Choice on Regional Economic Growth. *Review of Regional Studies* 35(3): 356–368.

Klump, Rainer, and Manuel Woersdoerfer. 2010. An Ordoliberal Interpretation of Adam Smith. *Jahrbuch für die Ordnung von Wirthschaft und Gesellschaft* 61: 29–51.

Labio, Catherine. 2006. The Solution Is in the Text: A Survey of the Recent Literary Turn in Adam Smith Studies. *Adam Smith Review* 2: 149–176.

Labio, Catherine. 2013. Adam Smith's Aesthetics. In *The Oxford Handbook of Adam Smith*, ed. Christopher Berry, Maria Pia Paganelli, and Craig Smith, 105–125. Oxford: Oxford University Press.

Lamb, Robert. 1973. Adam Smith's Concept of Alienation. *Oxford Economic Papers* 25(2): 275–285.

Lawson, John, and Harold Silver. 1973. *A Social History of Education in England*. London: Methuen & Co, Ltd.

Leathers, Charles, and Patrick Raines. 1992. Adam Smith on Competitive Religious Markets. *History of Political Economy* 24(2): 499–513.

Leathers, Charles, and Patrick Raines. 1999. Adam Smith and Thomas Chalmers on Financing Religious Instruction. *History of Political Economy* 31(2): 338–359.

Leathers, Charles, and Patrick Raines. 2003. *The Economics Institutions of Higher Education: Economic Theories of University Behavior*. Cheltenham, UK: Edward Elgar.

Lee, Young Joo. 2017. Understanding Higher Education Institutions' Publicness: Do Public Universities Produce More Public Outcomes than Private Universities? *Higher Education Quarterly* 71(2): 82–203.

Lindgren, Ralph. 1973. *The Social Philosophy of Adam Smith*. The Hague: Martinus Nijhoff.

Lissner, Will. 1986. Adam Smith as Philosopher and Social Scientist. *The American Journal of Economics and Sociology* 451(1): 92.

Lucas, Christopher. 1972. *Our Western Educational Heritage*. London: Macmillan.

Lund, Brian. 2002. *Understanding State Welfare: Social Justice or Social Exclusion?* London: Sage.

Lynn, Arthur. 1976. Adam Smith's Fiscal Ideas: An Eclectic Revisited. *National Tax Journal* 29(4): 369–378.

Macdonald, K. 2019. Of Shame and Poverty; and on Misreading Sen and Adam Smith. *Adam Smith Review* 11: 111–262.

Macfie, Alec. 1967. The Moral Justification of Free Enterprise: A Lay Sermon on an Adam Smith Text. *Scottish Journal of Political Economy* 14: 1–11.

Malloy, Robin. 1994a. Is Law and Economics Moral? In *Adam Smith and the Philosophy of Law and Economics*, ed. Robin Malloy and Jerry Evensky, 153–166. Dordrecht, Netherlands: Springer Science and Business Media.

Malloy, Robin. 1994b. Adam Smith and the Modern Discourse of Law and Economics. In *Adam Smith and the Philosophy of Law and Economics*, ed. Robin Malloy and Jerry Evensky, 113–150. Dordrecht, Netherlands: Springer Science and Business Media.

Martin, Christopher. 2015. Equity, Besides: Adam Smith and the Utility of Poverty. *Journal* *of the History of Economic Thought* 37(4): 559–581.

McNulty, Paul. 1973. Adam Smith's Concept of Labor. *Journal of History of Ideas* 34(3): 345–366.

Milgate, Murray, and Shannon Stimson. 2009. *After Adam Smith: A Century of Transformation in Politics and Political Economy*. Princeton, N.J.: Princeton University Press.

Miller, William. 1966. The Economics of Education in English Classical Economics. *Southern Economics Journal* 32(3): 294–309.

Minowitz, Peter. 1993. *Profits, Priests, and Princes: Adam Smith's Emancipation of Economics from Politics and Religion*. Stanford, Cal.: Stanford University Press.

Montes, Leonidas. 2003. Das Adam Smith Problem: Its Origins, the Stages of the Current Debate, and One Implication for Our Understanding of Sympathy. *Journal of the History of Economic Thought* 25(1): 63–90.

Montesquieu. 2001 [1752]. *The Spirit of the Laws*, trans. Thomas Nugent. Kitchener, Canada: Batoche Books.

Montgomery, George. 1949. *The Return of Adam Smith*. Caldwell, Idaho: Caxton Printers.

Morrow, Glenn. 1927. Adam Smith: Moralist and Philosopher. *Journal of Political Economy* 35(3): 321–342.

Mulhern, James. 1959. *A History of Education*. New York: Ronald Press.

Muller, Jerry. 1993. *Adam Smith in His Times and Ours: Designing the Decent Society*. New York: Free Press.

Muller, Jerry. 2002. *The Mind and the Market: Capitalism in Western Thought*. New York: First Anchor Books.

Musgrave, Peter. 1968. *Society and Education in England Since 1800*. New York: Routledge.

Naismith, D. 1988. Improving Educational Quality and Accountability. *Local Government Studies* 14(1): 21–30.

National Development and Security. 1994. *National Development and Security* (Foundation for Research on International Environment, National Development and Security, Rawalpindi, Pakistan) 2(3–4).

Norman, Jessie. 2018. *Adam Smith: Father of Economics*. New York: Basic Books.

Novak, Michael. 1986. *Will It Liberate? Questions About Liberation Theology*. Mahwah, N.J.: Paulist Press.

O'Rourke, P. J. 2007. *On the Wealth of Nations*. New York: Grove Press.

Ortman, Andreas. 1999. The Nature and Causes of Corporate Negligence, Sham Lectures, and Ecclesiastical Indolence: Adam Smith on Joint-Stock Companies, Teachers, and Preachers. *History of Political Economy* 31(2): 297–315.

Otteson, James. 2011. *Adam Smith*. New York: Continuum, International Publishing Group.

Pack, Spencer. 1991. *Capitalism as a Moral System: Adam Smith's Critique of the Free Market Economy*. Aldershot, UK: Edward Elgar.

Pack, Spencer. 2013. Adam Smith and Marx. In *The Oxford Handbook of Adam Smith*, ed. Christopher Berry, Maria Pia Paganelli, and Craig Smith, 522–543. Oxford: Oxford University Press.

Palley, Claire. 1991. *The United Kingdom and Human Rights*. London: Stevens and Sons.

Parr, Samuel. 1828. A Discourse on Education. In *The Works of Samuel Parr*, ed. J. Johnstone, vol. II. London: Longman, Reese, Orme, Brown, and Greene.

Paul, Ellen. 1979. *Moral Revolution and Economic Science*. London: Greenwood Press.

Peacock, Alan. 1975. The Treatment of the Principles of Public Finance in The Wealth of Nations. In *Essays on Adam Smith*, ed. Andrew Skinner and Thomas Wilson, 553–567. Oxford: Clarendon Press.

Perelman, Michael. 2010. Adam Smith: Class, Labor, and Industrial Revolution. *Journal of Economic Behavior and Organization* 76(3): 481–496.

Peterson, Scot M. 2009. Rational Choice, Religion, and the Marketplace: Where Does Adam Smith Fit In? *Journal for the Scientific Study of Religion* 48(1): 185–192.

Petrella, Frank. 1970. Individual, Group, or Government? Smith, Mill, and Sidgwick. *History of Political Economy* 2(1): 152–176.

Phelps, Edmund. 1997. *Rewarding Work*. Boston: Harvard University Press.

Phillipson, Nicholas. 2012. *Adam Smith: An Enlightened Life*. New Haven, Conn.: Yale University Press.

Pickering, Danby. 1762. *The Statutes at Large of the Magna Carta to the End of the Eleventh Parliament of Great Britain*, vol. XXXVII. Cambridge, UK: John Archdeacon.

Pike, E. Royston. 1965. *Adam Smith: Father of the Science of Economics*. New York: Hawthorn Books.

Pocock, J. G. A. 2006. Adam Smith and History, In *The Cambridge Companion to Adam Smith*, ed. Knud Haakonssen, 270–287. Cambridge, UK: Cambridge University Press.

Pollard, Hugh M. 1947. *Pioneers of Popular Education: 1760–1850*. Boston: Harvard University Press.

Priestley, Joseph. 1765. *An Essay on a Course of Liberal Education*. London: C. Henderson.

Quinn, Kevin. 2013. Adam Smith on Education. *Critical Review* 25(1): 120–129.

Rabushka, Alvin. 1985. *From Adam Smith to the Wealth of America*. New York: Transaction Books.

Raphael, D. D. 1985. *Adam Smith*. Oxford: Oxford University Press.

Rashid, Salim. 1998. *The Myth of Adam Smith*. Cheltenham, UK: Edward Elgar.

Rasmussen, Dennis. 2008. *The Problems and Promises of Commercial Society: Adam Smith's Response to Rousseau*. University Park, Pa.: Pennsylvania State University Press.

Rasmussen, Dennis. 2013. Adam Smith and Rousseau: Enlightenment and Counter-enlightenment. In *The Oxford Handbook of Adam Smith*, ed. Christopher Berry, Maria Pia Paganelli, and Craig Smith, 54–76. Oxford: Oxford University Press.

Rauhut, Daniel. 2005. Adam Smith—A Champion for the Poor! In *Economists and Poverty: From Adam Smith to Amartya Sen*, ed. Daniel Rauhut, Neelambar Hatti, and Carl-Axel Olsson, 21–40. New Delhi: Vedams.

Reisman, David. 1976. *Sociological Economics*. London: Routledge.

Reisman, David. 1998. Adam Smith on Market and State. *Journal of Institutional and Theoretical Economics* 154(2): 357–383.

Rimlinger, Gaston V. 1976. Smith and the Merits of the Poor. *Review of Social Economy* 34(3): 333–44.

Robbins, Lionel. 1965. *The Theory of Economic Policy in English Classical Political Economy*. London: Macmillan.

Robertson, John. 1983. Scottish Political Economy Beyond the Civic Tradition: Government and Economic Development in the Wealth of Nations. *History of Political Thought* 4(3): 451–482.

Rosenberg, Nathan. 1960. Some Institutional Aspects of the Wealth of Nations. *Journal of Political Economy* 68(6): 557–570.

Ross, Ian. 1984. Adam Smith and Education. *Studies in Eighteenth-Century Culture* 13: 173–187.

Rothschild, Emma. 1992. Adam Smith and Conservative Economics. *Economic History Review* 45(1): 74–96.

Rothschild, Emma. 1998. Condorcet and Adam Smith on Education and Instruction. In *Philosophers on Education: Historical Perspectives*, ed. A. O. Rorty, 209–226. London: Routledge.

Rothschild, Emma, and Amartya Sen. 2006. Adam Smith's Economics. In *The Cambridge Companion to Adam Smith*, ed. Knud Haakonssen, 319–365. Cambridge, UK: Cambridge University Press.

Ryan, Edward W. 1990. *In the Words of Adam Smith: The First Consumer Advocate*. Sun Lake, Ariz.: Thomas Horton and Daughters.

Sadler, Michael E. 1897. Sixty Years of Primary Education in England and Wales. *The Journal of Education* (London) 19(335): 387–390.

Sen, Amartya. 2009. Adam Smith's Market Never Stood Alone. *Financial Times*, March 10.

Sen, Amartya. 2013. The Contemporary Relevance of Adam Smith. In *The Oxford Handbook of Adam Smith*, ed. Christopher Berry, Maria Pia Paganelli, and Craig Smith, 581–591. Oxford: Oxford University Press.

Silver, Harold. 1965. *The Concept of Popular Education*. London: Routledge.

Skinner, Andrew. 1988. Adam Smith and Economic Liberalism. Hume Occasional Paper No. 9. Edinburgh: David Hume Institute.

Skinner, Andrew. 1995. Adam Smith and the Role of the State: Education as a Public Service. In *Adam Smith's Wealth of Nations: New Interdisciplinary Essays*, ed. Stephen Copley and Kathryn Sutherland, 70–96. Manchester, UK: Manchester University Press.

Skinner, Andrew. 2012. Adam Smith: Theory and Policy. In *Handbook of the History of Economic Thought: Insight on the Founders of Modern Economics*, ed. Jurgen Backhaus, 161–172. London: Springer.

Skinner, Quentin. 1969. Meaning and Understanding in the History of Ideas. *History and Theory* 8(1): 3–53.

Small, Albion. 1907. *Adam Smith and Modern Sociology*. Chicago: University of Chicago Press.

Smith, Adam. 1976 [1790]. *The Theory of Moral Sentiments*, eds. D. D. Raphael and A. L. Macfie. Oxford: Oxford University Press.

Smith, Adam. 1976 [1776] (WN). *An Inquiry into the Nature and Causes of the Wealth of Nations*, eds. R. H. Campbell and A. S. Skinner, 2 vols. Oxford: Oxford University Press.

Smith, Craig. 2006. Adam Smith on Progress and Knowledge. In *New Voices on Adam Smith*, ed. Leonidas Montes and Eric Schliesser, 293–312. London: Routledge.

Smith, Craig. 2012. Adam Smith: Left or Right? *Political Studies* 61(4): 784–798.

Smith, Craig. 2014. Smith, Justice, and the Scope of the Political. In *Propriety and Prosperity*, ed. David Hardwick, and Leslie Marsh, 254–274. New York: Palgrave Macmillan.

Smout, T. C. 1969. *A History of the Scottish People: 1560–1830*. New York: Charles Scribner's Sons.

Solomon, Frank. 2013. *Capitalism: An Analysis and Summary of Adam Smith's Wealth of Nations*. Bloomington, Ind.: Archway Publishing.

Spengler, Joseph. 1975. Adam Smith and Society's Decision Makers. In *Essays on Adam Smith*, ed. Andrew Skinner and T. Wilson. Oxford: Oxford University Press.

Spengler, Joseph. 1977. Adam Smith on Human Capital. *American Economic Review* 67(1): 32–36.

Spiegel, Henry. 1976. Adam Smith's Heavenly City. *History of Political Economy* 8(4): 478–493.

Stabile, R. Donald. 1997. Adam Smith and the Natural Wage: Sympathy, Subsistence, and Social Distance. *Review of Social Economy* 55(3): 292–311.

Stanfield, James. 2005. Adam Smith on Education. *Economic Affairs* 25(2).

Stephens, W. B. 1998. *Education in Britain 1750–1914*. New York: St. Martin's Press.

Stone, Richard. 2005. Public Economic Policy. In *Adam Smith's Legacy*, ed. Michael Fry, 65–88. New York: Routledge.

Stonier, Tom. 1988. Education: Society's Number-One Enterprise. In *Open Learning in Transition*, ed. Nigel Pain, 14–37. London: Kogan Page.

Taylor, Arthur. 1972. *Laissez-Faire and State Intervention in Nineteenth-Century Britain*. London: Macmillan.

Thomas, Alex. 2017. Adam Smith on the Philosophy and Provision of Public Education. *Journal of Interdisciplinary Economics* 30(1): 105–116.

Tribe, Keith. 1999. Adam Smith: Critical Theorist? *Journal of Economic Literature* 37(2): 609–632.

Tribe, Keith. 2008. 'Das Adam Smith Problem' and the Origins of Modern Smith Scholarship. *History of European Ideas* 34(4): 514–525.

Tu, Pierre. 1966. *The Economics of Educational Planning*. Ph.D. dissertation, Australian National University.

Vaughan, Michalina, and Margaret Scotford Archer. 1971. *Social Conflict and Educational Change in England and France 1789–1848*. Cambridge, UK: Cambridge University Press.

Ver Eecke, Wilfried. 2013. *Ethical Reflections on the Financial Crisis: Making Use of Smith, Musgrave, and Rajan*. Berlin: Springer.

Viner, Jacob. 1927. Adam Smith and Laissez-Faire. *Journal of Political Economy* 35(2): 198– 232.

Walsch, Brendan. 1998. Symposium on the Economic Returns to Education. *Journal of the Statistical and Social Inquiry Society of Ireland* 27(5): 139–158.

Weinstein, Jack Russell. 2006. Sympathy, Difference, and Education: Social Unity in the Work of Adam Smith. *Economics and Philosophy* 22: 79–111.

Weinstein, Jack Russell. 2007. Adam Smith's Philosophy of Education. *Adam Smith Review* 3: 51–74.

Weinstein, Jack Russell. 2013. *Adam Smith's Pluralism: Rationality, Education, and the Moral Sentiments*. New Haven, Conn.: Yale University Press.

Werhane, Patricia. 1991. *Adam Smith and His Legacy for Modern Capitalism*. New York: Oxford University Press.

West, E. G. n.d. Adam Smith's Proposal on Public Education. Unpublished manuscript.

West, E. G. 1964. Private versus Public Education: A Classical Economic Dispute. *Journal of Political Economy* 72(5): 465–475.

West, E. G. 1967. Tom Paine's Voucher Scheme for Public Education. *Southern Economic Journal* 22(3): 378–382.

West, E. G. 1977. Adam Smith's Public Economics: A Re-evaluation. *Canadian Journal of Economics* 10(1): 1–18.

West, E. G. 1980. Review of *Adam Smith's Politics: An Essay in Historiographic Revision* by Donald Winch. *Southern Economic Journal* 46(3): 997–999.

West, E. G. 1990. *Adam Smith and Modern Economics: From Market Behavior to Public Choice.* Aldershot, UK: Edward Elgar.

West, E. G. 1991. The Rise of the State in Education Policy: Part One: The Intellectual Background. *Policy: A Journal of Public Policy and Ideas* (Centre for Independent Studies, St. Leonards, Australia) 7(Autumn–Winter).

West, E. G. 1994. Interview with Adam Smith. *The Region* (Federal Reserve Bank of Minneapolis), June 1.

Wilson, James. 1989. Adam Smith on Business Ethics. *California Management Review*, Fall: 59–72.

Winch, Christopher. 1998. Two Rival Conceptions of Vocational Education: Adam Smith and Friedrich List. *Oxford Review of Education* 24(3): 365–378.

Winch, Donald. 1978. *Adam Smith's Politics: An Essay in Historiographic Revision.* Cambridge, UK: Cambridge University Press.

Winch, Donald. 1991. Adam Smith's Politics Revisited. *Quaderni di storia dell'economia politica* 9(1): 3–27.

Winch, Donald. 1996. *Riches and Poverty: An Intellectual History of Political Economy in Britain, 1750–1834.* Cambridge, UK: Cambridge University Press.

Wolcott, Gregory. 2018. The Rehabilitation of Adam Smith for Catholic School Teaching. *Journal of Business Ethics* 149(1): 57–82.

Wood, Anthony. 1792. *The History and Antiquities of the University of London.* Oxford: John Gutch.

Wright, Alexander. 1898. *The History of Education and the Old Parish Schools of Scotland.* Edinburgh: Thomas Adams and Sons.

Wright, Robert. 2017. A History of Socially Responsible Business, C. 1600–1950. In *Corporate Social Responsibility and the Rise of the Non-Profit Sector in America*, ed. William Pettigrew and David Chan Smith, 117–135. Hampshire, UK: Palgrave Macmillan.

Young, Jeffrey. 1997. *Economics as a Moral Science: The Political Economy of Adam Smith.* Cheltenham, UK: Edward Elgar Publishing.

Remarks from 1809 by Dupont de Nemours on Adam Smith

Foreword

Daniel B. Klein and Frederic Sautet

Here we provide a translation of some remarks about Adam Smith by Dupont de Nemours from 1809. During Smith's time in France (1764–66) the two men met and interacted. Published 18 years after Smith's death, the remarks repeatedly suggest that Smith, in writing *The Wealth of Nations*, engaged in what might variously be called hedging, moderating, compromising, bargaining, strategizing, being tactful, or even fudging, dissembling, or dissimulating. Dupont made his remarks as commentary placed within the collection of Turgot's work that he edited. The remarks say little about Turgot, and come across as a rather gratuitous speculation on Smith's fudging. James McLain (1977, 216 n.45), Ian Simpson Ross (1995, 214), and Emma Rothschild (2001, 66–67) have noted that Dupont here suggests that Smith moderated his support for liberalization, or at least wrote of certain taxes as less unfavorable than he really thought.

Dupont's remarks from 1809 make a good companion to his letter to Smith twenty years prior, 19 June 1788, a letter only recently translated. Robert Prasch and Thierry Warin (2009) take as the title of their translation and discussion a line from the letter, "Il est encore plus important de bien faire que de bien dire," or: It is more important to do well than to say well. The piece by Prasch and Warin, containing the 1788 letter, is available online, and we recommend it to anyone interested in Smith or in the compromising nature of political and economic discourse.

Dupont's 1788 letter to Smith accompanied a copy of a pamphlet that Dupont had recently published. Dupont explains to Smith that the "bright light" of political economy must be dimmed when "we announce to our traders, to our producers and to the cream of our civil administrators that it is useless and dangerous to give specific encouragement to firms and the export of their products." "By assaulting their eyes with a bright light, we would reconstitute their blindness." Thus, Dupont asks, "I hope you will forgive the deficiencies of my work that are not unknown to me and some of which were voluntarily committed" (Prasch and Warin 2009, 69).

Prasch and Warin (2009) and Rothschild (2001, 55, 271 n.29) show quite convincingly that this letter influenced Smith's additions to *The Theory of Moral Sentiments* contrasting the man of public spirit and the man of system. In the material translated here, we see Dupont returning to the "bright light" metaphor, ascribing to Smith the same kind of fudging he had confessed to Smith in 1788.

The literature on Smith has ample discussion of whether he fudged his views in the matter of religion—for example, Bittermann (1940, 710) suggesting "an element of deliberate deception in Smith's remarks about religion in the *Moral Sentiments.*" But discussions of Smith fudging his policy views, though hinted at by Dugald Stewart, have been less developed. A recent exploration is represented by the dissertation work of Michael J. Clark (2010; 2011).

Prompted by the splendid contribution of Prasch and Warin, we offer an English version of Dupont's 1809 remarks with minimal commentary. Dupont's economic argumentation here is poorly expressed and often dubious at best. We are inclined to think that Dupont pronounces Smith's compromises somewhat too eagerly, and somewhat too extravagantly; Dupont's remarks might reveal as much about Dupont as about Smith. But readers might find Dupont's remarks useful in interpreting Smith's words.

About Dupont de Nemours

The following biographical information comes from Ernest Mossner and Ian Simpson Ross (1977, 311 n.1): "Pierre-Samuel Dupont de Nemours (1739–1817), philanthropist, economist, Deputy to the National Assembly, and translator of Ariosto. He impressed the *économistes* by his *Réflexions sur l'écrit intitulé: Richesse de l'État* (1763), and publicized Quesnay's system in frequent articles for two journals he edited: *Journal de l'agriculture* (1765–6) and

Éphémérides du citoyen (1768–72), also he published Quesnay's writings together with an analysis in *Physiocratie* (1768). His treatise *De l'origine et du progrès d'une science nouvelle* (1767) and the *Tableau raisonné des principes de l'économie politique* (1775) are among his important contributions to the literature of economics. He became the friend and confidant of Turgot and served under him in the French Government, 1774–6; later he wrote memoirs of Turgot (1782), then enlarged these for an edition of Turgot's complete works (1808–11). As a practical politician he took part in the early stages of the French Revolution, but his views clashed with those of the Jacobins, and after running a clandestine press he was imprisoned, surviving this period solely as a result of the fall of Robespierre. In 1799 he emigrated to the United States and a year later, at Jefferson's request, he prepared a plan for national education. At this time his son, Eleuthère Irénée, set up a gunpowder mill in Delaware, thus founding the family chemical industry. The father returned to France in 1802 to assist in the negotiations for the Louisiana Purchase, and was active in bringing down Napoleon's regime in 1814, but a year later returned to America where he died."

About the 1809 text

Between 1808 and 1811 Dupont edited *Oeuvres de Turgot* and published them in nine volumes. The text translated is Dupont's commentary on Turgot's *Réflexions sur la Formation et la Distribution des Richesses*, and immediately follows that work. We have taken the text as found in a subsequent version of Turgot's collected works, edited by Eugène Daire and Hippolyte Dussard, a version that reproduces Dupont's commentaries, Paris, Guillaumin, 1844. The text is available online; see pp. 67–71.

About the translation

Frederic Sautet did the translation. Dupont's original text reads as though it were written hastily. The translation places faithfulness above enhancing clarity. Instead, we tried to enhance clarity by inserting clarifications in brackets [like this]. When we wish to put the clarification in our own voice we precede it with "K&S" for Klein and Sautet (as opposed to "Eds.", which a reader might read as Daire and Dussard).

About the difficult discussion of taxation

Where Dupont writes "The only criticism..." he embarks on matters that are difficult for us to make sense of, matters of what Smith said about taxation, of whether Smith makes sense, whether Dupont represents him fairly, and whether Dupont's analysis makes sense. We do not attempt to sort matters out, but the following notes may be useful:

1. Smith writes: "By necessaries I understand not only the commodities which are indispensably necessary for the support of life, but whatever the custom of the country renders it indecent for creditable people, even of the lowest order, to be without" (WN, 869.3—meaning page 869, paragraph 3). He then says: "All other things I call luxuries..." Thus, "luxuries" for Smith are simply non-necessaries.

2. It is important to recognize the population mechanism in Smith's theorizing of the taxation of necessaries—presumably, Smith holds that the employer feels impelled to employ only "creditable" people. When Smith says that consumption taxes on necessaries lead to corresponding increases in nominal wages (871.4), his period of analysis is at least the duration between human generations. Dupont, it seems at points, loses sight of that, and works from a shorter period of analysis.

3. In Smith's reasoning, the taxation of "luxuries" tends not to raise wages, because they do not figure into the population mechanism (871.6–9).

4. From our reading of Smith, we might say that Dupont's representation of Smith's Book V judgment on British taxation of "luxuries" is one-sided. Yes, Smith sometimes endorses or excuses the practice (871–873; see also 936.75), but Smith later devotes several pages (896–990) to how "[t]axes upon luxuries...offend in every respect the fourth" maxim of taxation, in that "[s]uch taxes, in proportion to what they bring into the publick treasury of the state, always take out or keep out of the pockets of the people more than almost any other

taxes" (899.60–61).

5. Dupont argues that taxing "luxuries" leads to an increase in nominal wages via the following mechanism: Laborers find that their real wage is reduced, and hence less readily seek work, reducing the competition among workers, and leading to higher wages. The 1844 text includes a footnote, which we have translated and reproduced, by editor Hippolyte Dussard that criticizes Dupont's reasoning.

We see a certain irony in that Dupont, who was inclined to look between the lines, focused mainly on Smith's discussion of certain consumption taxes. The tax that Smith in fact seems most enthusiastic about is some kind of land-value or ground-rent/"geo-rent" tax (see Foldvary 2005), but his arguments for it are oddly dispersed, occurring principally at 832–834, 840–844, 848–850, 934.70. Interestingly, when Smith first describes the tax that he feels should "be established as a perpetual and unalterable regulation, or as what is called a fundamental law of the commonwealth" (834), that is, the discussion on pages 832–834, he avoids altogether the word "ground-rent," which then surfaces prominently from 840ff. In this fashion he never confronts the radical nature of the proposal, but, rather, remarks nonchalantly that "such a system of administration" does not appear likely to occasion any inconveniency to the landlord "except always the unavoidable one being obliged to pay the tax" (834). That Smith may have fudged on the matter is suggested by Henry George (1887, 8–9, 14, 292; 1898, 160–169, 182), although George seems to understate the degree to which Smith wrote favorably of ground-rent taxation.

Now we turn to Dupont's 1809 commentary.

Some Comments on the Points of Agreement and Disagreement Between Smith and Turgot

Pierre-Samuel Dupont de Nemours
edited by Daniel B. Klein and Frederic Sautet
translated by Frederic Sautet

This eternally classical work [Turgot's *Reflections*], which was written nine years before Adam Smith's famous magnum opus and published five years before the time when Smith set to work on his own, shows how the two authors [Turgot and Smith] are in complete agreement on the following points: the principles of agriculture and commerce; the progress of society due to the division of labor (including the advantages that resulted from that division and will result from it in the future); the composing elements of the prices of goods, including design and marketing; the introduction and the usefulness of money; the formation of capital; the distribution and use of capital; the effect of IOUs when they are of repute; the interest rate on monetary credit; the necessity to leave commerce and social norms absolute freedom.

They differ chiefly in the sense they give to the notion that some works are *wealth producing* when they are only *conservative* [of the wealth] and help in the accumulation of capital.

Indeed, *accumulation* should not be confused with *production* by such a mind as that of Smith.

He makes the not well-founded distinction between the type of works that produce goods for durable consumption, which he sees as being the only productive ones because they stabilize the value of the worker's total consumption, and those that produce goods for immediate consumption and which do not create much satisfaction in the long run.

If one admits that distinction, then one may be led to conclude that the work of a music composer whose work is printed and kept is always productive, whereas that of a gardener who produces fruits for immediate consumption is not.

It wouldn't have been necessary to insist on that point.

Philosophers and statesmen who are worthy of reading Smith's work and know how to admire it will understand.

This is especially true since his mistake is mostly in the expression and does not take away the general beauty of Smith's doctrine, as it does not affect Smith's fundamental principles of freedom in commerce and labor. The only criticism that can be leveled against his work is a weakness or perhaps some complacency, in the second section of the second chapter of his fifth book [K&S: Dupont presumably means especially V.ii.k, "Taxes upon consumable Commodities," 869–906], with the vices of English public finance, and the inconveniencies, the dangers, and actual negative impacts of its taxes.

It appears that he may have been frightened that the severe judgment implied in his book would upset the numerous perceptions in England that contribute to reduce freedom in matters of labor, commerce, but also in more mundane and innocent actions that a citizen in the republic of Great Britain should enjoy in the privacy of his own home; as well as the abuses that these opinions create.

After having shown in his first four books how these opinions were contrary to wealth creation, he must have wanted to show that they were not so destructive after all.

He went as far as saying, in a surprising way for a genius like him, that [K&S: the following words attributed to Smith are not an actual quotation; Dupont has perhaps in mind 871–873, and possibly 936.75] "taxes on consumption, especially taxes on sugar, tea, beer, and tobacco, do not increase wage rates; they [those taxes] have the same effect as luxury laws [taxes on luxury goods]; and through forced frugality, they even turn out to be advantageous for the wage earner's family."

His skilled French translator, Senator Germain Garnier, has already refuted Smith's mistakes, which were not and could not have been the result of his great mind, but rather a sacrifice to popular opinion, a sacrifice that he thought was useful in his homeland. — Under the circumstances in which he found himself at the time (and in which his government is still to be found), he thought that in order to maintain public peace, one should not assault infirm eyes with a bright light turned too directly towards them.

Smith's tact did not fit the state of English public finance, and we do not believe that it was as useful as Smith thought it would be. — Errors are not only detrimental to those who commit them but also to their neighbors. We [the French] are the neighbors of the English, and we also have a fatherland [K&S: that is, Smith's errors produce mischief in France, where his writings are also influential].

Luxury laws prohibit freedom. No one has shown it as well as Smith did: such laws weaken social conventions and stop or slow down labor's efforts and the incentives to work. — Is there any resemblance between scarcity caused by poverty and the injunctions caused by such laws, which affect consumption of product of low utility or for pure pleasure? To think of these two categories in the same way is to be rather inexact. And what should we think when this confusion happens to a writer like Smith who is normally extremely specific and exact?

Goods for mundane daily consumption cannot be thought of in the same way as luxury goods, which don't fulfill real needs and over which luxury laws apply, but which must be discouraged through the example of statesmen, social norms, and not by legislation.

Consumption taxes are generally levied on goods that are necessary to everyone, and especially to the poor, because taxes that would be levied on luxury goods would not pay for their enforcement costs.

Forced frugality cannot be beneficial to the family that is reduced to it.

England's social mores and climate make beer and tea primary goods, including for those in great poverty. And in every country, people know that the habit of smoking tobacco can become an addiction.

Even if the laborer's consumption was less general and less necessary, isn't it a principle demonstrated by Smith that the laborer works only to obtain his wage, that is, the capacity to obtain what competition from other laborers enables him to get?

If some authority seizes temporarily a portion of that income, the entrepreneur may increase the laborer's income to compensate him for that lack; this increase, in addition to the reimbursement of the amount he [the laborer] was forced to pay in taxes, should also compensate him [the entrepreneur] for the trouble, the embarrassment, and the costs of being constrained to advance the money. The only condition that cannot be violated is the integrity of one's income or what competition enables one to get.

If we were to imagine circumstances that would make possible the taxation of a portion of the wage destined to the laborer's enjoyment, it would follow that competition to obtain that salary would decline, which would force again the entrepreneur to compensate the laborers.

And it remains obvious that the less the laborer gets taxed on his consumption, the fiercer the competition among laborers will be, and the more each of them, being assured to enjoy his present state, will be satisfied with what he can obtain without asking for a greater wage.

Smith gets by only by stating a fact that appears sensible only when it is poorly examined; and he was one of the most capable men to examine and discuss a fact: "wages, he said, have not been increased in England since taxes were introduced and increased, which confiscated part of the proceeds" [K&S: again, the words attributed to Smith are not an actual quotation and perhaps correspond to words at 871.6].

What does it prove? — This state of affairs has two causes.

On the one hand, the increase in the population, which has been important and certainly does not come from taxes on consumption, has, with the help of a strengthened competition, reduced the laborers' desire to demand higher salaries. On the other hand, improvements in arts and the division of labor have reduced the production costs of many of the goods that laborers use, and have helped them keep more or less the same real standards of living, in spite of a portion of their wages being diverted away.

But if wages were not taxed, it is clear that competition restraining the wage to the laborer's needs, that is to say what the laborer really obtains from his wage, this wage would reduce in an amount at least similar to the tax itself.

Taxation [K&S: of "luxuries"] thus increases the wage.

Smith seen in private, in his room or in that of a friend, as I saw him when we were co-disciples at Mr. Quesnay's, would not deny that view.

He who reasoned so well, didn't reason in favor of the kind of taxes that his country used exaggeratedly [K&S: that is, "luxury" consumption taxes]. He only states the following vague idea: *England prospered.* He knew better than anyone else that England prospered in spite of it [such taxation] and not because of it.

The last part of his fifth book, in great opposition to his own doctrine and to the rest of the book, could be summarized in those terms: "In spite of what I proved against the obstacles to development, industry, work, the free use of capital, and the ease of communication, the inadequate English tax system, which local circumstances render less confiscatory than similar systems in other countries (proposition that he has not proven), has not hampered the progress, even rapid, in the accumulation of riches witnessed in my nation" [K&S: again, not an actual quotation; the ideas perhaps correspond to material at 899.66–900.69, 929.58].

No one more than he would have calculated what general progress and wealth would have been without those obstacles.

As soon as a nation witnesses the formation of capital and land becoming arable, it is impossible not to witness wealth and progress. It's easy to understand.

No work can be done without the worker being paid enough to maintain a level of subsistence and to maintain his capital.

No capital can be used in production or to pay laborers without the capitalist being reimbursed for the principal plus interest; for no one would want to advance any capital without making a profit.

When land is arable, the one who has some capital that he can use to buy land will not allocate his means to another use if he cannot make a profit at least equal to that he could make in land.

No good can be produced, no merchandise can be made, and none of them can be sold without their price ensuring an interest for the capital advanced by the capitalist.

But all the laborers and the maintenance of all the capital goods and plants are necessarily paid from the proceeds of sales, payments made before the interest has been paid; thus there is always in every business venture that survives the profit of the capitalist, and in addition to his personal remuneration for his work, an interest paid on the capital that he advanced and which he could not renounce without renouncing to his venture. If the capital generates enough interest beyond what the capitalist invested, the capitalist can enjoy his capital with the interest accumulating along with the principal and thus progressively growing.

This is what Mr. Turgot established with the greatest accuracy in his paragraphs 57–63, 67, 68, 71, 72, 87–90, and 92.

The power of compounded interest to increase capital, to reduce the interest on monetary credit, to offer new means to start useful businesses, and to ceaselessly perfect work, is such that the greatest errors of governments, or even the horrors of war, when they are not a devastation of barbarians, can only rarely hamper riches; and the use of science thanks to the accumulation of riches, and all the practical progress in daily life that results from it, increase from centuries to centuries the affluence and happiness of humankind.

From the wealth of a nation that increases, or at least does not diminish, one should not infer that its government is without fault. It can only be said is that it is not bad enough to bring about a retrograde trend to the all the ventures or at least to the most useful ones.

The laws of nature and the goodness of Providence fight, generally with success, against the follies and even the crimes of men; they mend their sad consequences. What will it be like when men become enlightened enough not to hamper, or only slightly, the laws of nature, and to enjoy peacefully and thankfully the blessings of heaven!

Footnote by the 1844 editor Hippolyte Dussard

This note by Dupont de Nemours presents a very interesting critique of Adam Smith's opinion on the effect of indirect taxation on wages [K&S: that is, taxes on consumption]. Turgot and Dupont de Nemours were strong supporters of direct taxation [K&S: that is, taxes on income and capital]. They correctly believed that consumption taxation is an impediment to wealth creation; and Dupont explains perfectly that this tax, to be productive, must be levied, not on luxury goods, but on bare necessities, or (and this is the same), on general goods.

We believe this antipathy [to indirect taxation] has gone too far. Some goods are taxable in essence, and among those are tobacco products. — Following Dupont's advice, we would obtain this result: tobacco products could be taxed as long as they are not widely consumed, but once they become part of general consumption, they couldn't be taxed anymore.

What Dupont de Nemours adds, when he explains that the entrepreneur must increase the laborer's wage when the latter is taxed, proves that he didn't have a very clear theory of wage determination; for this is not the way it is determined. The wage only depends on the portion of capital dedicated to labor. Wages are higher when laborers, compared to the amount of capital, are fewer; and it is lower in the opposite situation. If taxation destroys part of that capital, wages will necessarily go down, not up.

This conclusion, that [consumption] taxation increases wages, is not founded, and it would be more exact to say that consumption taxation, by *increasing* prices of essential goods, limits the laborer's consumption potential, and thereby reduces production, and brings more labor force on the market. — This is not, however, a cause for wage increase.

As to the end of the note, regarding the use of capital and the increase in wealth, it is perfect. [K&S: Thus ends Dussard's footnote on Dupont's comments.]

References

Bittermann, Henry J. 1940. Adam Smith's Empiricism and the Law of Nature: II. *Journal of Political Economy* 48(5): 703–734.

Clark, Michael J. 2010. Adam Smith's Approach to Public Policy: Astounding Deviation or Artful Moderation? Working paper.

Clark, Michael J. 2011. The Virtuous Discourse of Adam Smith: A Liberal Regard for Prevailing Prejudice. *Mercatus Center Working Paper* 11-16. George Mason University (Fairfax, Va.).

Foldvary, Fred E. 2005. Geo-Rent: A Plea to Public Economists. *Econ Journal Watch* 2(1): 106–132.

George, Henry. 1887. *Protection or Free Trade*. New York: Henry George.

George, Henry. 1898. *The Science of Political Economy*. New York: Doubleday.

McLain, James J. 1977. *The Economic Writings of Du Pont de Nemours*. Newark: University of Delaware Press.

Mossner, Ernest Campbell and Ian Simpson Ross. 1977. *The Correspondence of Adam Smith*. Oxford: Oxford University Press.

Prasch, Robert, and Thierry Warin. 2009. 'Il est encore plus important de bien faire que de bien dire': A Translation and Analysis of Dupont de Nemours' 1788 Letter to Adam Smith. *History of Economics Review* 49: 67–75.

Ross, Ian Simpson. 1995. *The Life of Adam Smith*. New York: Oxford University Press.

Rothschild, Emma. 2001. *Economic Sentiments: Adam Smith, Condorcet, and the Enlightenment*. Cambridge: Harvard University Press.

Smith, Adam. 1981 [1776]. *An Inquiry Into the Nature and Causes of the Wealth of Nations*. Ed. R. H. Campbell and A. S. Skinner. Indianapolis: Liberty Fund.

Glimpses of Adam Smith

Foreword

Daniel B. Klein

On May 21, 2015, Ian Simpson Ross passed away in Vancouver at the age of 84. A tender, informative notice in *Herald Scotland* (1 June 2015), by Harry McGrath, says that Ross "was a Scots-born academic, lecturer and writer who became Professor Emeritus of English at the University of British Columbia. He was also the author of the much-lauded Life of Adam Smith, which was the first full-scale biography of Smith in a century when it was published in 1995." Ross was a student of Ernest Mossner, who enlisted Ross to co-edit, with Mossner, Adam Smith's correspondence, for the Glasgow Edition of Smith's works published by Oxford University Press and later reprinted by Liberty Fund. Ross's *The Life of Adam Smith* (Oxford University Press, 1995, 2nd ed. 2010) is one of the great biographies of Adam Smith, and by far the longest, consisting of 589 rather dense pages. It is meticulously packed with detail. Here we present selections from the second edition (2010), enumerated with Roman numerals. In reproducing material, we have sometimes inserted information to provide context; since Ross himself sometimes used brackets [like these], we instead use braces {like these}. Omitted intermittent material is replaced with an ellipsis. All of the ellipses in what follows are our insertions, except those that appear inside the quotations of Smith within excerpts I and XXVI, which are Ross's own ellipses. We have retained Ross's footnotes and in-line citations (but reformatting them, and in a few cases correcting, clarifying, or adding them), collecting the published sources cited in a References section that appears at the end of this article (archival sources used by Ross are not listed in the References here, but details on those can be found in the book).

Glimpses of Adam Smith: Excerpts from the Biography by Ian Simpson Ross[1]

Ian Simpson Ross

I. (p. 22)

In January 1736 {Adam Smith at the time being 12 years old} there was excitement over the apprehension of the 'free-trader' Andrew Wilson, who had attempted to recoup his smuggling losses by robbing an excise collector at nearby Pittenweem. Subsequently he failed in an attempt to escape from the Tolbooth in Edinburgh, and tried again to escape during morning service in the Tolbooth Kirk, a scene witnessed by Smith's friend, Alexander Carlyle. At Wilson's execution, Captain Porteous of the Edinburgh City Guard ordered his men to fire on the mob. When Porteous was pardoned by the Government for this crime, a disciplined mob, said to have included many men from Fife, seized him on the night of 7 September 1736 and hanged him at the scene of Wilson's death, showing their detestation of the revenue system Wilson fought, and their utter defiance of official authority (Scott 1818, ch. vii; Carlyle 1973, 18–20; Roughead 1909). In *WN*, Smith considers the lot of the smuggler with some sympathy and understanding, representing him as a 'person who, though no doubt highly blameable for violating the laws of his country, is frequently incapable of violating those of natural justice, and would have been, in every respect, an excellent citizen, had not the laws of his country made that a crime which nature never meant to be so'. We might think that the fate of Alexander Wilson fits precisely what Smith paints as typical of the smuggler: someone who 'from being at first, perhaps, rather imprudent than criminal...at last too often becomes one of the hardiest and most determined violators of the laws of society' (V.ii.k.64).

II. (p. 52)

Regarding {Francis} Hutcheson's teaching of politics as part of the moral

---

1. *Econ Journal Watch* gratefully acknowledges Oxford University Press for its grant of permission to reprint these excerpts from *The Life of Adam Smith*, 2nd ed., 2010.

philosophy course, an inspiration for Smith must have been his professor's stress on the 'Old Whig' and civic humanist theme of the importance of civil and religious liberty for human happiness:

> as a warm love of liberty, and manly zeal for promoting it, were ruling principles in his {that is, Hutcheson's} own breast, he always insisted upon it at great length, and with the greatest strength of argument and earnestness of persuasion: and he had such success on this important point, that few, if any, of his pupils, whatever contrary prejudices they might bring along with them, ever left him without favourable notions of that side of the question which he espoused and defended. (Leechman 1755, xxxv–xxxvi)

Smith seems to have absorbed his teacher's arguments for economic and political liberty, as we shall see, but he never pushed them as far as Hutcheson.

III. (pp. 114–115)

The teaching of moral philosophy was at the core of the Scottish university education of Smith's time, and of the Scottish Enlightenment as a movement, as much recent scholarship has demonstrated (Stewart-Robertson 1983; Emerson 1990; Sher 1990; Wood 1990; Haakonssen 1996). Though there was a measure of philosophical and religious freedom and diversity in Scotland, the kirk could still exercise control over appointments, as Hume's failure to get a Chair at Edinburgh and Glasgow illustrates. But absent from the Scottish academic scene were the monolithic tendencies in the state-administered universities of absolutist Protestant Germany, for example, Jena, Leipzig, Halle, and, from 1737, Göttingen (Nissen 1989). Men of letters were certainly supported in these institutions, as *WN* notes (V.i.g.39), but they faced political and religious restrictions, and also, for many decades, the intellectual stranglehold of Christian Wolff's philosophy (Boyle 1992, 17–18).

The Glasgow tradition of a broad approach to moral philosophy went back to the sixteenth century, when in the early decades John Mair taught the *Ethics of Aristotle*, publishing an edition of this text in 1530, as well as taking up economic issues in lectures on the Sentences of Peter Lombard. In addition, Andrew Melville and his nephew James Melville in the 1570s taught the moral philosophy of Aristotle (Durkan and Kirk 1977, 158, 279). Gershom Carmichael and Hutcheson had broken away from neo-Aristotelianism to introduce, between them, the natural-law tradition of {Hugo} Grotius and {Samuel} Pufendorf, Stoic ethics, and Shaftesbury's philosophy of benevolence and moral sense. The distribution of {Thomas} Craigie's duties, in which Smith participated, indicated the range—and liberal nature—of the public course in moral philosophy at Glasgow by 1751.

IV. (p. 116)

Orthodox religious opinion was not impressed by Smith's handling of the first part of his course, a state of affairs reflected in the comments of the anecdotalist John Ramsay of Ochtertyre:

> [Smith's] speculations upon natural religion, though not extended to any great length, were no less flattering to human pride than those of Hutcheson. From both the one and the other presumptuous striplings took upon themselves to draw an unwarranted conclusion—namely, that the great truths of theology, together with the duties which man owes of God and his neighbours, may be discovered by the light of nature without any special revelation.

Ramsay also mentioned that doubts were entertained about the soundness of Smith's principles, in view of the company he kept, an allusion to his friendship with Hume. Smith was also described as being 'very guarded in conversation', and Ramsay noted that he seemed to find it disagreeable to pray in public when opening his class, also that he petitioned unsuccessfully to be excused from this duty. The prayer he offered 'savoured strongly of natural religion', and it was further reported that Smith gave up Hutcheson's practice of convening the moral philosophy class on Sundays for an improving discourse (Ramsay 1888, i.461–462).

V. (pp. 124–125)

{John} Millar also noted in Smith that crucial interest in his subject which 'never failed to interest his hearers'. Very likely recalling the ethics or jurisprudence courses he attended, Millar described a characteristic pattern of organization which seems to reflect Smith's account of 'didactic eloquence' (LRBL, ii.125–126), also a love of paradox which Smith claimed in his 'History of Astronomy' (iv.34) was 'so natural to the learned':

Each discourse consisted commonly of several distinct propositions, which [Smith] successively endeavoured to prove and illustrate. These propositions, when announced in general terms, had, from their extent, not unfrequently something of the air of a paradox. In his attempts to explain them, he often appeared, at first, not to be sufficiently possessed of the subject, and spoke with some hesitation. As he advanced, however, the matter seemed to crowd upon him, his manner became warm and animated, and his expression easy and fluent. In points susceptible of controversy, you could easily discern, that he secretly conceived an opposition to his opinions, and that he was led upon this account to support them with greater energy and vehemence. By the fulness and variety of his illustrations, the subject gradually swelled in his hands, and acquired a dimension which, without a tedious repetition of the same views, was calculated to seize the attention of his audience, and to afford them pleasure, as well as instruction, in following the same object, through all the diversity of shades and aspects in which it was presented, and afterwards in tracing it backwards to that original proposition or general truth from which this beautiful train of speculation had proceeded. (Millar, quoted in Stewart 1980/ 1793, I.21)

We might think of Smith expounding his ethical doctrine concerning the objects of reward and punishment in this fashion, or the economic one of free trade (on 6 April 1763, for example, see *LJ*(A) vi.87). There could be added to this picture in our mind's eye details of Smith's reliance on signs of the sympathy or lack of it of a selected hearer for gauging the effect of what he was saying. Smith described his practice thus to Archibald Alison the elder, an Edinburgh magistrate and Lord Provost:

During one whole session a certain student with a plain but expressive countenance was of great use to me in judging of my success. He sat conspicuously in front of a pillar: I had him constantly under my eye. If he leant forward to listen all was right, and I knew that I had the ear of my class; but if he leant back in an attitude of listlessness I felt at once that all was wrong, and that I must change either the subject or the style of my address.[2]

Thus, all the contemporary reports we have suggest that Adam Smith found the best situation for his abilities as a professor at Glasgow. His years of study, and preliminary experience as a lecturer at Edinburgh, came to fruition in excellent and appreciated teaching of seminal ideas. Of particular significance

2. Anecdote told by Smith's student Archibald Alison to Archdeacon John Sinclair, reported by him (1875, 9).

was his growing sophistication of economic analysis in the jurisprudence lectures, as he extended the natural-law tradition of Grotius and Pufendorf, relayed through Carmichael and Hutcheson, in discussing value and exchange, and added his perspective to the comparative vision of Montesquieu and Hume concerning social and institutional transformation. It must indeed have been inspiring for his students to hear Smith expound his views on the dynamics of the creation of civil society and the alteration of values in its successive stages.

VI. (p. 160)

An anecdotal obituary of Smith in the *St James's Chronicle* (31 July 1790) recorded that he took {Charles} Townshend on a tour of manufactures in Glasgow, and they visited a tannery.... Smith fell into the pit—a noisome pool containing fat from hides, lime, and the gas generated by the mixture. He was dragged out, stripped, covered in blankets, placed in a sedan chair, and sent home.... The anecdote alleges that he was 'talking warmly on his favourite subject, the division of labour', and forgot the dangerous nature of the ground on which he stood.

VII. (p. 162)

Regarding Smith's influence at this time, his former pupil and colleague, John Millar, testified as follows: 'those branches of science which [Smith] taught became fashionable at [Glasgow], and his opinions were the chief topics of discussion in clubs and literary societies. Even the small peculiarities in his pronunciation or manner of speaking, became frequently the objects of imitation' (Millar, quoted in Stewart 1980/1793, I.22).

VIII. (p. 178)

Smith...finds the same outlook in the black people of the coast of Africa, suggesting that their magnanimity far exceeds any conception of their 'sordid' slave-masters. His indignation then flashes out against the enslavement of these people by the Europeans:

> Fortune never exerted more cruelly her empire over mankind, than when she subjected those nations of heroes to the refuse of the jails of Europe, to wretches who possess the virtues neither of the countries which they came from, nor of those which they go to, and whose levity, brutality, and baseness, so justly expose them to the contempt of the vanquished. (*TMS* 1759, 398; 1790, V.2.9)

It is to be hoped that the withers were wrung of readers in Glasgow and elsewhere engaged in business ventures profiting from slavery, and no doubt Smith as a moralist was helping to build the case of the anti-slavery movement.

IX. (p. 224)

Smith...felt that Hume should not publish anything about it {Rousseau's quarrelsomeness toward Hume}. Smith begins a letter to Hume, then in London, on 6 July by teasing him that he is as 'great a Rascal' as Rousseau, then continues with characteristically prudent advice not to 'unmask before the Public this hypocritical Pedant'...

X. (p. 240)

While in London, Smith moved in the same social circle that welcomed David Hume.... One of Hume's and Smith's hostesses of this period was Lady Mary Coke.... She kept a lively journal of her life, and her entry for Sunday 8 February 1767 paints Smith in a characteristic domestic scene:

> While Lady George Lennox was with me Sir Gilbert Elliot came in: they talked of Mr Smith, the Gentleman that went abroad with the Duke of Buccleugh, I said many things in his praise, but added he was the most Absent Man that ever was. Lady George gave us an instance that made me laugh. Mr Damer [son of Lord Milton, who married the sculptress, Anne Conway, encouraged by Hume] She said, made him a visit the other morning as he was going to breakfast, and falling into discourse, Mr Smith took a piece of bread and butter, which, after he rolled round and round, he put into the teapot and pour'd the water upon it; some time after he poured it into a cup, and when he had tasted it, he said it was the worst tea he had ever met with. (Coke 1889, 141)

XI. (p. 243)

Smith explained his situation in Kirkcaldy thus to Hume: 'My Business here is Study in which I have been very deeply engaged for about a month past. My Amusements are long, solitary walks by the Sea side. You may judge how I spend my time. I feel myself, however, extremely happy, comfortable and contented. I never was, perhaps, more so in all my life'.

The letter ends with requests for information about Rousseau's activities: 'Has he gone abroad, because he cannot get himself sufficiently persecuted in Great Britain?'

XII. (pp. 250–251)

One anecdote has it that in his study in his mother's home in Kirkcaldy Smith dictated sections of *WN* to an amanuensis, either Reid or Gillies perhaps. He did so standing and had the curious habit of rubbing his head against the wall above the chimney-piece. This is supposed to have left a mark on the wall from the pomatum of his wig, and the reporter of this anecdote, Robert Chambers, alleged in his *Picture of Scotland* (1827) that the traces remained until the wall was repainted.

XIII. (p. 254)

As this state of affairs was protracted his health seems to have suffered, and he fought against this by going on long walks. Also, it is reported that he took up swimming again in the Firth of Forth. This pursuit very likely gave rise to the anecdote of his arriving in Dunfermline in his dressing gown, one Sunday morning as the bells were ringing and people were going to the kirk. He may have walked the fifteen miles from Kirkcaldy in a fit of abstraction, perhaps upon taking a wrong turning after a douse in the North Sea (Scott 1937, 325 n.1; Rae 1965, 259–260).

XIV. (p. 257)

Hume on returning to Scotland in 1769 sought to draw his friend into some relaxation and refreshing companionship. On 20 August, he wrote to

Smith that he was 'glad to have come within sight' of him by having a view of Kirkcaldy from his window in James's Court, but he also wished to be on speaking terms, and since he declared himself to be as tired of travelling as Smith 'ought naturally to be, of staying at home', he suggested that Smith should come to join him in his 'Solitude' in Edinburgh:

> I want to know what you have been doing, and propose to exact a rigorous Account of the method, in which you have been employed yourself during your Retreat. I am positive you are in the wrong in many of your Speculations, especially where you have the Misfortune to differ from me. All these are Reasons for our meeting, and I wish you would make me some reasonable Proposal for the Purpose.

He then pointed out that there was the island of Inchkeith in the 'great Gulph' that lay between them, but it was uninhabited otherwise he would challenge Smith to meet him there, and 'neither [of] us ever to leave the Place, till we were fully agreed on all points of Controversy' (*Corr.*, No. 121).

XV. (p. 258)

Writing on 28 January 1772, Hume mentions a promise from Smith to visit him at Christmas, whose performance he had not 'challenged' because his sister Katherine, who lived with him and of whom he was very fond, had fallen 'dangerously ill of a Fever'. She has now recovered and Hume looks for Smith's 'Company', teasing him about his pleas of ill health:

> I shall not take any Excuse from your own State of Health, which I suppose only a Subterfuges invented by Indolence and Love of Solitude. Indeed, my Dear Smith, if you continue to hearken to Complaints of this Nature, you will cut Yourself out entirely from human Society, to the great Loss of both Parties. (*Corr.*, No. 129)

XVI. (p. 262)

Smith and Hume labored the point of the solitude of Kirkcaldy, perhaps dwelling on a Rousseauistic theme, but Smith had the companionship of his cousin Janet Douglas and his mother, both women of character who were well connected with the Fife gentry, and there were neighbours such as

Robert Beatson of Vicars Grange, who were certainly capable of instructive conversation about economics (*Corr.*, No. 266). Also, there is a report that during his evening walks along the Kirkcaldy foreshore, Smith had the company of a blind boy from the neighbourhood, Henry Moyes, who displayed great intellectual ability. Smith adopted the role of teacher of this boy, and sent him on to Hume, who secured a bursary for him at Edinburgh University, thus paving the way for a notable career as a popular lecturer on chemistry and the philosophy of natural history (Viner 1965, 74–77).

XVII. (p. 268)

On 14 September 1779, Boswell confided in his Journal: 'Since [Smith's] absurd eulogium on Hume, and his ignorant, ungrateful attack on the English University education, I have no desire to be much with him. Yet I do not forget that he was very civil to me at Glasgow' (Middendorf 1961; Boswell 1976, xc–xcii).

XVIII. (pp. 272–273)

There is circumstantial evidence that {Smith} was often in {Benjamin} Franklin's company at this time, and even that he showed chapters of *WN* to him (see Viner 1965, 44–47). This is not impossible. ... Certainly, Smith and Franklin had views in common. The theory of free trade is to be found in an unsystematic way in the economic writings of Franklin, and Smith shared the American's vision of an incorporating political union to end the disputes between their respective countries. Franklin left London in March 1775 to begin his career as one of the founding fathers of revolutionary America. This included taking a hand in drafting the Declaration of Independence of 4 July 1776, four months after Smith had struck his blow for economic independence with the publication of *WN*.

XIX. (p. 306)

Another of the literati who congratulated Smith was {William} Robertson the historian, writing on 8 April to give his views on *WN*. Like {Hugh} Blair, he commented on Smith's achievement in forming 'into a regular and complete system one of the most important and intricate parts of political science', and ventured the opinion that 'if the English be capable of extending their ideas beyond the narrow and illiberal arrangements introduced by the mercantile supporters of the {Glorious} Revolution, and countenanced by Locke and some of their favourite writers', then *WN* will bring about a 'total change' in economic policy and finance.

XX. (pp. 329–330)

Within a few months of Smith's removal to Edinburgh in 1778, he took into his care David Douglas, the 9-year-old youngest son of another cousin, Col. Robert Douglas of Strathendry (Rae 1965, 326). Smith delighted in the company of this boy, occupied his leisure hours in helping to educate him (Stewart 1980/1793, V.18), and secured the mathematician and natural philosopher John Leslie to be his tutor, 1785–7 (*Corr.*, No. 275). David Douglas would be a blink of sunshine in that house of elderly people, and perhaps recreated for Smith what he seems to have enjoyed at Glasgow, contact with the expanding mind of youth.

It is from this period that we have some images of Smith and can visualize him in his Edinburgh surroundings (Pl. 10). In general terms, we are told by William Smellie the antiquarian printer and naturalist, who knew him well, that 'in stature he somewhat exceeded the ordinary size; and his countenance was manly and agreeable'. He was not an ostentatious man, and remarked once, 'I am a beau in nothing but my books' (Smellie 1800, 297).

XXI. (p. 332)

John Kay, whose engraver's shop was at the corner of Parliament Close, and who must have seen Adam Smith many times going towards the Royal Exchange opposite, on whose upper floors was the Custom-house, issued a print dated 1787 showing him in a broad-brimmed hat, wearing a light linen coat and carrying in his left hand a bunch of flowers, perhaps to ward off the notorious Edinburgh effluvia (Pl. 11: Kay 1842, i.72, 75; Evans and Evans 1973). In his right hand he grasps his cane by the middle, sloping it against his shoulder, according to Smellie, 'as a soldier carries his musket'. He also described Smith's strange gait, his head moving in a gentle manner from side to side, and his body swaying 'vermicularly' (a nice touch from a naturalist) as if with each step 'he meant to alter his direction, or even to turn back'. Meantime, his lips would move and form smiles as if he were deep in conversation with persons unseen (Smellie 1800, 293). Edinburgh anecdote had it that an old market-woman observing him in these oddities exclaimed:

> 'Hegh, sirs!' and shook her head, to which a companion answered by sighing compassionately, then observed: 'and he is well put on too', thus expressing surprise that an obviously well-to-do lunatic would be allowed to wander freely. (Scott 1887/1827, 388)

XXII. (pp. 332–333)

At the entrance of the Exchange in Smith's time, to convey visitors on Custom-house business to what is now denominated the Old Council Room (Gifford et al. 1988 rpt.), was the doorkeeper, Adam Matheson. He appears in the official records, desiring on Christmas Eve 1778 more accommodation for his family in the garrets (SRO, Customs Board Minutes vol. 16), and getting a replacement for his scarlet gown bedecked with frogs of worsted lace. He was armed with a seven-foot wooden staff, and when the Board sat he saluted each arriving Commissioner with the kind of drill infantry officers used to perform with their spontoons or halberds, then conducted them up the great staircase to the first floor boardroom to deliberate on Customs business. Walter Scott heard from one of the other Commissioners a tale of Smith being so mesmerized by the doorkeeper's salute that he returned it compulsively with his cane, to the servant's amazement (Scott 1887/1827, 388–389).

A suggestion has been made that this happened because Smith had been subjected to drill routine after becoming an Honorary Captain of the Trained Bands of Edinburgh—the City Guard—on 4 June 1781 (Graham 1908, 169; Rae 1965, 374). It is more likely, however, that Smith was deep in thought coming up the High Street and simply entranced by a military manoeuvre. The story is of a piece with another one Scott presents of Smith taking a long time to sign a Customs document, and being found to have imitated laboriously the signature of the colleague going before him.

XXIII. (pp. 342–343)

A point to be made about this {that is, Smith's work as a Customs Commissioner}, however, is that Smith was one member of a Board guided by government and office policy and tradition, and he would have limited room for swaying his colleagues in the direction of putting into practice his own ideas about revenue collection and economic policy. The letters to {Henry} Dundas and {Lord} Carlisle about free trade for Ireland (*Corr.*, Nos. 201, 202), also to {William} Eden about raising revenue and American commerce (Nos. 203, 233), and to {John} Sinclair of Ulbster about the economic drain of empire and realistic duties (Nos. 221, 299) all indicate that Smith made no secret of his views to influential people asking for his comments and advice which, if taken, would affect practice in the Customs service.

He was invited to present his ideas about reducing smuggling to a House of Commons Committee dealing with this topic in 1783, and there is some evidence that {William} Pitt's Commutation Act of 1784 did embody Smith's principles in part at least in connection with duty on tea, also that by 1789 the contraband trade in that commodity had been dealt a severe blow (*Corr.*, app. D, p. 411). When Smith had a free hand to negotiate reformation of Customs duties, as we shall hear, he certainly did uphold his principles, but he also showed sensitivity about the effect of such a reformation would have on the livelihood of the Customs officers in Scotland. Moreover, as a Commissioner he did hear representations from concerned bodies that reflected the ideas expressed in *WN*.

XXIV. (p. 347)

Regarding answers to the evil of smuggling, the Excise Board, with tact but nevertheless at the outset of their recommendations, suggests that lowering duties would reduce the temptation to smuggle. Smith was thus not alone in thinking along these lines, and later on firm support for free trade even came from members of official bodies enforcing monopolies, the tariff system, and the Navigation Acts.[3]

---

3. Mathias (1983, 91, 269), citing James Mill (East India Co.), James Deacon Hume (Customs Service and Board of Trade), and John McGregor (Board of Trade); account of abolition of the Navigation Acts in 1849 (p. 275); Rule (1992, 316).

The Customs Board effected some of these suggestions to control smuggling in the south-west of Scotland, as appears from a letter co-signed by Adam Smith on 7 April 1785.

XXV. (pp. 348, 349)

{One} proposal Smith made for reforming the customs, that of warehousing imports under close inspection, with duty to be paid on goods when drawn out for home consumption, and to be duty-free if exported, was an extension of the excise practice in levying duties on rum (*WN*, V.ii.k.37). ...

In connection with the warehousing proposal, Smith acted in concert with his colleagues, though we may think the wording of their report has something of the flavour of his style, and may in part have been composed by him. On at least one occasion, however, he had a free hand in making recommendations about Custom-house practice in Scotland, and apparently altering policy in the direction of his reforming and even free-trade principles.

XXVI. (p. 350)

{Smith} believed that what the Royal Burghs wanted was freedom of trade in the inland waters from variable fees for certificates relating to taxable goods. Agreeable to his principles, he finds no difficulty with this:

> I have always been of opinion that not only the Trade within such Rivers and Firths but the whole Coasting Trade of Great Britain so far as it is carried on in Goods [not prohibited to be exported, or not liable to any duty...upon exportation], may with great conveniency to the Merchants and with Security to the Revenue of the Customs be exempted from the formality of Bonds and Cockets.

He noted that a Bill to this end had been drafted for the Customs Board applicable to the Firth of Forth, and accordingly he argued that 'it would be not only much shorter, but much more just and equal, to extend this exemption at once to the whole Coasting Trade of Great Britain' (PRO, Kew, Treasury T1/570).

Predictably, the officers of the Customs service petitioned against the loss of income threatened by these proposals; but they did go into effect in large part....

XXVII. (p. 351)

On 23 January 1781, the physician and merchant, also confidant of Lord Shelburne, Benjamin Vaughan, gave his Lordship an account of a visit to Edinburgh. He reported that he found Adam Smith 'more to his relish than I know some hold he ought to be in the South...he is among the best of them [the Edinburgh literati], though with peculiarities of manners well enough known here'. He continued: '[Smith] is very well provided for in the customs, where he does not innovate; but I believe he at times wishes he had kept in his college, where he had both more time and more respect and perhaps more company'. ...

Despite the disclaimer about Smith as an innovator in the Customs service, we have some evidence that in the course of his career as a Commissioner, his insights as an economic theorist, as well as his knowledge of practical affairs, led him to promote changes he viewed as both useful and just. It may be observed also that he was as scrupulous in his attention to his civil service duties, and role as a Commissioner, as he had been as a Glasgow professor.

XXVIII. (p. 358)

Yet the publication of Smith's supplement to Hume's *My Own Life*, in the form of a letter to {William} Strahan detailing Hume's last illness, had aroused a storm of protest from Christians. They were infuriated because Smith had adapted as an epitaph for Hume the last sentence of the *Phaedo* (*Corr.*, No. 178; quoted Ch. 17). The most unchristian fury evoked in England by this linking of Hume to Socrates as truly virtuous and wise men in secular terms is well represented by *A Letter to Adam Smith, LL.D. on the Life, Death, and Philosophy of His Friend David Hume Esq. By One of the People Called Christians*, published anonymously by the Clarendon Press, Oxford, in 1777 (4th ed., 1784), by no less a personage than the President of Magdalen College, George Horne (Aston, *ODNB-O*, 2004), who ended his career as Bishop of Norwich. ... In so many words (p. 7), Horne accuses Smith of promoting atheism and denying there is a life to come of rewards and punishments, but he must have overlooked Smith's passage on the Atonement and Calvinist penal substitution theory retained in *TMS* until 1790 (Ch. 12 above). As for the shock felt in Scotland by 'every sober Christian' about Smith's Letter to Strahan, this was registered by the anecdotalist Ramsay of Ochtertyre (1888, i.466–467). Attacks such as Horne's led Smith to make his sardonic remark of October 1780: a 'single, and as, I thought, a very harmless Sheet of paper, which I happened to Write concerning the death of our late friend Mr Hume, brought upon me ten times more abuse than the very violent attack I had made upon the whole commercial system of Great Britain' (*Corr.*, No. 208).

XXIX. (pp. 374–375)

To be sure, Smith could be critical of {Edmund} Burke's efforts as a legislator. Thus, in the first edition of *WN* he had commented adversely on a Bill that Burke had devised to improve but essentially maintain bounties on the export of a grain, a subject still exercising him in preparing the third edition. Concerning certain features of what was enacted (13 Geo. III, c. 43, 1772), Smith wrote: 'The bounty ought certainly either to have been withdrawn at a much lower price, or exportation ought to have been allowed at a much higher. So far, therefore, this law seems to be inferior to the antient system' (IV.v.b. 52–53). Burke is said to have answered this criticism of not bringing about a repeal of the corn bounty with one of those metaphorical flights for which he was famous. He neatly distinguished between Smith's role as theorist with a tendency to model his systems on geometry, as Dugald Stewart perceived, and his own role as the practical man seeking to get a law through Parliament:

> it was the privilege of philosophers to conceive their diagrams in geometrical accuracy; but the engineer must often impair the symmetry as well as the simplicity of his machine, in order to overcome the irregularities of friction and resistance. (quoted in Horner 1957, 98; Viner 1965, 23)

Smith allowed the justice of this answer, and had added to the second edition of *WN* (1778) a balanced comment on Burke's legislation:

> With all its imperfections, however, we may perhaps say of it what was said of the laws of Solon, that, though not the best in itself, it is the best which the interests, prejudices, and temper of the times would admit of. It may perhaps in

due time prepare the way for a better. (IV.v.b.53)

In the final revisions for the 1790 *TMS*, Smith included in the new section on Virtue a discussion of the 'man of system', making clear that the point Burke brought up about the Corn Bounty Act was germane to his own outlook:

> Some general, and even systematical, idea of the perfection of policy and law, may no doubt be necessary for directing the views of the statesman [this being the drive of *WN*]. But to insist upon establishing, and upon establishing all at once, and in spite of all opposition, every thing which that idea may seem to require, must often be the highest degree of arrogance.

As in the 1778 *WN*, Smith evokes in the last edition of *TMS* the example of Solon as a legislator who, short of establishing the best system of laws, enacted the 'best the people can bear' (VI.ii.2.16, 18).

XXX. (p. 377)

But after the merriment and stimulation of Burke's visit, and the excitement of the general election, came a sad event for Smith, the death of his mother on 23 May {1784}. He writes of this in a letter to Strahan dated 10 June, in which he comments on receiving the proofs of the new third edition of *WN* by the cheaper conveyance of the coach, when he would have preferred the proofs of the MS 'additions', at least, to have been sent by post:

> I should immediately have acknowledged the receipt of the fair sheets; but I had just then come from performing the last duty to my poor old Mother; and tho' the death of a person in the ninetieth year of her age was no doubt an event most agreable to the course of nature; and, therefore, to be foreseen and prepared for; yet I must say to you, what I have said to other people, that the final separation from a person who certainly loved me more than any other person ever did or ever will love me; and whom I certainly loved and respected more than I ever shall either love or respect any other person, I cannot help feeling, even at this hour, as a very heavy stroke upon me. (*Corr.*, No. 237)

XXXI. (p. 379)

To be sure, {Jeremy} Bentham claims in the *Defence of Usury* that in refuting Smith's arguments about the 'policy of the laws fixing the rate of interest', he is turning his master's weapons against himself (*Corr.*, No. 388). He means that the tendency of *WN* is to show that economic growth has been created in spite of the laws made by governments, rather than as a result of them, and that this demonstration can be extended to interest-rate controls against which the 'prudent projectors' who sustain growth have struggled with varying degrees of success (*Corr.*, No. 391).

It is difficult not to agree with Bentham's reading of *WN* and even to see the message about the detrimental effect of most economic legislation intensified in the third edition.

XXXII. (p. 399)

It was in this letter {of 23 September 1788} that Smith wrote movingly of his grief at the impending death of his cousin Janet Douglas, who had looked after his mother and him for so many years (*Corr.*, app. E, p).

XXXIII. (pp. 402–403)

There was an Edinburgh tradition that on one occasion during this London visit Smith was one of the last gentlemen to come into the room in Dundas's Wimbledon villa, where Pitt, {William Wyndham} Grenville, Henry Addington, and William Wilberforce were other guests. The company rose to receive Smith, and he asked them to be seated. Pitt is represented as saying: 'No, we will stand till you are first seated, for we are all your scholars' (Kay 1842, i.75; Rae 1965, 405). Smith had advance notice of Pitt's good opinion of him, and had come round to valuing his ministry, despite his own adherence to the remnants of the Rockingham Whigs. Answering on 14 November 1786 a letter from the reform-minded MP Henry Beaufoy, he wrote:

> I think myself much honoured by the slightest mark of Mr Pitts approbation. You may be assured that the long and strict friendship in which I have lived with some of his opponents, does not hinder me from discerning courage, activity, probity, and public spirit in the great outlines of his administration. (Piero Sraffa Collection B5/3, Trinity College, Cambridge)

Addington, later to be Grenville's successor as Speaker of the House of Commons, 1789–1801, and thereafter a stopgap Prime Minister until Pitt regained control of affairs in 1804, is said to have returned home after the Wimbledon meeting and composed verses to the 'author of the Wealth of Nations, etc.: on his visit to London and its neighbourhood in the month of June, 1787':

> I welcome you, whose wise and patriot page
> The road to wealth and peace hath well defin'd,
> Hath strove to curb and soften hostile rage,
> And to unite, with int'rest's tie, mankind:
> Dragg'd from his lonely den, and at thy feet
> The bloated fiend Monopoly is thrown:
> And with thy fame, its splendor to compleat,
> The pride and hope of Britain blends his own.
> Proceed, great soul, and error's shades disperse,
> Perfect and execute the glorious plan;
> Extend your view wide as the Universe,
> Burst every bar that sep'rates man from man,
> And ne'er may war's curst banner be unfurled,
> But commerce harmonize a jarring world!

This effusion was communicated to Smith early in 1790, and since the great man was a sound critic of poetry, Ernest Mossner once claimed it 'may well have hastened the end' (1969, 20–21).

XXXIV. (pp. 428–429)

The talk then turned to French writers, in particular Voltaire and Turgot. It was on this occasion that Smith would not hear of some 'clever but superficial author' being called by {Samuel} Rogers 'a Voltaire'. Smith banged the table and declared energetically, 'Sir, there is only one Voltaire.' Regarding Turgot, he was described to Rogers by Smith as an excellent, absolutely honest, and well-intended person, who was not well-versed in human nature with all its selfishness, stupidity, and prejudice.

XXXV. (p. 430)

{Samuel} Rogers was greatly impressed with Smith's kindness: 'he is a very friendly, agreeable man, and I should have dined and supped with him every day, if I had accepted all his invitations'. He seemed quite oblivious to the disparity in age between himself and the poet, who was then 23, and he was free with information and opinions. His manner Rogers described as 'quite familiar'; he would ask, for example: 'Who should we have to dinner?' Rogers did not see in him the absent-mindedness others stressed. Compared to Robertson, Smith seemed to Rogers far more a man of the world (*BL* Add. MSS 32,566; Dyce 1856, 45; Clayden 1887, 90, 96).

XXXVI. (p. 432)

Smith anticipates that after the death {in 1788) of his cousin {Janet Douglas} he will suffer emotional destitution, and this is an indication that she had partly filled the gap in his life left by the death of his mother, to whom he was so strongly attached. As for other ladies in his life, Dugald Stewart tells us that as a young man Smith was in love with a beautiful and accomplished young woman, but unknown circumstances prevented their marriage, and both apparently afterwards decided not to marry (Stewart 1980/1793, n. K). Anecdotage reports that Smith beamed at her in company later in life, and his cousin Janet Douglas is supposed to have said: 'Don't you know, Adam, this is your ain Jeannie?' But the smile was one of general kindness rather than special favour, and nothing came of the re-encounter (Mackay 1896, 209). In France he had sighed unavailingly for an Englishwoman named Mrs Nichol, and a French marquise pursued him without success, as far as we know, but he seems to have been entirely content with his existence as a bachelor.

XXXVII. (p. 436)

In any event, satisfied about the protection of his reputation or the safe-guarding of moral and political truth, after the burning of his papers on that long-ago July Sunday in Panmure House, Smith felt well enough to welcome his friends in the evening with his usual equanimity. A considerable number of them came to be with him then, but he did not have strength to sit with them through supper, so he retired to bed before it. Henry Mackenzie recorded his parting words in the form: 'I love your company, gentlemen, but I believe I must leave you to go to another world' (quoted in Clayden 1887, 168). {James} Hutton gave Stewart some different wording: 'I believe we must adjourn this meeting to some other place' (quoted in Stewart 1980/1793, V.8 n., p. 328).

XXXVIII. (p. 437)

Since Smith lived in a hospitable but modest way, his friends wondered at the limited nature of the bequests, though no one has been detected censuring the will, as Beatson feared. We may believe that Smith left instructions to his heir that his servant was to be looked after properly, also that he had given away generous sums from his income in secret charity, hence his slender resources at the end. The instance has been mentioned of Smith giving £200 in 1783 to a 'Welch nephew' to save him from having to sell his army commission (*Corr.*, No. 231). Stewart obtained first-hand information that strengthens belief that Smith was markedly generous in an unostentatious fashion:

> Some very affecting instances or Mr Smith's beneficence, in cases where he found it impossible to conceal entirely his good offices, have been mentioned to me by a near relation of his, and one of his most confidential friends, Miss Ross, daughter of the late Patrick Ross, Esq., of Innernethy. They were all on a scale much beyond what might have been expected from his fortune; and they were accompanied with circumstances equally honourable to the delicacy of his feelings and the liberality of his heart. (Stewart 1980/1793, V.4 n., p. 326)

XXXIX. (p. 438)

Samuel Romilly, then a young barrister concerned with law reform, who had been added to the group of Whig liberals surrounding Lord Shelburne, and who was an admirer of Smith's advanced ideas, wrote {on 20 August 1790} to a French lady in response to her request for a copy of the latest edition of *TMS*:

> I have been surprised and, I own, a little indignant to observe how little impression [Smith's] death {17 July 1790} has made here. Scarce any notice has been taken of it, while for above a year together after the death of Dr Johnson [1784] nothing was to be heard but panegyrics of him,—lives, letters, and anecdotes,—and even at this moment there are two more lives of him to start into existence [possibly Boswell's, 1791; and Arthur Murphy's, 1792].

Indeed, one ought not perhaps to be very much surprised that the public does not do justice to the works of A. Smith since he did not do justice to them himself, but always considered his *TMS* a much superior work to his [*WN*]. (Romilly 1840, i.403)

XL. (pp. 444–445)

Nature did not favour Smith in his mode of expression, it seems, for we read of his harsh voice with an almost stammering impediment, and a conversational style that amounted to lecturing (Carlyle 1973, 141). His friends understood this, and made allowances for his disposition. According to Stewart, they 'were often led to concert little schemes, in order to engage him in the discussions most likely to interest him'. They were greatly diverted when he expatiated in his social hours in his characteristically original way on subjects relatively unfamiliar to him, or advanced extreme positions or judgements on relatively slight grounds, and then just as readily withdrew them when countervailing views were put to him. When with strangers, apparently, his manner was sometimes an embarrassed one, because he was conscious of, and perhaps on guard about, his customary absence of mind; also, he had very high speculative notions of propriety, yet an imperfect ability to live up to them. What shines through all accounts of his character and characteristics, particularly as they were displayed in his relationships with young people, was his essential kindness. Samuel Rose, grieving for the death of his father William, an old friend of Smith's from the time of his notice of *TMS* in the *Monthly Review* in 1759, wrote to a relative that 'Commissioner Smith has treated me with uncommon tenderness' (GUL MS Accession No. 4467 to Edward Foss, 19 July 1786). Somewhat in the same vein, Stewart wrote of Smith that 'in the society of those he loved, his features were often brightened with a smile of inexpressible benignity' (Stewart 1980/1793, V.17).

References

Boswell, James. 1976. *The Correspondence of James Boswell with Certain Members of The Club*, ed. Charles N. Fifer. London: Heinemann.

Boyle, Nicholas. 1992. *Goethe: The Poet and the Age, Vol. I: The Poetry of Desire (1749–1790)*. Oxford: Oxford University Press.

Carlyle of Inversek, Alexander. 1973. *Anecdotes and Characters of the Times*, ed. James Kinsley. London: Oxford University Press.

Chambers, Robert. 1827. *Pictures of Scotland*. Edinburgh: William Tait.

Clayden, P. W. 1887. *The Early Life of Samuel Rogers*. London: Smith, Elder.

Coke, Mary. 1889. *The Letters and Journals of Lady Mary Coke: Volume First, 1756–1767*. London: Kingsmead.

Durkan, John, and James Kirk. 1977. *The University of Glasgow 1451–1577*. Glasgow: University of Glasgow Press.

Dyce, Alexander, ed. 1856. *Recollections of the Table-Talk of Samuel Rogers*. New York: Appleton.

Emerson, Roger L. 1990. Science and Moral Philosophy in the Scottish Enlightenment. In *Studies in the Philosophy of the Scottish Enlightenment*, ed. M. A. Stewart, 11–36. Oxford: Oxford University Press.

Evans, Hilary, and Mary Evans. 1973. *John Kay of Edinburgh: Barber, Miniaturist and Social Commentator, 1742–1826*. Aberdeen: Impulse Publications.

Gifford, John, Colin McWilliam, David Walker, and Christopher Wilson. 1988. *Edinburgh: The Buildings of Scotland*. Harmondsworth, UK: Penguin.

Graham, Henry Gray. 1908. *Scottish Men of Letters in the Eighteenth Century*. London: Adam & Charles Black.

Haakonssen, Knud. 1996. *Natural Law and Moral Philosophy: From Grotius to the Scottish Enlightenment*. Cambridge, UK: Cambridge University Press.

Horne, George. 1777. *A Letter to Adam Smith LL.D. on the Life, Death, and Philosophy of his Friend David Hume Esq., by One of the People Called Christians*. Oxford: Clarendon Press.

Horner, Francis. 1957. *The Economic Writings of Francis Horner in the Edinburgh Review 1802–6*, ed. Frank Whitson Fetter. London: London School of Economics and Political Science.

Kay, John. 1842. *A Series of Portraits and Character Etchings*, 2 vols. Edinburgh: Hugh Paton.

Leechman, William. 1969 [1755]. The Preface, Giving Some Account of the Life, Writings, and Character of the Author. In *A System of Moral Philosophy*, vol. 1, by Francis Hutcheson. Hildersheim: G. Olms.

Mackay, A. J. G. 1896. *A History of Fife and Kinross*. Edinburgh: Blackwood.

Mathias, Peter. 1983. *The First Industrial Nation: An Economic History of Britain 1700–1914*, 2nd ed. London: Methuen.

Middendorf, John. 1961. Dr Johnson and Adam Smith. *Philological Quarterly* 40: 281–296.

Mossner, Ernest Campbell. 1969. *Adam Smith: The Biographical Approach*. Glasgow: University of Glasgow.

Nissen, Walter. 1989. *Kulturelle Beziehungen zwischen den Universitätsstäden Halle/Wittenburg und Göttingen im Zeitalter der Aufklärung*. Göttingen: Sparkasse Göttingen.

Rae, John. 1965 [1895]. *Life of Adam Smith*. New York: Augustus M. Kelley.

Ramsay of Ochtertyre, John. 1888. *Scotland and Scotsmen in the Eighteenth Century*, 2 vols., ed. A. Allardyce. Edinburgh and London: William Blackwood.

Romilly, Samuel. 1840. *Memoirs of the Life of Sir Samuel Romilly*. London: Murray.

Roughead, William, ed. 1909. *Trial of Captain Porteous*. Glasgow: William Hodge.

Rule, John. 1992. *The Vital Century: England's Developing Economy 1714–1815*. London: Longman.

Scott, Walter. 1818. *The Heart of Midlothian*. Edinburgh: Archibald Constable.

Scott, Walter. 1887 [1827]. Life and Works of John Home. In *Essays on Chivalry, Romance, and the Drama*, 356–403. London: Frederick Warne.

Scott, William R. 1937. *Adam Smith as Student and Professor.* Glasgow: Jackson, Son & Company.

Sher, Richard B. 1990. Professors of Virtue: The Social History of the Edinburgh Moral Philosophy Chair. In *Studies in the Philosophy of the Scottish Enlightenment*, ed. M. A. Stewart, 87–126. Oxford: Oxford University Press.

Sinclair, John. 1875. *Sketches of Old Times and Distant Places.* London: John Murray.

Smellie, William. 1800. *Literary and Characteristical Lives of John Gregory, M. D., Henry Home, Lord Kames, David Hume, Esq., and Adam Smith, L. L. D.* Edinburgh: A. Smellie.

Smith, Adam. 1811–1812. *The Works of Adam Smith, LL.D., with an Account of His Life and Writings by Dugald Stewart*, 5 vols. London: T. Cadell & W. Davies; Edinburgh: W. Creech.

Smith, Adam. 1976 [1776] (*WN*). *An Inquiry Into the Nature and Causes of The Wealth of Nations*, 2 vols., eds. R. H. Campbell and A. S. Skinner. Oxford: Clarendon Press.

Smith, Adam. 1976 [1790] (*TMS*). *The Theory of Moral Sentiments*, eds. D. D. Raphael and A. L. Macfie. Oxford: Clarendon Press.

Smith, Adam. 1977 (*Corr.*). *The Correspondence of Adam Smith*, eds. Ernest C. Mossner and Ian Simpson Ross. Oxford: Clarendon Press.

Smith, Adam. 1978 (*LJ*(A)). *Lectures on Jurisprudence: Report of 1762–3.* In *Lectures on Jurisprudence*, by Adam Smith, eds. R. L. Meek, D. D. Raphael, and P. G. Stein, 1–394. Oxford: Clarendon Press.

Smith, Adam. 1980. The History of Astronomy. In *Essays on Philosophical Subjects*, by Adam Smith, eds. W. P. D. Wightman and J. C. Bryce, 33–105. Oxford: Clarendon Press.

Smith, Adam. 1983 (*LRBL*). *Lectures on Rhetoric and Belles Lettres*, ed. J. C. Bryce. Oxford: Clarendon Press.

Stewart, Dugald. 1980 [1793]. *Account of the Life and Writings of Adam Smith*, ed. Ian Simpson Ross. In *Essays on Philosophical Subjects*, by Adam Smith, eds. W. P. D. Wightman and J. C. Bryce, 269–351. Oxford: Clarendon Press.

Stewart-Robinson, J. C. 1983. Cicero Among the Shadows: Scottish Prelections of Virtue and Duty. *Rivista critica di storia della filosofia* 38: 25–49.

Viner, Jacob. 1965. Guide to John Rae's *Life of Adam Smith*. In *Life of Adam Smith*, by John Rae, 5–145. New York: Augustus M. Kelley.

Wood, Paul B. 1990. Science and the Pursuit of Virtue in the Aberdeen Enlightenment. In *Studies in the Philosophy of the Scottish Enlightenment*, ed. M. A. Stewart, 127–149. Oxford: Oxford University Press.

Thoughts and Details on Scarcity

Foreword

Daniel B. Klein

Edmund Burke's literary executors French Laurence and Walker King issued "Thoughts and Details on Scarcity" in 1800, three years after Burke's death in 1797. The document—reproduced in entirety here though without their informative Preface[1]—comes principally from a memorial Burke wrote to Prime Minister William Pitt in 1795, but almost half comes from other draft material, intended for the public but to be framed as letters addressed to Burke's friend Arthur Young.[2]

The material began as a timely warning against interventionist measures in the face of dearth, including a locally administered minimum-wage scheme (referred to as a "tax" by Burke, because employers pay more for labor). But the interpolations from the letters are more of the nature of general political economy. The final document, "Thoughts and Details on Scarcity," then, is an admixture—"Details," the more specific facts from the memorial, including testimony of Burke the farmer, which work as illustration of the "Thoughts," formulated especially in the material that the executors had drawn from the subsequent draft letters.

We have made a few very minor corrections to Burke's text, and we include most of the footnotes added by Francis Canavan for the Liberty Fund edition (Burke 1999), which relate the text to affairs of the moment. We thank Liberty Fund for their kind permission to reproduce Canavan's notes.

Why do we draw attention to "Thoughts and Details on Scarcity"?

Adam Smith's "liberal plan" or "liberal system" (WN, 664, 538–539) is centered on the idea of liberty, which is a flipside of commutative justice.

---

1. Their Preface can be found online.
2. In the Liberty Fund edition of the work (Burke 1999), editor Francis Canavan indicates the three interpolations (pages 64–72, 73–76, 90–92) added to the original memorial to Pitt.

Liberty is others not messing with one's stuff, or as Smith puts it "allowing every man to pursue his own interest his own way" (WN, 664; cf. 687). A presumption of liberty is central to the original political meaning of "liberal."

Presupposed by that liberalism, however, is a stable, integrated, functional polity. Smith's "science of a legislator" (WN, 468) is a philosophy of *policy reform*, within a settled and integrated system of political authority.

Burke is famous for decrying the French Revolution and worrying about the destabilization of political systems. He often speaks to matters outside of what Smithian liberalism presupposes. Many of Burke's writings concern not policy reform so much as *polity* reform. On the basis of his writings in this domain he may aptly be considered conservative—although one should not imagine that Burke favors the conservation of constitutional or fundamental political institutions per se, that is, even terrible ones. And when polity reform seems ripe, he may favor it, as he came to favor letting the American colonies go their own way.

But conservatism in polity reform may coexist with liberalism in policy reform. Burke was indeed a liberal. Burke's *policy* sensibilities were liberal, seen throughout his life and career, notably in "Thoughts and Details on Scarcity."

In philosophy and political ideology, David Hume, Smith, and Burke are three peas in a pod (see, e.g., Miller 1981, 196–203). But Hume and Smith operated in philosophy, speculation, scholarship, science, offering among other things "the science of a legislator." Burke operated in practical legislating and advising. Burke was "that insidious and crafty animal, vulgarly called a statesman or politician, whose councils are directed by the momentary fluctuations of affairs" (WN, 468). Burke did, of course, also have a foot in philosophy, as well as one in journalism, publishing, and propaganda.

Alexis de Tocqueville (1856, 145) suggested that Britain, especially in contrast to France, was exceptional in the coordination between these two groups of players, the philosophers and the politicos: "In England writers on the theory of government and those who actually governed co-operated with each other, the former setting forth their new theories, the latter amending or circumscribing these in light of practical experience." The present document by Edmund Burke helps us appreciate the outlook common to liberals at work in both realms, and it might inspire such cooperation today in all countries.

When reading Burke, we should mind whether he is treating polity reform or policy reform, and we should keep track of his multiple roles: Sometimes, somewhat the philosopher who treats what is relatively timeless, but also the politico or publicist, tending the timely and fluctuating.

Even in the latter, though, there's a timelessness in the manner of his words and deeds.

Thoughts and Details on Scarcity

Edmund Burke

Of all things, an indiscreet tampering with the trade of provisions is the most dangerous, and it is always worst in the time when men are most disposed to it:—that is, in the time of scarcity. Because there is nothing on which the passions of men are so violent, and their judgment so weak, and on which there exists such a multitude of ill-founded popular prejudices.

The great use of Government is as a restraint; and there is no restraint which it ought to put upon others, and upon itself too, rather than on the fury of speculating under circumstances of irritation. The number of idle tales spread about by the industry of faction, and by the zeal of foolish good-intention, and greedily devoured by the malignant credulity of mankind, tends infinitely to aggravate prejudices, which, in themselves, are more than sufficiently strong. In that state of affairs, and of the publick with relation to them, the first thing that Government owes to us, the people, is *information*; the next is timely coercion:—the one to guide our judgment; the other to regulate our tempers.

To provide for us in our necessities is not in the power of Government. It would be a vain presumption in statesmen to think they can do it. The people maintain them, and not they the people. It is in the power of Government to prevent much evil; it can do very little positive good in this, or perhaps in any thing else. It is not only so of the state and statesman, but of all the classes and descriptions of the Rich—they are the pensioners of the poor, and are maintained by their superfluity. They are under an absolute, hereditary, and indefeasible dependance on those who labour, and are miscalled the Poor.

The labouring people are only poor, because they are numerous. Numbers in their nature imply poverty. In a fair distribution among a vast multitude, none can have much. That class of dependant pensioners called the rich, is so extremely small, that if all their throats were cut, and a distribution made of all they consume in a year, it would not give a bit of bread and cheese for one night's supper to those who labour, and who in reality feed both the pensioners and themselves.

But the throats of the rich ought not to be cut, nor their magazines plundered; because, in their persons they are trustees for those who labour, and their hoards are the banking-houses of these latter. Whether they mean it or not, they do, in effect, execute their trust—some with more, some with less fidelity and judgment. But on the whole, the duty is performed, and every thing returns, deducting some very trifling commission and discount, to the place from whence it arose. When the poor rise to destroy the rich, they act as wisely for their own purposes as when they burn mills, and throw corn into the river, to make bread cheap.

When I say, that we of the people ought to be informed, inclusively I say, we ought not to be flattered: flattery is the reverse of instruction. The *poor* in that case would be rendered as improvident as the rich, which would not be at all good for them.

Nothing can be so base and so wicked as the political canting language, "The Labouring *Poor*." Let compassion be shewn in action, the more the better, according to every man's ability, but let there be no lamentation of their condition. It is no relief to their miserable circumstances; it is only an insult to their miserable understandings. It arises from a total want of charity, or a total want of thought. Want of one kind was never relieved by want of any other kind. Patience, labour, sobriety, frugality, and religion, should be recommended to them; all the rest is downright *fraud*. It is horrible to call them "The *once happy* labourer."

Whether what may be called moral or philosophical happiness of the laborious classes is increased or not, I cannot say. The seat of that species of happiness is in the mind; and there are few data to ascertain the comparative state of the mind at any two periods. Philosophical happiness is to want little. Civil or vulgar happiness is to want much, and to enjoy much.

If the happiness of the animal man (which certainly goes somewhere towards the happiness of the rational man) be the object of our estimate, then I assert, without the least hesitation, that the condition of those who labour (in all descriptions of labour, and in all gradations of labour, from the highest to the lowest inclusively) is on the whole extremely meliorated, if more and better food is any standard of melioration. They work more, it is certain; but

271

they have the advantage of their augmented labour; yet whether that increase of labour be on the whole a *good* or an *evil*, is a consideration that would lead us a great way, and is not for my present purpose. But as to the fact of the melioration of their diet, I shall enter into the detail of proof whenever I am called upon: in the mean time, the known difficulty of contenting them with any thing but bread made of the finest flour, and meat of the first quality, is proof sufficient.

I further assert, that even under all the hardships of the last year, the labouring people did, either out of their direct gains, or from charity, (which it seems is now an insult to them) in fact, fare better than they did, in seasons of common plenty, 50 or 60 years ago; or even at the period of my English observation, which is about 44 years. I even assert, that full as many in that class, as ever were known to do it before, continued to save money; and this I can prove, so far as my own information and experience extend.

It is not true that the rate of wages has not encreased with the nominal price of provisions. I allow it has not fluctuated with that price, nor ought it; and the Squires of Norfolk[3] had dined, when they gave it as their opinion, that it might or ought to rise and fall with the market of provisions. The rate of wages in truth has no *direct* relation to that price. Labour is a commodity like every other, and rises or falls according to the demand. This is in the nature of things; however, the nature of things has provided for their necessities. Wages have been twice raised in my time, and they bear a full proportion, or even a greater than formerly, to the medium of provision during the last bad cycle of twenty years. They bear a full proportion to the result of their labour. If we were wildly to attempt to force them beyond it, the stone which we had forced up the hill would only fall back upon them in a diminished demand, or, what indeed is the far lesser evil, an aggravated price of all the provisions, which are the result of their manual toil.

There is an implied contract, much stronger than any instrument or article of agreement, between the labourer in any occupation and his employer—that the labour, so far as that labour is concerned, shall be sufficient to pay to the employer a profit on his capital, and a compensation for his risk; in a word, that the labour shall produce an advantage equal to the payment. Whatever is

3. Burke may have mistakenly written Norfolk when he meant Suffolk, where the Justices of the Peace recommended that the wages of laborers should be adjusted in proportion to the price of corn.

above that, is a direct *tax*; and if the amount of that tax be left to the will and pleasure of another, it is an *arbitrary tax*.

If I understand it rightly, the tax proposed on the farming interest of this kingdom,[4] is to be levied at what is called the discretion of justices of peace.

The questions arising on this scheme of arbitrary taxation are these—Whether it is better to leave all dealing, in which there is no force or fraud, collusion or combination, entirely to the persons mutually concerned in the matter contracted for; or to put the contract into the hands of those, who can have none, or a very remote interest in it, and little or no knowledge of the subject.

It might be imagined that there would be very little difficulty in solving this question; for what man, of any degree of reflection, can think, that a want of interest in any subject closely connected with a want of skill in it, qualifies a person to intermeddle in any the least affair; much less in affairs that vitally concern the agriculture of the kingdom, the first of all its concerns, and the foundation of all its prosperity in every other matter, by which that prosperity is produced?

The vulgar error on this subject arises from a total confusion in the very idea of things widely different in themselves;—those of convention, and those of judicature. When a contract is making, it is a matter of discretion and of interest between the parties. In that intercourse, and in what is to arise from it, the parties are the masters. If they are not completely so, they are not free, and therefore their contracts are void.

But this freedom has no farther extent, when the contract is made; then their discretionary powers expire, and a new order of things takes its origin. Then, and not till then, and on a difference between the parties, the office of the judge commences. He cannot dictate the contract. It is his business to see that it be *enforced*; provided that it is not contrary to pre-existing laws, or obtained by force or fraud. If he is in any way a maker or regulator of the contract, in so much he is disqualified from being a judge. But this sort

---

4. The reference is to the so-called Speenhamland system, which inspired Burke to write this memorandum to William Pitt. In 1782, Parliament had enacted Gilbert's Act, which authorized local governments to grant allowances in aid of wages. Subsidizing the wages of the poor was not even then a new departure in English law. On this basis, in 1795 the magistrates of Berkshire, a county adjacent to Burke's Buckinghamshire, met in the Pelican Inn in Speenhamland, and adopted a scheme to ensure laborers a living wage. A minimum wage was fixed, which varied with the price of corn; if the wages actually paid fell below that, they would be supplemented from the poor rates.

of confused distribution of administrative and judicial characters, (of which we have already as much as is sufficient, and a little more) is not the only perplexity of notions and passions which trouble us in the present hour.

What is doing, supposes or pretends that the farmer and the labourer have opposite interests;—that the farmer oppresses the labourer; and that a gentleman called a justice of peace, is the protector of the latter, and a controul and restraint on the former; and this is a point I wish to examine in a manner a good deal different from that in which gentlemen proceed, who confide more in their abilities than is fit, and suppose them capable of more than any natural abilities, fed with no other than the provender furnished by their own private speculations, can accomplish. Legislative acts, attempting to regulate this part of œconomy, do, at least, as much as any other, require the exactest detail of circumstances, guided by the surest general principles that are necessary to direct experiment and enquiry, in order again from those details to elicit principles, firm and luminous general principles, to direct a practical legislative proceeding.

First, then, I deny that it is in this case, as in any other of necessary implication, that contracting parties should originally have had different interests. By accident it may be so undoubtedly at the outset; but then the contract is of the nature of a compromise; and compromise is founded on circumstances that suppose it the interest of the parties to be reconciled in some medium. The principle of compromise adopted, of consequence the interests cease to be different.

But in the case of the farmer and the labourer, their interests are always the same, and it is absolutely impossible that their free contracts can be onerous to either party. It is the interest of the farmer, that his work should be done with effect and celerity: and that cannot be, unless the labourer is well fed, and otherwise found with such necessaries of animal life, according to its habitudes, as may keep the body in full force, and the mind gay and cheerful. For of all the instruments of his trade, the labour of man (what the ancient writers have called the *instrumentum vocale*) is that on which he is most to rely for the re-payment of his capital. The other two, the *semivocale* in the ancient classification, that is, the working stock of cattle, and the *instrumentum mutum*, such as carts, ploughs, spades, and so forth, though not all inconsiderable in themselves, are very much inferiour in utility or in expence; and without a given portion of the first, are nothing at all. For in all things whatever, the mind is the most valuable and the most important; and in this scale the whole of agriculture is in a natural and just order; the beast is as an informing principle to the plough and cart; the labourer is as reason to the beast; and the farmer is as a thinking and presiding principle to the labourer. An attempt to break this chain of subordination in any part is equally absurd; but the absurdity is the most mischievous in practical operation, where it is the most easy, that is, where it is the most subject to an erroneous judgment.

It is plainly more the farmer's interest that his men should thrive, than that his horses should be well fed, sleek, plump, and fit for use, or than that his waggon and ploughs should be strong, in good repair, and fit for service.

On the other hand, if the farmer ceases to profit of the labourer, and that his capital is not continually manured and fructified, it is impossible that he should continue that abundant nutriment, and cloathing, and lodging, proper for the protection of the instruments he employs.

It is therefore the first and fundamental interest of the labourer, that the farmer should have a full incoming profit on the product of his labour. The proposition is self-evident, and nothing but the malignity, perverseness, and ill-governed passions of mankind, and particularly the envy they bear to each other's prosperity, could prevent their seeing and acknowledging it, with thankfulness to the benign and wise disposer of all things, who obliges men, whether they will or not, in pursuing their own selfish interests, to connect the general good with their own individual success.

But who are to judge what that profit and advantage ought to be? certainly no authority on earth. It is a matter of convention dictated by the reciprocal conveniences of the parties, and indeed by their reciprocal necessities.—But, if the farmer is excessively avaricious?—why so much the better—the more he desires to increase his gains, the more interested is he in the good condition of those, upon whose labour his gains must principally depend.

I shall be told by the zealots of the sect of regulation, that this may be true, and may be safely committed to the convention of the farmer and the labourer, when the latter is in the prime of his youth, and at the time of his health and vigour, and in ordinary times of abundance. But in calamitous seasons, under accidental illness, in declining life, and with the pressure of a numerous offspring, the future nourishers of the community but the present drains and blood-suckers of those who produce them, what is to be done? When a man cannot live and maintain his family by the natural hire of his labour, ought it not to be raised by authority?

On this head I must be allowed to submit, what my opinions have ever been; and somewhat at large.

And, first, I premise that labour is, as I have already intimated, a commodity, and as such, an article of trade. If I am right in this notion, then labour must be subject to all the laws and principles of trade, and not to regulations foreign to them, and that may be totally inconsistent with those principles and those laws. When any commodity is carried to market, it is not the necessity of the vender, but the necessity of the purchaser that raises the price. The extreme want of the seller has rather (by the nature of things with which we shall in vain contend) the direct contrary operation. If the goods at market are beyond the demand, they fall in their value; if below it, they rise. The impossibility of the subsistence of a man, who carries his labour to a market, is totally beside the question in this way of viewing it. The only question is, what is it worth to the buyer?

But if authority comes in and forces the buyer to a price, who is this in the case (say) of a farmer, who buys the labour of ten or twelve labouring men, and three or four handycrafts, what is it, but to make an arbitrary division of his property among them?

The whole of his gains, I say it with the most certain conviction, never do amount any thing like in value to what he pays to his labourers and artificers; so that a very small advance upon what *one* man pays to *many*, may absorb the whole of what he possesses, and amount to an actual partition of all his substance among them. A perfect equality will indeed be produced;—that is to say, equal want, equal wretchedness, equal beggary, and on the part of the partitioners, a woeful, helpless, and desperate disappointment. Such is the event of all compulsory equalizations. They pull down what is above. They never raise what is below: and they depress high and low together beneath the level of what was originally the lowest.

If a commodity is raised by authority above what it will yield with a profit to the buyer, that commodity will be the less dealt in. If a second blundering interposition be used to correct the blunder of the first, and an attempt is made to force the purchase of the commodity (of labour for instance), then one of these two things must happen, either that the forced buyer is ruined, or the price of the product of the labour, in that proportion, is raised. Then the wheel turns round, and the evil complained of falls with aggravated weight on the complainant. The price of corn, which is the result of the expence of all the operations of husbandry, taken together, and for some time continued, will rise on the labourer, considered as a consumer. The very best will be, that he remains where he was. But if the price of the corn should not compensate the price of labour, what is far more to be feared, the most serious evil, the very destruction of agriculture itself, is to be apprehended.

Nothing is such an enemy to accuracy of judgment as a coarse discrimination; a want of such classification and distribution as the subject admits of. Encrease the rate of wages to the labourer, say the regulators—as if labour was but one thing and of one value. But this very broad generic term, *labour*, admits, at least, of two or three specific descriptions: and these will suffice, at least, to let gentlemen discern a little the necessity of proceeding with caution in their coercive guidance of those whose existence depends upon the observance of still nicer distinctions and sub-divisions, than commonly they resort to in forming their judgments on this very enlarged part of economy.

The labourers in husbandry may be divided: 1st. into those who are able to perform the full work of a man; that is, what can be done by a person from twenty-one years of age to fifty. I know no husbandry work (mowing hardly excepted) that is not equally within the power of all persons within those ages, the more advanced fully compensating by knack and habit what they lose in activity. Unquestionably, there is a good deal of difference between the value of one man's labour and that of another, from strength, dexterity, and honest application. But I am quite sure, from my best observation, that any given five men will, in their total, afford a proportion of labour equal to any other five within the periods of life I have stated; that is, that among such five men there will be one possessing all the qualifications of a good workman, one bad, and the other three middling, and approximating to the first and the last. So that in so small a platoon as that of even five, you will find the full complement of all that five men *can* earn. Taking five and five throughout the kingdom, they are equal: therefore, an error with regard to the equalization of their wages by those who employ five, as farmers do at the very least, cannot be considerable.

2dly. Those who are able to work, but not the complete task of a day-labourer. This class is infinitely diversified, but will aptly enough fall into principal divisions. *Men*, from the decline, which after fifty becomes every year more sensible, to the period of debility and decrepitude, and the maladies that precede a final dissolution. *Women*, whose employment on husbandry is but occasional, and who differ more in effective labour one from another than men do, on account of gestation, nursing, and domestic management, over and above the difference they have in common with men in advancing, in stationary, and in declining life. *Children*, who proceed on the reverse order, growing from less to greater utility, but with a still greater disproportion of nutriment to labour than is found in the second of these sub-divisions; as is visible to those who will give themselves the trouble of examining into the interior economy of a poor-house.

This inferior classification is introduced to shew, that laws prescribing, or magistrates exercising, a very stiff, and often inapplicable rule, or a blind and rash discretion, never can provide the just proportions between earning and salary on the one hand, and nutriment on the other: whereas interest, habit, and the tacit convention, that arise from a thousand nameless circumstances, produce a *tact* that regulates without difficulty, what laws and magistrates cannot regulate at all. The first class of labour wants nothing to equalize it; it equalizes itself. The second and third are not capable of any equalization.

But what if the rate of hire to the labourer comes far short of his necessary subsistence, and the calamity of the time is so great as to threaten actual famine? Is the poor labourer to be abandoned to the flinty heart and griping hand of base self-interest, supported by the sword of law, especially when there is reason to suppose that the very avarice of farmers themselves has concurred with the errors of Government to bring famine on the land.

In that case, my opinion is this. Whenever it happens that a man can claim nothing according to the rules of commerce, and the principles of justice, he passes out of that department, and comes within the jurisdiction of mercy. In that province the magistrate has nothing at all to do: his interference is a violation of the property which it is his office to protect. Without all doubt, charity to the poor is a direct and obligatory duty upon all Christians, next in order after the payment of debts, full as strong, and by nature made infinitely more delightful to us. Pufendorf, and other casuists do not, I think, denominate it quite properly, when they call it a duty of imperfect obligation. But the manner, mode, time, choice of objects, and proportion, are left to private discretion; and perhaps, for that very reason it is performed with the greater satisfaction, because the discharge of it has more the appearance of freedom; recommending us besides very specially to the divine favour, as the exercise of a virtue most suitable to a being sensible of its own infirmity.

The cry of the people in cities and towns, though unfortunately (from a fear of their multitude and combination) the most regarded, ought, in *fact*, to be the *least* attended to upon this subject; for citizens are in a state of utter ignorance of the means by which they are to be fed, and they contribute little or nothing, except in an infinitely circuitous manner, to their own maintenance. They are truly *"Fruges consumere nati."*[5] They are to be heard with great respect and attention upon matters within their province, that is, on trades and manufactures; but on any thing that relates to agriculture, they are to be listened to with the same *reverence* which we pay to the dogmas of other ignorant and presumptuous men.

If any one were to tell them, that they were to give in an account of all the stock in their shops; that attempts would be made to limit their profits, or raise the price of the labouring manufacturers upon them, or recommend to Government, out of a capital from the publick revenues, to set up a shop of the same commodities, in order to rival them, and keep them to reasonable dealing, they would very soon see the impudence, injustice, and oppression of such a course. They would not be mistaken; but they are of opinion, that agriculture is to be subject to other laws, and to be governed by other principles.

A greater and more ruinous mistake cannot be fallen into, than that the trades of agriculture and grazing can be conducted upon any other than the common principles of commerce; namely, that the producer should be permitted, and even expected, to look to all possible profit which, without fraud or violence, he can make; to turn plenty or scarcity to the best advantage he can; to keep back or to bring forward his commodities at his pleasure; to account to no one for his stock or for his gain. On any other terms he is the slave of the consumer; and that he should be so is of no benefit to the consumer. No slave was ever so beneficial to the master as a freeman that deals with him on an equal footing by convention, formed on the rules and principles of contending interests and compromised advantages. The consumer, if he were suffered, would in the end always be the dupe of his own tyranny and injustice. The landed gentleman is never to forget, that the farmer is his representative.

It is a perilous thing to try experiments on the farmer. The farmer's

---

5. "Born to consume the fruits [of the earth]." Horace *Epistles* 1.2.27.

capital (except in a few persons, and in a very few places) is far more feeble than commonly is imagined. The trade is a very poor trade; it is subject to great risks and losses. The capital, such as it is, is turned but once in the year; in some branches it requires three years before the money is paid. I believe never less than three in the turnip and grass-land course, which is the prevalent course on the more or less fertile, sandy and gravelly loams, and these compose the soil in the south and south-east of England, the best adapted, and perhaps the only ones that are adapted, to the turnip husbandry.

It is very rare that the most prosperous farmer, counting the value of his quick and dead stock, the interest of the money he turns, together with his own wages as a bailiff or overseer, ever does make twelve or fifteen *per centum* by the year on his capital. I speak of the prosperous. In most of the parts of England which have fallen within my observation, I have rarely known a farmer, who to his own trade has not added some other employment or traffic, that, after a course of the most unremitting parsimony and labour (such for the greater part is theirs), and persevering in his business for a long course of years, died worth more than paid his debts, leaving his posterity to continue in nearly the same equal conflict between industry and want, in which the last predecessor, and a long line of predecessors before him, lived and died.

Observe that I speak of the generality of farmers who have not more than from one hundred and fifty to three or four hundred acres. There are few in this part of the country within the former, or much beyond the latter, extent. Unquestionably in other places there are much larger. But, I am convinced, whatever part of England be the theatre of his operations, a farmer who cultivates twelve hundred acres, which I consider as a large farm, though I know there are larger, cannot proceed, with any degree of safety and effect, with a smaller capital than ten thousand pounds; and that he cannot, in the ordinary course of culture, make more upon that great capital of ten thousand pounds, than twelve hundred a year.

As to the weaker capitals, an easy judgment may be formed by what very small errors they may be farther attenuated, enervated, rendered unproductive, and perhaps totally destroyed.

This constant precariousness and ultimate moderate limits of a farmer's fortune, on the strongest capital, I press, not only on account of the hazardous speculations of the times, but because the excellent and most useful works of my friend, Mr. Arthur Young, tend to propagate that error (such I am very certain it is), of the largeness of a farmer's profits. It is not that his account of the produce does often greatly exceed, but he by no means makes the proper allowance for accidents and losses. I might enter into a convincing detail, if other more troublesome and more necessary details were not before me.

This proposed discretionary tax on labour militates with the recommendations of the Board of Agriculture: they recommend a general use of the drill culture.[6] I agree with the Board, that where the soil is not excessively heavy, or incumbered with large loose stones (which however is the case with much otherwise good land), that course is the best, and most productive, provided that the most accurate eye; the most vigilant superintendance; the most prompt activity, which has no such day as to-morrow in its calendar; the most steady foresight and pre-disposing order to have every body and every thing ready in its place, and prepared to take advantage of the fortunate fugitive moment in this coquetting climate of ours—provided, I say, all these combine to speed the plough, I admit its superiority over the old and general methods. But under procrastinating, improvident, ordinary husbandmen, who may neglect or let slip the few opportunities of sweetening and purifying their ground with perpetually renovated toil, and undissipated attention, nothing, when tried to any extent, can be worse, or more dangerous: the farm may be ruined, instead of having the soil enriched and sweetened by it.

But the excellence of the method on a proper soil, and conducted by an husbandman, of whom there are few, being readily granted, how, and on what conditions, is this culture obtained? Why, by a very great encrease of labour; by an augmentation of the third part, at least, of the hand-labour, to say nothing of the horses and machinery employed in ordinary tillage. Now, every man must be sensible how little becoming the gravity of Legislature it is to encourage a Board, which recommends to us, and upon very weighty reasons unquestionably, an enlargement of the capital we employ in the operations of the land, and then to pass an act which taxes that manual labour, already at a very high rate; thus compelling us to diminish the quantity of labour which in the vulgar course we actually employ.

What is true of the farmer is equally true of the middle man; whether the middle man acts as factor,[7] jobber, salesman, or speculator, in the markets of

---

6. To drill is to sow seeds or seedlings along a shallow furrow.
7. One who acts for another as an agent, deputy, or representative; more narrowly, an agent who buys or sells for another; a commission merchant.

grain. These traders are to be left to their free course; and the more they make, and the richer they are, and the more largely they deal, the better both for the farmer and consumer, between whom they form a natural and most useful link of connection; though, by the machinations of the old evil counsellor, *Envy*, they are hated and maligned by both parties.

I hear that middle men are accused of monopoly. Without question, the monopoly of authority is, in every instance and in every degree, an evil; but the monopoly of capital is the contrary. It is a great benefit, and a benefit particularly to the poor. A tradesman who has but a hundred pound capital, which (say) he can turn but once a year, cannot live upon a *profit* of 10 *per cent.* because he cannot live upon ten pounds a year; but a man of ten thousand pounds capital can live and thrive upon 5 *per cent.* profit in the year, because he has five hundred pounds a year. The same proportion holds in turning it twice or thrice. These principles are plain and simple; and it is not our ignorance, so much as the levity, the envy, and the malignity of our nature, that hinders us from perceiving and yielding to them: but we are not to suffer our vices to usurp the place of our judgment.

The balance between consumption and production makes price. The market settles, and alone can settle, that price. Market is the meeting and conference of the *consumer* and *producer*, when they mutually discover each other's wants. Nobody, I believe, has observed with any reflection what market is, without being astonished at the truth, the correctness, the celerity, the general equity, with which the balance of wants is settled. They who wish the destruction of that balance, and would fain by arbitrary regulation decree, that defective production should not be compensated by encreased price, directly lay their *axe* to the root of production itself.

They may even in one year of such false policy, do mischiefs incalculable; because the trade of a farmer is, as I have before explained, one of the most precarious in its advantages, the most liable to losses, and the least profitable of any that is carried on. It requires ten times more of labour, of vigilance, of attention, of skill, and let me add, of good fortune also, to carry on the business of a farmer with success, than what belongs to any other trade. Seeing things in this light, I am far from presuming to censure the late circular instruction of Council to Lord Lieutenants[8]—but I confess I do not clearly

---

8. A circular letter sent by the Council through the Home Secretary to the Lords Lieutenant

discern its object. I am greatly afraid that the enquiry will raise some alarm as a measure, leading to the French system of putting corn into requisition. For that was preceded by an inquisition somewhat similar in its principle, though, according to their mode, their principles are full of that violence, *which here* is not much to be feared. It goes on a principle directly opposite to mine: it presumes, that the market is no fair *test* of plenty or scarcity. It raises a suspicion, which may affect the tranquillity of the public mind, "that the farmer keeps back, and takes unfair advantages by delay;" on the part of the dealer, it gives rise obviously to a thousand nefarious speculations.

In case the return should on the whole prove favourable, is it meant to ground a measure for encouraging exportation and checking the import of corn? If it is not, what end can it answer? And, I believe, it is not.

This opinion may be fortified by a report gone abroad, that intentions are entertained of erecting public granaries, and that this enquiry is to give Government an advantage in its purchases.

I hear that such a measure has been proposed, and is under deliberation, that is, for Government to set up a granary in every market town, at the expence of the state, in order to extinguish the dealer, and to subject the farmer to the consumer, by securing corn to the latter at a certain and steady price.

If such a scheme is adopted, I should not like to answer for the safety of the granary, of the agents, or of the town itself, in which the granary was erected—the first storm of popular phrenzy would fall upon that granary.

So far in a political light.

In an economical light, I must observe, that the construction of such granaries throughout the kingdom, would be at an expence beyond all calculation. The keeping them up would be at a great charge. The management and attendance would require an army of agents, store-keepers, clerks, and servants. The capital to be employed in the purchase of grain would be enormous. The waste, decay, and corruption, would be a dreadful drawback on the whole dealing; and the dissatisfaction of the people, at having decayed, tainted, or corrupted corn sold to them, as must be the case, would be serious.

This climate (whatever others may be) is not favourable to granaries,

---

asking them to hold magistrates' meetings in their counties to ascertain the produce of the recent harvest.

where wheat is to be kept for any time. The best, and indeed the only good granary, is the rick-yard of the farmer, where the corn is preserved in its own straw, sweet, clean, wholesome, free from vermin and from insects, and comparatively at a trifle of expence. This, with the barn, enjoying many of the same advantages, have been the sole granaries of England from the foundation of its agriculture to this day. All this is done at the expence of the undertaker, and at his sole risk. He contributes to Government; he receives nothing from it but protection; and to this he has a *claim*.

The moment that Government appears at market, all the principles of market will be subverted. I don't know whether the farmer will suffer by it, as long as there is a tolerable market of competition; but I am sure that, in the first place, the trading government will speedily become a bankrupt, and the consumer in the end will suffer. If Government makes all its purchases at once, it will instantly raise the market upon itself. If it makes them by degrees, it must follow the course of the market. If it follows the course of the market, it will produce no effect, and the consumer may as well buy as he wants—therefore all the expence is incurred gratis.

But if the object of this scheme should be, what I suspect it is, to destroy the dealer, commonly called the middle man, and by incurring a voluntary loss to carry the baker to deal with Government, I am to tell them that they must set up another trade, that of a miller or a mealman, attended with a new train of expences and risks. If in both these trades they should succeed, so as to exclude those who trade on natural and private capitals, then they will have a monopoly in their hands, which, under the appearance of a monopoly of capital, will, in reality, be a monopoly of authority, and will ruin whatever it touches. The agriculture of the kingdom cannot stand before it.

A little place like Geneva, of not more than from twenty-five to thirty thousand inhabitants, which has no territory, or next to none; which depends for its existence on the good-will of three neighbouring powers, and is of course continually in the state of something like a *siege*, or in the speculation of it, might find some resource in state granaries, and some revenue from the monopoly of what was sold to the keepers of public-houses. This is a policy for a state too small for agriculture. It is not (for instance) fit for so great a country as the Pope possesses, where, however, it is adopted and pursued in a greater extent, and with more strictness. Certain of the Pope's territories, from whence the city of Rome is supplied, being obliged to furnish Rome and the granaries of his Holiness with corn at a certain price, that part of the papal territories is utterly ruined. That ruin may be traced with certainty to this sole cause, and it appears indubitably by a comparison of their state and condition with that of the other part of the ecclesiastical dominions not subjected to the same regulations, which are in circumstances highly flourishing.

The reformation of this evil system is in a manner impracticable; for, first, it does keep bread and all other provisions equally subject to the chamber of supply, at a pretty reasonable and regular price, in the city of Rome. This preserves quiet among the numerous poor, idle, and naturally mutinous people, of a very great capital. But the quiet of the town is purchased by the ruin of the country, and the ultimate wretchedness of both. The next cause which renders this evil incurable, is, the jobs which have grown out of it, and which, in spite of all precautions, would grow out of such things, even under governments far more potent than the feeble authority of the Pope.

This example of Rome which has been derived from the most ancient times, and the most flourishing period of the Roman empire (but not of the Roman agriculture) may serve as a great caution to all Governments, not to attempt to feed the people out of the hands of the magistrates. If once they are habituated to it, though but for one half-year, they will never be satisfied to have it otherwise. And, having looked to Government for bread, on the very first scarcity they will turn and bite the hand that fed them. To avoid that *evil*, Government will redouble the causes of it; and then it will become inveterate and incurable.

I beseech the Government (which I take in the largest sense of the word, comprehending the two Houses of Parliament) seriously to consider that years of scarcity or plenty, do not come alternately or at short intervals, but in pretty long cycles and irregularly, and consequently that we cannot assure ourselves, if we take a wrong measure, from the temporary necessities of one season; but that the next, and probably more, will drive us to the continuance of it; so that in my opinion, there is no way of preventing this evil which goes to the destruction of all our agriculture, and of that part of our internal commerce which touches our agriculture the most nearly, as well as the safety and very being of Government, but manfully to resist the very first idea, speculative or practical, that it is within the competence of Government, taken as Government, or even of the rich, as rich, to supply to the poor, those necessaries which it has pleased the Divine Providence for a while to with-hold from them. We, the people, ought to be made sensible, that it is not in breaking the laws of commerce, which are the laws of nature, and consequently the laws of God, that we are to place our hope of softening the Divine displeasure to remove any calamity under which we suffer, or which hangs over us.

So far as to the principles of general policy.

As to the state of things which is urged as a reason to deviate from them, these are the circumstances of the harvest of 1795 and 1794. With regard to the harvest of 1794, in relation to the noblest grain, wheat, it is allowed to have been somewhat short, but not excessively; and in quality, for the seven and twenty years, during which I have been a farmer, I never remember wheat to have been so good. The world were, however, deceived in their speculations upon it—the farmer as well as the dealer. Accordingly the price fluctuated beyond any thing I can remember; for, at one time of the year, I sold my wheat at 14l. a load, (I sold off all I had, as I thought this was a reasonable price), when at the end of the season, if I had then had any to sell, I might have got thirty guineas for the same sort of grain. I sold all that I had, as I said, at a comparatively low price, because I thought it a good price, compared with what I thought the general produce of the harvest; but when I came to consider what my own *total* was, I found that the quantity had not answered my expectation. It must be remembered, that this year of produce, (the year 1794) short, but excellent, followed a year which was not extraordinary in production, nor of a superior quality, and left but little in store. At first this was not felt, because the harvest came in unusually early—earlier than common, by a full month.

The winter, at the end of 1794, and beginning of 1795, was more than usually unfavourable both to corn and grass, owing to the sudden relaxation of very rigorous frosts, followed by rains, which were again rapidly succeeded by frosts of still greater rigour than the first.

Much wheat was utterly destroyed. The clover grass suffered in many places. What I never observed before, the rye-grass, or coarse bent, suffered more than the clover. Even the meadow-grass in some places was killed to the very roots. In the spring, appearances were better than we expected. All the early sown grain recovered itself, and came up with great vigour; but that, which was late sown, was feeble, and did not promise to resist any blights, in the spring, which, however, with all its unpleasant vicissitudes passed off very well; and nothing looked better than the wheat at the time of blooming:—but at that most critical time of all, a cold dry east wind, attended with very sharp frosts, longer and stronger than I recollect at that time of year, destroyed the flowers, and withered up, in an astonishing manner, the whole side of the ear next to the wind. At that time I brought to town some of the ears, for the purpose of shewing to my friends the operation of those unnatural frosts, and according to their extent I predicted a great scarcity. But such is the pleasure of agreeable prospects, that my opinion was little regarded.

On threshing, I found things as I expected—the ears not filled, some of the capsules quite empty, and several others containing only withered hungry grain, inferior to the appearance of rye. My best ears and grains were not fine; never had I grain of so low a quality—yet I sold one load for 21l. At the same time I bought my seed wheat (it was excellent) at 23l. Since then the price has risen, and I have sold about two load of the same sort at 23l. Such was the state of the market when I left home last Monday. Little remains in my barn. I hope some in the rick may be better; since it was earlier sown, as well as I can recollect. Some of my neighbours have better, some quite as bad, or even worse. I suspect it will be found, that wherever the blighting wind and those frosts at blooming time have prevailed, the produce of the wheat crop will turn out very indifferent. Those parts which have escaped, will, I can hardly doubt, have a reasonable produce.

As to the other grains, it is to be observed, as the wheat ripened very late, (on account, I conceive, of the blights) the barley got the start of it, and was ripe first. The crop was with me, and wherever my enquiry could reach, excellent; in some places far superior to mine.

The clover, which came up with the barley, was the finest I remember to have seen.

The turnips of this year are generally good.

The clover sown last year, where not totally destroyed, gave two good crops, or one crop and a plentiful feed; and, bating the loss of the rye-grass, I do not remember a better produce.

The meadow-grass yielded but a middling crop, and neither of the sown or natural grass was there in any farmer's possession any remainder from the year worth taking into account. In most places, there was none at all.

Oats with me were not in a quantity more considerable than in commonly good seasons; but I have never known them heavier, than they were in other places. The oat was not only an heavy, but an uncommonly abundant crop. My ground under pease did not exceed an acre, or thereabouts, but the crop was great indeed. I believe it is throughout the country exuberant.

It is however to be remarked, that as generally of all the grains, so particularly of the pease, there was not the smallest quantity in reserve.

The demand of the year must depend solely on its own produce; and the price of the spring-corn is not to be expected to fall very soon, or at any time very low.

Uxbridge is a great corn market. As I came through that town, I found that at the last market-day, barley was at forty shillings a quarter; oats there were literally none; and the innkeeper was obliged to send for them to London. I forgot to ask about pease. Potatoes were 5s. the bushel.

In the debate on this subject in the House, I am told that a leading member of great ability, *little conversant in these matters*, observed, that the general uniform dearness of butcher's meat, butter, and cheese, could not be owing to a defective produce of wheat; and on this ground insinuated a suspicion of some unfair practice on the subject, that called for enquiry.

Unquestionably the mere deficiency of wheat could not cause the dearness of the other articles, which extends not only to the provisions he mentioned, but to every other without exception.

The cause is indeed so very plain and obvious, that the wonder is the other way. When a properly directed enquiry is made, the gentlemen who are amazed at the price of these commodities will find, that when hay is at six pound a load, as they must know it is, herbage, and for more than one year, must be scanty, and they will conclude, that if grass be scarce, beef, veal, mutton, butter, milk, and cheese, *must* be dear.

But to take up the matter somewhat more in detail—if the wheat harvest in 1794, excellent in quality, was defective in quantity, the barley harvest was in quality ordinary enough; and in quantity deficient. This was soon felt in the price of malt.

Another article of produce (beans) was not at all plentiful. The crop of pease was wholly destroyed, so that several farmers pretty early gave up all hopes on that head, and cut the green haulm as fodder for the cattle, then perishing for want of food in that dry and burning summer. I myself came off better than most—I had about the fourth of a crop of pease.

It will be recollected, that, in a manner, all the bacon and pork consumed in this country, (the far largest consumption of meat out of towns) is, when growing, fed on grass, and on whey, or skimmed milk; and when fatting, partly on the latter. This is the case in the dairy countries, all of them great breeders and feeders of swine; but for the much greater part, and in all the corn countries, they are fattened on beans, barley meal, and pease. When the food of the animal is scarce, his flesh must be dear. This, one would suppose, would require no great penetration to discover.

This failure of so very large a supply of flesh in one species, naturally throws the whole demand of the consumer on the diminished supply of all kinds of flesh, and, indeed, on all the matters of human sustenance. Nor, in my opinion, are we to expect a greater cheapness in that article for this year, even though corn should grow cheaper, as it is to be hoped it will. The store swine, from the failure of subsistence last year, are now at an extravagant price. Pigs, at our fairs, have sold lately for fifty shillings, which, two years ago, would not have brought more than twenty.

As to sheep, none, I thought, were strangers to the general failure of the article of turnips last year; the early having been burned as they came up, by the great drought and heat; the late, and those of the early which had escaped, were destroyed by the chilling frosts of the winter, and the wet and severe weather of the spring. In many places a full fourth of the sheep or the lambs were lost, what remained of the lambs were poor and ill-fed, the ewes having had no milk. The calves came late, and they were generally an article, the want of which was as much to be dreaded as any other. So that article of food, formerly so abundant in the early part of the summer, particularly in London, and which in a great part supplied the place of mutton for near two months, did little less than totally fail.

All the productions of the earth link in with each other. All the sources of plenty, in all and every article, were dried or frozen up. The scarcity was not as gentlemen seem to suppose, in wheat only.

Another cause, and that not of inconsiderable operation, tended to produce a scarcity in flesh provision. It is one that on many accounts cannot be too much regretted, and, the rather, as it was the sole *cause* of scarcity in that article, which arose from the proceedings of men themselves. I mean the stop put to the distillery.

The hogs (and that would be sufficient) which were fed with the waste wash of that produce, did not demand the fourth part of the corn used by farmers in fattening them. The spirit was nearly so much clear gain to the nation. It is an odd way of making flesh cheap, to stop or check the distillery.

The distillery in itself produces an immense article of trade almost all over the world, to Africa, to North America, and to various parts of Europe. It is of great use, next to food itself, to our fisheries and to our whole navigation. A great part of the distillery was carried on by damaged corn, unfit for bread, and by barley and malt of the lowest quality. These things could not be more unexceptionably employed. The domestic consumption of spirits, produced, without complaints, a very great revenue, applicable, if we pleased, in bounties to the bringing corn from other places, far beyond the value of that consumed in making it, or to the encouragement of its encreased production at home.

As to what is said, in a physical and moral view, against the home consumption of spirits, experience has long since taught me very little to respect the declamations on that subject—whether the thunder of the laws, or the thunder of eloquence, "is hurled *on gin*,"[9] always I am thunder-proof. The alembic,[10] in my mind, has furnished to the world a far greater benefit and blessing, than if the *opus maximum*[11] had been really found by chemistry, and, like Midas, we could turn every thing into gold.

Undoubtedly there may be a dangerous abuse in the excess of spirits; and at one time I am ready to believe the abuse was great. When spirits are cheap, the business of drunkenness is atchieved with little time or labour; but that evil I consider to be wholly done away. Observation for the last forty years, and very particularly for the last thirty, has furnished me with ten instances of drunkenness from other causes, for one from this. Ardent spirit is a great medicine, often to remove distempers—much more frequently to prevent them, or to chase them away in their beginnings. It is not nutritive in *any great* degree. But, if not food, it greatly alleviates the want of it. It invigorates the stomach for the digestion of poor meagre diet, not easily alliable to the human constitution. Wine the poor cannot touch. Beer, as applied to many

---

9. See Alexander Pope's *Epilogue to the Satires*, Dialogue 1, lines 129–31, deploring the presumptuousness of the lower classes in imitating the vices of their social superiors: "This, this, my friend, I cannot, must not bear; / Vice thus abused demands a nation's care; / This calls the Church to deprecate our sin, / And hurls the thunder of the laws on gin."
10. An apparatus used in distilling spirits.
11. The greatest work or art, that of realizing alchemy's dream of turning base metals into gold.

occasions, (as among seamen and fishermen for instance) will by no means do the business. Let me add, what wits inspired with champaign and claret, will turn into ridicule—it is a medicine for the mind. Under the pressure of the cares and sorrows of our mortal condition, men have at all times, and in all countries, called in some physical aid to their moral consolations,—wine, beer, opium, brandy, or tobacco.

I consider therefore the stopping of the distillery, œconomically, financially, commercially, medicinally, and in some degree morally too, as a measure rather well meant than well considered. It is too precious a sacrifice to prejudice.

Gentlemen well know whether there be a scarcity of partridges, and whether that be an effect of hoarding and combination. All the tame race of birds live and die as the wild do.

As to the lesser articles, they are like the greater. They have followed the fortune of the season. Why are fowls dear? was not this the farmer's or jobber's fault. I sold from my yard to a jobber, six young and lean fowls, for four and twenty shillings; fowls, for which, two years ago, the same man would not have given a shilling a-piece.—He sold them afterwards at Uxbridge, and they were taken to London to receive the last hand.

As to the operation of the war in causing the scarcity of provisions, I understand that Mr. Pitt has given a particular answer to it—but I do not think it worth powder and shot.

I do not wonder the papers are so full of this sort of matter, but I am a little surprised it should be mentioned in parliament. Like all great state questions, peace and war may be discussed, and different opinions fairly formed, on political grounds, but on a question of the present price of provisions, when peace with the regicides is always uppermost, I can only say, that great is the love of it.

After all, have we not reason to be thankful to the giver of all good? In our history, and when "The labourer of England is said to have been once happy," we find constantly, after certain intervals, a period of real famine; by which, a melancholy havock was made among the human race. The price of provisions fluctuated dreadfully, demonstrating a deficiency very different from the worst failures of the present moment. Never since I have known England, have I known more than a comparative scarcity. The price of wheat, taking a number of years together, has had no very considerable fluctuation, nor has it risen exceedingly until within this twelvemonth. Even now, I do not know of one man, woman, or child, that has perished from famine; fewer, if any, I believe, than in years of plenty, when such a thing may happen by accident. This is owing to a care and superintendance of the poor, far greater than any I remember.

The consideration of this ought to bind us all, rich and poor together, against those wicked writers of the newspapers, who would inflame the poor against their friends, guardians, patrons, and protectors. Not only very few (I have observed, that I know of none, though I live in a place as poor as most) have actually died of want, but we have seen no traces of those dreadful exterminating epidemics, which, in consequence of scanty and unwholesome food, in former times, not unfrequently, wasted whole nations. Let us be saved from too much wisdom of our own, and we shall do tolerably well.

It is one of the finest problems in legislation, and what has often engaged my thoughts whilst I followed that profession, "What the State ought to take upon itself to direct by the public wisdom, and what it ought to leave, with as little interference as possible, to individual discretion." Nothing, certainly, can be laid down on the subject that will not admit of exceptions, many permanent, some occasional. But the clearest line of distinction which I could draw, whilst I had my chalk to draw any line, was this: That the State ought to confine itself to what regards the State, or the creatures of the State, namely, the exterior establishment of its religion; its magistracy; its revenue; its military force by sea and land; the corporations that owe their existence to its fiat; in a word, to every thing that is *truly and properly* public, to the public peace, to the public safety, to the public order, to the public prosperity. In its preventive police it ought to be sparing of its efforts, and to employ means, rather few, unfrequent, and strong, than many, and frequent, and, of course, as they multiply their puny politic race, and dwindle, small and feeble. Statesmen who know themselves will, with the dignity which belongs to wisdom, proceed only in this the superior orb and first mover of their duty, steadily, vigilantly, severely, courageously: whatever remains will, in a manner, provide for itself. But as they descend from the state to a province, from a province to a parish, and from a parish to a private house, they go on accelerated in their fall. They *cannot* do the lower duty; and, in proportion as they try it, they will certainly fail in the higher. They ought to know the different departments of things; what belongs to laws, and what manners alone can regulate. To these, great politicians may give a leaning, but they cannot give a law.

Our Legislature has fallen into this fault as well as other governments; all have fallen into it more or less. The once mighty State, which was nearest to us locally, nearest to us in every way, and whose ruins threaten to fall upon our heads, is a strong instance of this error.[12] I can never quote France without a foreboding sigh—ΕΣΣΕΤΑΙʻΗΜΑΡ![13] Scipio said it to his recording Greek friend amidst the flames of the great rival of his country.[14] That state has fallen by the hands of the parricides of their country, called the Revolutionists, and Constitutionalists, of France, a species of traitors, of whose fury and atrocious wickedness nothing in the annals of the phrenzy and depravation of mankind had before furnished an example, and of whom I can never think or speak without a mixed sensation of disgust, of horrour, and of detestation, not easy to be expressed. These nefarious monsters destroyed their country for what was good in it: for much good there was in the constitution of that noble monarchy, which, in all kinds, formed and nourished great men, and great patterns of virtue to the world. But though its enemies were not enemies to its faults, its faults furnished them with means for its destruction. My dear departed friend,[15] whose loss is even greater to the public than to me, had often remarked, that the leading vice of the French monarchy (which he had well studied) was in good intention ill-directed, and a restless desire of governing too much. The hand of authority was seen in every thing, and in every place. All, therefore, that happened amiss in the course even of domestic affairs, was attributed to the Government; and, as it always happens in this kind of officious universal interference, what began in odious power, ended always, I may say without an exception, in contemptible imbecillity. For this reason, as far as I can approve of any novelty, I thought well of the Provincial Administrations. Those, if the superior power had been severe, and vigilant, and vigorous, might have been of much use politically in removing

---

12. That of the fixing of prices by government.

13. The first words of a passage in Homer (*Iliad* 6.448–49), in which Hector tells his wife that he knows that Troy is doomed: "The day will come when sacred Troy will perish, / And Priam and his people shall be slain."

14. The Roman general Scipio, who had finally and fully conquered Carthage, repeated Hector's words, "The day will come," when his Greek friend, the historian Polybius, asked him why he wept when he saw Carthage in flames. He feared for Rome, too, says Polybius, "when he reflected on the fate of all things human." *Histories* 38.22.1–3.

15. His son Richard, who had died the year before, on August 2, 1794.

government from many invidious details. But as every thing is good or bad, as it is related or combined, government being relaxed above as it was relaxed below, and the brains of the people growing more and more addle with every sort of visionary speculation, the shiftings of the scene in the provincial theatres became only preparatives to a revolution in the kingdom, and the popular actings there only the rehearsals of the terrible drama of the republic.

. Tyranny and cruelty may make men justly wish the downfall of abused powers, but I believe that no government ever yet perished from any other direct cause than its own weakness. My opinion is against an over-doing of any sort of administration, and more especially against this most momentous of all meddling on the part of authority; the meddling with the subsistence of the people.

FINIS

References

Burke, Edmund. 1800. *Thoughts and Details on Scarcity*. London: Rivington.

Burke, Edmund. 1999. *Selected Works of Edmund Burke: Miscellaneous Writings*, ed. Francis Canavan. Indianapolis: Liberty Fund.

Miller, David. 1981. *Philosophy and Ideology in Hume's Political Thought*. Oxford: Clarendon.

Smith, Adam. 1976 [1776] (WN). *An Inquiry Into the Nature and Causes of the Wealth of Nations*, eds. R. H. Campbell and A. S. Skinner, 2 vols. Oxford: Oxford University Press.

Tocqueville, Alexis de. 1955 [1856]. *The Old Régime and the French Revolution*, trans. S. Gilbert. New York: Doubleday Anchor.

Edmund Burke's "Scattered Hints Concerning Philosophy and Learning"

Foreword

Daniel B. Klein

In 1957, Cambridge University Press published a slim volume titled *A Note-Book of Edmund Burke: Poems, Characters, Essays and Other Sketches in the Hands of Edmund and William Burke Now Printed for the First Time in Their Entirety and Edited by H. V. F. Somerset*. Here we reproduce an abridgement of one of the items by Edmund Burke, the full title of which is "Several Scattered Hints Concerning Philosophy and Learning Collected Here from My Papers," pp. 81–98.

We have omitted three segments thought not worthwhile, a total of about 1290 words. The abridged version here is about 4460 words. Hence, about 22 percent of the original (about 5750 words) has been omitted. Bracketed comments indicated where the omissions occur. And a few other insertions are in brackets.

The essay itself probably derives from notations that Burke made in the 1750s. The *Note-Book* includes a Foreword by Sir Ernest Barker. He writes, "we may therefore use the general substance of the Note-Book as evidence of Burke's thought and the development of his ideas during his early youth, from the age of 21 (he was 21 when he came to England) to the age of 27, when he published his first work" (1957, x). Barker calls the essay we abridge slightly here "the longest and finest of the essays" in the book (ibid., xi).

We inquired with Cambridge University Press, through PLS Clear, about reproducing what follows here, and received no response, which tends to confirm that Burke's words are not under copyright. We thank Jacob Hall for typing up the piece as printed in 1957.

Within the *Note-Book*, Somerset (1957, 81) writes: "This piece, clearly by Edmund Burke, and inscribed as being so, is one of the most typical of his style and thought in the note-book." In the piece, Burke warns against "confined" learning. He writes: "The End of learning is not knowledge but virtue; as the End of all speculation should be practice of one sort or another."

Several Scattered Hints Concerning Philosophy and Learning Collected Here from My Papers

Edmund Burke

[About 100 words omitted here.]

The appearance from real learning is like a complexion had from sound health; it looks lively and natural, and is only the sign of something better.

It signifies much less what we read than how we read, and with a view to what end. To study only for its own sake is a fruitless labour; to learn only to be learned is moving in a strange Circle. The End of learning is not knowledge but virtue; as the End of all speculation should be practice of one sort or another. It is owing to inattention to this that we so often see men of great Erudition immersed as deeply as any in the passions, prejudices, and vain opinions of the vulgar; nay we often see them more servile, more proud, more opinionative, fonder of money, more governed by vanity, more afraid of Death, and captivated more by little appearances and trifling distinctions. In these two last particulars I have often observed it, and always with wonder.

It is worth observing that when anything not a principal itself, and culti-vated only as an accessory to something else, is diverted from its proper end, it not only does not promote that end, but it goes a great way to destroy it. The Gymnastic exercises among the Greeks were undoubtedly designed to form their people to war; and they seem well calculated for that purpose. But when they forgot that purpose, when they made that art acquiesce in itself, when they sought a reputation from the exercise alone, it lost its use; and the professed Wrestlers always made the worst Soldiers. Those who make a trade of Tumbling are never very remarkable for their agility in any other way; and in the little Course of my own experience, I have always observed of your prodigious and ostentatious memories that they served for little else than prodigy and ostentation. It has happened in a manner not unlike this to learning. Knowledge is the Culture [cultivation] of the mind; and he who rested there, would be just as wise as he who should plough his field without any intention of sowing or reaping.

[About 290 words omitted here.]

As learning in some measure answers to the experience of Old age, it seems to produce something of its querulous disposition too. I do not know any discourse worse received than complaints of the times; and I think with some reason; as they usually begin with our own misfortunes and end with them. But such complaints least of all become men of Learning, who by some fatality are always stunning us with the reproaches of the age they live in, and the little encouragement they receive. And it will ever be so whilst men propose to themselves any other views in Learning than the regulation of their minds and their own inward content and repose. If we consider the matter rightly, what reward should I expect for doing myself the greatest service imaginable? If I complain of want of encouragement in this way, it is a sure sign I deserve none. If my Studies are not of such a nature as to enable me to make a figure in the world, or to acquire some better possession instead of it, what have I been doing? And in what a light do I present myself?

We ought rather to be learned *about* Sciences than *in* them (I don't speak here of the particular profession of any). That is, we ought, if possible, rather to master those principles that govern almost all of them than to sift into those particulars that direct and distinguish each of them separately. By these means we can extend our views much more considerably; we keep our minds open, and prevent that littleness and narrowness that almost inevitably attends a confined commerce with any Art or Science however noble in itself. I remember a preface to some book of Heraldry wherein the Author, after giving due commendation to his own Studies, passes a severe Censure on those who are weak enough to mis-spend their time in such trivial pursuits as those of philosophy and poetry, neglecting an art of so much delight in the Study, and advantage in the application, as Heraldry.

Confined reading and company are the Greatest Sources of pride that I know; and I am sure any knowledge that carries this taint along with it does not make amends for the mischief it brings. If a man be a poor narrow minded Creature what does it avail whether he is a Logician or a Shoemaker, a Geometrician or a Taylor? If he has the narrow views of a Mechanic, he is as far from being a philosopher as the mechanic, and farther too, if the other chances to have from nature a more generous way of thinking.

There is inseparably annexed to any confined Studies a number of false admirations that a more general knowledge would go a great way to Cure. When a man is conversant in all the variety of Arts and Sciences, in the Stories, opinions, Customs, manners, atchievements of all ages and all nations, it must by a sure consequence wear away those little prejudices of little parties that Cause such heats and animosities amongst mankind; it must lessen something of that extravagant admiration of power and riches that intoxicates us to our ruin, and overturns the peace and innocence of our lives. It might perhaps humble us, and abate something of our confidence in our opinions, if, after taking a view of the rise and fall of kingdoms, we observed those of science; to see it rise from chance, grow by industry, strengthen by contention, refine by subtilty and ease, fall then into nicety, Error, Guess,—and, dissolving at last, make way for new Systems, which rise by the same means, and fall by the same fortune. Whatever tends to humble us, tends to make us wiser. Whatever makes us wiser, makes us better, and easier, and happier.

I would make an ingenuous and liberal turn of mind the End of all learning and wherever I don't see it I should doubt the reality of the knowledge. For the End of all knowledge ought to be the bettering us in some manner; and whoever has a sour, splenetick, unsocial, malevolent Temper; who is haughty in his own acquirements and contemptuous of others; ostentatious of his knowledge, positive in his Tenets, and abusive to those who differ from him; he may be a Scholar,—and indeed most of those called Scholars are something in this Character,—but sure he is not a man of learning, nor a philosopher. The more he vaunts his reading, the more loudly he proclaims his ignorance. If a deep and general knowledge does not make a man diffident and humble, no human means, I believe, can do it.

To attempt a general knowledge ought not to be thought too bold an undertaking; to have many things in hand will rather advance us in Each, whilst they relieve one another; and prevent that satiety which arises from a confined application, and which can have no relief but in Idleness or some other Study, And which is to be preferred, everyone may judge.

There is certainly, besides, some connexion in all the Sciences which makes them mutually advance one another; though I allow not so much as some contend for. But one of the Strongest reasons I have for admitting great variety into our Studies, and a passing in a pretty Quick Succession from one to another, is that it helps to form that *versatile ingenium* which is of very great use in Life,—Not to be so possessed with any subject, but that we should be able at pleasure to quit it, to turn to another, so to a third, to resume the first again, and to follow the occasion with a suppleness that may suit the infinite intricacy that occurs in many sorts of Business and employments. For we ought if possible to keep all our talents subservient to the uses of Life, and not to make ourselves the Slaves of any of them. Those who lay out their whole time on any one Science, are apt to be carried away by it; and are no longer their own masters so far as to decide when and where, and in what measure they shall indulge their Speculations; and therefore are not so generally fit for the world.

There is great reason to believe that being engaged in business is rather of Service to Speculative knowledge than otherwise; because perhaps the mind can do more in sudden starts than in an even progression. Experience may show that an entire application to study alone is apt to carry men into unprofitable Subtilities and whimsical notions. Man is made for Speculation and action; and when he pursues his nature he succeeds best in both.

I am not moved with what it is common for people to advance about superficial learning. A man who does not seek a reputation from his knowledge, will be indifferent whether it be thought deep or shallow provided it be of any real use to him. One may know all the maxims of a Science, be perfectly conversant in their Grounds, ready in the reasonings about them, and know all that has been thought, written, or experimented on that Subject, and yet have but a superficial knowledge in that Science. Another who knows but few of its principles, if yet he can extend them, can multiply their resources, can strike out something new, can remedy some defect, he has a deeper knowledge in the Science than the other, if this other should not be able to advance its landmarks,—as thousands well conversant in Arts cannot do, and who therefore have a more superficial knowledge, because a less useful one. And such is the weakness of the human mind, that it is found, a great acquaintance and readiness in what is already known in any branch of Learning is rather of prejudice than use in extending it.

It is common with men of a small understanding to think nothing of any use, that is not particularly and avowedly designed for use, and apparently so. But in fact there are things that aim obliquely at their end that often hit it more surely. I speak this of such who depreciate the ornamental parts of Learning as Eloquence, Poetry, and such like—and consider them merely as matter of ornament. I look on them in quite a different light, because I always consider the Chief use of Learning is to implant an elegant disposition into the mind and manners and to root out of them everything sordid, base or illiberal. I conceive that the polite arts are rather better calculated for this purpose than any others; and this for the very reason that some condemn them; because they apply to the passions, in which, more than in any faults of reasoning, the Sources of all our Errors lie.

Those who speak in favour of these studies, on the other hand, do not seem to me truly to discern wherein their advantage consists. Say they, moral precepts when graced with the advantages of Eloquence, invite the inattentive, and by being mixed with something pleasureable, make a deeper impression. It is true they do so; but in fact the great powers of Eloquence and poetry, and the great Benefits that result from them, are not in giving precepts but creating habits. For the preceptive part of poetry makes but a small part of it in all poems; and none at all in many; and yet they all have their use. For the mind when it is entertained with high fancies, elegant and polite sentiments, beautiful language, and harmonious sounds, is modelled insensibly into a disposition to elegance and humanity. For it is the bias the mind takes that gives direction to our lives; and not any rules or maxims of morals and behavior. It imitates what is called the natural Temper best; and this is the best guide and guard we can have in every Virtue. For though rules, fear, interest, or other motives may induce us to virtue, it is the virtue of a bad soil, harsh and disagreeable.

Most Books, prove, affirm, demonstrate; they come with settled notions to us, and make us settle ours too early. We are too apt to take our parties in everything when our Judgement is very unripe and make the reasoning of our mature years subservient to the rashness of our Youth. I am almost tempted to think we ought to learn not so much to cure our Doubts, of which we have too few, as to learn how to doubt.

We daily hear the words, 'tis impossible, 'tis absurd, 'tis unreasonable, 'tis contradiction, used on many occasions with equal hardiness and ignorance; and that on every side of Questions extremely dark and puzzling, and which seem as it were calculated to suspend and confound the human understanding. If a man seriously set about regarding his opinions of things in several periods of his life, he would see what he thought in one part of it impossible was easy; what he thought absurd, he now finds highly reasonable; how his experience reverses his notions; makes him adopt what he rejected and reject what he was fondest of. These considerations one would think might tend to humble the understanding and make it Cautious and diffident.—Such a review is sometimes made; but with a very different Effect; we view the littleness of our former notions with an exultation on our present Growth; we Triumph in the comparison; and never recollect that we are to tread the same Circle again; affording matter of contempt in our present Triumph to our later, God knows whether wiser, Schemes of things. We should take a quite contrary Course—I once was sure; I now find I was mistaken; I am going to be very positive again; can I say a few years more may not show me that I was positive in an Error?

To have the mind a long time lost in Doubts and uncertainties may have the same Effect on our understandings that fermentation has on liquors. It disturbs them for a while, but it makes them both the Sounder and clearer ever after.

We read too much; and our studies being remote from the occasions of Life cannot so easily be mixt with them afterwards. It were to be wished that matters of moment made a larger part in the conversations even of the greatest men. It is but reasonable that our general conduct should be a good deal modelled by the general Sense of the publick; and that unfortunately leads to amusements, trivial or worse; but I would willingly give something to reason as well as Custom; I would be its humble Servant but not its Slave. What we learn in Conversation is in some way of a better kind than that we draw from Books; and it certainly goes further towards influencing our Conduct. Discourse is nearer to action and mixes more with it than mere reading, and surely Philosophy of every sort is naturally pleasing to the mind; it is not excluded from conversation because it is sour and pedantick, but it is apt to be sour and pedantick, when it is excluded from conversation.

The more a man's mind is elevated above the vulgar the nearer he comes to them in the simplicity of his appearance, speech, and even not a few of his Notions. He knows his reason very well and therefore he is suspicious of it. He trusts his passions more on some occasions; he reins them, but does not fetter them. A man who considers his nature rightly will be diffident of any reasonings that carry him out of the ordinary roads of Life; Custom is to be regarded with great deference especially if it be an universal Custom; even popular notions are not always to be laughed at. There is some general principle operating to produce Customs, that is a more sure guide than our Theories. They are followed indeed often on odd motives, but that does not make them less reasonable or useful. A man is never in greater danger of being wholly wrong than when he advances far in the road of refinement; nor have I ever that diffidence and suspicion of my reasonings as when they seem to be most curious, exact, and conclusive. Great subtelties and refinements of reasoning are like spirits which disorder the brain and are much less useful than ordinary liquors of a grosser nature; I never would have our reasoning too much dephlegmatic, much less would I have its pernicious activity exerted on the forms and ceremonies that are used in some of the material Businesses and more remarkable changes of Life. I find them in all nations, and at all times; and therefore I judge them suitable to our nature, and do not like to hear them called fopperies. Our fathers, ruder indeed than we, and, if not instructed, at least not misled, practised them; we should follow them. But they ought not to affect us beyond their just value. When Diogenes was dying, his friends desired to know how he would have his Body disposed of. 'Throw it into the fields,' says he. They objected that it might be liable to be devoured by wild Beasts. 'Then set my Staff by me to drive them off.' One answered, 'You will be then insensible and unable to do it.' 'So shall I be' (sayd he) 'of their injuries.'

I like the vivacity of the Turn in this Story. The philosophy is shewy but has no substance; for to what would he persuade us by this odd example? Why, that our Bodies being after Death neither capable of pain nor pleasure, we should not trouble our heads about them. But let this pass into a general principle, and thence into a general practice, and the ill consequence is obvious. The wisdom of nature, or rather providence, is very worthy of admiration in this, as in a thousand other things, by working its ends by means that seem directed to other purposes. A man is anxious and sollicitous about the fate of his body which he knows can have no feeling. He never considers what a nuisance it would be to Society if it was exposed. He considers such an event as personally terrible; and he does piously for others what he would wish done for himself.

It is not easily conceived what use funeral ceremonies (for my story led me to think) are to mankind. Triffling as they may seem, they nourish humanity, they soften in some measure the rigour of Death, and they inspire humble, sober and becoming thoughts. They throw a decent Veil over the weak and dishonourable circumstances of our Nature. What shall we say to that philosophy, that would strip it naked? Of such sort is the wisdom of those who talk of the Love, the sentiment, and the thousand little dalliances that pass between the Sexes, in the gross way of mere procreation. They value themselves as having made a mighty discovery; and turn all pretences to delicacy into ridicule. I have read some authors who talk of the Generation of mankind as getting rid of an excrement; who lament bitterly their being subject to such a weakness. They think they are extremely witty in saying it is a dishonourable action and we are obliged to hide it in the obscurity of night. It is hid it's true, not because it is dishonourable but because it is mysterious. There is no part of our condition, but we ought to submit to with Cheerfulness. Why should I desire to be more than man? I have too much reverence for our nature to wish myself divested even of the weak parts of it. I would not wish, as I have heard some do, that I could live without eating or sleeping. I rather thank providence that has so happily united the subsistence of my body with its satisfaction. When we go into another State we shall have means fitted to it, with equal wisdom no doubt. At the present we ought to make the best of our Condition; and improve our very necessities, our wants, and imperfections, into Elegancies;—if possible, into virtues.

The common people are puzzled about extraordinary Phenomena, and wonder at nothing else. The learned wonder not at uncommon things; 'tis about the most ordinary things they are puzzled and perplexed. They can account for earthquakes and eclipses, but doubt of their seeing feeling hearing etc. In reasoning about abstruse matters and the assent we give to Propositions concerning them, we don't sufficiently distinguish between a Contrariety and a Contradiction. No man in his Senses can agree to a Contradiction; but an apparent, nay a real, Contrariety in things, may not only be proposed and believed, but proved beyond any reasonable doubt. Most of our Enquiries, when carried beyond the very Superficies of things, lead us into the greatest Difficulties and we find qualities repugnant to each other whenever we attempt to dive into the Manner of Existence.

Nec tamen istas questiones Physicorum contemnandas puto. Est enim Animarum Ingeniorumque naturale quoddam quasi pabulum, consideratio contemplatioque Naturae.[1]

Perhaps the bottom of most things is unintelligible; and our surest reasoning, when we come to a certain point, is involved not only in obscurity but contradiction.

[About 900 words omitted here.]

Sapere aude—it requires some boldness to make use of one's reason.
We ought to be earnest not anxious in our Business.

That seems to me the most uneasy state of Life when Men are placed where the high and the low meet—where they [are] distracted with the Ambition and vast Desires of the greatest and have scarce more than the Enjoyment of the lowest State.

The Information[s] we receive from Books about Business and Men are, I believe, to be but cautiously trusted; because even if they should be right, yet being written at a distance of time, tho' Nature be justly described, yet a Variation in Customes, in the Characters and Manners of the Age, of which every Age has its own, makes a great variation in the Conduct to be pursued in the Management of Affairs.

A Man is not invariably and obstinately to [be] swayed by his own Opinion, but in affairs it is still worse to have no Dependence on your own Opinion. The first may [make in MS.] make you sometimes act wrong, the second will prevent your ever acting steadily. And steadiness is the Soul of all action. But there are Men so weak that they suffer themselves to be persuaded out of

---

1. The quotation is from Cicero's *Academica*, though the original reads a bit differently: *Nec tamen istas quaestiones physicorum exterminandas puto. Est enim animorum ingeniorumque naturale quoddam quasi pabulum consideratio contemplatioque naturae.* Harris Rackham's translation is: "And all the same I do not think that these physical investigations of yours should be put out of bounds. For the study and observation of nature affords a sort of natural pasturage for the spirit and intellect."

their own resolution by those whom they thought to have persuaded. And they are always unsuccessful; because, in imagining themselves always ready to be informed of their Errors, they can by no possibility see their great Error, which is their being easily persuaded that their own Opinions are always Erroneous.

In writing, the wisdom of Nature ought to be strictly imitated; which has made all things necessary to our preservation in the highest Degree pleasing to our Appetites. Dry precepts and reasoning do little. It is from the imagination and will that our Errors rise, and in them, as in their first beginnings, they ought to be attacked. Men are full as inclined to Vice as to Virtue. Now suppose a piece was written describing the Nature and extent of any Vice, suppose that it shewed its Limits, described its several Species, gave Directions about the encrease and furtherance of it;—suppose this done in such a manner as to avoid carefully the Affecting any of our passions, and then see how little the reader shall be incited to profit from the Lecture. I believe very little. But then, try what a Lascivious Song will do. This is directed to the imagination and in a Moment the Desires are raised. And so undoubtedly and much more will it hold in Virtue. Therefore they who would introduce new Religions must aim at the Imagination not the Understanding. Thus Mahomet's paradise is famed for the Indulgence of all the soft Eastern passions; While in our colder Climates the Methodist, by painting hell torments in all its terrors,—like the Rattle-Snake does the Squirrel—terrifies the poor wretch into his Snare. But neither Mahomet nor the Methodist have anything to do with the Understanding. To instance in the Methodist;—all their terms with a wicked wisdom, are chosen by them too unintelligible and inexplicable, for fear the Understanding should have any play. Thus '*the new light*', '*the inward feeling*', '*born again*'. When a reason of their faith is demanded, this cant is the answer you receive. A plain man who can make neither head nor tail of this, desires it to be explained. They are embarrassed. By the pride natural to the Mind of Man they chuse rather to think you reprobate, than themselves absurd. And thus, wraped up in terms which themselves do not understand, but by which their Imagination is engaged, they continue their folly.

The Action of a play ought to be like a Rack to make Actors discover the bottom of their Souls, the most hidden part of their Characters. Else 'tis good for little.

It is not enough that the discourses of the Actors should be such as are not unnatural. They ought to be natural for the time, the occasion, the person who speaks, the person spoken to. But above all they ought to be natural to the End i.e. such as is proper to carry on the principle Action; and natural in such an Action.

As there are different manners of expressing knowledge, why not a different manner of gaining it too? Quacks prescribe but one remedy for all Constitutions. We see the Absurdity, yet expect that the school method should suit all Geniuses. Their Masters are too much above them, their play-fellows too much on a level. From the first they will not learn much, from the latter they can learn nothing. They are expected to be more at their Books than they chuse; and less is attempted in Conversation with them than they are capable of.

As those who draw charts mark the Sands and Rocks as well as the safe harbours, why should not Philosophers tell us the ill success, as well as the good, of their Experiments?

It is much more common with Men to contend in violent disputes about the Excellence of their Studies, their profession and their Countrys, than to exert themselves to do anything that may be for the Credit or advantage of them.

An Economic Dream[1]

Erik Gustaf Geijer
edited by Björn Hasselgren
translated by Peter C. Hogg

Once a rare occurrence, I have for some time now often dreamt. These dreams are not usually disjointed and fantastical. On the contrary, they are distinguished by a logical context, which unfolds, seemingly autonomously, behind the eyes of the dreamer. It is as if the machinery of the mind had of its own volition crafted the subject.

Recently, this was economic and left the, perhaps rare, example of an economic dream; therefore I wish to tell of it, briefly. It is a dream of national economy, which may be added to the others.

The question concerned the influence of the natural features of a country on its finances and the answering of it undertaken with respect to the fatherland.

In that connection it emerged that the expanse of Sweden, with all its natural dissimilarities, could not avoid exerting a profound influence on the economies of especial places in the fatherland. The different lives of the plainsman and the mountain-dweller were displayed. The miner, the farmer, the manufacturer, the merchant, the hunter, the fisherman stepped forward, all under the various conditions that the place and the distinct needs arising therefrom prescribed for their activities. They gathered into groups accordingly. The various groups were scattered, separated by great distances, in that way isolated within themselves. It is no wonder that each regarded itself as *a whole unto itself!* Different needs and circumstances had shaped each one. The

---

1. "En ekonomisk dröm" ("An Economic Dream") was published in *Dagligt Allehanda* on February 26, 1847. Its author Erik Gustaf Geijer (pronounced "yay-yer"), then 64 years old, died less than two months later; "En ekonomisk dröm" was the last of his publications during his lifetime. The piece is translated into English for the first time by Peter C. Hogg, and appears in *Freedom in Sweden: Selected Works of Erik Gustaf Geijer*, edited by Björn Hasselgren (Stockholm: Timbro, 2017): 441–445. The text is used by permission of Björn Hasselgren.

force of habit had cemented it and erected a wall, as it were, around each domain, beyond whose horizon the gazes of the inhabitants need not extend. I said to myself: behold the origins of *corporative and guild privileges!* — These are the children first of *need*, second of *habit* and finally of *prejudice*. As *such*, they exist long in the imagination, because their true validity has dissipated long before this. The various domains, by reason of an omniprevalent enterprise, are now drawn together. Their relationships to each other are utterly changed. He whose gaze encompasses several such areas will see this at once. He who lives by charity under the old conditions, however, does not see the change, or considers it a disorder and thus cries out incessantly for order, the *old* order, that is; even as the *new* is already, unnoticed by him, in full swing.

It is clear that he whose enterprise extends to *several* objects of human industry will more easily arrive at this insight, than he who is confined to one. For the insight is a *comparative* insight and arises through the comparison. So, it manifests itself soonest to the merchant, the manufacturer; latest, most reluctantly to the artisan, in whose life change usually comes before he notices it, much less has any inkling of its causes. Therein, he is like an animal startled out of its hibernation, which charges its enemy to its own destruction. Thereof the recently so common uprisings of workers against their masters. It is a blind impulse, made yet blinder and angrier of the unaccustomed light. And this usually turns out to the detriment of those who surrender themselves in that direction and rush headlong into new conditions, alien to them, which will soon take them further than they could have imagined. What has been the result of all these assemblies? *Improved working methods*, in which *science* replaces the shortage of *reduced manual power* many times over; further, as a consequence thereof, *reduced wages*, and yet—oddly enough—*increased production and consumption* to the extent that the *freer distribution* puts food in the hands of many more than under the old, barbaric order. It is the leap into the midst of the new order of things, to which each and every one must resign himself. — Often, certainly, a hazardous endeavour. The transition reaps many victims. All who live in such a transition period must then be prepared—happily if he does not have eyes only for his losses, but also for the manifold and vital sources of new enterprise that run to meet him. Because that which is happening in the world now is: the *liberation of labour*—a true incarnation of the so-often odious *principle of personality*, which is increasingly encroaching upon reality. Judgments vary according to point of view! This *liberty* is tantamount with *disorder*, a thousand voices shout. On the contrary, she is a new, self-evolving order; so do others comfort themselves, the more industrious, the wiser. That liberty, even if she brings disorder for a passing while, follows her own rules and develops from within, implanted in her by the Creator, her own *law*: that is the full faith of *liberalism* and it leads to salvation. What is a *conservatism* that rejects this gift of God? A holding on to the corruptible in its corruption, no less fruitless than perfectly and immeasurably absurd. This way of thinking may very well console itself with its own, higher wisdom, incomprehensible to most. This wisdom shuns the rising light. To the degree this lowers itself from the heights to the vales, the faith of the many in the same is lost, as the sunbeam vanishes in the fog; and thus is the supremely unnatural alliance between the so-called *conservative* and *popular* interests severed, whose loathsome delusion is still, on both sides, the so often invoked support for the most ignorant superstition.

What is the *new order of things?* With each day, its *law* evolves more clearly; its *substance* is already so apparent that one can thereof judge its nature and the spirit of progress. This substance is the *day-by-day, constantly evolving, all-encompassing fellowship and interaction of human powers and needs*. This new, but actually ancient law of labour is that of *intelligence*, which works in expanding circles. From there comes the dependency, from there the interaction in all occupations, equally familiar and acknowledged, and which, to the extent of this increasingly ardent acknowledgement, communicates ever more directly with its own essence and from this new, greater powers emerge, day-by-day and without surcease. Therefore, every seeming defeat is a true victory for it. It needs hardly touch the earth to feel at home and rise again with renewed vigour.

One needs only to regard this immortal principle in detail in its effects to find oneself in the field of an infinite project that reaches in all directions and returns from all directions to its centre. — How could any occupation, any area of human enterprise, now be able to isolate itself? In so doing, it cuts itself off from its very breath of life, withers and inevitably dies. It thrives, flourishes, feels happy and promotes happiness utterly to the same extent that it both communicates and receives based on an enlivening influence.

And so, the separated groups of industries and trades finally flowed together before my eye. The artisan, not merely with his bodily strength, but with his intelligence, was the foundation of it all, for an enterprise that the factory owner used and distributed, that the merchant spread across the earth. I saw a new day ascend above it. It was the rising sun; and the Dancing Hours moving around the sun, in measured heavenly-harmonious orbits, were the beautiful performance at which I wakened from my dream.

The Social Theories of Classical Political Economy and Modern Economic Policy

Foreword

Erwin Dekker and Stefan Kolev

In 1890, the centenary of Adam Smith's death was used by Carl Menger as a touchstone for a reflection on the economic thought of Menger's time and the liberal tradition of Smith and classical political economy. This reflection was published in two parts, on the 6th and the 8th of January, 1891, in the most respected newspaper of the Habsburg Empire, the *Neue Freie Presse*. Never before translated into English, it is presented here under the title "The Social Theories of Classical Political Economy and Modern Economic Policy."[1]

To give some context to Menger's essay, let us draw on Friedrich Hayek's contextualization of Menger's career. Hayek writes that in the decades after 1848, classical political economy experienced mixed fortunes across Europe: "critical attacks and attempts at reconstruction multiplied in most countries." He continues:

> Nowhere, however, had the decline of the classical school of economists been more rapid and complete than in Germany. Under the onslaught of the Historical School not only were the classical doctrines completely abandoned— they had never taken very firm root in that part of the world—but any attempt

---

1. The German title differs between the first and second parts of the newspaper article. The first title speaks of the social theories of the classical political economist (!) (*des classischen National-Ökonomen*), a reference to Smith, and the second title of classical political economy (*classischen National-Ökonomie*). The original articles are available online from the Österreichische Nationalbibliothek and are reprinted in the *Collected Works of Carl Menger*, vol. 3.

at theoretical analysis came to be regarded with deep distrust. This was partly due to methodological considerations. But even more it was due to the intense dislike of the practical conclusions of the classical English School—which stood in the way of the reforming zeal of the new group, which prided itself on the name of the 'ethical school.' (Hayek 1992/1934, 63–64)

"The 'ethical school'" is a reference to the school of *Social-Politik*, the movement of economists across German-speaking Europe for social reform, later called the 'Younger' Historical School.

Menger, who had started out as an economic correspondent, was not only an economic theorist of great significance, he was also a prominent Viennese liberal. In 1883 he published his second book, on methodology, which was critical of the 'Younger' Historical School. Its leader Gustav Schmoller caustically replied, Menger caustically rejoined, and Schmoller published a dismissive letter about Menger's rejoinder. The exchange constitutes the textual core of what is known as the *Methodenstreit*. Hayek tells of "the passion which this controversy aroused" and "what the break with the ruling school in Germany meant to Menger and his followers":

Schmoller, indeed, went so far as to declare publicly that members of the 'abstract' school were unfit to fill a teaching position in a German university, and his influence was quite sufficient to make this equivalent to a complete exclusion of all adherents to Menger's doctrines from academic positions in Germany. (Hayek 1992/1934, 81)

Menger did not perceive himself as a revolutionary in economic theory. The article presented here shows that Menger was spiritually close to Adam Smith and classical political economy. Likewise, Menger's tutorial instruction from 1876 to the Crown Prince Rudolf of Austria closely followed *The Wealth of Nations* (particularly Book I). As Erich Streissler writes, "Carl Menger was much more of a classical economist than is commonly recognized" (1994, 24).

The article presented here is one of the best sources we have for understanding Menger's position on questions of economic policy (Böhm 1985; Streissler 1990). It is part of a larger effort, from Menger and his students, to defend classical political economy and to draw a connection between their theoretical contributions and that of the classical school. Two other important contributions to that effort are, first, Eugen Böhm-Bawerk's lengthy review of Lujo Brentano's Viennese inaugural lecture on the classical school (Böhm-

Bawerk 1924/1889), and, second, a dissertation written under Menger's supervision by Richard Schüller (1895) with the clearly programmatic title *Die klassische Nationalökonomie und ihre Gegner* (*Classical Political Economy and Its Enemies*).

Menger's article, as well as Böhm-Bawerk's review and Schüller's dissertation, were written on the defensive. Reacting to the low standing accorded to the classical school, Menger, Böhm-Bawerk, and Schüller were primarily occupied with correcting and refuting the arguments of their opponents. The debate over the standing of classical political economy is closely connected to the *Methodenstreit*, with a similar separation between camps. But the debate about the standing of political economy is more directly tied to economic policy and the advent of the *Verein für Socialpolitik* (VfS) and what Menger throughout the piece calls the school of *Social-Politik*. In Menger's article we have to wait until the final pages to get a good sense of what he himself favors.

The VfS, the German equivalent of the American Economic Association, was founded in 1872 by a group of economists, and was soon dominated by Gustav Schmoller, who was two years Menger's senior. Schmoller's agenda for the decades to come aimed at generating policy solutions to the 'social question.' His reformist goals were reflected in the name of the association, with its emphasis on social and economic policy. The substance of the agenda might be described as an attempt to establish a 'third way' between the *Manchestertum* and state or Marxist socialisms (Grimmer-Solem 2003, 171–186). *Manchestertum*, a pejorative term coined by the German socialist activist Ferdinand Lassalle in the 1860s to attack the allegedly anti-social attitudes of British liberals like Richard Cobden, was soon widely used by socialists and conservatives alike to attack liberalism as an extremist ideology that was imported from Britain and was bereft of any sympathy for the poor and the working class (Doering 2004, 18–21). The VfS was explicitly founded as a counterweight to the *Volkswirtschaftlicher Kongreß* (Economic Congress), a convention of Manchesterist liberal public figures like Hermann Schulze-Delitzsch and John Prince-Smith (Henderson 1950, 297–301; Hentschel 1975; Oschina 2010, 14–16). In the article Menger repeatedly distances himself from these individuals and the ideas associated with *Manchestertum*.

The VfS, eventually successful in crowding out the Economic Congress, was one of Schmoller's weapons—Schmoller being a gifted academic entrepreneur—to consolidate large parts of German economists around his agenda and, after forming alliances with powerful bureaucrats in the university administration of the new Reich, to dominate the nomination of appointees to chairs of political economy in Germany as well as in Austria-Hungary (Blumenthal 2007, 66–75). That included the appointment of Brentano, his fellow *Social-Politiker*, to Vienna in 1888 (Backhaus 1993, 12–13), which ignited heavy opposition from the burgeoning Austrian School.[2] The VfS and its intellectual climate had effects reaching well beyond Central Europe: The many American students at German-speaking universities, described by Richard T. Ely as "the group of young rebels who returned from Germany about 1880," had a direct and significant impact on the formative decades of the American Economic Association, founded in 1885 (Ely 1936, 143; see also Seager 1893). Both the VfS and the AEA were, during these decades, part of what in America has come to be called progressivism (Bernstein 2001; Leonard 2016).

This context of the rise of progressive politics is of crucial importance in interpreting Menger's article. He writes: "It is not true that the newer school of *Social-Politik* in Germany stands in substantive contrast to classical political economy." Quoted out of context this sentence can be seriously misleading, and a proper understanding of the article depends on what Menger is trying to convey here. He is trying to convey a similarity in spirit, or inclination—"*Tendenz*," he calls it—of the classical school and that of the modern *Social-Politiker*. It is Menger's central message that one can be for the poor, for the workers, and be a teacher and writer in the tradition of classical political economy. Indeed, toward the end of the article the guise falls away to some extent: The well-being of society requires that tradition.

All classical political economists, he argues, were convinced that many of the injustices of their time harmed the poor and the workers. The final pages of the article make it clear that this would entail a policy program quite different than that proposed by the *Social-Politiker*. But Menger has an even more important issue on his mind. He wants to make clear that the classical political economists were every bit as much concerned with advancing justice through economic reform. In practical terms this meant that economists working in the classical tradition could just as much belong to the VfS. Menger argues that there is a fundamental similarity between the

---

2. Brentano occupied his chair in Vienna for less than a year between 1888 and 1889, when he moved to Leipzig. Menger was strongly opposed to Brentano's appointment, telling Brentano: "You cannot imagine what bitterness your appointment has filled me with" (quoted in Grimmer-Solem 2003, 265).

classical economists, himself, and the *Social-Politiker* of his time. That is why he argues that Smith and his disciples could well be described as the *Social-Politiker* of their age, and why he extols their accomplishments in the policy arena, especially their success in breaking down privileges. But from these shared goals, this shared purpose, quite different social policies could result, based on differing economic theories. It is this shared purpose that is also the subject of Böhm-Bawerk's opening article *"Unsere Aufgaben"* ("Our Mission") (1924/ 1892) in the newly founded journal *Zeitschrift für Volkswirtschaft, Socialpolitik und Verwaltung (Journal of Economics, Social Policy and Public Administration)*. This journal, in combination with the reactivation around 1890 of the *Gesellschaft Österreichischer Volkswirte* ("Society of Austrian Economists," which was initially organized in 1875; see Egger 2001, 4–7), constituted the Austrian answer to the efforts by the VfS.

The fact that Menger is on the defensive results in descriptions of Smith and the other classical economists that seem one-sided, even distorted. In his efforts to argue that their sympathy is with the poor and workers and their intention is to further justice, he eagerly seizes upon passages in which the classical economists accept state interventions. It is up to us, as readers, to interpret what Menger means precisely. But the end of the article should make perfectly clear that Menger was squarely at odds with the economic program of the *Social-Politiker* of his age. He makes clear that the "negative program" of the classical economists, aimed at breaking down existing privileges and moving toward a system of natural liberty, was of an importance in improving the position of the worker far greater than modern interventionist measures. Moreover, he also criticizes a number of interventions promoted by the *Social-Politiker* that create new privileges and effectively harm the lower classes.

Another remarkable aspect of Menger's work around this period is his concern with establishing a lineage for the work being done by him and his students and associates. Around the same time he writes several commemorative articles, for a variety of occasions, in which he relates the contributions of Austrian economists to those of others. Menger clearly develops a preference for Adam Smith, whom he here calls the "consummate master" (*"Vollender"*) of classical political economy, and in the other commemorative articles Menger praises Smith as the most important classical political economist, who eschewed dogmatism and whose inclinations were always sound. Later accounts of Austrian economics have sometimes accorded a pioneering and revolutionary role to Menger himself, but Menger is clear that he saw himself as continuing the tradition in which Smith was paramount, and which included the important economic theorists of the nineteenth century, including David Ricardo, Jean-Baptiste Say, John Stuart Mill, William Stanley Jevons, and Léon Walras. Menger's frequent reference to Smith's disciples in this article should certainly be read as an indication that Menger considered himself to be one of them.

The Social Theories of Classical Political Economy and Modern Economic Policy[3]

Carl Menger
translated by Erwin Dekker and Stefan Kolev

I.

The centenary of Adam Smith's death has passed virtually unnoticed on German soil. The progressive German press has bestowed only few wreaths of grateful memory upon the grave of this man, who for a century provided that very press with the weapons it has used in the battle against the oppressive economic privileges of the once-favored societal groups. German science, too, which until the middle of our century[4] followed the great master more with piousness than with critical independence, has only honored him timidly. Alas, on this occasion Smith has been struck by the cruel fate of being "historically interpreted," and being "defended" from too much diminution, by the representatives of a hostile group, which has meanwhile gained dominance at German universities. What we witnessed on the 17th of July of last year was an unenthusiastic, almost hesitant commemoration of the man who was once praised as the father, yes, even the consummate master of scientific political economy.

But even so, the miserable centenary we witnessed is only a minor stroke in the decline in the German public reputation of the "old" or classical political

---

3. This essay is a translation from German of a two-part article published in the *Neue Freie Presse*, Vienna, January 6 (pages 8–9) and January 8 (page 8), 1891. The parts are indicated here by the roman numeral headers.
4. The nineteenth century.

economy and its founder. When Babeuf, no longer fearful of death, stood in front of the guillotine, he worried only that his opponents would write the history of his endeavors. Classical political economy really has been struck by this fate. The role that the school plays in current public opinion in Germany has been "created" by its hateful opponents, by agitators pursuing practical goals, by Friedrich List, and in other respects by Ferdinand Lassalle. This reputation of classical political economy has been eagerly reinforced by the scientific opponents of the progressive bourgeoisie, working in the spirit of Prince Bismarck. Thereafter in German science classical political economy is regarded as capitalistic, atomistic, abstract, and against the people,[5] it is considered to be refuted and dismissed.

The reversal in the public opinion of Smith and classical political economy that has occurred in Germany has not remained restricted to academia. German economic policy has also renounced the teachings of Smith and his disciples, "the economic party doctrines of individualism and liberalism." Prince Bismarck defended himself, and allowed himself to be defended by others, against the charge of being a politician in the spirit of *The Wealth of Nations*, as if he defended himself from an intellectual and moral failing, and ever since there is hardly a statesman in Germany who does not place special emphasis on his emancipation from Smith's theories. Smith is not only a dethroned prince of science in Germany, he is—like another Delbrück[6]—pushed aside because of outdated views and has consequently fallen from grace as advisor to leading German statesmen. If Smith—a man once praised as the sixth great power[7]—could have witnessed the fate of his scholarly fame in Germany, he would cry out, with Hecuba:

Quondam maxima rerum
Nunc trahor exul, inops[8]

---

5. "*Volksfeindlich*," literally 'hostile to the people,' has no equivalent in English; we opted for 'against the people.' In 1891 this word did not yet have the nationalistic connotations it would later have, when it would be closer to 'unpatriotic.'

6. A reference to Hans Delbrück (1848–1929), a scholar who was repudiated by Bismarck-admiring historian Heinrich von Treitschke (1834–1896).

7. That is alongside the five great powers: United Kingdom, Prussia, France, Russia, and Austria.

8. Ovid, *Metamorphoses* 13:508–510: "modo maxima rerum, tot generis natisque potens nuribusque viroque nunc trahor exul, inops." In F. J. Miller's translation (Harvard University

Such a reversal does not fail to leave a deep impact on the political parties of Germany and Austria. The liberal party had, from the moment when it secured basic political rights for the population, drawn its main force from its economic program. Questions of fiscal and socioeconomic policy were its primary concern. A close attention to particular economic interests had won it the hearts of the nations.[9] But from the time that Smithian thought was believed to be refuted and dismissed, the liberal party has—like an Antaeus—lost that ground from which it mainly drew its force. The decline of the old, and the victory of the new political economy has caused, more than any other shift in public opinion, a shift in the power relations between the political parties, a roll-back of liberalism, even in the noblest sense of that word. The dominant opinion among scientists and practitioners that the Smithian system had been refuted by the new developments in German science, that classical political economy had been dismissed, is a fact of wide-ranging political significance. The liberal party lost its erstwhile connection with economic science and consequently its footing and leadership in economic matters as well as its belief in its own economic program.

I am well aware of the fact that overcoming scientific fallacies entrenched in academic minds, even when they clearly contradict facts, is one of the most cumbersome tasks of scientific criticism, especially when the dominant fallacies are supported by the interests of powerful groups in society. But time not only dampens passions, it also has a corrective impact on men's fallacies. Thus the dominant legend in Germany of the relationship between the "new" political economy and the Smithian doctrine will eventually be replaced by a better understanding. I believe we would do well not to condemn classical political economy based on the authority of its opponents, but instead to not spare efforts to evaluate it without bias, perhaps ideally to let it speak for itself once more. That is what should take place here, even at the risk of concluding that the supposed victory of the school of *Social-Politik*[10] over Smith and

---

Press, 1916): "But late on the pinnacle of fame, strong in my many sons, my daughters, and my husband, now, exiled, penniless [...] I am dragged away."

9. Nations ("*Völker*") here probably refers to the different nationalities in Germany and Austria-Hungary.

10. When referring to this school, its ideas, etc., Menger uses the adjective form "*social-politische*" and noun "*Social-Politik*." We opt to use "*Social-Politik*" throughout, for both parts of speech.

the classical authors of political economy is based on a confusion between classical political economy and Manchesterism, and is thus a victory not over classical political economy, but over the one-sidedness of the doctrines of Manchesterism.

It is not true that the newer school of *Social-Politik* in Germany stands in substantive contrast to classical political economy.

In every conflict of interest between the rich and the poor, the strong and the weak, Smith sides *without exception* with the latter. I use the term "without exception" with proper consideration, as one cannot find one single instance in the works of Smith in which he represents the interests of the rich and the powerful against the poor and the weak. As highly as Smith praises the free initiative of the individual in economic matters, does he energetically promote state interventions[11] to abolish laws, or the execution of the laws, which oppress the poor and the weak in favor of the rich and the powerful.

Smith fights against the industrial policy of the mercantile system because it favors the industries of the rich while neglecting and oppressing those branches of industry which guarantee the sustenance of the poor and the weak. He demands free mobility because its limitation hurts labor much more than capital, as the rich merchant can obtain the right to settle down anywhere much easier than the poor craftsman. He is against the regulation of the so-called legal settlement laws, because they primarily hurt the poor and violate natural liberty and justice when expelling someone from a parish who has chosen the very place as his residence; he favors high wages, in which he sees both an imperative of humanity and of prudence. Smith is against state meddling with the wage contract, especially when the intervention proves to be to the *disadvantage* of the worker and to harm "the holiest and most inalienable right of the worker, the right to his labor."[12] He speaks so infre-

---

11. *"Eingriffe"* might have a slightly different connotation from our modern use of the word *interventions*. Nonetheless we opted for 'interventions' here, not only because it is the literal translation of *Eingriffe*, but from the other occurrences of the term it also becomes clear that Menger refers to positive state action, not to a more general idea of economic reform.

12. Not all quotations by Menger are literal. This one is most likely a reference to: "The property which every man has in his own labour, as it is the original foundation of all other property, so it is the most sacred and inviolable. The patrimony of a poor man lies in the strength and dexterity of his hands; and to hinder him from employing this strength and dexterity in what manner he thinks proper without injury to his neighbour, is a plain violation of this most sacred property" (Smith 1976/1776, 138).

quently against state intervention *advantageous* to the poor and weak that he rather endorses it in all cases when he expects it to be *favorable* (and not oppressive) for the propertyless classes. Smith even favors legal provisions on the wage level when they are set at such a level that they *favor* the workers, and he *always* declares such fixed wages as just and fair.[13] Smith also favors the law which forces in some trades the masters to pay the workers in money and not in kind.[14] Yes, Smith goes so far as to argue that, while *capital profits are a deduction from the full product of labor, rents are the incomes of those* who wish to reap without having sown. When matters concern the protection of the poor and the weak, the basic principled standpoint of Smith sometimes is more progressive than that of any of the modern *"Social-Politiker."*[15] At various points in his work, his views touch upon those of the modern socialists. As is well known, Louis Blanc, Ferdinand Lassalle, and Karl Marx constantly refer to the theories of Smith and those of his disciples, not to those of their opponents.

From the above, every unbiased reader can discern the true inclination of Smith's *Social-Politik*. He identifies laws and execution of laws which oppress the workers and the propertyless to the favor of the propertied classes, and which harm "the holiest and most inalienable right, the right of the worker to his labor." Therefore he stands, in line with *his* historical task, for the liberation of the propertyless classes from the harmful influence of the state on the labor contract and, if I may say so, of odious privileges. However, Smith does not stop there. He demands in numerous cases positive regulations in favor of the workers. To consider Smith an enemy of labor, or even to be a doctrinaire indifferent to the working class, is a falsification of

---

13. Menger uses the word *"Lohntaxen,"* which has since fallen out of use. This mercantilist institution was used by many medieval cities to regulate the wage levels for the different branches of employment in the sense of 'fair wages' for these different branches, mostly in the form a fixed wage or of a maximum wage. The aim of a maximum wage was to prevent inflation due to excessive wage dynamics in the sense of wage-price spirals, and of a fixed wage to prevent downward spirals of wages if employers in a guild colluded against the employees.

14. In Smith's original: "Thus the law which obliges the masters in several different trades to pay their workmen in money and not in goods, is quite just and equitable. It imposes no real hardship upon the masters. It only obliges them to pay that value in money, which they pretended to pay, but did not always really pay, in goods" (1976/1776, 158).

15. Adherents or practitioners of *Social-Politik*.

history. The complete opposite is correct.

It should not be thought that it was just Smith whose view, in the spirit of the liberality of the eighteenth century, was shaped by the duty of the individual and of society to the workers. Rather, it is also the disciples of the great friend of humanity [Smith] who energetically speak up for the property-less classes.

According to Ricardo, "the general happiness" depends primarily on the fate of the working classes. The wage level, he argues, determines the welfare of the largest part of society. Every shift in the distribution of income which gives the workers a greater part of the national income is a very desirable improvement in the condition of society, because through such a shift easily the most important class of society, the working class, gains. "However," says Ricardo, "one could state that with this the income of the capitalist will not increase, or that the million which falls to the workers in the form of the increased wages, is deducted from the rents of the landlords. Even so!" says Ricardo, "This cannot shake my argumentation. The condition of society is still improved. My argument proves that it is even more desirable that the single most important class of society gains through this new distribution of national income."[16]

The labor-friendly attitude appears least in Robert Malthus, the representative among the classical economists of agrarian interests. He too demands help in cases of need, even when this can be offered by a sacrifice from the propertied classes: "At least then the evil will be generalized, tempered, and made bearable for all."[17] I know, Malthus says, of nothing more miserable

---

16. In Ricardo's original: "But it may be said, that the capitalist's income will not be increased; that the million deducted from the landlord's rent, will be paid in additional wages to labourers! Be it so; this will make no difference in the argument: the situation of the society will be improved, and they will be able to bear the same money burthens with greater facility than before; it will only prove what is still more desirable, that the situation of another class, and by far the most important class in society, is the one which is chiefly benefited by the new distribution" (1821, 32.51).

17. In Malthus's original: "Yet even in this way of employing labour, the benefit to some must bring with it disadvantages to others. That portion of each person's revenue which might go in subscriptions of this kind, must of course be lost to the various sorts of labour which its expenditure in the usual channels would have supported; and the want of demand thus occasioned in these channels must cause the pressure of distress to be felt in quarters which might otherwise have escaped it. But this is an effect which, in such cases, it is impossible to avoid; and, as a temporary measure, it is not only charitable but just, to spread the evil

than the idea to condemn workers to dress themselves in rags and to live in miserable huts, in order to be able to sell a few more of our cloths and calicos abroad. He demands the employment of the unemployed through public works. Every friend of humanity, he argues in another passage, must wholeheartedly wish Robert Owen success in his efforts to pass a parliamentary act limiting the number of working hours for children and prohibiting their employment at too young an age. He even declares that he would immediately favor eliminating the corn tariffs if this permanently improved the condition of workers. However, he is not convinced of the utility of this measure (just like our current agrarians don't believe that the abolition of corn tariffs improves the position of the workers). However, it should not be overlooked that Malthus is fundamentally influenced in these doctrines by his patriotic concern over the independence of his home country, which he considers threatened by England's dependence on imported corn during war times.

The head of French classical political economy, Jean-Baptiste Say, argues much in the same spirit as the current *Social-Politiker*. "The entrepreneurs," he argues, "claim to have the right to assemble to resist the undue pretensions of the workers. But when one believes that the coalitions of workers who fight for the assertion of their rights are blameworthy, how come that one does not hold the same opinion of the coalitions of entrepreneurs opposing the workers who demand sufficient wages? The employers already have enough instruments of influence through their wealth and social position and are not entitled to even more influence. When the authorities side with one camp in such struggles of interest, the other side will invariably be oppressed."[18] "A humanitarian perspective," he argues in another passage, "makes it desirable that workers and their families can dress themselves as is fitting given the climate and the season; that they have spacious, airy and heated rooms; and

---

over a larger surface, in order that its violence on particular parts may be so mitigated as to be made bearable by all" (1826, III.VII.13).

18. Say's *Cours complet d'économie politique pratique* has not been translated, and we can thus only refer to the French original: "Les maîtres ont prétendu qu'ils étaient obligés de se rassembler pour résister aux injustes prétentions de leurs ouvriers; mais si l'on trouve répréhensibles les coalitions d'ouvriers qui se concertent pour faire valoir leurs droits en commun, pourquoi ne trouve-t-on pas telle la réunion des maîtres qui s'entendent pour refuser un salaire suffisant? Les maîtres, par leur fortune, par leur position sociale, ont déjà des moyens d'influence qu'il ne convient pas de fortifier" (Say 1840, 556).

that they have healthy, abundant, and somewhat varied food."[19] "When it is the custom of a nation that it is unconditionally necessary that every worker has the duty to save for old age, then this will undoubtedly increase the wages. *However, in the eyes of every friend of mankind it must look outright appalling that this has not already been the case for a long time.* One must lament that the worker not only does not save for old age, but not even *for accidents, for illness and incapacity for work.*"[20] In some of his writings, Say goes further. He writes that one must combat the problems of the working classes according to their causes. He suggests, regarding important matters, that the state should make positive interventions in favor of the workers. "M. de Sismondi", he writes, "who in general recognizes the harmfulness of state interventions in private affairs, nonetheless believes that the law should offer protection for that contracting party (the worker) which, in the nature of things, finds itself in such a precarious and subordinated position that it is frequently forced to accept irksome conditions. It is impossible not to share the opinion of Sismondi as well as not to agree with the currently emerging trend in English legislation to fix the age under which children are not allowed to be drawn to work in factories."[21]

Such are the "anti-labor doctrinaires," the men whose teachings are notori-

---

19. "Humanity, indeed, would rejoice to see them and their families dressed in clothing suitable to the climate and season; houses in roomy, warm, airy, and healthy habitations, and fed with wholesome and plentiful diet, with perhaps occasional delicacy and variety." Say continues with a serious caveat: "But there are very few countries, where wants, apparently so moderate, are not considered far beyond the limits of strict necessity, and therefore not to be gratified by the customary wages of the mere laboring class" (Say 1855, II.VII.51).

20. "Did the habitual practice of society imperatively subject every family to the obligation of laying by some provision for age, as it commonly does for infancy, our ideas of necessity would be somewhat enlarged, and the minimum of wages somewhat raised. It must appear shocking to the eye of philanthropy, that such is not always the case. It is lamentable to think of the little providence of the laboring classes against the season of casual misfortune, infirmity, and sickness, as well as against the certain helplessness of old age" (Say 1855, II.VII.52–53).

21. "M. de Sismondi, convenant en principe des inconvénients qui résultent de l'intervention de l'autorité dans les conventions particulières, pense néanmoins que la loi doit prêter quelque force à celui des deux contractants qui est nécessairement dans une position tellement précaire et dominée, qu'il est quelquefois force d'accepter des conditions onéreuses. Il est impossible de ne pas partager en ce point l'opinion de M. de Sismondi, et de ne pas approuver une disposition récente de la législation anglaise, qui fixe l'âge au-dessous duquel il n'est pas permis à un manufacturier de faire travailler les enfants dans ses ateliers" (Say 1852, 50).

ously denounced as capitalist, against the people, and refuted, against which our modern *"Social-Politiker"* rail, and against whose affinity Poschinger seeks to defend Prince Bismarck, as if against a disgrace inflicted on the latter.[22] It is no less an outrage against the historical truth when the doctrines of those who develop Smith's doctrines in *his* spirit are made to appear as representatives of a cruel and exploitative capitalism, than when it is done with Smith himself.

The same lack of unbiasedness and truthfulness that is present in the critique of classical political economy by the newer schools of *Social-Politik* is also present in relation to numerous other matters of economic policy.

It is not true, it is a falsification of history, that Smith is a doctrinaire of *"laisser faire, laisser aller,"* or that he thought that the only way to advance the economic well-being of society was the completely free play of individual interests. He recognizes on numerous occasions in his works that the endeavors and interests of single individuals and entire societal classes can contradict the general interest, and in such cases he not only does not reject state interventions but rather lets them appear as an imperative of humanity and consideration for the common good. He expects so little of implementing the principle of *"laisser faire"* that he, on the contrary, points to a number of organizations and institutions *which are to a great extent advantageous to the common good, and which would never be possibly established by the free play of competition.* He explicitly declares that in these cases the state has *the important duty to establish and maintain the offices* and organizations which foster the common good. Smith is not only for interventions by the state in the economy in favor of the poor and weak, especially the workers. He also endorses, proportional to the circumstances,[23] corn tariffs in favor of agriculture, export subsidies for wool to raise the national production, and, yes, moderate tariffs on all manufacturing products, to secure an advantage for national labor on the domestic market. But unlike our modern *Social-Politiker* he never neglects the advantages of the international division of labor, and he recognizes the

---

22. In his foreword to *Aktenstücke zur Wirthschaftspolitik des Fürsten Bismarck* (*Documents on the Economic Policy of Prince Bismarck*), Heinrich von Poschinger wrote that Bismarck derived his power, in part, "from the gradually spreading belief in the German Reich that his economic policy was based not on *The Wealth of Nations*, but on the well-being of every single man" (1890, ix, our translation).

23. The German *"nach Maßgabe der Verhältnisse,"* might alternatively be translated as "if reasonable given the circumstances."

destructiveness of protective tariffs that steer national production in an inappropriate direction. He is so far from advocating a complete freedom of trade that he declares it equally absurd as the realization of some Utopia.[24] Smith declares that the state has the task to provide roads, canals, harbors, public warehouses, etc., and yes, under certain circumstances he even favors the state fixing the prices of basic foodstuffs, etc.

This point of view is essentially shared by the other authors of the classical school. They too are anything but supporters of the principle of *laisser faire*. In fact they sometimes go even further in their support of positive interventions by the state in the interest of the common good. J. B. Say demands forestry legislation, which protects the land from wood shortage and the water courses from depletion; he endorses measures of the government favoring agriculture and preventive measures against unsound practices of industrialists. In trade policy he not only argues for some consideration for existing industries and a gradual shift toward freedom of trade, he also demands state support for such industries which initially operate at a loss but offer the prospect of becoming profitable in the course of time—the support of industrial education of the people by the state—fundamentally anticipating the ideas of Friedrich List. In the same manner, Malthus supports protective tariffs, insofar as they have the goal to let specific lines of production in a country develop, to prevent great fluctuations in the economic life of a people, or to restore the equilibrium between different classes of society. He argues that protective tariffs are an important means in an economic policy aimed at the common good. Ricardo believes that tax-balancing tariffs and subsidies are necessary, and he supports the famous Corn Laws. It is an antihistorical legend that classical political economy supports the unrestrained rule of individual self-interest and the passivity of the government in economic matters.

The newer school of *Social-Politik* in Germany has not refuted and dismissed classical political economy—it has, rather, continued its develop-

---

24. Menger presumably has in mind the following passage of *The Wealth of Nations*: "To expect, indeed, that the freedom of trade should ever be entirely restored in Great Britain, is as absurd as to expect that an Oceana or Utopia should ever be established in it. Not only the prejudices of the publick, but what is much more unconquerable, the private interests of many individuals, irresistibly oppose it" (Smith 1976/1776, 471). But assuming that is indeed the referent passage, the meaning which Menger ascribes to it seems to us not to have been Smith's intended meaning.

ment in certain respects, and in other respects, as I will show, it has lagged behind. In the fight of the school of *Social-Politik* with the proponents of capitalistic Manchesterism—its caricature of Classicism—it was partly right, *but not against Smith and classical political economy*. The final configuration of classical political economy cannot be found in Cobden, Bright, Bastiat, Prince-Smith, and Schulze-Delitzsch, but rather in John Stuart Mill, the social philosopher, who, next to Sismondi, must be considered the most important founder behind the modern direction of *Social-Politik*, as far as it has an objective scientific character. Whoever reads the writings of the classical school as an interrelated whole will find the above judgment to be confirmed in every respect.

Classical political economy has erred in many respects, and in some decisive respects for the further development of economic theory. The current fashion in the newer German political economy which underestimates Smith and his school is based upon misunderstandings and misinterpretations of the classical authors, the correcting of which is the duty of objective science. This underestimation has even led Roscher to the noteworthy remark that the future "will restore the honor of men like Ricardo and Malthus as scientists."[25]

II.

The real difference between classical political economy and the modern school of *Social-Politik* in the workers question is not their inclination. Both recognize the unfavorable economic position of a large part of the workers within the population, both demand changes in favor of the workers, and neither fundamentally denies state help. The contrast is that the Smithian school believes that the improvement of the economic position of the workers lies primarily in the elimination of all state and social institutions which are disadvantageous for the workers' employment and their income, and only

---

25. "Recent science has endeavored, and successfully, to examine the facts which contradict the Ricardian and Malthusian formulations of the laws in question, and to extend the formulas accordingly. ... [I]t is not hard to comprehend that, while this process of elucidation is going on, most scholars, those especially possessed more of a dogmatic than of a historical turn of mind, should estimate these two leaders more in accordance with their few defects than with the great merits of their discoveries. ... For my own part, I have no doubt that, when the process of elucidation above referred to shall have been thoroughly finished, the future will accord both to Ricardo and Malthus their full meed of honor as political economists and discoverers of the first rank" (Roscher 1878, p. x).

deems positive interventions by the state in the economy advisable where the self-help of the workers and their free associations do not suffice for attaining the above purpose. Our modern *Social-Politiker* on the other hand—I mean those who are serious about improving the workers' lot—place the main emphasis on positive measures of the state, now that a large part of the laws of past ages which oppressed the poor and the weak in favor of the propertied classes have already been abolished. In this difference we cannot recognize a fundamental opposition, no different inclination, but only a difference in the evolution of circumstances regarding the continued development of the efforts to improve the position of the working class. The economic policy of classical political economy was precisely dedicated to the most immediate and urgent needs of the time in which it came into being, a time full of unjust class privileges and detrimental restrictions on the poor and weak, full of irrational and self-interested over-regulation. Smith and his disciples recognized the needs of *Social-Politik* in their time very precisely when they first pressed for the abolition of the harmful restrictions on workers and when they opposed the state interventions in the economy detrimental to the poor.

Smith and his disciples were *"Social-Politiker"* for their time at least to the same degree as those economists who currently claim for themselves the honor of this title as against the Smithian school. The men who stood up for the elimination of serfdom, feudal labor,[26] arbitrary justice, exclusive and exploitative guilds, monopolies, tax privileges, etc., have, when we look back at the conditions that had been there before their activities started, even with regard to their "negative program," at least an equal claim to the honorary title of *Social-Politiker* as do any economists of the present.

But that negative part does not exhaust the program of Smith and his disciples. We have seen that those same men spoke out for the necessity of positive measures by the state in all fields of economic life as soon as the free conduct of the individual proves insufficient for or harmful to the common good. No unbiased observer would believe that either Smith or his disciples would, from the spirit of their teachings, if they were asked today, oppose the more recent positive regulations which are truly aimed at the well-being of the workers class,[27] but probably they would oppose the corn tariffs, the

---

26. Menger refers to the institution of *"Frohnden."*
27. Menger uses in the context of workers the word *"Arbeiterstand"*, literally "workers' estate," even though other contexts he also uses *"Classe."*

progressive increase in indirect consumption taxes, the cartel laws, and various other laws and institutions of "*Social-Politik.*" It would be unfair to question the "inclination" of these men.

One could at most pose the question which group of social philosophers has actually *achieved more* for the protection of the needy classes, if this way of posing the question should not be dismissed as unhistorical. The goal of both schools is, considering the circumstances of their time, improving the economic position of the weak and the oppressed. But if the acceptance of theories of *Social-Politik* by the least privileged classes is taken as the correct measure of their relative merit, then the issue can hardly be decided in favor of our modern *Social-Politiker*. Wherever I look, the working class even today does not rely on the newer economic theories, according to which we should not be certain that high corn tariffs (imposed by grain-importing countries!) raise the price of bread, that petrol tariffs raise the price of the most important source of light for the worker, or that indirect taxes raise the cost of living of the worker and lower his standard of life. Rather, I find to this day that the workers, almost without exception, base their efforts on the theories of classical political economy, on the price theory of the classical school, on the land rent theory and the wage law of Ricardo, on the maxims of the classics that favor direct taxes, etc.

The same can be said for the newer positive measures for the improvement of the working classes. I do not want to doubt the inclination from which they owe their origin, nor their expected successes. But I must state the following two things: that the laws which protect the worker originate from England, the land of "classical political economy," and secondly—what I believe is more important—that nowhere is there a considerable group of workers who would be willing to exchange the right of self-determination and in particular the right of free association for the sum of all of the positive measures of modern *Social-Politik*. And that is, I believe, for good reasons. However highly one wants to value the worker-insurance as has already partly been introduced in Germany and in Austria, plus the entire sum of the *Social-Politik* measures aimed at the improvement of the working classes, an unbiased observer would have to recognize that the liberation of the workers from the former oppressive laws that favored the propertied classes, and the freedom of association for which the classical school argued, are, in their practical effects, to the present day, of immeasurably greater value. The intellectual leaders of the workers movement have also recognized that at all times. They accepted the improvements of modern *Social-Politik*, but they expect a more substantial improvement of the position of the workers from the freedom of association. Only recently, the English leader of the workers, Burns,[28] declared at the Liverpool congress that the freedom of association gives the workers a means of power which should enable the workers to achieve all their goals and which initially should be used with some caution for the very sake of the workers' own interests. The measures of *positive* state assistance favoring the working classes have not been met with the same enthusiasm by the representatives of the working classes, and have not given rise to the same great hopes. The merits that classical political economy has earned for the situation of the needy classes certainly do not lag behind those of newer schools of *Social-Politik*. The supposedly purely "negative program" of Smith and his disciples is still met with a higher esteem by the representatives of the needy classes than is the "positive program" of the newer *Social-Politiker*. This is even more the case since the latter is bound up with a system of other measures of *Social-Politik* that are decidedly detrimental for the working classes, and against which Smith and his disciples would vehemently object in the name of those same propertyless classes.

Where the classical economists are certainly equal to the modern *Social-Politiker* with respect to their worker-friendly inclination, I believe that in another respect the perspective of classical political economy is without a doubt significantly superior to that of the new *Social-Politiker*. By that, I mean the correct insight into the causes of the well-being of the working classes. That the position of the workers does not only depend on the positive legal interventions, but at least as much on the progressive accumulation of capital and on the entrepreneurial spirit of those who possess it, is too often completely overlooked nowadays. The one-sided tendency against everything which is named capital and enterprise has seemingly blinded the newer schools of *Social-Politik* to the recognition of this truth and its practical consequences. It is true that the distribution of income between capital and labor is in itself a problem of the utmost importance and every measure through which labor gains a greater proportion of the fruits of production, as long as it

---

28. John Elliot Burns (1858–1943) was a British unionist, MP, and minister of the Liberal Party.

does not threaten the continued existence of industries, should be applauded as welcome social progress. But with equal certainty would I argue that a significant increase in wages can only be the consequence of the progressive accumulation and productive use of capital. Indeed, the employment of a growing labor force with increasing wages or even at the current wage level can only go hand in hand with capital accumulation and an increase of productive activities. They who, too one-sidedly, only have an eye for a maximally beneficial distribution between the entrepreneur and the worker of the value of production, fail to see that the expected benefits from this for the working class, however important they may be, are severely limited. The expected benefits which arise automatically from the accumulation of capital and its productive use are of far greater importance.

Our age has often been accused of the fact that, unlike the propertied classes of antiquity, we do not enjoy life leisurely, but instead continuously strive for the acquisition of more wealth—that the propertied classes have been inflicted by an irrational pleonexia, which is not so much guided by a striving for leisurely enjoyment but rather from striving to possess more than others. It is this accusation which, especially with respect to the bourgeois classes of contemporary society, is not completely unjustified, and which matters even more when we take into account that the abstract drive for the accumulation of capital is partly cancelled out, in its effects for the capital owners, by the reduction of the interest rate. However, it seems to me that it is overlooked by those who make this accusation that this pleonexia is a kind of economic remedy for the progressive growth of the labor population, for it is among the most important means to provide this very population with employment and wages. However one might think about the "abstract capitalist drive" of the bourgeois classes of society, from the perspective of *Social-Politik* it is beneficial. At the very least it does not deserve the loud reproach of those who do not voice one word of reproach toward the waste of capital that takes place among other social classes, sometimes in ruinous ways, for example through the mortgaging of increased rents from land and the use of this money for consumption purposes.

So classical political economy certainly does not lag behind the newer school of *Social-Politik* in its worker-friendly inclination, and with respect to the correct insight into the causes of the more or less satisfactory fate of the propertyless classes, classical political economy is far superior. Classical political economy does not overlook the importance of capital, the entrepreneurial spirit, and commercial intelligence for the well-being of the working class. It is free from doctrinaire spitefulness towards capital and enterprise, which the newer doctrines of the *Social-Politiker* have adopted from socialist agitators. It does not lose sight of the fact that even an unequally distributed wealth of capital is less harmful for the working classes than is a lack of capital, and that the worker is never more helpless than when the "cursed money" dries up for the entrepreneurs, or when an intimidated entrepreneurial spirit shies away from capital investments.

I have argued that the newer measures of *Social-Politik* to lift up the needy classes are already contained in the program of classical political economy. But I should have added a caveat to this argument, which I believe, also, lends a great superiority to the Smithian perspective over those of the new *Social-Politiker*. Adam Smith and his disciples always stood up for the *common good*, not for class interests, and they were even less prone to advocate favorable measures for particular factions within social classes, an accusation from which the newer *Social-Politik* cannot be completely spared.

Our rural population has been badly hit by the decline in prices of agricultural products. They are supposed to be assisted by disinheriting a part of them, with this adding a new artificial rural proletariat to the already existing proletariat. The class of farmers is supposed to be assisted by pushing the overwhelming majority of the farmers into the proletariat. Artisans and craftsmen wage a heavy fight with big industry. The cure against their decline is supposed to lie in setting up excessively high protective measures for the existing businesses while making it more difficult for self-employed new entrants to start a business, so that the class of dependent wage laborers would be artificially increased. The position of the workers, clearly, leads to highly sophisticated thoughts from the *Social-Politiker*. The solution should, according to some, come from associations of workers, which, through exclusion of the poorest and the neediest, would lead to a certain worker aristocracy, which would be granted the advantages of petty bourgeois existence, but which would at the same time make the struggle for existence hopeless for the remaining workers. The creation of privileged factions within the individual classes of society—a preferred *numerus clausus*—where the rest of society is completely neglected, would supposedly cure the social afflictions of our times! And all of this is propagated not from the perspective of one-sided factional interests, but from that of a popular *Social-Politik*! The task of helping the weak and disinherited shall be met by artificially increasing them in number, and especially by increasing the wealth and employment advantages of particular factions within social classes through "positive legal measures," while those outside these factions would not only be denied access to property but also to employment. Even the cartels of the industrialists—the configurations of the roughest, most collectivist Manchesterism—have finally found their apologists, and finally are they recognized as beneficial institutions of *Social-Politik*, yes, even as universal means for the solution to our social problem. In this way the social ills of the world are supposed to be eliminated, and the encroachment of socialist elements in the armies, which are cited as a threat to our current legal and social order, stopped!

Social-Politik measures of this "positivism" are as alien to Smith, to his teachings, and to those disciples who have continued to work in his spirit, as the importance for society of capital and entrepreneurial spirit is alien to the modern *Social-Politiker*.

Thus, again, classical political economy does not lag behind the newer schools of *Social-Politik* in its sympathy toward the poor and the weak, and with respect to the correct understanding of the nature and the causes of economic phenomena—the correct theoretical insight—classical political economy is far superior.

The effects of the new doctrines on the classes of the population who are to be supported have been felt. The striving for a better position in society through thrift and personal industriousness, a striving that no unbiased observer can deny is responsible for the most important economic improvements of all classes of the population, is visibly disappearing in large parts of the people, while all their thoughts and intentions are directed towards the struggle of individual classes to secure a maximum share of the total production of the economy. The striving for personal industriousness has given way to a class struggle that, as seen from the perspective of society as a whole, is unproductive. Self-interest, so much despised by the *Social-Politiker*, has not disappeared from the world, but rather has degenerated into a collectivist, a national and a class egoism, which does not strive for an increase in the total production (that which is to be shared!) but rather for the maximal part of the total production for every individual social class.

The school of *Social-Politik* in Germany suffers from a doctrinarism, which in its one-sidedness vividly brings to mind the doctrinarism of Manchesterism, only that the latter uncritically expects everything from the free play of individual interests, while the former expects everything from artificial "organizations" and the interventions of state authority. There was a time when the reputation of a competent economist was granted to anybody who declared an intention to destroy anything that smacked of state influence or organization. To receive the highest praise of the current representatives of one strand of *Social-Politik*, no more is needed than to display blind animosity against capital, entrepreneurial spirit, and any form of individual initiative and responsibility in economic matters.

The doctrinarism of the one and of the other have equally distanced themselves from an objective science which recognizes the role of state authority as consisting in the equally important tasks of improving the position of the working class and a just income distribution, but at least to the same degree also in promoting individual industry, thrift, and the entrepreneurial spirit.

References

Backhaus, Jürgen G. 1993. The University as an Economic Institution: The Political Economy of the Althoff System. *Journal of Economic Studies* 20(4–5): 8–29.

Bernstein, Michael A. 2001. *A Perilous Progress: Economists and Public Purpose in Twentieth-Century America.* Princeton, N.J.: Princeton University Press.

Blumenthal, Karsten von. 2007. *Die Steuertheorien der Austrian Economics: Von Menger zu Mises.* Marburg: Metropolis Verlag.

Böhm, Stephan. 1985. The Political Economy of the Austrian School. In *Gli economisti e la politica economica,* ed. Piero Roggi, 243–260. Naples: Edizioni Scientifiche Italiane.

Böhm-Bawerk, Eugen von. 1924 [1889]. Die klassische Nationalökonomie. In *Gesammelte Schriften von Eugen von Böhm-Bawerk,* ed. Franz X. Weiss, 144–157. Vienna: Hölder-Pichler-Tempsky.

Böhm-Bawerk, Eugen von. 1924 [1892]. Unsere Aufgaben. In *Gesammelte Schriften von Eugen von Böhm-Bawerk,* ed. Franz X. Weiss, 129–143. Vienna: Hölder-Pichler-Tempsky.

Doering, Detmar. 2004. *Mythos Manchestertum: Ein Versuch über Richard Cobden und die Freihandelsbewegung.* Potsdam: Liberales Institut der Friedrich-Naumann-Stiftung.

Egger, Hans Christian. 2001. *Die "Gesellschaft österreichischer Volkswirte" im Spiegel ihrer Publikationen.* Munich: Grin.

Ely, Richard T. 1936. The Founding and the Early History of the American Economic Association. *American Economic Review* 26(1): 141–150.

Grimmer-Solem, Erik. 2003. *The Rise of Historical Economics and Social Reform in Germany 1864–1894.* Oxford: Oxford University Press.

Hayek, Friedrich A. 1992 [1934]. Carl Menger. In *The Fortunes of Liberalism (The Collected*

Works of F. A. Hayek, vol. 4), ed. Peter G. Klein, 61–95. Chicago: University of Chicago Press.

Henderson, W. O. 1950. Prince Smith and Free Trade in Germany. *Economic History Review* 2(3): 295–302.

Hentschel, Volker. 1975. *Die deutschen Freihändler und der Volkswirtschaftliche Kongreß 1858 bis 1885*. Stuttgart: Klett.

Leonard, Thomas C. 2016. *Illiberal Reformers: Race, Eugenics, and American Economics in the Progressive Era*. Princeton, N.J.: Princeton University Press.

Malthus, Thomas R. 1826. *An Essay on the Principle of Population*, 6th ed. London: John Murray.

Oschina, Susanne. 2010. *Die Entwicklung des Vereins für Socialpolitik von seiner Gründung bis 1980*. Master's thesis, University of Graz.

Poschinger, Heinrich von. 1890. Vorwort. In *Aktenstücke zur Wirthschaftspolitik des Fürsten Bismarck*, ed. Heinrich von Poschinger, vii–ix. Berlin: Verlag von Paul Hennig.

Ricardo, David. 1821. *On the Principles of Political Economy and Taxation*, 3rd ed. London: John Murray.

Roscher, Wilhelm G. F. 1878. *Principles of Political Economy*, trans. John J. Lalor, vol. 1. New York: Henry Holt & Co.

Say, Jean-Baptiste. 1840. *Cours complet d'économie politique pratique*, 2nd ed., vol. 1. Paris: Guillaumin.

Say, Jean-Baptiste. 1852. *Cours complet d'économie politique pratique*, 3rd ed., vol. 2. Paris: Guillaumin.

Say, Jean-Baptiste. 1855. *A Treatise on Political Economy*, ed. Clement C. Biddle, trans. C. R. Prinsep, 6th ed. Philadelphia: Lippincott, Grambo & Co.

Schüller, Richard. 1895. *Die klassische Nationalökonomie und ihre Gegner*. Berlin: Carl Heymans Verlag.

Seager, H. R. 1893. Economics at Berlin and Vienna. *Journal of Political Economy* 1(2): 236–262.

Smith, Adam. 1976 [1776]. *An Inquiry Into the Nature and Causes of the Wealth of Nations*. Oxford: Oxford University Press.

Streissler, Erich W. 1990. Carl Menger on Economic Policy: The Lectures to Crown Prince Rudolf. In *Carl Menger and His Legacy in Economics*, ed. Bruce J. Caldwell, 107–130. Durham, N.C.: Duke University Press.

Streissler, Erich W. 1994. Menger's Treatment of Economics in the Rudolf Lectures. In *Carl Menger's Lectures to Crown Prince Rudolf of Austria*, eds. Erich W. Streissler and Monika Streissler, 3–25. Cheltenham, UK: Edward Elgar.

About the Authors, Editors, and Translators

Benoît Malbranque, a research fellow at Institut Coppet, is studying French classical liberalism. He is the author of *Les théoriciens français de la liberté humaine* (Institut Coppet, 2020).

René Louis de Voyer de Paulmy, Marquis d'Argenson (1694–1757), was a minister in France; in a letter, Voltaire wrote that he was "the best citizen that had ever tasted the ministry." He was, along with Boisguilbert and Vincent de Gournay, one of the main promoters of the laissez-faire stance in French economics leading up to the Physiocrats. He wrote numerous essays and kept a journal, in which he discussed how the social and economic conditions of France could be revived through a policy of non-intervention. His views influenced numerous economists, including the Physiocrats.

An **anonymous** author who had previously published in *Journal Œconomique* a summary of Girolamo Belloni's *Del commercio*.

Tobias Smollett (1721–1771) was a Scottish poet and author.

Authorship by **"Hew Dalrymple"** is purported on the last page of the 1758 pamphlet "Information for the Hair Dressers in Edinburgh; Against the Incorporation of Barbers—The Second Edition." The British Library has deemed the work pseudonymous. Further investigation, however, suggests that perhaps the pamphlet is a rollicking variant on a no-longer-extant legal document, the author of which may well have been a Hew Dalrymple.

David Hume (1711–1776) was a Scottish political theorist, moral philosopher, historian, and essayist. Adam Smith wrote of him as a "never to be forgotten friend."

Daniel Klein is the chief editor of *Econ Journal Watch* and professor of economics and JIN Chair at the Mercatus Center at George Mason University, where he and Erik Matson lead a program in Adam Smith. He has published numerous scholarly works on David Hume, most recently with Matson "Convention Without Convening," in *Constitutional Political Economy*.

Jason Briggeman is the managing editor of *Econ Journal Watch*, an adjunct associate professor of economics at Austin Community College, an associate editor for *Liberal Currents*, and an adjunct fellow of the Niskanen Center.

Jacob Hall is an economics Ph.D. student at George Mason University. He is a Ph.D. fellow at the Mercatus Center and a fellow of the Adam Smith Program at George Mason University. His academic research is in economic history. He also does work on the writings of David Hume, especially the *History of England*.

F. E. Guerra-Pujol received his J.D. from Yale Law School and teaches business law and ethics at the University of Central Florida. His areas of research include markets, property rights, and the history of legal ideas. Dr. Guerra-Pujol is the author of many scholarly papers and book chapters including "Gödel's Loophole," "Buy or Bite?," and "The Poker-Litigation Game," and he is currently writing a book on probability and the law.

Scott Drylie is an assistant professor and the director of the graduate program for Cost Analysis at the Air Force Institute of Technology in Dayton, Ohio. He is also an active-duty finance officer for the United States Air Force. He teaches economic principles, mathematical economics, and acquisitions cost estimating. His research focuses on the role of learning, expertise, and innovation in organizations and systems. He has a B.S. in Economics from Montana State University, an M.Ed. in Education, an M.S. in Cost Analysis, and a Ph.D. in Economics from George Mason University.

Frederic Sautet studied at the University of Paris, the Paris Institute of Political Studies ("Sciences Po") and New York University (post-doc). He is an associate professor at the Busch School of Business at the Catholic University of America in Washington D.C. where he is the co-founder of the Art and Carlyse Ciocca Center for Principled Entrepreneurship, and the director of the Röpke-Wojtyła Fellowship. Dr. Sautet is the co-editor of Israel Kirzner's *Collected Works* published by Liberty Fund.

The following biographical information comes from Mossner and Ross (1977, 311 n.1): "**Pierre-Samuel Dupont de Nemours** (1739–1817), philanthropist, economist, Deputy to the National Assembly, and translator of Ariosto. He impressed the *économistes* by his *Réflexions sur l'écrit intitulé: Richesse de l'État* (1763), and publicized Quesnay's system in frequent articles for two journals he edited: *Journal de l'agriculture* (1765–6) and *Éphémérides du citoyen* (1768–72), also he published Quesnay's writings together with an analysis in *Physiocratie* (1768). His treatise *De l'origine et du progrès d'une science nouvelle* (1767) and the *Tableau raisonné des principes de l'économie politique* (1775) are among his important contributions to the literature of economics. He became the friend and confidant of Turgot and served under him in the French Government, 1774–6; later he wrote memoirs of Turgot (1782), then enlarged these for an edition of Turgot's complete works (1808–11). As a practical politician he took part in the early stages of the French Revolution, but his views clashed with those of the Jacobins, and after running a clandestine press he was imprisoned, surviving this period solely as a result of the fall of Robespierre. In 1799 he emigrated to the United States and a year later, at Jefferson's request, he prepared a plan for national education. At this time his son, Eleuthère Irénée, set up a gunpowder mill in Delaware, thus founding the family chemical industry. The father returned to France in 1802 to assist in the negotiations for the Louisiana Purchase, and was active in bringing down Napoleon's regime in 1814, but a year later returned to America where he died."

Ian Simpson Ross (1930–2015) was Professor Emeritus of English at the University of British Columbia. A native of Scotland, he was educated at St. Andrews and Oxford prior to earning his Ph.D. at the University of Texas. Ross authored not only the biography of Adam Smith, excerpted here, but also biographies of the poet William Dunbar and Henry Home, Lord Kames. Ross's many works of scholarship related to Smith include his editorship of *The Correspondence of Adam Smith* (1977, with Ernest Mossner) and *On the Wealth of Nations: Contemporary Responses to Adam Smith* (1998).

Edmund Burke (1729–1797) was an author, statesman, and publicist, born in Dublin. He was an MP in the House of Commons between 1766 and 1794. His writings include *A Vindication of Natural Society*, *A Philosophical Enquiry into the Origin of Our Ideas of the Sublime and Beautiful*, *Thoughts on the Cause of the Present Discontents*, *Reflections on the Revolution in France*, *Appeal from the New to the Old Whigs*, *Letters on a Regicide Peace*, and *Thoughts and Details on Scarcity*.

Erik Gustaf Geijer (1783–1847) was an eminent figure in Sweden, a celebrated poet, a musician and composer, a moralist, an historian, a political philosopher, a public intellectual, and a Member of Parliament. He was professor at Uppsala University and its Chancellor. His work and thinking have defied classification, as he straddled, shifted between, or, arguably, integrated, enlightenment and romantic tendencies, nationalistic and liberal, scientific and poetic. Works in English translation by Peter C. Hogg are available in *Freedom in Sweden: Selected Works of Erik Gustaf Geijer*, edited by Björn Hasselgren (Stockholm: Timbro, 2017), which also contains an essay by Lars Magnusson on Geijer's life, works, and influence. In discussing influences on Geijer and the formation of his outlook, Magnusson brings to light British currents and especially Scottish moral philosophers and historians.

Erwin Dekker is a Senior Research Fellow at the Mercatus Center at George Mason University. Previously he taught at Erasmus University in Rotterdam. He is the author of *The Viennese Students of Civilization* (2016), from his Erasmus PhD dissertation, and *Jan Tinbergen and the Rise of Economic Expertise* (2021), and coeditor of *Governing Markets as Knowledge Commons* (2021), all of which are published by Cambridge University Press. He is now working on a history of the intellectual descendants of the German Historical School as well as an economic sociology analysis of so-called grey zones: markets and communities operating at the fringes of society.

Stefan Kolev is professor of political economy at the University of Applied Sciences Zwickau, Germany, and the deputy director of the Wilhelm Röpke Institute in Erfurt. He serves as co-editor of the *Journal of Contextual Economics—Schmollers Jahrbuch* and of the *ORDO Jahrbuch für die Ordnung von Wirtschaft und Gesellschaft*. He is among the co-founders of Network for

Constitutional Economics and Social Philosophy (NOUS) and is in charge of the NOUS young scholars seminar series. His research focuses on the link between the history of liberalism and the history of German-language political economy. Stefan has published on the connections among Friedrich A. Hayek, the "Old Chicago" School, and the ordoliberals, as well as on the revitalization of ordoliberal thought today and tomorrow. Currently, his interests focus on the German Historical School, on early German-language economic sociology, especially Max Weber, as well as on the connection of the Bloomington School to ordoliberalism.

Carl Menger (1840–1921) was an influential thinker and professor at the University of Vienna. His *Principles of Economics* of 1871 was a breakthrough in economic theory, notably for its marginalist approach and its subjectivist approach to value. His individual-centered conception of the economy was soon perceived as revolutionary and has ever since attracted generations of scholars to expand on this conception, with his immediate and closest associates being Eugen von Böhm-Bawerk (1851–1914) and Friedrich von Wieser (1851–1926). Following the publication of his *Investigations into the Method of the Social Sciences with Special Reference to Economics* in 1883, Menger engaged in what later would become known as the Methodenstreit, a controversy which, among others, addressed the relative roles of theory and history in economics. His principal opponent was the head of the Younger Historical School, Gustav Schmoller (1838–1917). In the decades after the Methodenstreit, Menger remained influential, both as teacher and as a public figure, but did not publish any new treatises. After the birth of his son Karl in 1902, Menger increasingly withdrew from public life, and Wieser succeeded him at the University of Vienna as the professor of economic theory. After his death, his partner Hermine Andermann sold his library to Hitotsubashi University in Japan. His archives are preserved at Duke University. Between 1933 and 1936, Friedrich A. Hayek edited the four-volume *Collected Works of Carl Menger*. Menger is widely credited as one of the founders of the Austrian School of economics.

CL Press
A Fraser Institute Project
https://clpress.net/

Professor Daniel Klein (George Mason University, Economics and Mercatus Center) and Dr. Erik Matson (Mercatus Center), directors of the Adam Smith Program at George Mason University, are the editors and directors of CL Press. CL stands at once for classical liberal and conservative liberal.

CL Press is a project of the Fraser Institute (Vancouver, Canada).

People:

- Dan Klein and Erik Matson are the co-editors and executives of the imprint.
- Jane Shaw Stroup is Editorial Advisor, doing especially copy-editing and text preparation.
- An Advisory Board:
  - Jordan Ballor, *Center for Religion, Culture, and Democracy*
  - Donald Boudreaux, *George Mason Univ.*
  - Caroline Breashears, St. *Lawrence Univ.*
  - Ross Emmett, *Arizona State Univ.*
  - Knud Haakonssen, *Univ. of St. Andrews*
  - Björn Hasselgren, *Timbro, Univ. of Uppsala*
  - Karen Horn, *Univ. of Erfurt*
  - Jimena Hurtado, *Univ. de los Andes*
  - Nelson Lund, *George Mason Univ.*
  - Daniel Mahoney, *Assumption Univ.*
  - Deirdre N. McCloskey, *Univ. of Illinois-Chicago*
  - Thomas W. Merrill, *American Univ.*

- James Otteson, *Univ. of Notre Dame*
- Catherine R. Pakaluk, *Catholic Univ. of America*
- Sandra Peart, *Univ. of Richmond*
- Mario Rizzo, *New York Univ.*
- Loren Rotner, *Univ. of Austin*
- Marc Sidwell, *New Culture Forum*
- Emily Skarbek, *Brown Univ.*
- Craig Smith, *Univ. of Glasgow*
- David Walsh, *Catholic Univ. of America*
- Barry Weingast, *Stanford Univ.*
- Richard Whatmore, *Univ. of St. Andrews*
- Lawrence H. White, *George Mason Univ.*
- Amy Willis, *Liberty Fund*
- Bart Wilson, *Chapman Univ.*
- Todd Zywicki, *George Mason Univ.*

Why start CL Press?

CL Press publishes good, low-priced work in intellectual history, political theory, political economy, and moral philosophy. More specifically, CL Press explores and advances discourse in the following areas:

- The intellectual history and meaning of liberalism.
- The relationship between liberalism and conservatism.
- The role of religion in disseminating liberal understandings and institutions including: humankind's ethical universalism, the moral equality of souls, the rule of law, religious liberty, the meaning and virtues of economic life.
- The relationship between religion and economic philosophy.
- The political, social, and economic philosophy of the Scottish Enlightenment, especially Adam Smith.
- The state of classically liberal ideas and policies across the world today.

CPSIA information can be obtained
at www.ICGtesting.com
Printed in the USA
BVHW081011150922
647127BV00014B/1427